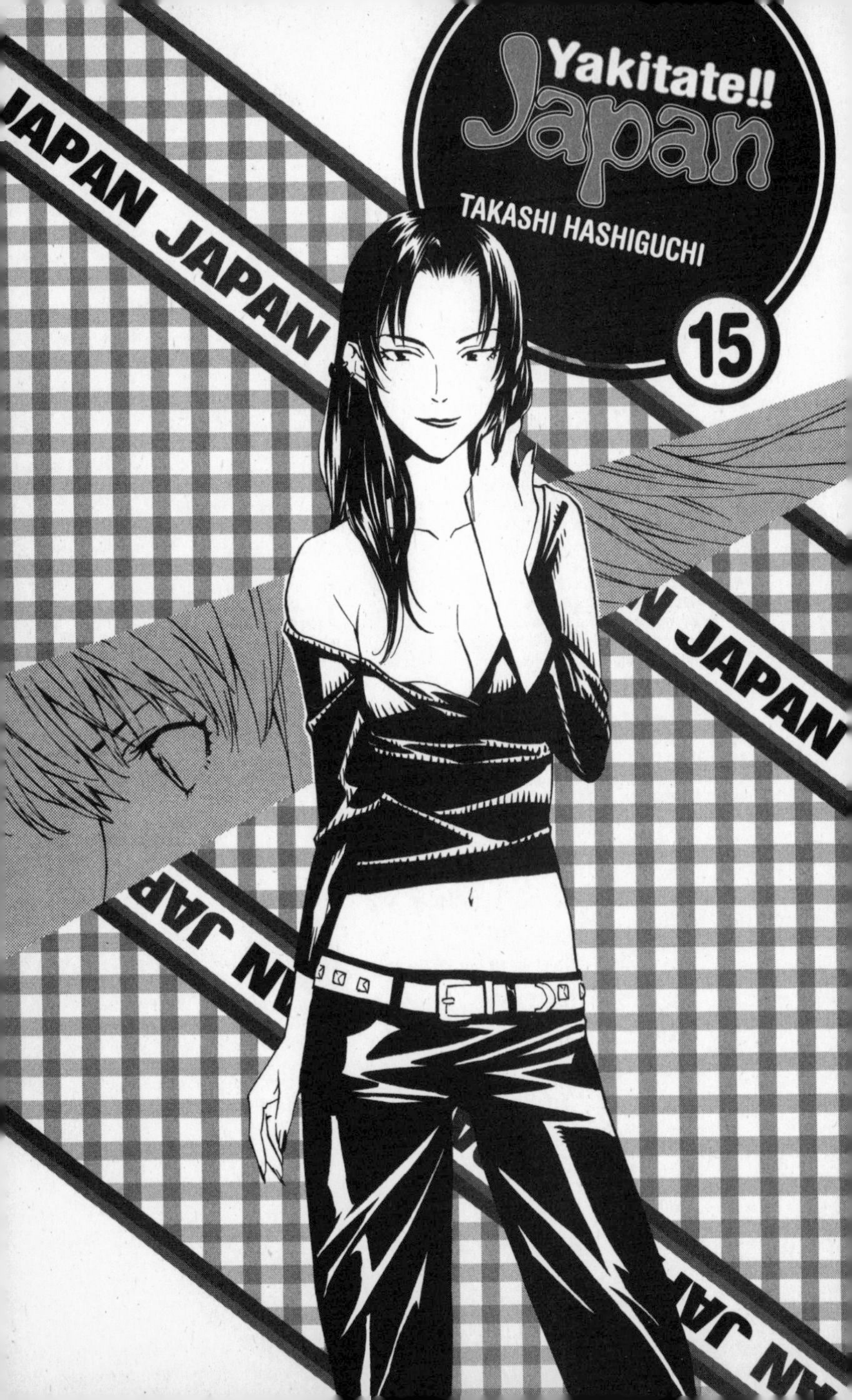
Yakitate!! Japan
TAKASHI HASHIGUCHI
15
JAPAN JAPAN
JAPAN

JAPAN JAPAN JAPAN JAPAN

YAKITATE!! JAPAN 15

VIZ Media Edition

★The Story Thus Far★

As the Monaco Cup enters the final match, Kazuma Azuma and American representative Shadow face off in making breads that use the flavors of their countries to the fullest.

Shadow, it turns out, is not a baker at all, but a world-class pantomime! Mimicking the techniques of St. Pierre's insidious owner Kirisaki, Shadow creates a "Go-pan" bagel with a taste so supreme, it sends judge Pierrot into outer space for a reunion with the mother he never met!

Unfazed, Azuma attempts to make the ultimate donut, Hemp Ja-pan, which brilliantly utilizes hempseed, an ingredient with a centuries-old history in Japan. When Pierrot tastes Azuma's bread, he is sent back in time to the Monaco Royal Palace, just before he was born. Not only is he given the chance to spend a few blissful months living alongside the family he never knew, but his actions prevent his royal parents from ever dying at all!

Pierrot declares Azuma the winner of the match because he made a bread that literally changed history. With that, Japan wins the Monaco Cup championship at last! But for the friends of Pantasia's South Branch, the victory means more than prestige—it means they can collect the 12 billion yen in winnings from the bet they placed to save the store. Finally Azuma and friends can toast to their success... or can they? Kirisaki's shadow (the figurative kind, not the crazy mime) looms...

CONTENTS

Research Assistance: "Pan No Mimi," Koichi Uchimura/
Writer, Shigeyuki Kimura

JAPAN JAPAN JAPAN JAPAN

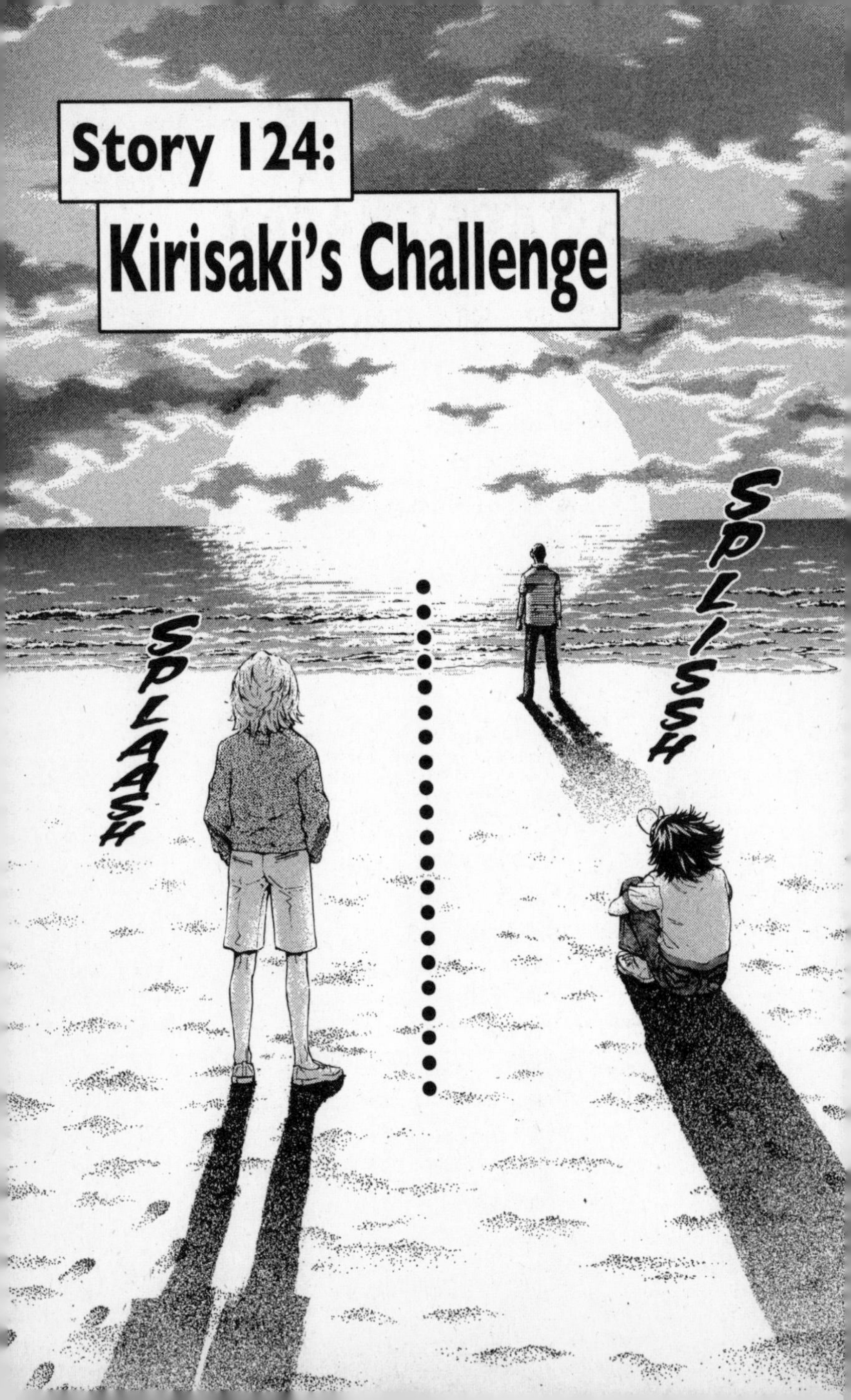
Story 124:
Kirisaki's Challenge
SPLISSH
....
SPLAASH

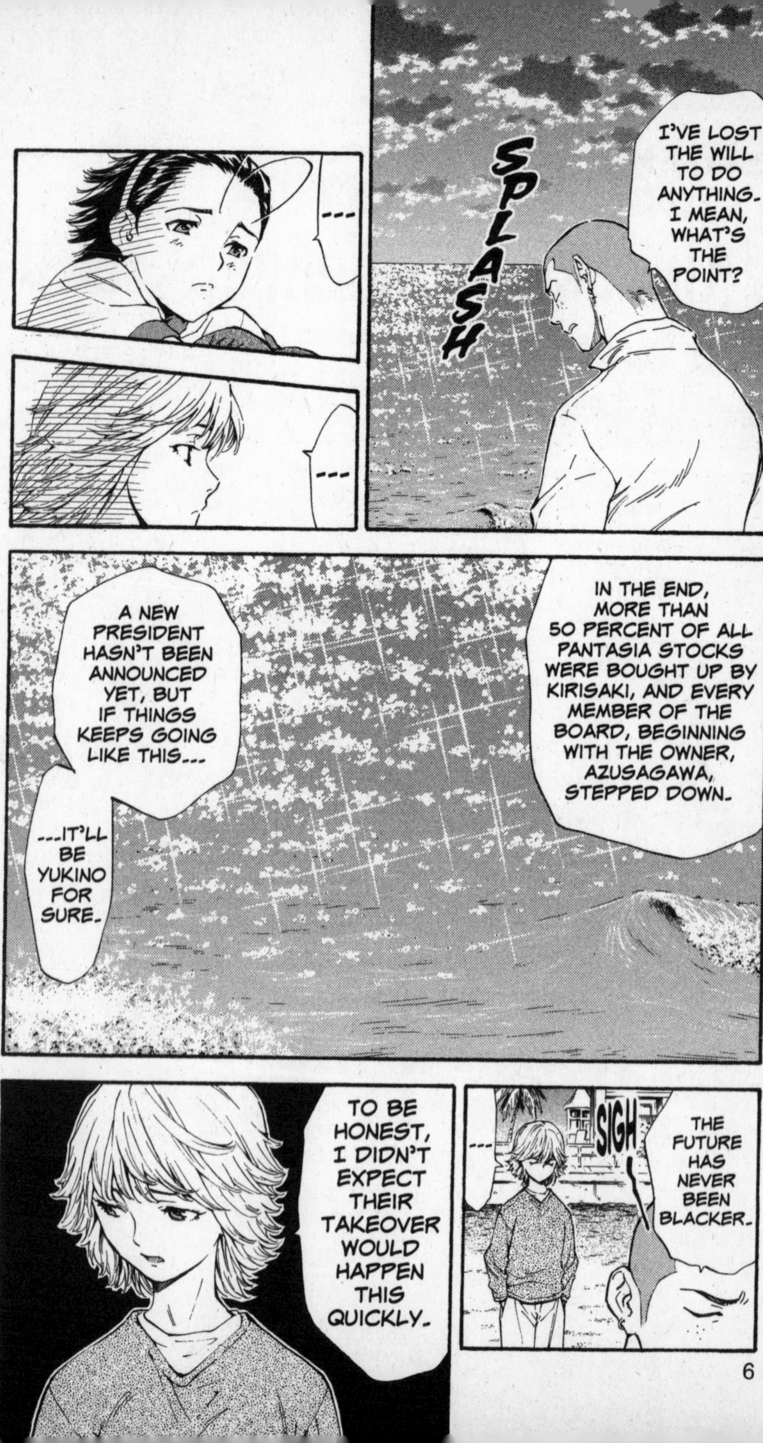
I'VE LOST THE WILL TO DO ANYTHING. I MEAN, WHAT'S THE POINT?
SPLASH
...
...
IN THE END, MORE THAN 50 PERCENT OF ALL PANTASIA STOCKS WERE BOUGHT UP BY KIRISAKI, AND EVERY MEMBER OF THE BOARD, BEGINNING WITH THE OWNER, AZUSAGAWA, STEPPED DOWN.
A NEW PRESIDENT HASN'T BEEN ANNOUNCED YET, BUT IF THINGS KEEPS GOING LIKE THIS...
...IT'LL BE YUKINO FOR SURE.
THE FUTURE HAS NEVER BEEN BLACKER.
SIGH
...
TO BE HONEST, I DIDN'T EXPECT THEIR TAKEOVER WOULD HAPPEN THIS QUICKLY.

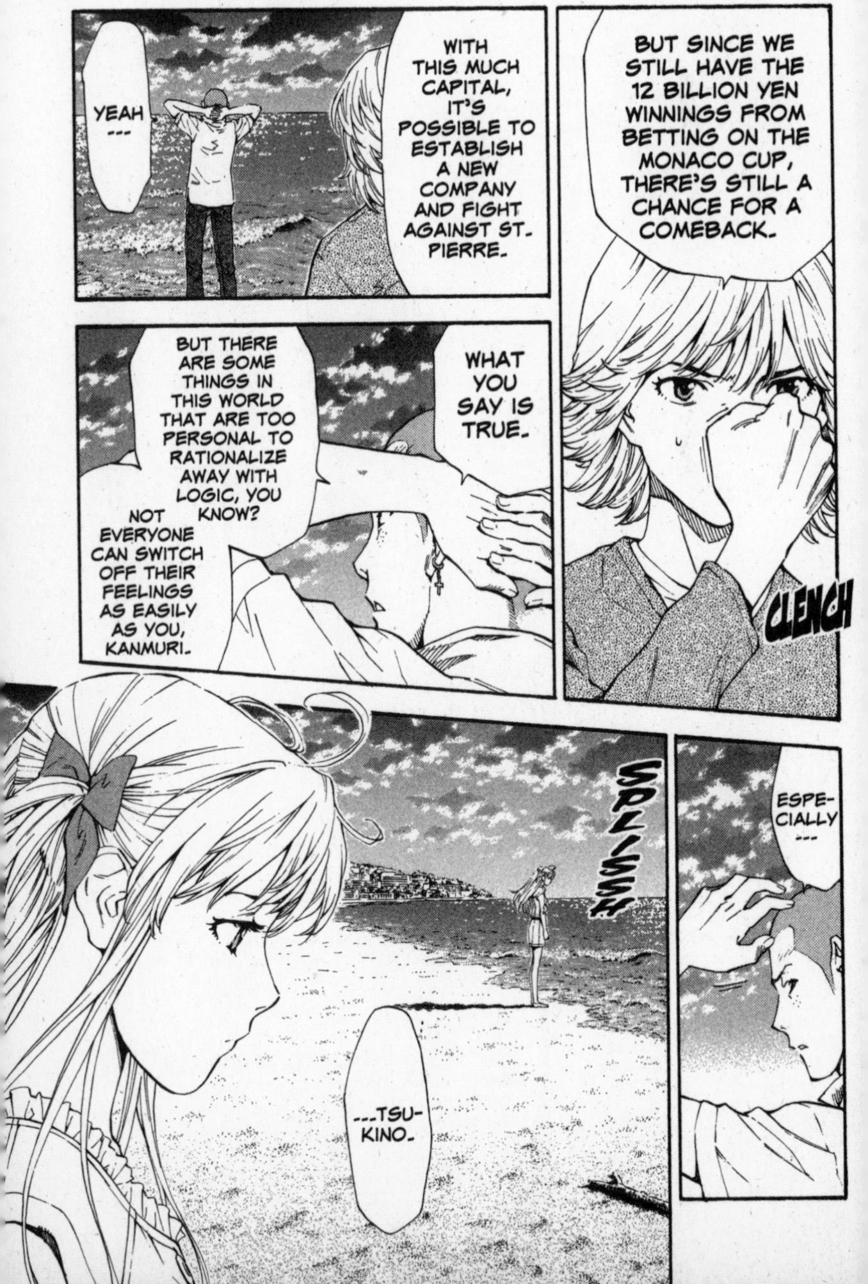
BUT SINCE WE STILL HAVE THE 12 BILLION YEN WINNINGS FROM BETTING ON THE MONACO CUP, THERE'S STILL A CHANCE FOR A COMEBACK.
CLENCH
WITH THIS MUCH CAPITAL, IT'S POSSIBLE TO ESTABLISH A NEW COMPANY AND FIGHT AGAINST ST. PIERRE.
YEAH---
WHAT YOU SAY IS TRUE.
BUT THERE ARE SOME THINGS IN THIS WORLD THAT ARE TOO PERSONAL TO RATIONALIZE AWAY WITH LOGIC, YOU KNOW?
NOT EVERYONE CAN SWITCH OFF THEIR FEELINGS AS EASILY AS YOU, KANMURI.
ESPE-CIALLY---
SPLISSH
---TSU-KINO.

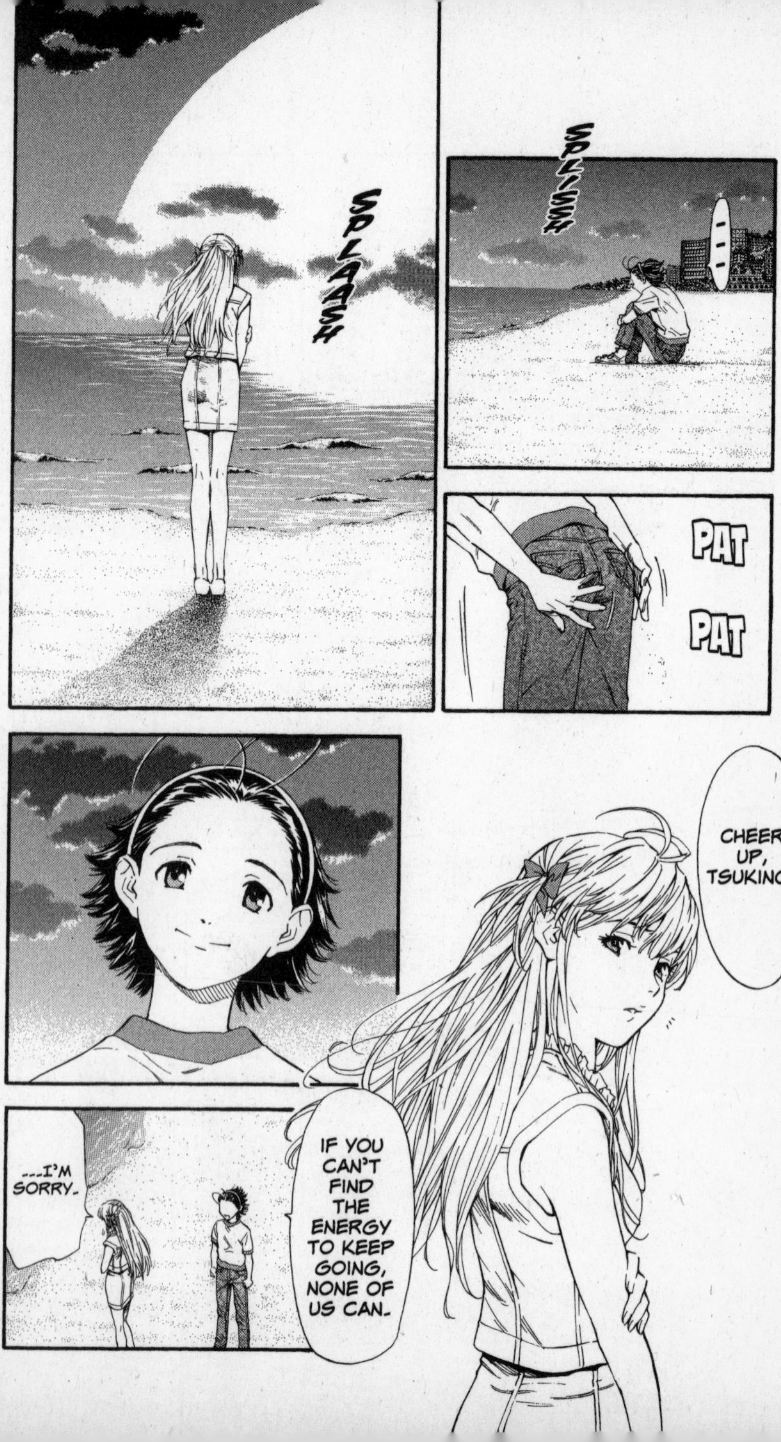
SPLISSH
...
PAT
PAT
SPLAASH
CHEER UP, TSUKINO!
IF YOU CAN'T FIND THE ENERGY TO KEEP GOING, NONE OF US CAN.
...I'M SORRY.

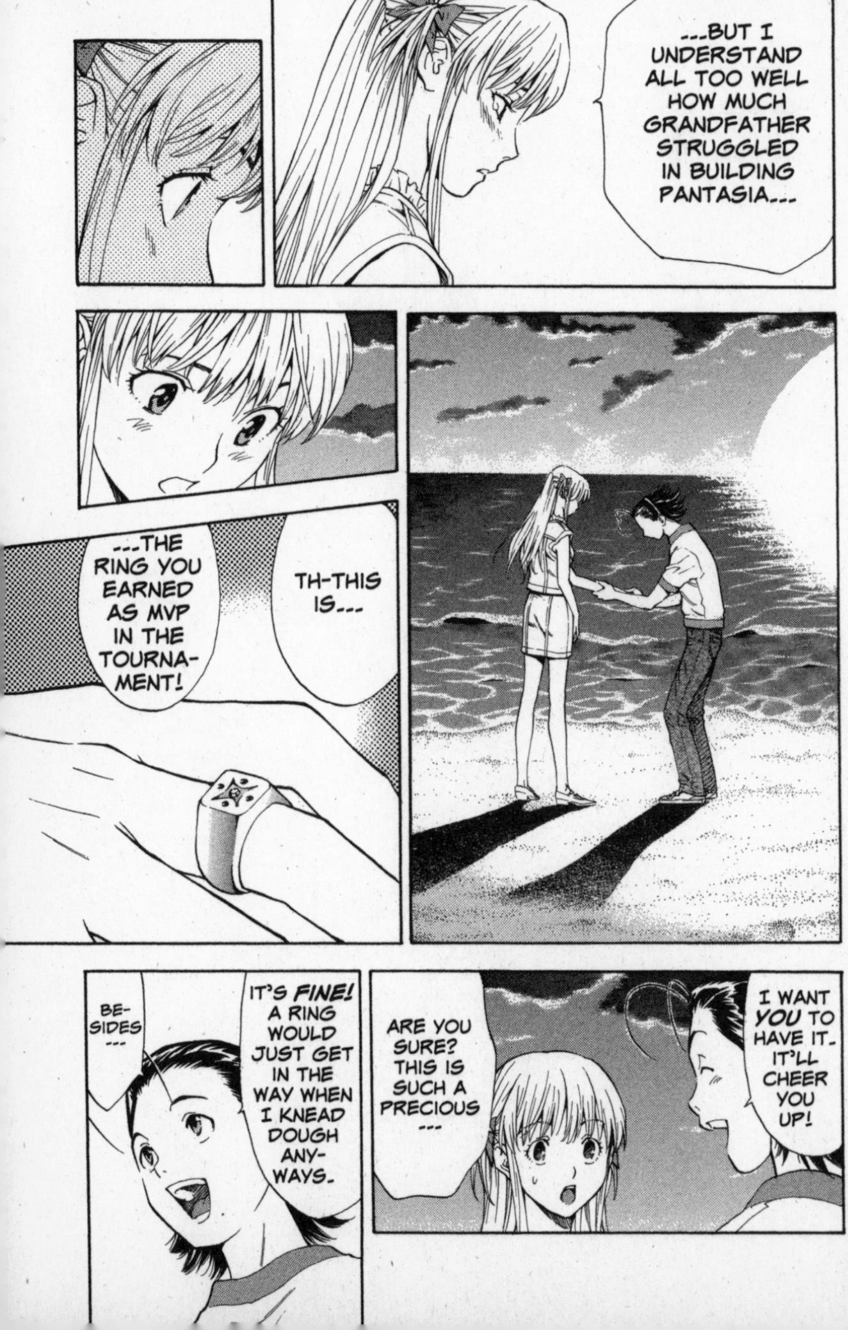
...BUT I UNDERSTAND ALL TOO WELL HOW MUCH GRANDFATHER STRUGGLED IN BUILDING PANTASIA...
TH-THIS IS...
...THE RING YOU EARNED AS MVP IN THE TOURNAMENT!
I WANT *YOU* TO HAVE IT. IT'LL CHEER YOU UP!
ARE YOU SURE? THIS IS SUCH A PRECIOUS ...
IT'S *FINE!* A RING WOULD JUST GET IN THE WAY WHEN I KNEAD DOUGH ANYWAYS.
BESIDES ...

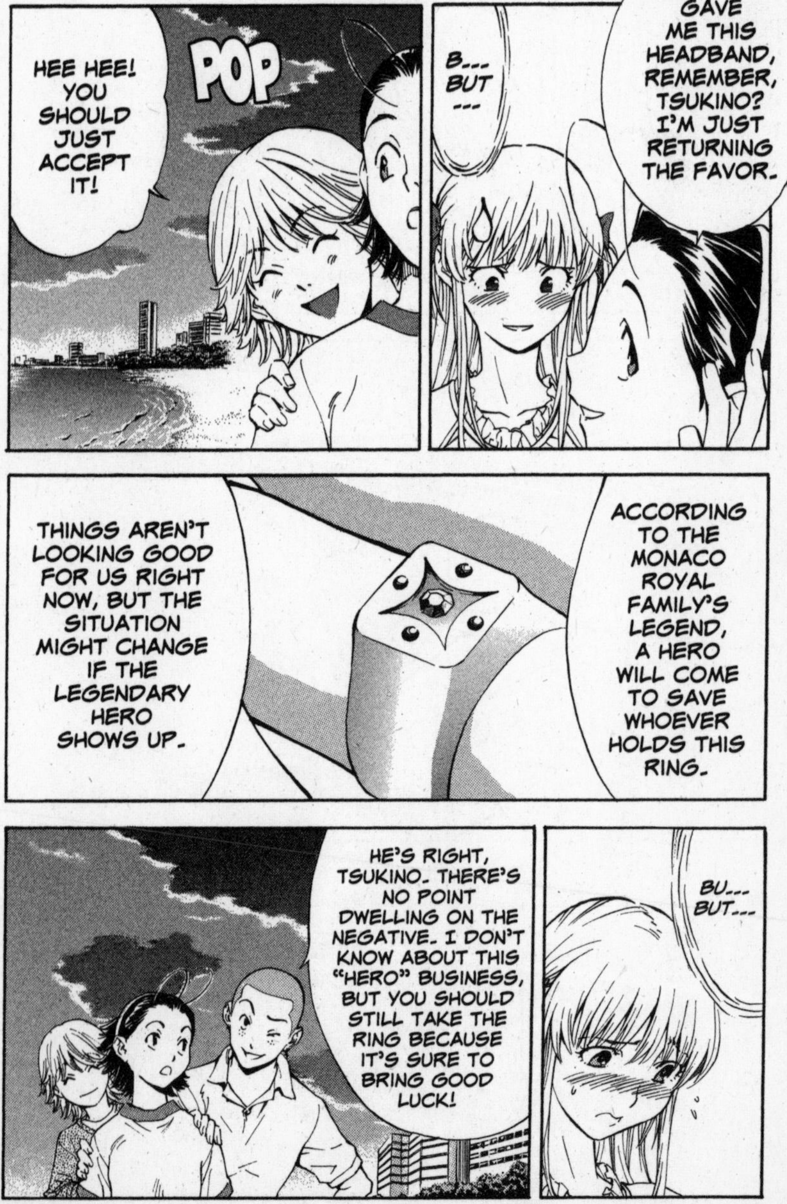
...YOU GAVE ME THIS HEADBAND, REMEMBER, TSUKINO? I'M JUST RETURNING THE FAVOR.
B... BUT ...
POP
HEE HEE! YOU SHOULD JUST ACCEPT IT!
ACCORDING TO THE MONACO ROYAL FAMILY'S LEGEND, A HERO WILL COME TO SAVE WHOEVER HOLDS THIS RING.
THINGS AREN'T LOOKING GOOD FOR US RIGHT NOW, BUT THE SITUATION MIGHT CHANGE IF THE LEGENDARY HERO SHOWS UP.
BU... BUT...
HE'S RIGHT, TSUKINO. THERE'S NO POINT DWELLING ON THE NEGATIVE. I DON'T KNOW ABOUT THIS "HERO" BUSINESS, BUT YOU SHOULD STILL TAKE THE RING BECAUSE IT'S SURE TO BRING GOOD LUCK!

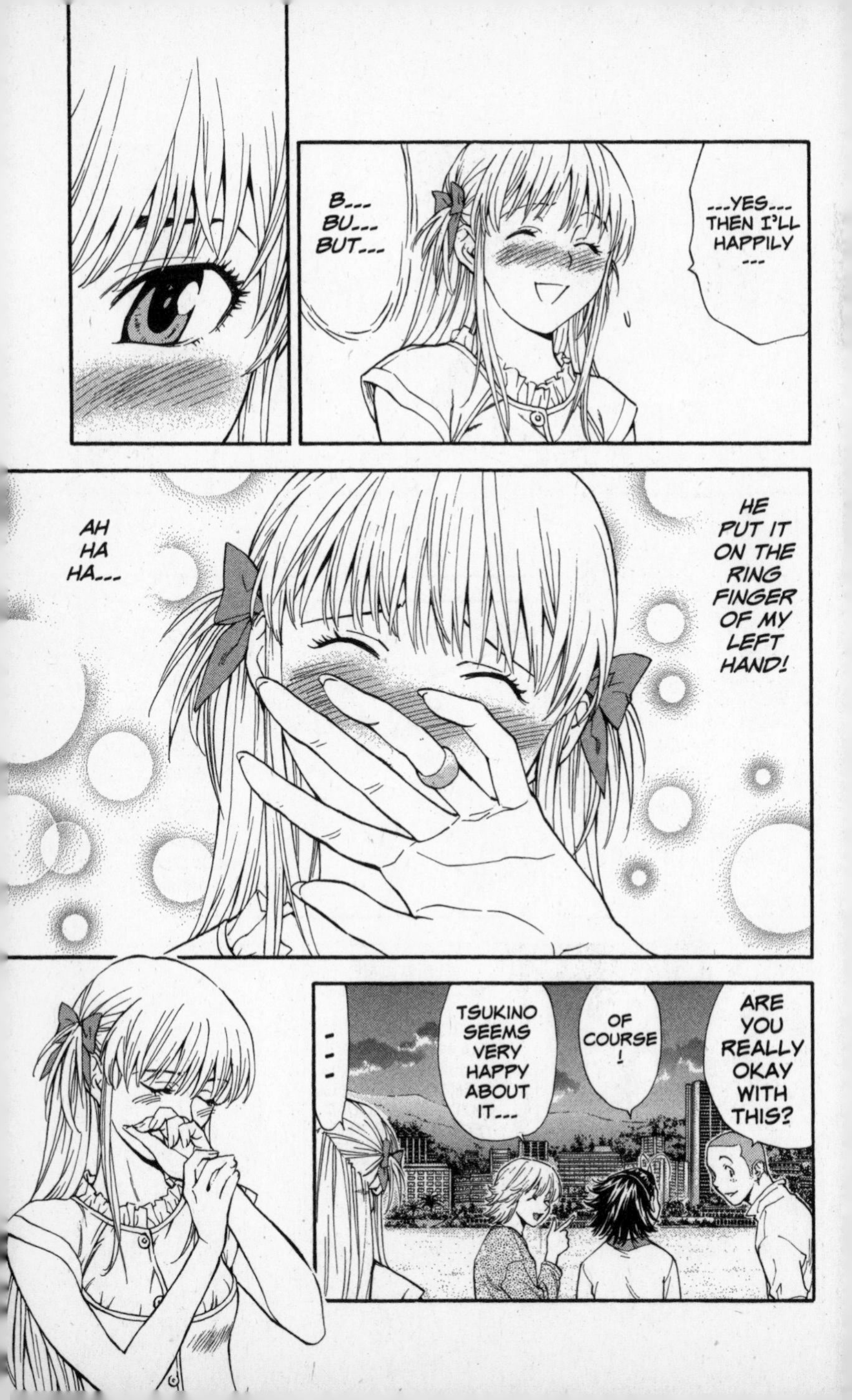
...YES... THEN I'LL HAPPILY ---
B... BU... BUT...
HE PUT IT ON THE RING FINGER OF MY LEFT HAND!
AH HA HA...
ARE YOU REALLY OKAY WITH THIS?
OF COURSE!
TSUKINO SEEMS VERY HAPPY ABOUT IT...
...

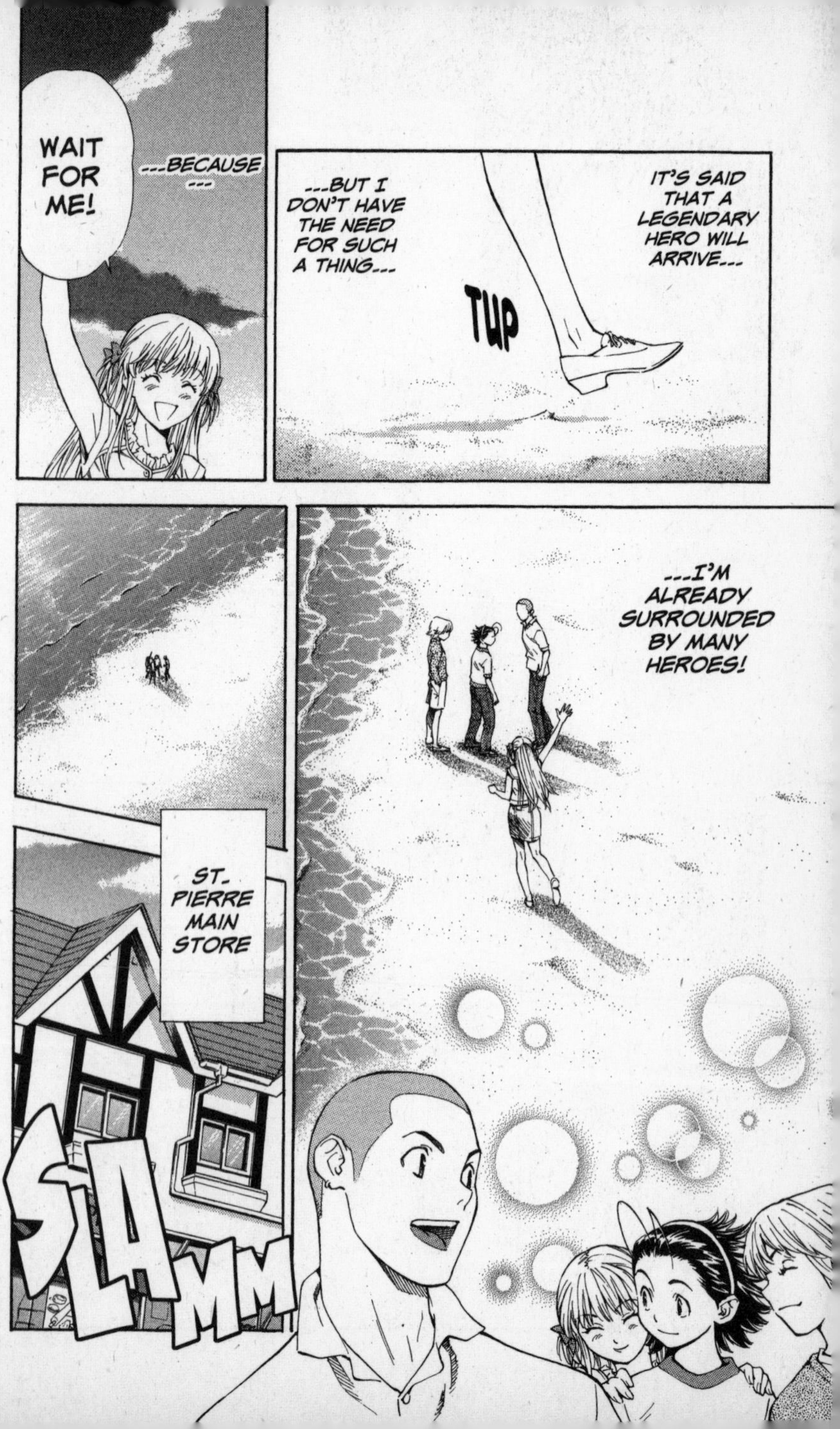
IT'S SAID THAT A LEGENDARY HERO WILL ARRIVE...
...BUT I DON'T HAVE THE NEED FOR SUCH A THING...
TUP
...BECAUSE ...
WAIT FOR ME!
...I'M ALREADY SURROUNDED BY MANY HEROES!
ST. PIERRE MAIN STORE
SLAMM

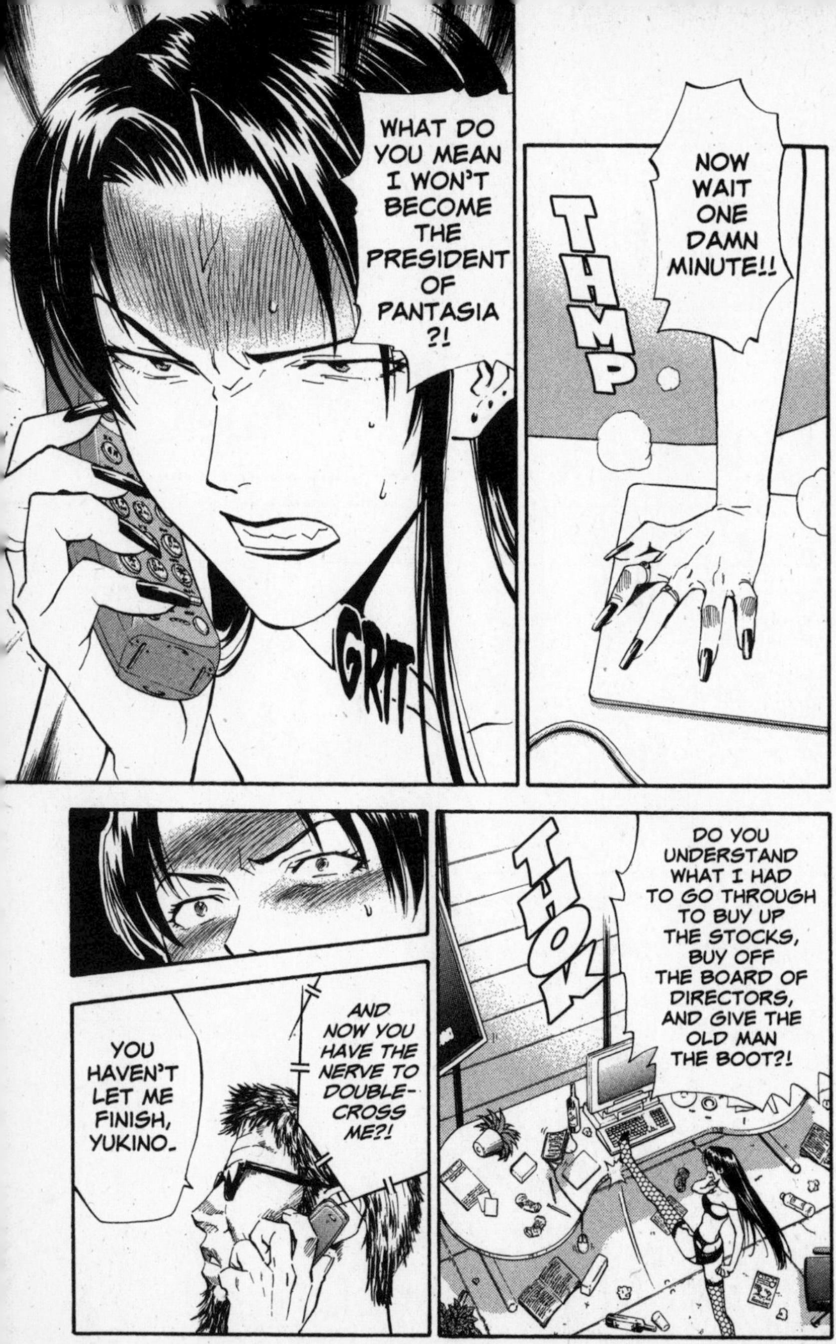
NOW WAIT ONE DAMN MINUTE!!
THMP
WHAT DO YOU MEAN I WON'T BECOME THE PRESIDENT OF PANTASIA ?!
GRIT
THOK
DO YOU UNDERSTAND WHAT I HAD TO GO THROUGH TO BUY UP THE STOCKS, BUY OFF THE BOARD OF DIRECTORS, AND GIVE THE OLD MAN THE BOOT?!
AND NOW YOU HAVE THE NERVE TO DOUBLE-CROSS ME?!
YOU HAVEN'T LET ME FINISH, YUKINO.

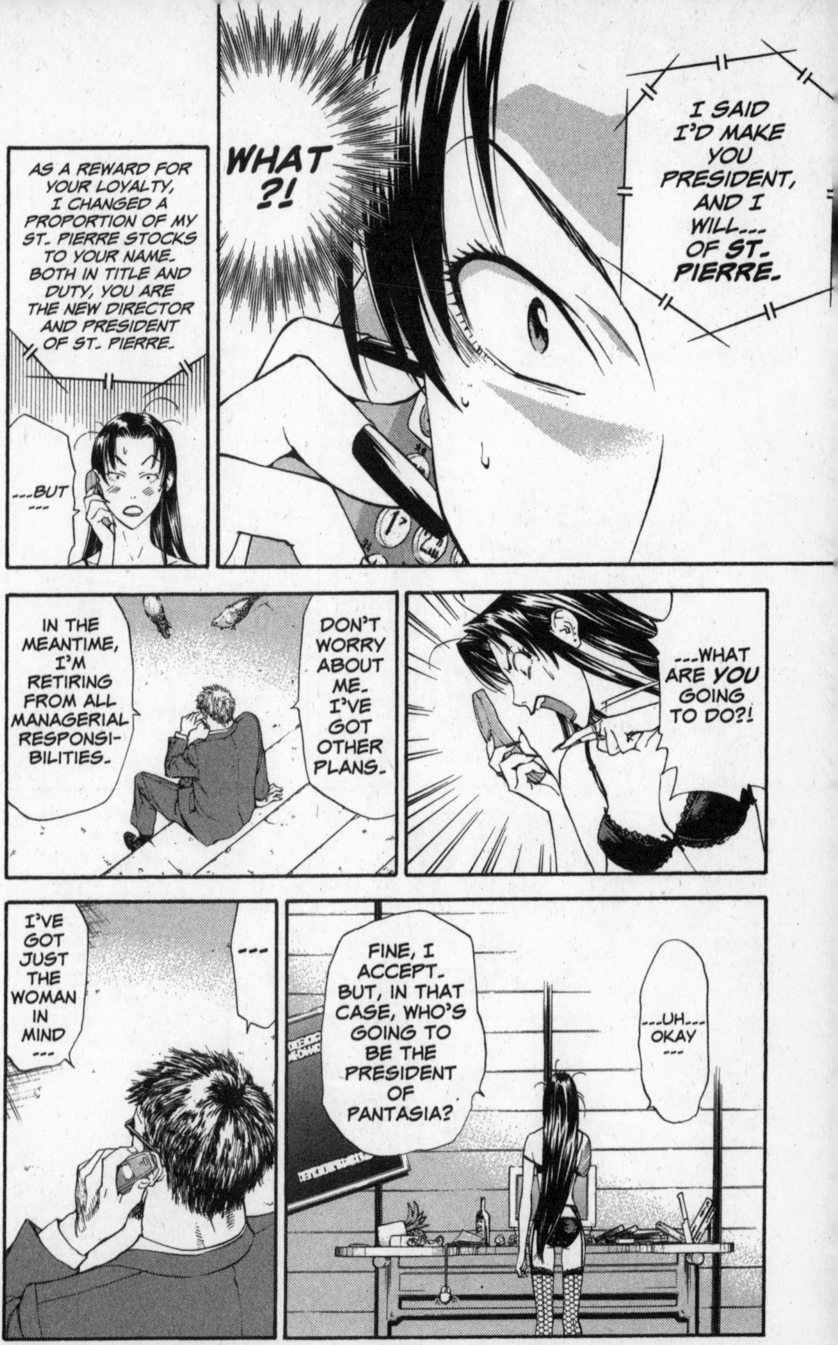
I SAID I'D MAKE YOU PRESIDENT, AND I WILL... OF ST. PIERRE.
WHAT?!
AS A REWARD FOR YOUR LOYALTY, I CHANGED A PROPORTION OF MY ST. PIERRE STOCKS TO YOUR NAME. BOTH IN TITLE AND DUTY, YOU ARE THE NEW DIRECTOR AND PRESIDENT OF ST. PIERRE.
...BUT...
...WHAT ARE YOU GOING TO DO?!
DON'T WORRY ABOUT ME. I'VE GOT OTHER PLANS.
IN THE MEANTIME, I'M RETIRING FROM ALL MANAGERIAL RESPONSI-BILITIES.
...UH... OKAY...
FINE, I ACCEPT. BUT, IN THAT CASE, WHO'S GOING TO BE THE PRESIDENT OF PANTASIA?
...
I'VE GOT JUST THE WOMAN IN MIND...

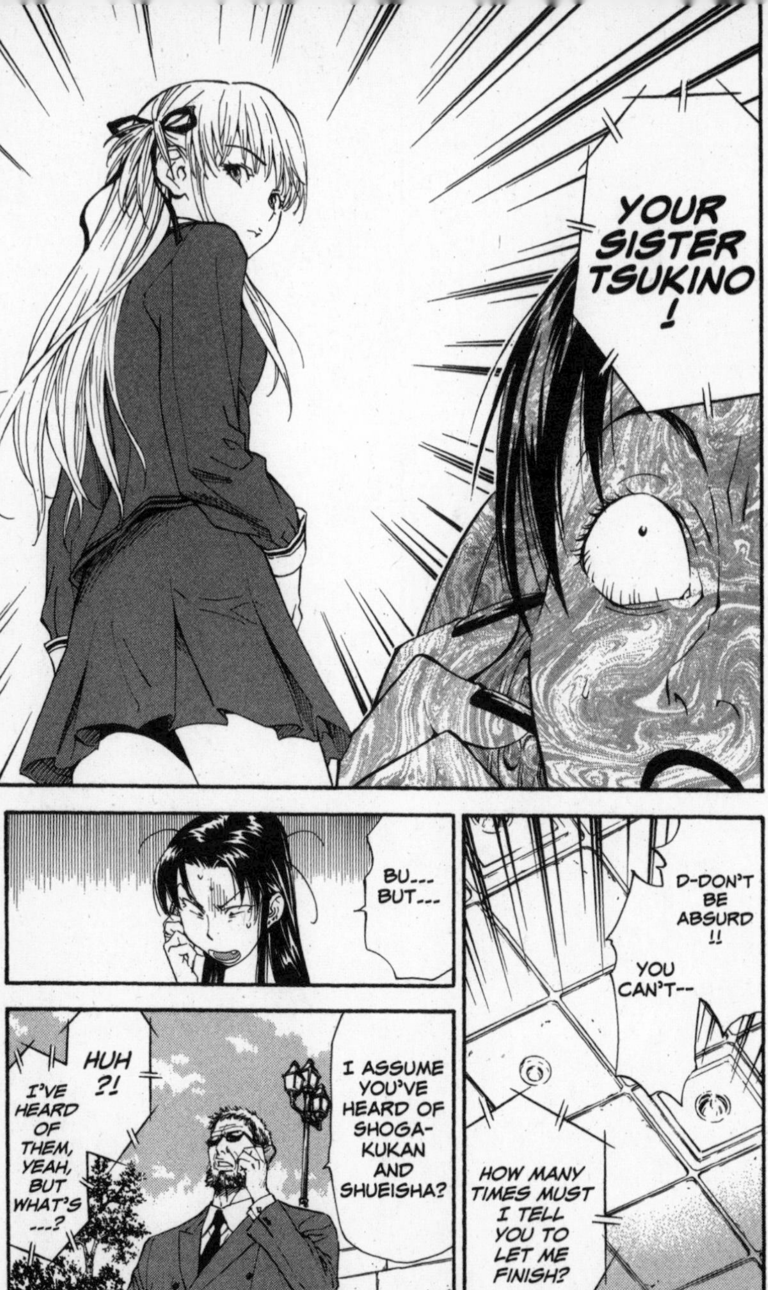
YOUR SISTER TSUKINO!
D-DON'T BE ABSURD!!
YOU CAN'T--
HOW MANY TIMES MUST I TELL YOU TO LET ME FINISH?
BU... BUT...
I ASSUME YOU'VE HEARD OF SHOGA-KUKAN AND SHUEISHA?
HUH?!
I'VE HEARD OF THEM, YEAH, BUT WHAT'S...?

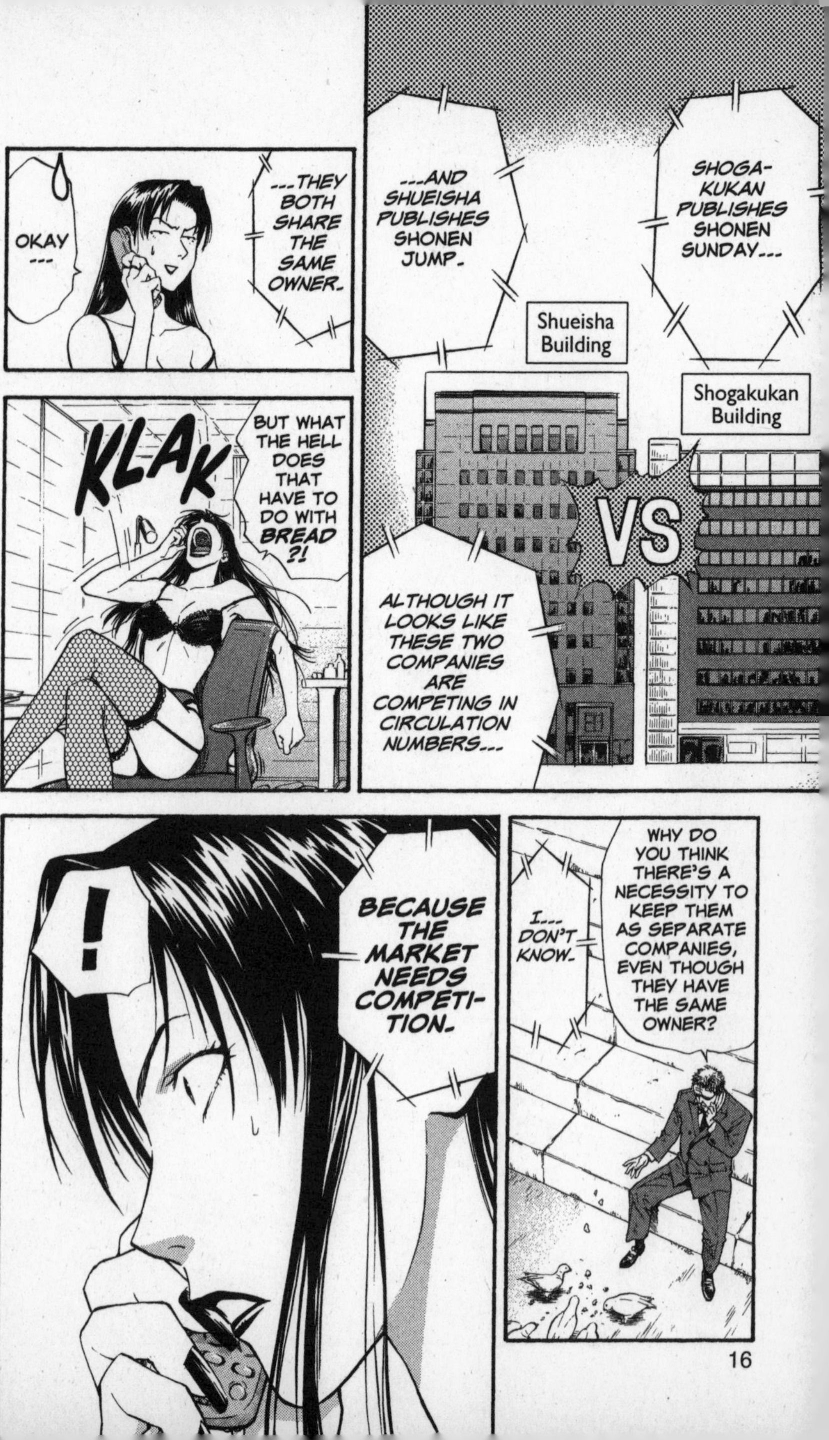
SHOGAKUKAN PUBLISHES SHONEN SUNDAY...
...AND SHUEISHA PUBLISHES SHONEN JUMP.
Shogakukan Building
Shueisha Building
VS
ALTHOUGH IT LOOKS LIKE THESE TWO COMPANIES ARE COMPETING IN CIRCULATION NUMBERS...
...THEY BOTH SHARE THE SAME OWNER.
OKAY...
KLAK
BUT WHAT THE HELL DOES THAT HAVE TO DO WITH BREAD?!
WHY DO YOU THINK THERE'S A NECESSITY TO KEEP THEM AS SEPARATE COMPANIES, EVEN THOUGH THEY HAVE THE SAME OWNER?
I... DON'T KNOW.
BECAUSE THE MARKET NEEDS COMPETITION.
!

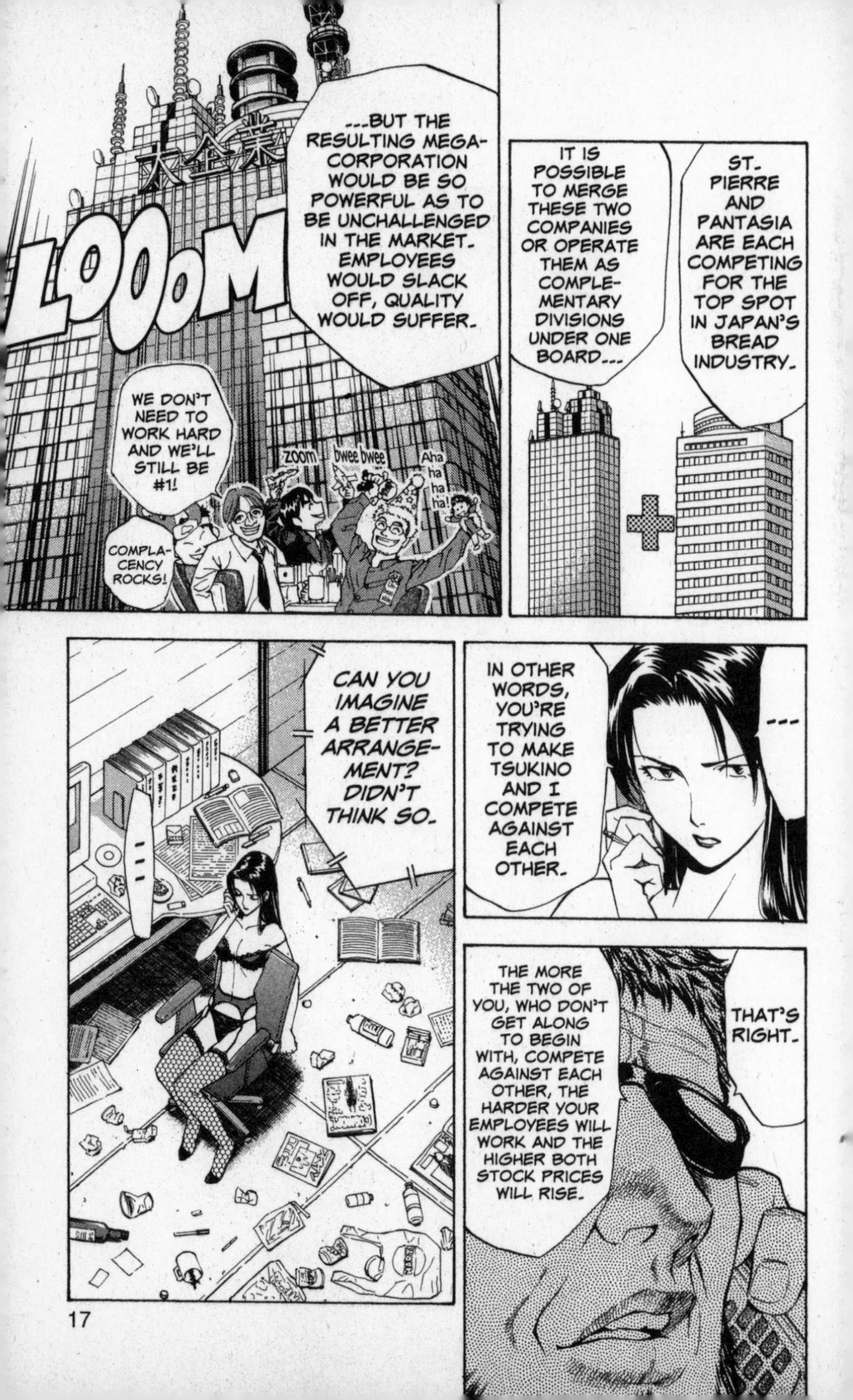
ST. PIERRE AND PANTASIA ARE EACH COMPETING FOR THE TOP SPOT IN JAPAN'S BREAD INDUSTRY.
IT IS POSSIBLE TO MERGE THESE TWO COMPANIES OR OPERATE THEM AS COMPLE-MENTARY DIVISIONS UNDER ONE BOARD...
...BUT THE RESULTING MEGA-CORPORATION WOULD BE SO POWERFUL AS TO BE UNCHALLENGED IN THE MARKET. EMPLOYEES WOULD SLACK OFF, QUALITY WOULD SUFFER.
LOOOM
zoom
bwee bwee
Aha ha ha ha!
WE DON'T NEED TO WORK HARD AND WE'LL STILL BE #1!
COMPLA-CENCY ROCKS!
...
IN OTHER WORDS, YOU'RE TRYING TO MAKE TSUKINO AND I COMPETE AGAINST EACH OTHER.
THAT'S RIGHT.
THE MORE THE TWO OF YOU, WHO DON'T GET ALONG TO BEGIN WITH, COMPETE AGAINST EACH OTHER, THE HARDER YOUR EMPLOYEES WILL WORK AND THE HIGHER BOTH STOCK PRICES WILL RISE.
CAN YOU IMAGINE A BETTER ARRANGE-MENT? DIDN'T THINK SO.
...

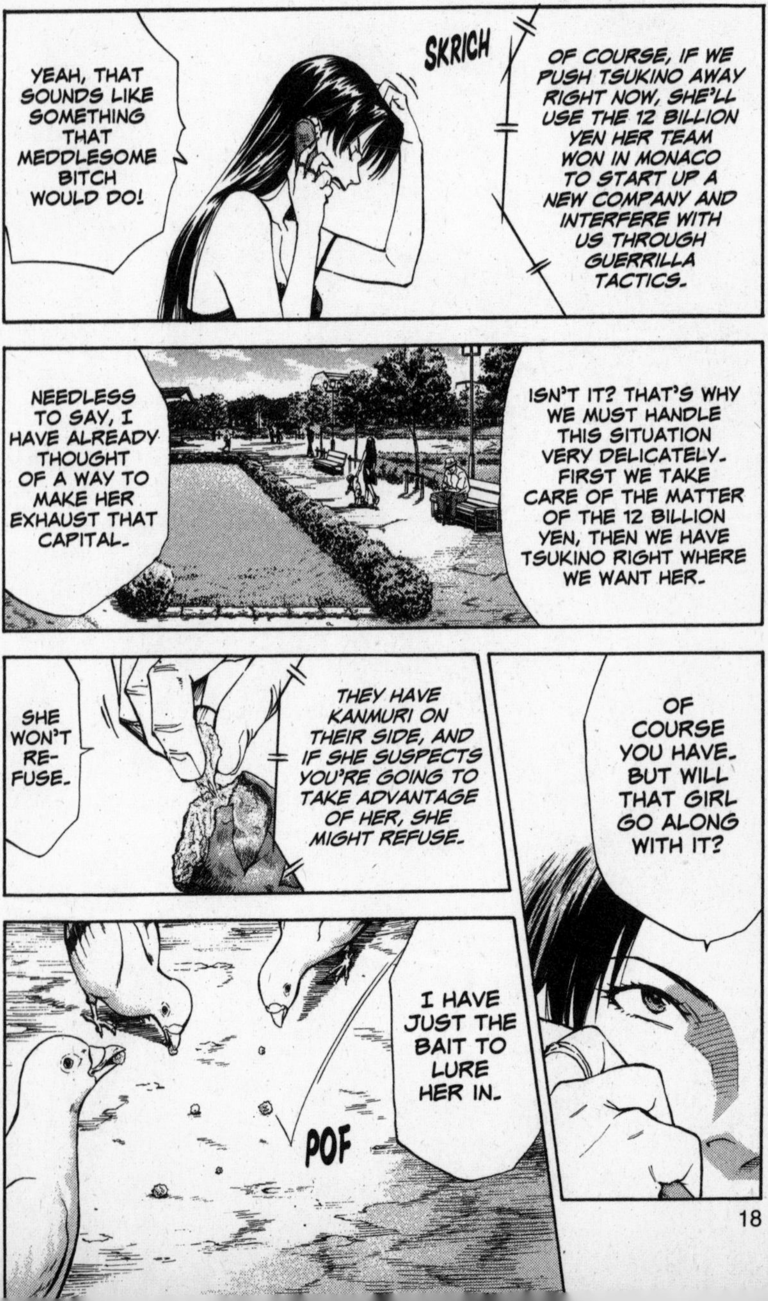
OF COURSE, IF WE PUSH TSUKINO AWAY RIGHT NOW, SHE'LL USE THE 12 BILLION YEN HER TEAM WON IN MONACO TO START UP A NEW COMPANY AND INTERFERE WITH US THROUGH GUERRILLA TACTICS.
SKRICH
YEAH, THAT SOUNDS LIKE SOMETHING THAT MEDDLESOME BITCH WOULD DO!
ISN'T IT? THAT'S WHY WE MUST HANDLE THIS SITUATION VERY DELICATELY. FIRST WE TAKE CARE OF THE MATTER OF THE 12 BILLION YEN, THEN WE HAVE TSUKINO RIGHT WHERE WE WANT HER.
NEEDLESS TO SAY, I HAVE ALREADY THOUGHT OF A WAY TO MAKE HER EXHAUST THAT CAPITAL.
OF COURSE YOU HAVE. BUT WILL THAT GIRL GO ALONG WITH IT?
THEY HAVE KANMURI ON THEIR SIDE, AND IF SHE SUSPECTS YOU'RE GOING TO TAKE ADVANTAGE OF HER, SHE MIGHT REFUSE.
SHE WON'T RE-FUSE.
I HAVE JUST THE BAIT TO LURE HER IN.
POF

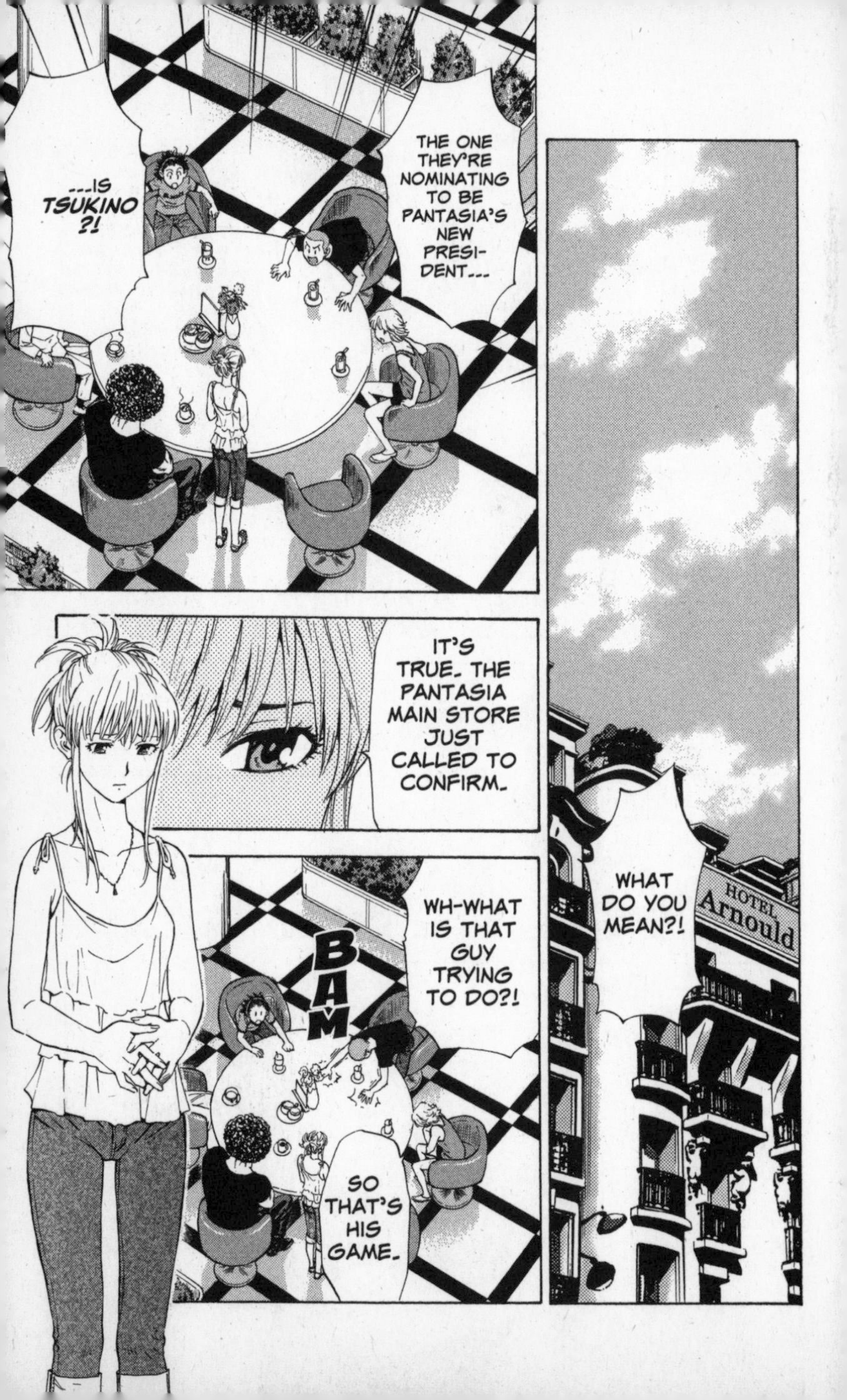

WHAT DO YOU MEAN?!
HOTEL Arnould
THE ONE THEY'RE NOMINATING TO BE PANTASIA'S NEW PRESI-DENT...
...IS TSUKINO ?!
IT'S TRUE. THE PANTASIA MAIN STORE JUST CALLED TO CONFIRM.
WH-WHAT IS THAT GUY TRYING TO DO?!
BAM
SO THAT'S HIS GAME.

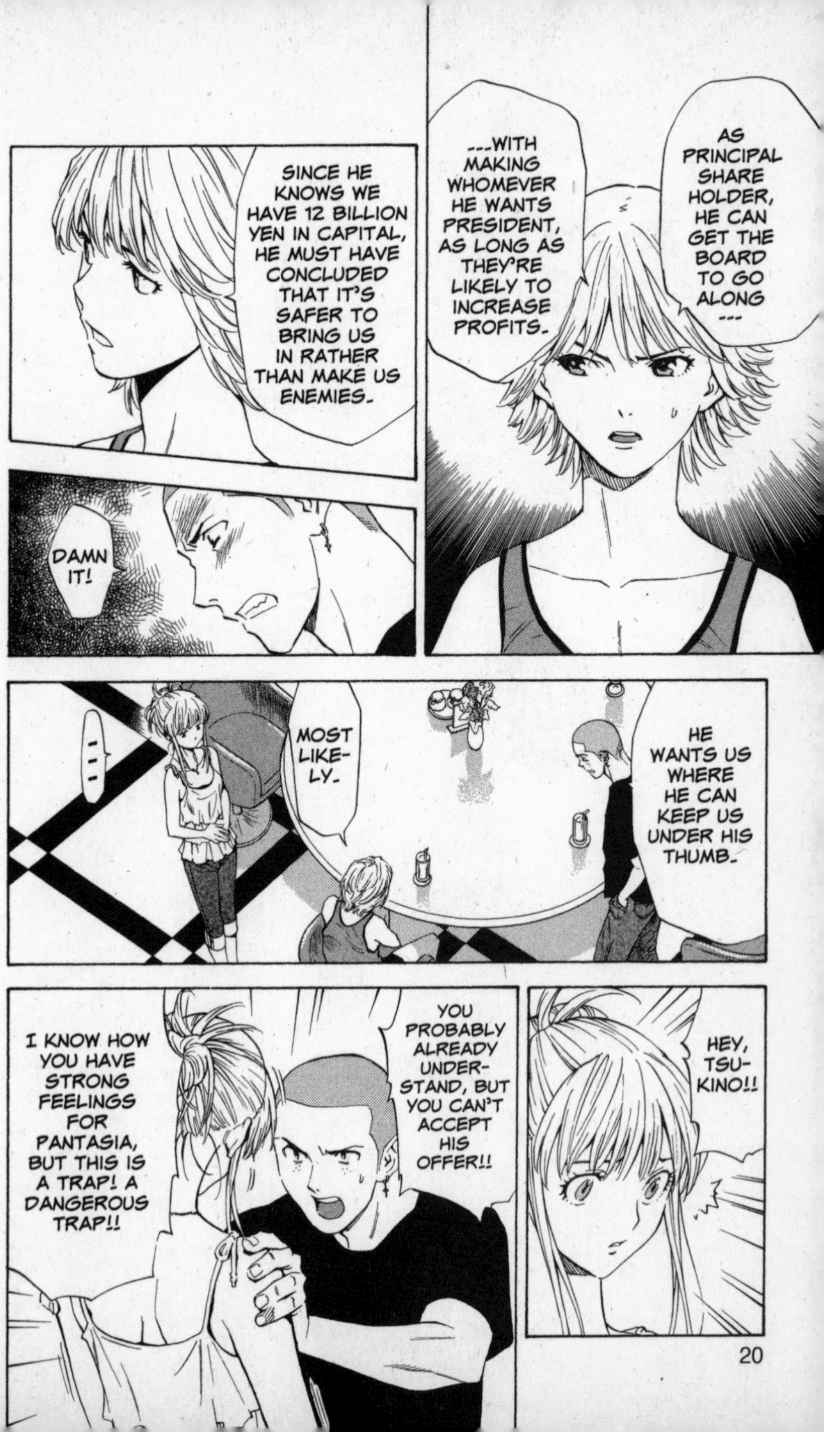
AS PRINCIPAL SHARE HOLDER, HE CAN GET THE BOARD TO GO ALONG ---
---WITH MAKING WHOMEVER HE WANTS PRESIDENT, AS LONG AS THEY'RE LIKELY TO INCREASE PROFITS.
SINCE HE KNOWS WE HAVE 12 BILLION YEN IN CAPITAL, HE MUST HAVE CONCLUDED THAT IT'S SAFER TO BRING US IN RATHER THAN MAKE US ENEMIES.
DAMN IT!
HE WANTS US WHERE HE CAN KEEP US UNDER HIS THUMB.
MOST LIKE-LY.
...
HEY, TSU-KINO!!
YOU PROBABLY ALREADY UNDER-STAND, BUT YOU CAN'T ACCEPT HIS OFFER!!
I KNOW HOW YOU HAVE STRONG FEELINGS FOR PANTASIA, BUT THIS IS A TRAP! A DANGEROUS TRAP!!

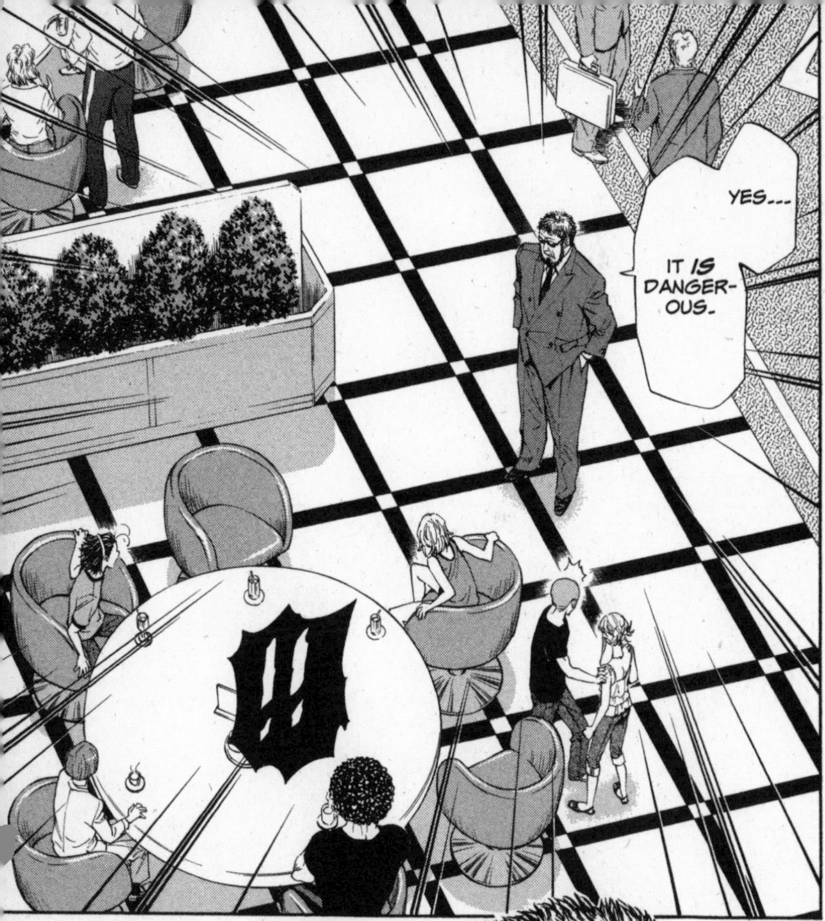
YES...
IT IS DANGER-OUS.
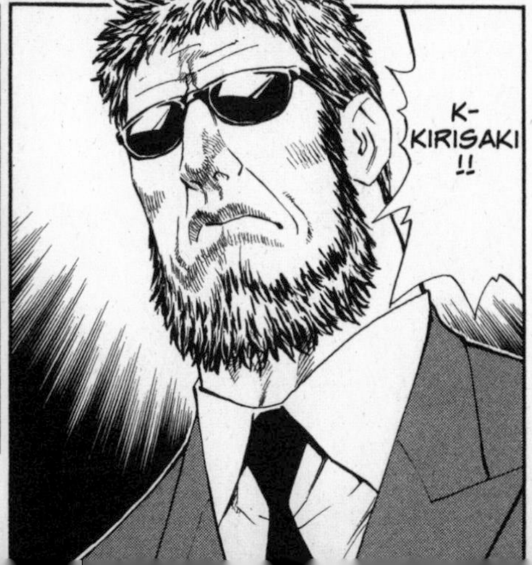
K-KIRISAKI!!
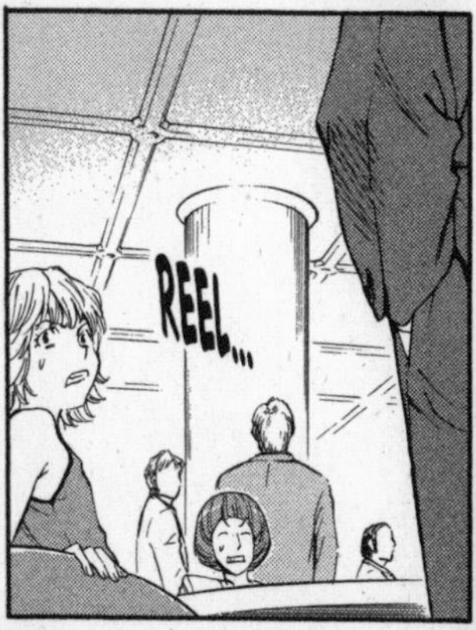
REEL...

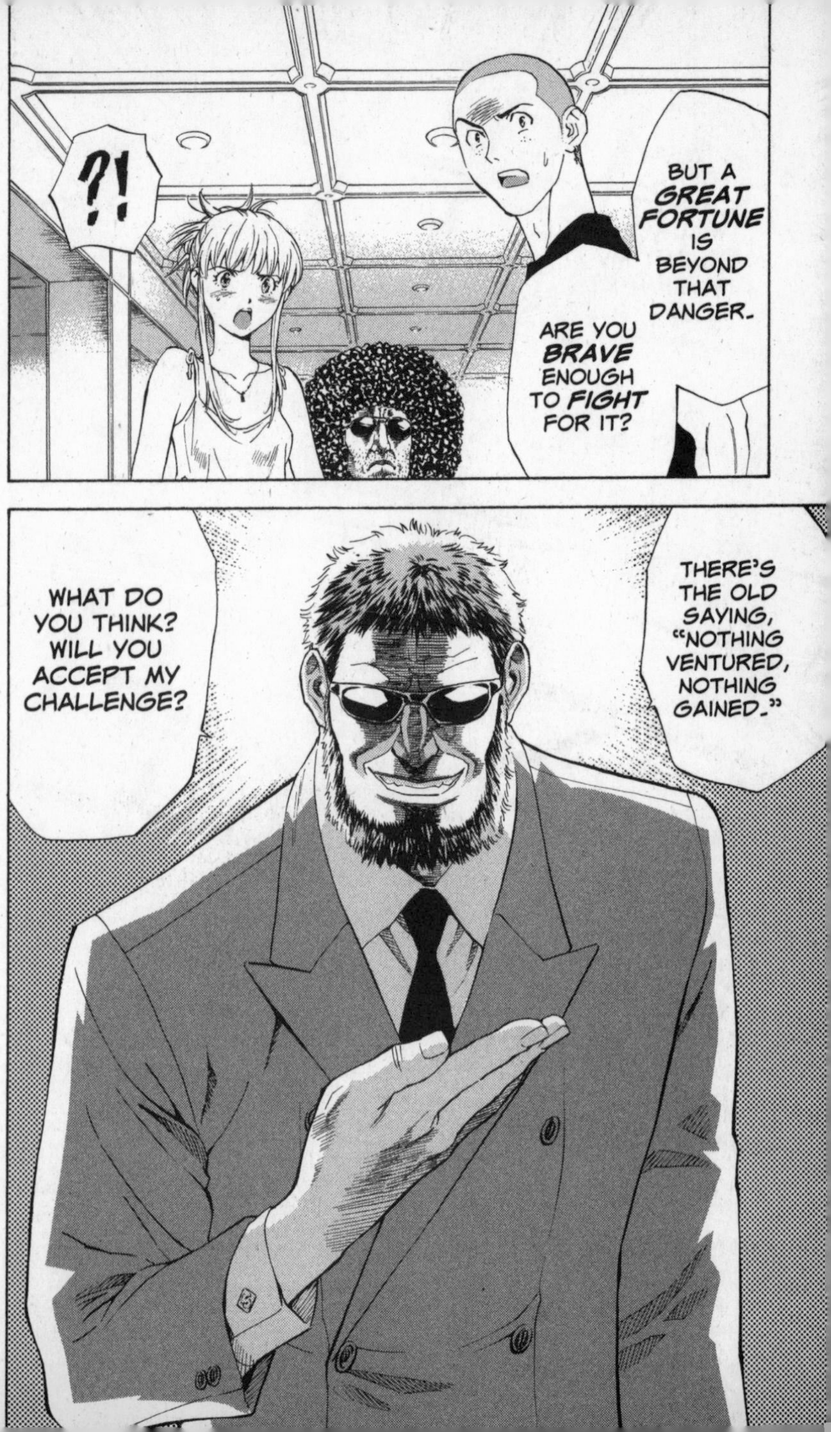
BUT A GREAT FORTUNE IS BEYOND THAT DANGER...
ARE YOU BRAVE ENOUGH TO FIGHT FOR IT?
?!
THERE'S THE OLD SAYING, "NOTHING VENTURED, NOTHING GAINED..."
WHAT DO YOU THINK? WILL YOU ACCEPT MY CHALLENGE?

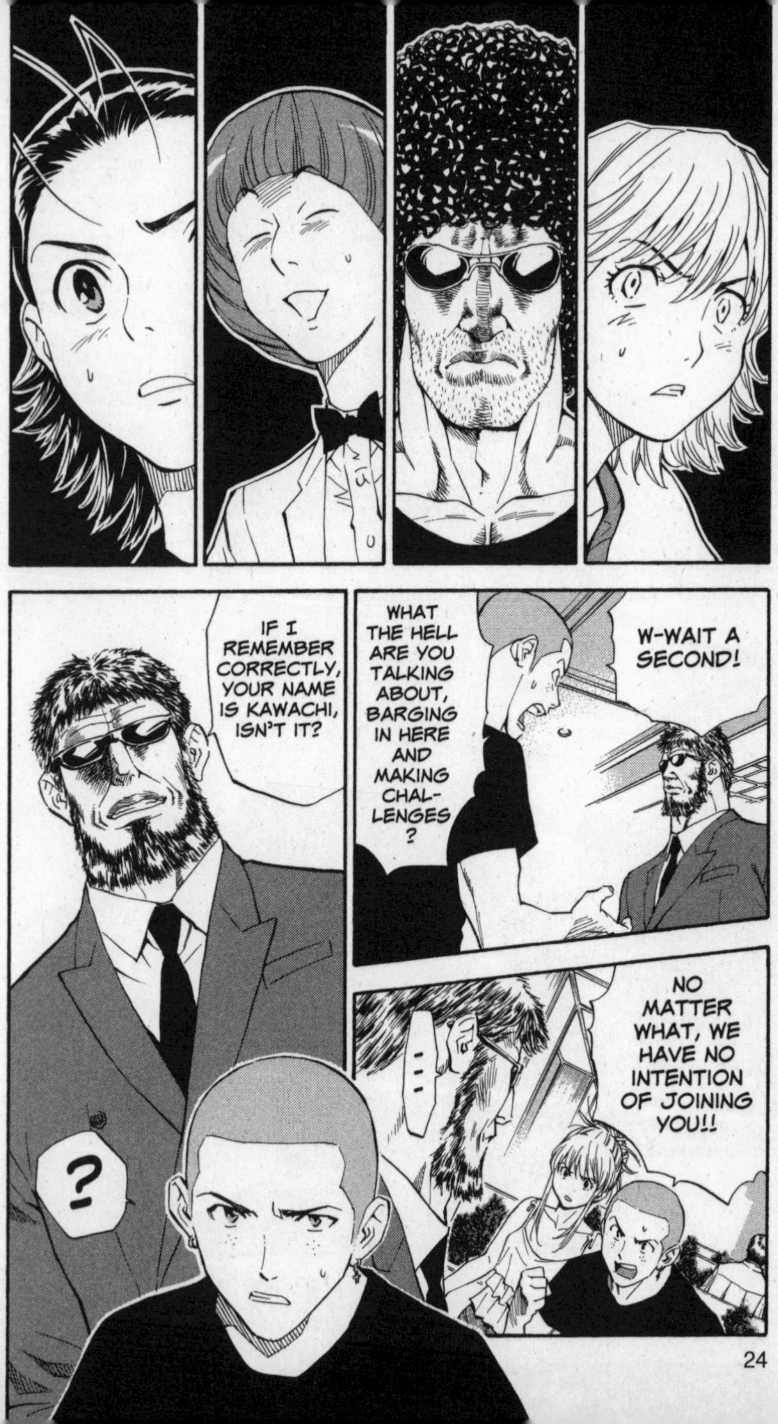
W-WAIT A SECOND!
WHAT THE HELL ARE YOU TALKING ABOUT, BARGING IN HERE AND MAKING CHAL-LENGES?
NO MATTER WHAT, WE HAVE NO INTENTION OF JOINING YOU!!
...
IF I REMEMBER CORRECTLY, YOUR NAME IS KAWACHI, ISN'T IT?
?

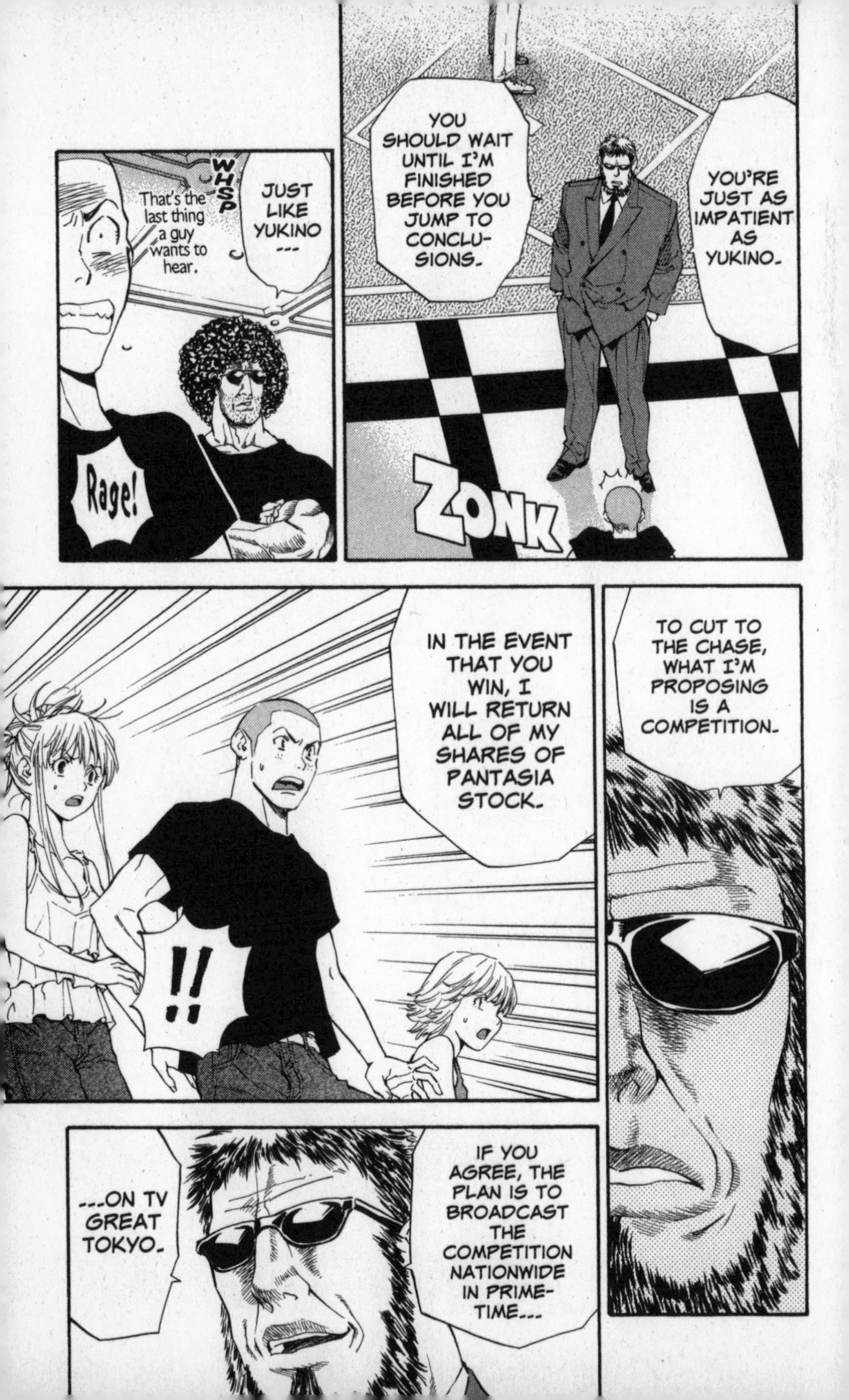

YOU'RE JUST AS IMPATIENT AS YUKINO.
YOU SHOULD WAIT UNTIL I'M FINISHED BEFORE YOU JUMP TO CONCLUSIONS.
ZONK
JUST LIKE YUKINO...
WHSP
That's the last thing a guy wants to hear.
Rage!
TO CUT TO THE CHASE, WHAT I'M PROPOSING IS A COMPETITION.
IN THE EVENT THAT YOU WIN, I WILL RETURN ALL OF MY SHARES OF PANTASIA STOCK.
!!
IF YOU AGREE, THE PLAN IS TO BROADCAST THE COMPETITION NATIONWIDE IN PRIME-TIME...
...ON TV GREAT TOKYO.

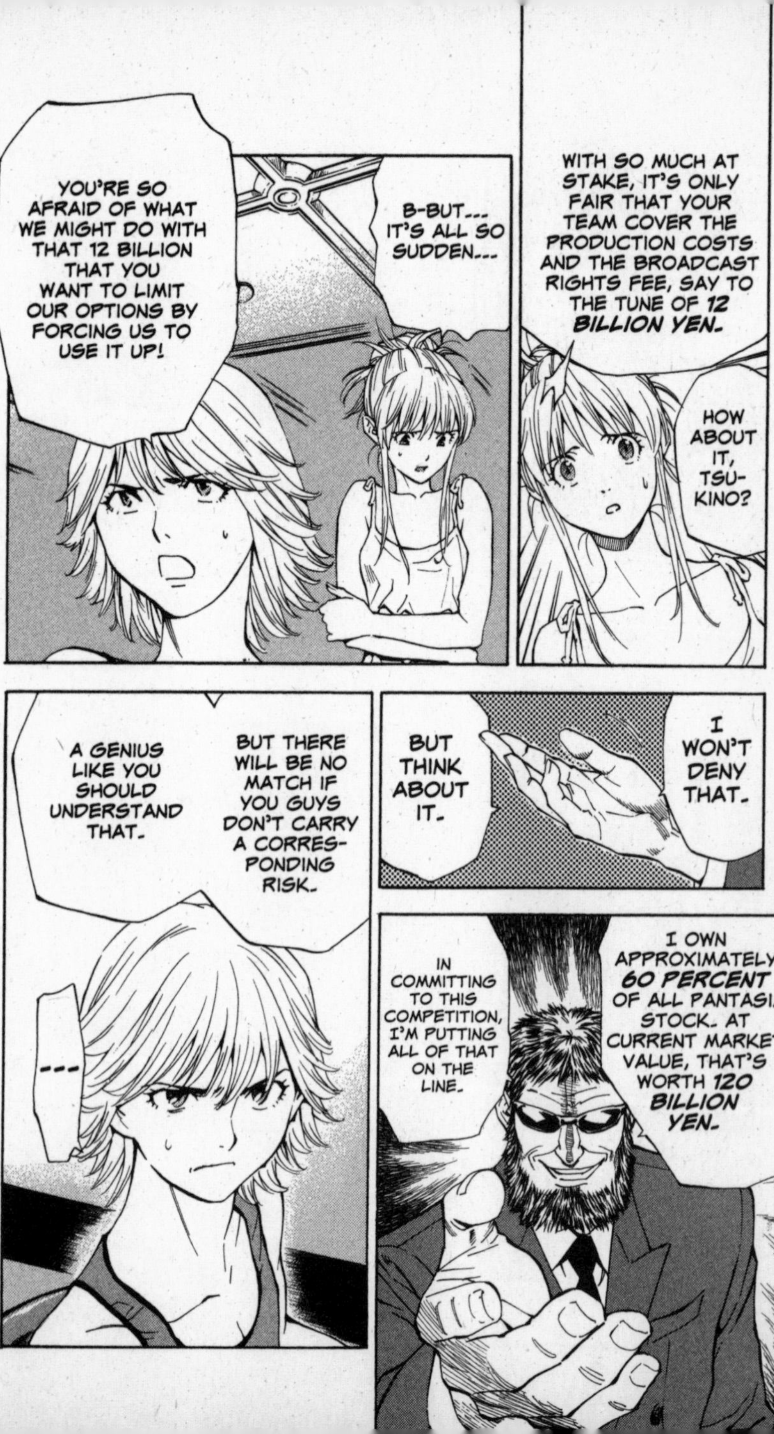
WITH SO MUCH AT STAKE, IT'S ONLY FAIR THAT YOUR TEAM COVER THE PRODUCTION COSTS AND THE BROADCAST RIGHTS FEE, SAY TO THE TUNE OF *12 BILLION YEN.*
HOW ABOUT IT, TSU-KINO?
B-BUT... IT'S ALL SO SUDDEN...
YOU'RE SO AFRAID OF WHAT WE MIGHT DO WITH THAT 12 BILLION THAT YOU WANT TO LIMIT OUR OPTIONS BY FORCING US TO USE IT UP!
I WON'T DENY THAT.
BUT THINK ABOUT IT.
I OWN APPROXIMATELY *60 PERCENT* OF ALL PANTASIA STOCK. AT CURRENT MARKET VALUE, THAT'S WORTH *120 BILLION YEN.*
IN COMMITTING TO THIS COMPETITION, I'M PUTTING ALL OF THAT ON THE LINE.
BUT THERE WILL BE NO MATCH IF YOU GUYS DON'T CARRY A CORRES-PONDING RISK.
A GENIUS LIKE YOU SHOULD UNDERSTAND THAT.
...

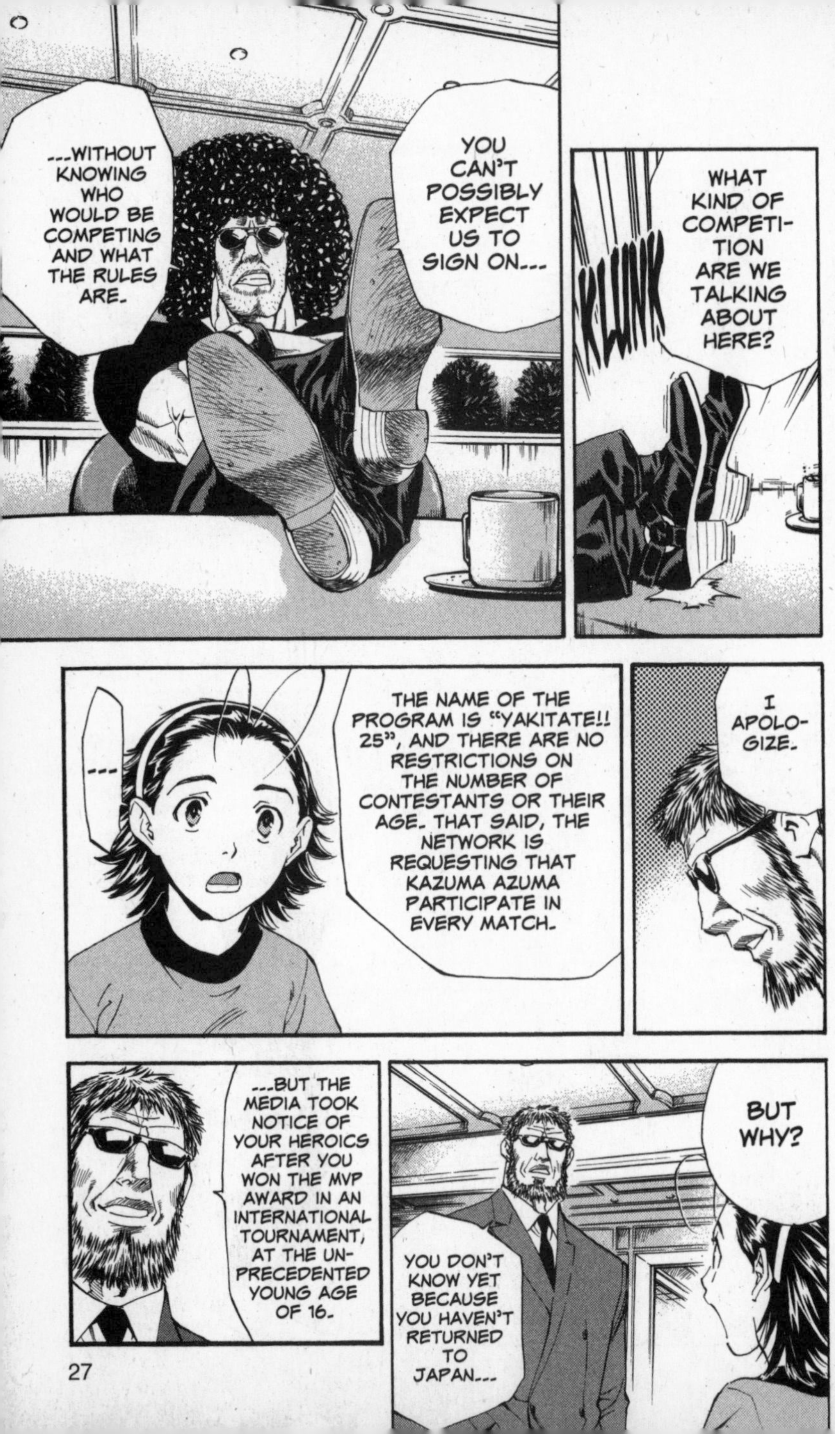
WHAT KIND OF COMPETITION ARE WE TALKING ABOUT HERE?
KLUNK
YOU CAN'T POSSIBLY EXPECT US TO SIGN ON...
...WITHOUT KNOWING WHO WOULD BE COMPETING AND WHAT THE RULES ARE.
I APOLOGIZE.
THE NAME OF THE PROGRAM IS "YAKITATE!! 25", AND THERE ARE NO RESTRICTIONS ON THE NUMBER OF CONTESTANTS OR THEIR AGE. THAT SAID, THE NETWORK IS REQUESTING THAT KAZUMA AZUMA PARTICIPATE IN EVERY MATCH.
...
BUT WHY?
YOU DON'T KNOW YET BECAUSE YOU HAVEN'T RETURNED TO JAPAN...
...BUT THE MEDIA TOOK NOTICE OF YOUR HEROICS AFTER YOU WON THE MVP AWARD IN AN INTERNATIONAL TOURNAMENT, AT THE UNPRECEDENTED YOUNG AGE OF 16.

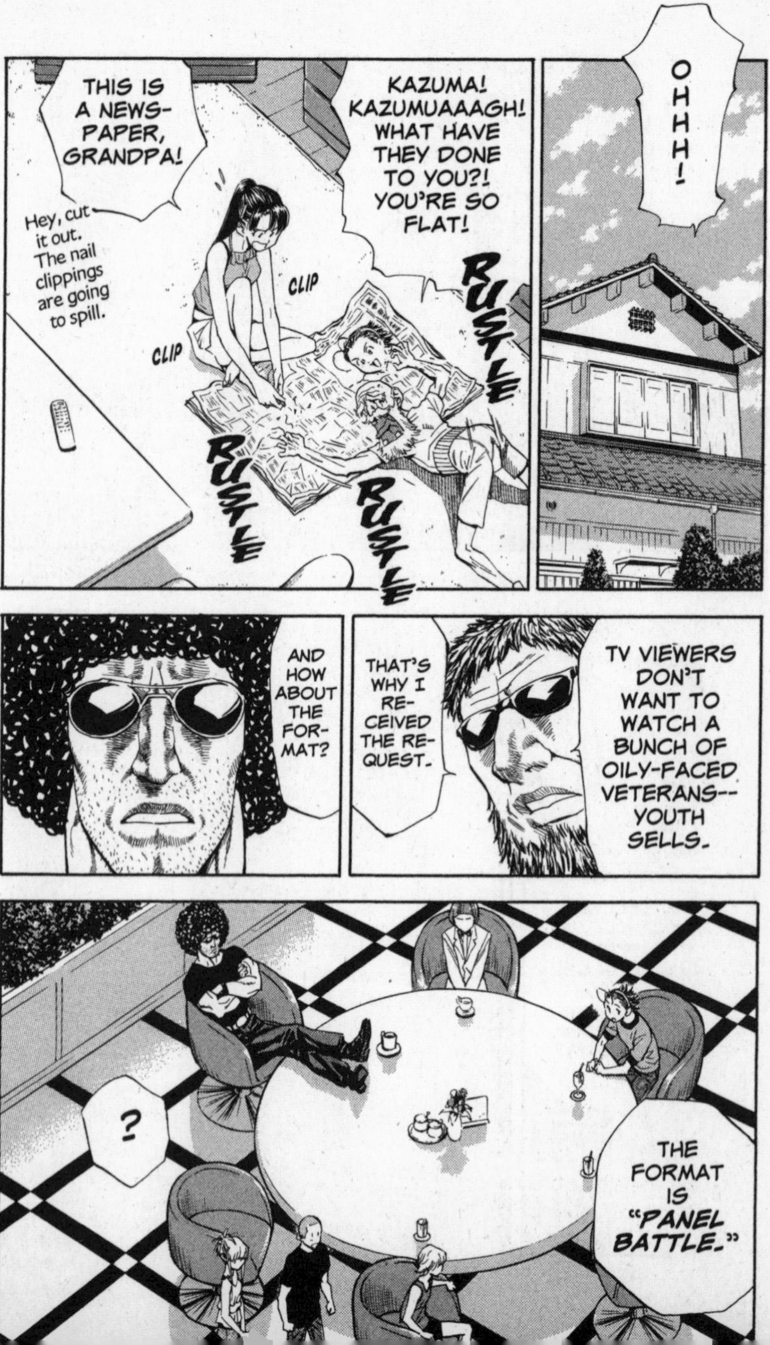
OHHHH!
KAZUMA! KAZUMUAAAGH! WHAT HAVE THEY DONE TO YOU?! YOU'RE SO FLAT!
RUSTLE
THIS IS A NEWS-PAPER, GRANDPA!
Hey, cut it out. The nail clippings are going to spill.
CLIP
CLIP
RUSTLE
RUSTLE
TV VIEWERS DON'T WANT TO WATCH A BUNCH OF OILY-FACED VETERANS-- YOUTH SELLS.
THAT'S WHY I RE-CEIVED THE RE-QUEST.
AND HOW ABOUT THE FOR-MAT?
THE FORMAT IS "PANEL BATTLE."
?

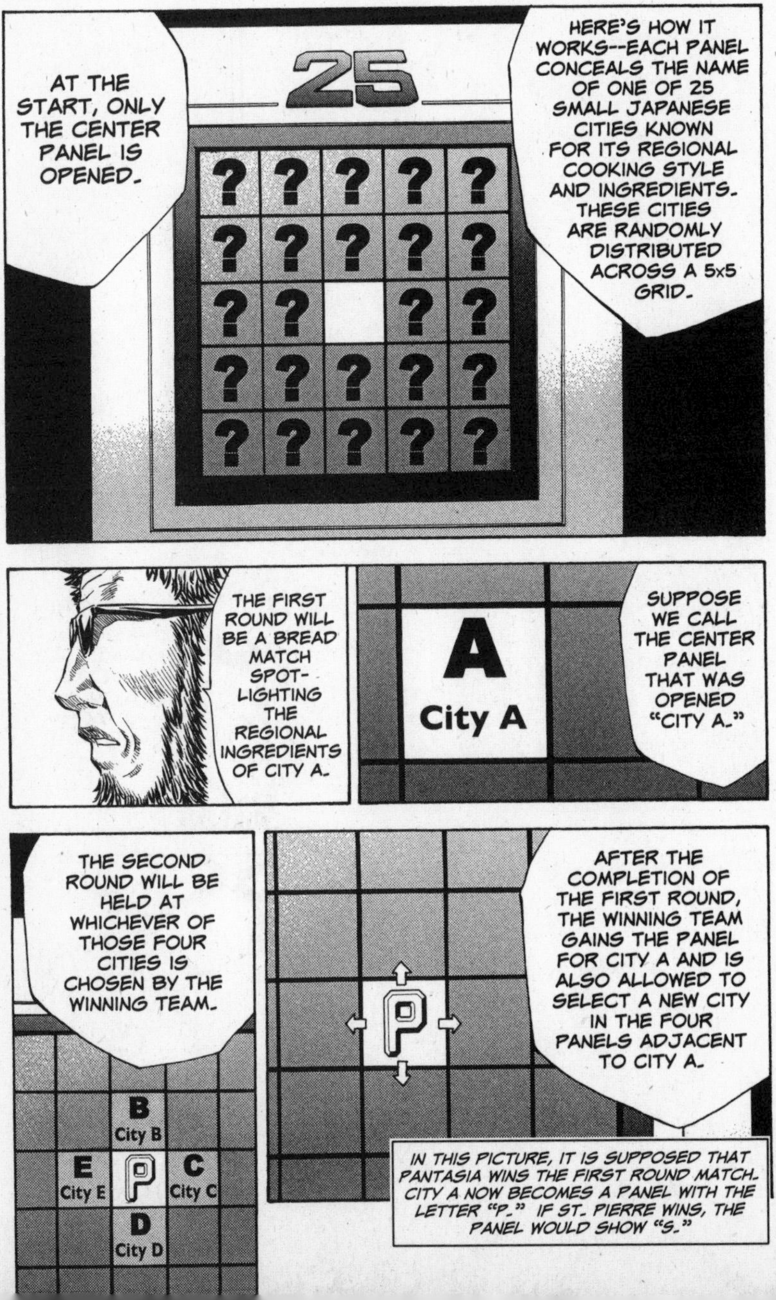

HERE'S HOW IT WORKS--EACH PANEL CONCEALS THE NAME OF ONE OF 25 SMALL JAPANESE CITIES KNOWN FOR ITS REGIONAL COOKING STYLE AND INGREDIENTS. THESE CITIES ARE RANDOMLY DISTRIBUTED ACROSS A 5x5 GRID.
25
AT THE START, ONLY THE CENTER PANEL IS OPENED.
SUPPOSE WE CALL THE CENTER PANEL THAT WAS OPENED "CITY A."
A
City A
THE FIRST ROUND WILL BE A BREAD MATCH SPOT-LIGHTING THE REGIONAL INGREDIENTS OF CITY A.
AFTER THE COMPLETION OF THE FIRST ROUND, THE WINNING TEAM GAINS THE PANEL FOR CITY A AND IS ALSO ALLOWED TO SELECT A NEW CITY IN THE FOUR PANELS ADJACENT TO CITY A.
P
IN THIS PICTURE, IT IS SUPPOSED THAT PANTASIA WINS THE FIRST ROUND MATCH. CITY A NOW BECOMES A PANEL WITH THE LETTER "P." IF ST. PIERRE WINS, THE PANEL WOULD SHOW "S."
THE SECOND ROUND WILL BE HELD AT WHICHEVER OF THOSE FOUR CITIES IS CHOSEN BY THE WINNING TEAM.
B
City B
E
City E
P
C
City C
D
City D

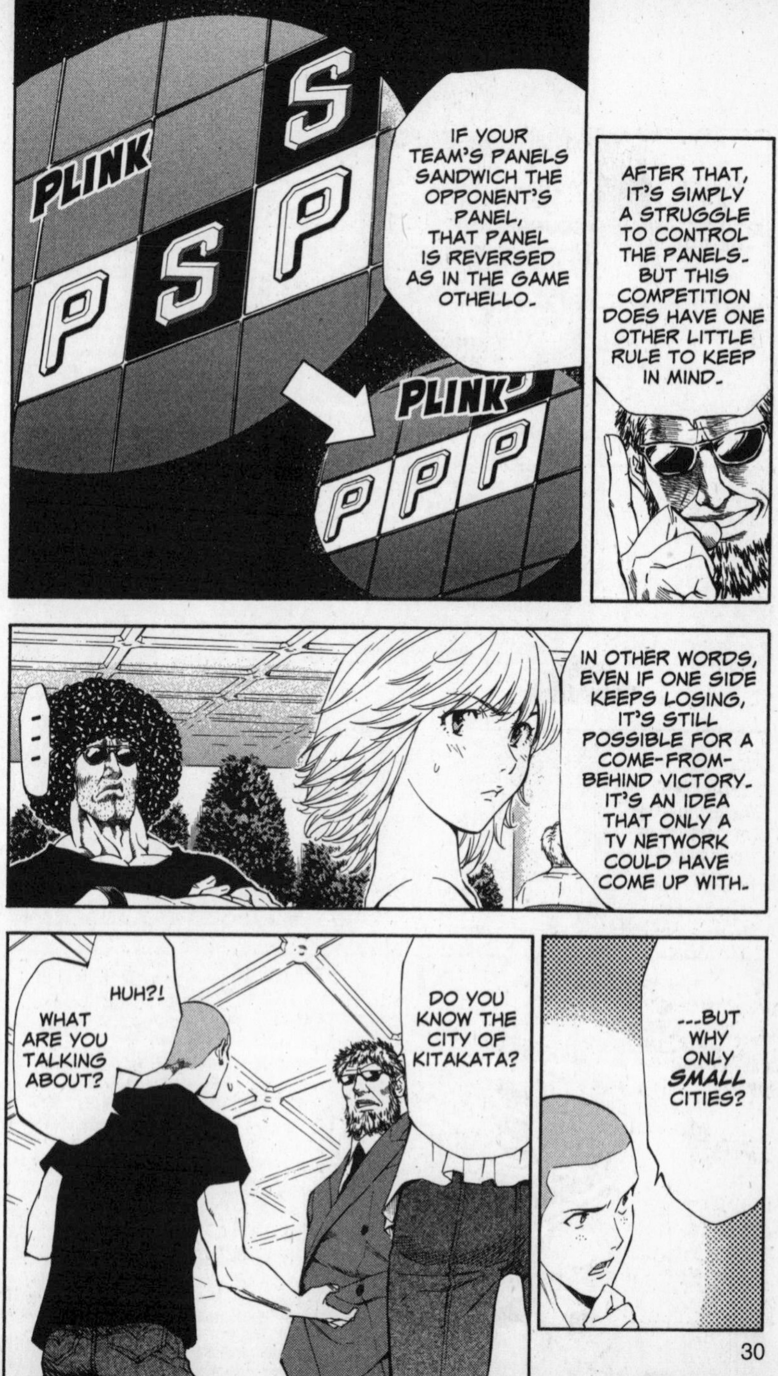
AFTER THAT, IT'S SIMPLY A STRUGGLE TO CONTROL THE PANELS. BUT THIS COMPETITION DOES HAVE ONE OTHER LITTLE RULE TO KEEP IN MIND.
IF YOUR TEAM'S PANELS SANDWICH THE OPPONENT'S PANEL, THAT PANEL IS REVERSED AS IN THE GAME OTHELLO.
PLINK
PLINK
IN OTHER WORDS, EVEN IF ONE SIDE KEEPS LOSING, IT'S STILL POSSIBLE FOR A COME-FROM-BEHIND VICTORY. IT'S AN IDEA THAT ONLY A TV NETWORK COULD HAVE COME UP WITH.
...
...BUT WHY ONLY SMALL CITIES?
DO YOU KNOW THE CITY OF KITAKATA?
HUH?! WHAT ARE YOU TALKING ABOUT?

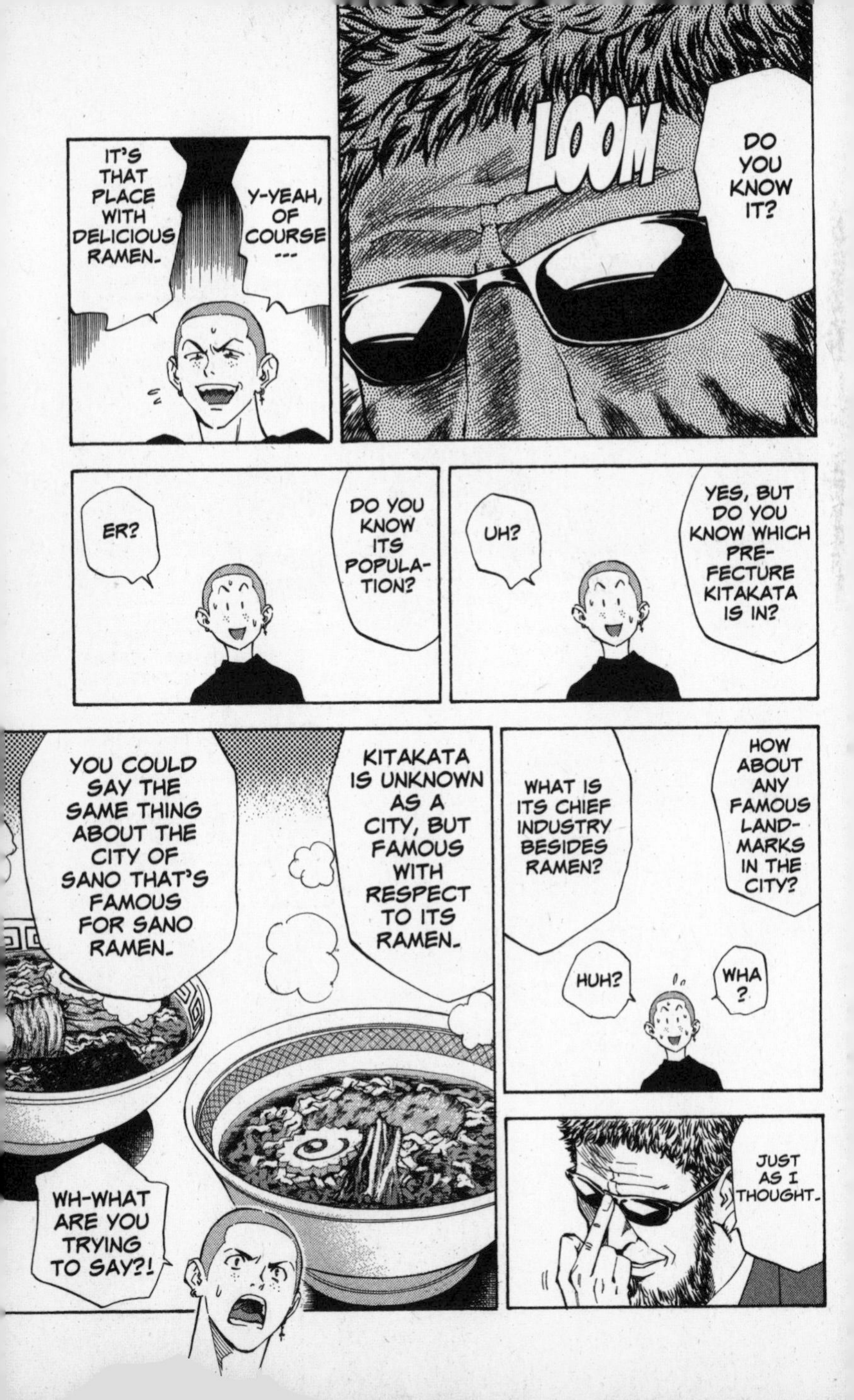
LOOM
DO YOU KNOW IT?
Y-YEAH, OF COURSE---
IT'S THAT PLACE WITH DELICIOUS RAMEN.
YES, BUT DO YOU KNOW WHICH PREFECTURE KITAKATA IS IN?
UH?
DO YOU KNOW ITS POPULATION?
ER?
HOW ABOUT ANY FAMOUS LANDMARKS IN THE CITY?
WHAT IS ITS CHIEF INDUSTRY BESIDES RAMEN?
WHA?
HUH?
JUST AS I THOUGHT.
KITAKATA IS UNKNOWN AS A CITY, BUT FAMOUS WITH RESPECT TO ITS RAMEN.
YOU COULD SAY THE SAME THING ABOUT THE CITY OF SANO THAT'S FAMOUS FOR SANO RAMEN.
WH-WHAT ARE YOU TRYING TO SAY?!

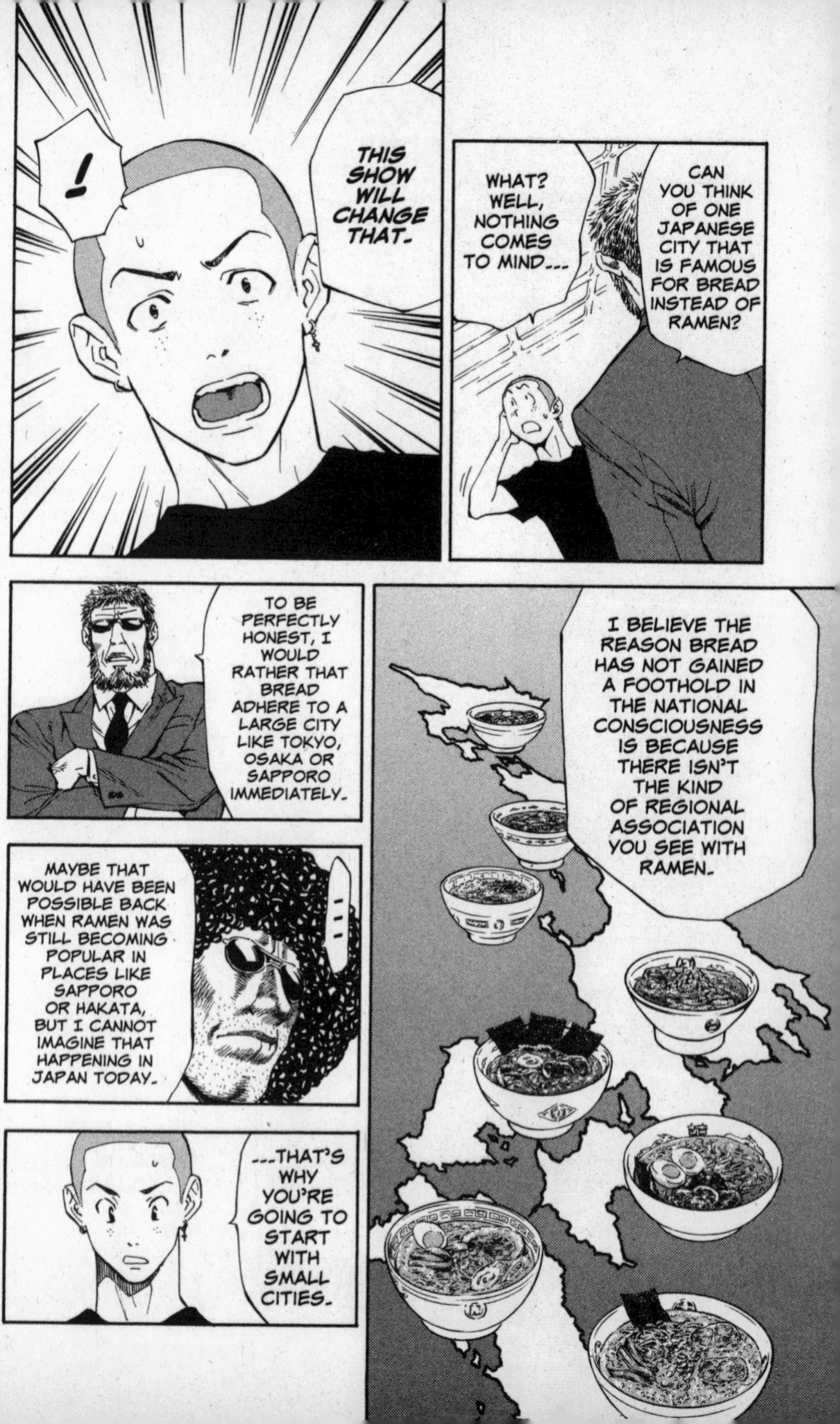
CAN YOU THINK OF ONE JAPANESE CITY THAT IS FAMOUS FOR BREAD INSTEAD OF RAMEN?
WHAT? WELL, NOTHING COMES TO MIND...
THIS SHOW WILL CHANGE THAT.
!
I BELIEVE THE REASON BREAD HAS NOT GAINED A FOOTHOLD IN THE NATIONAL CONSCIOUSNESS IS BECAUSE THERE ISN'T THE KIND OF REGIONAL ASSOCIATION YOU SEE WITH RAMEN.
TO BE PERFECTLY HONEST, I WOULD RATHER THAT BREAD ADHERE TO A LARGE CITY LIKE TOKYO, OSAKA OR SAPPORO IMMEDIATELY.
MAYBE THAT WOULD HAVE BEEN POSSIBLE BACK WHEN RAMEN WAS STILL BECOMING POPULAR IN PLACES LIKE SAPPORO OR HAKATA, BUT I CANNOT IMAGINE THAT HAPPENING IN JAPAN TODAY.
...THAT'S WHY YOU'RE GOING TO START WITH SMALL CITIES.

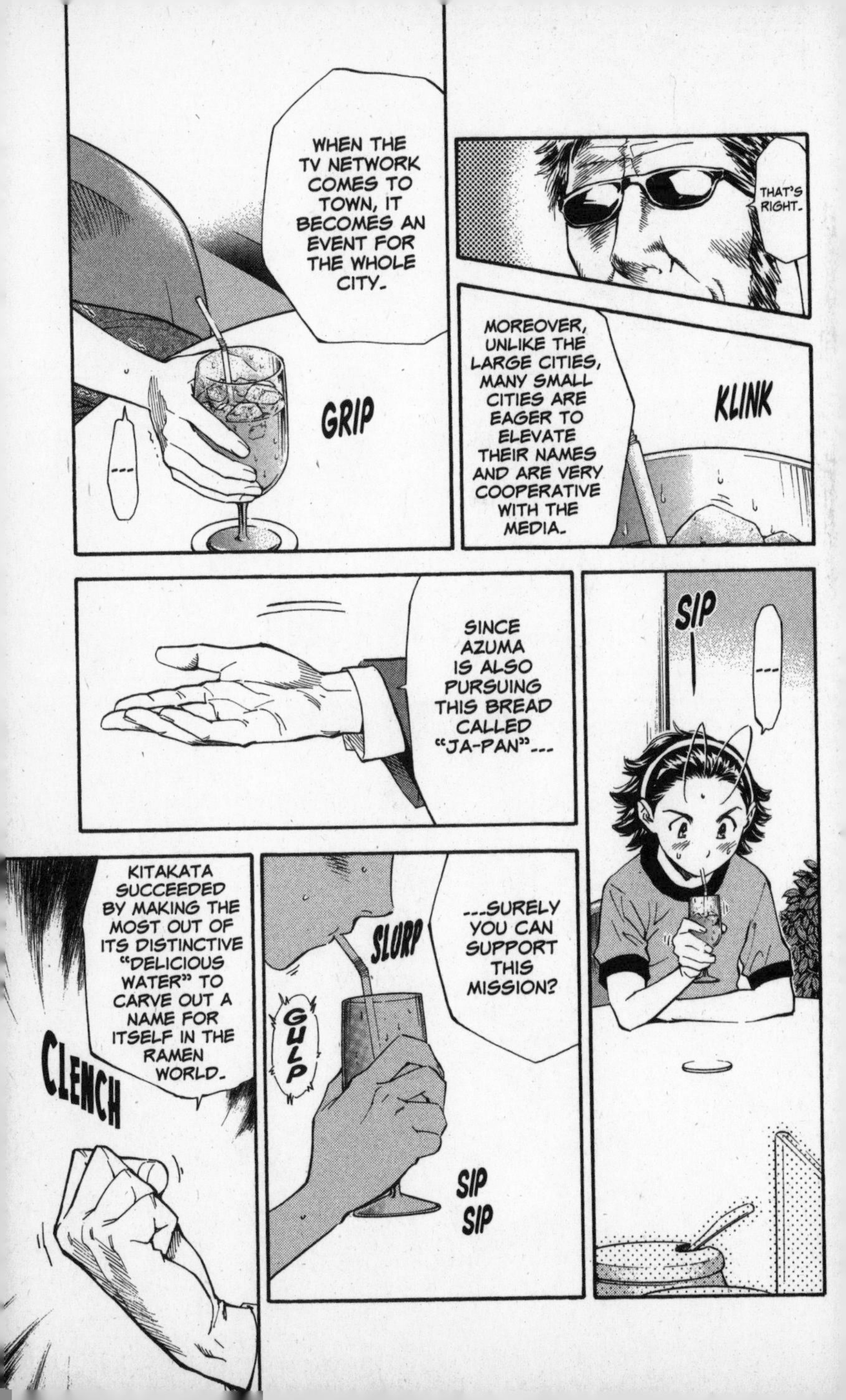
THAT'S RIGHT.
MOREOVER, UNLIKE THE LARGE CITIES, MANY SMALL CITIES ARE EAGER TO ELEVATE THEIR NAMES AND ARE VERY COOPERATIVE WITH THE MEDIA.
KLINK
WHEN THE TV NETWORK COMES TO TOWN, IT BECOMES AN EVENT FOR THE WHOLE CITY.
GRIP
...
SIP
...
SINCE AZUMA IS ALSO PURSUING THIS BREAD CALLED "JA-PAN"...
...SURELY YOU CAN SUPPORT THIS MISSION?
SLURP
GULP
SIP SIP
KITAKATA SUCCEEDED BY MAKING THE MOST OUT OF ITS DISTINCTIVE "DELICIOUS WATER" TO CARVE OUT A NAME FOR ITSELF IN THE RAMEN WORLD.
CLENCH

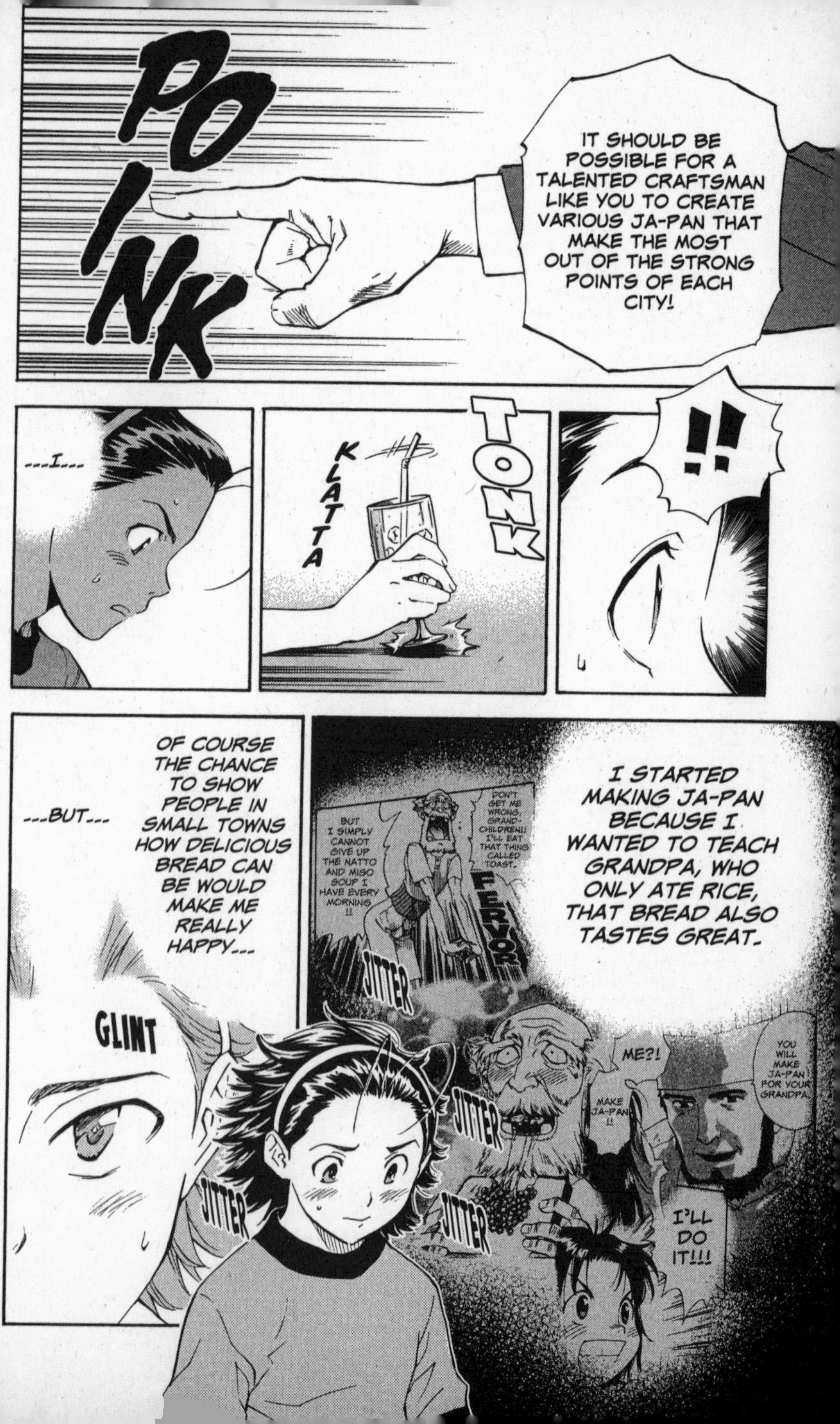
POINK
IT SHOULD BE POSSIBLE FOR A TALENTED CRAFTSMAN LIKE YOU TO CREATE VARIOUS JA-PAN THAT MAKE THE MOST OUT OF THE STRONG POINTS OF EACH CITY!
!!
TONK
KLATTA
...I...
I STARTED MAKING JA-PAN BECAUSE I WANTED TO TEACH GRANDPA, WHO ONLY ATE RICE, THAT BREAD ALSO TASTES GREAT.
DON'T GET ME WRONG, GRAND-CHILDREN!! I'LL EAT THAT THING CALLED TOAST.
BUT I SIMPLY CANNOT GIVE UP THE NATTO AND MISO SOUP I HAVE EVERY MORNING!!
FERVOR
JITTER
YOU WILL MAKE JA-PAN FOR YOUR GRANDPA.
ME?!
MAKE JA-PAN!!
I'LL DO IT!!!
JITTER
JITTER
JITTER
OF COURSE THE CHANCE TO SHOW PEOPLE IN SMALL TOWNS HOW DELICIOUS BREAD CAN BE WOULD MAKE ME REALLY HAPPY...
...BUT...
GLINT

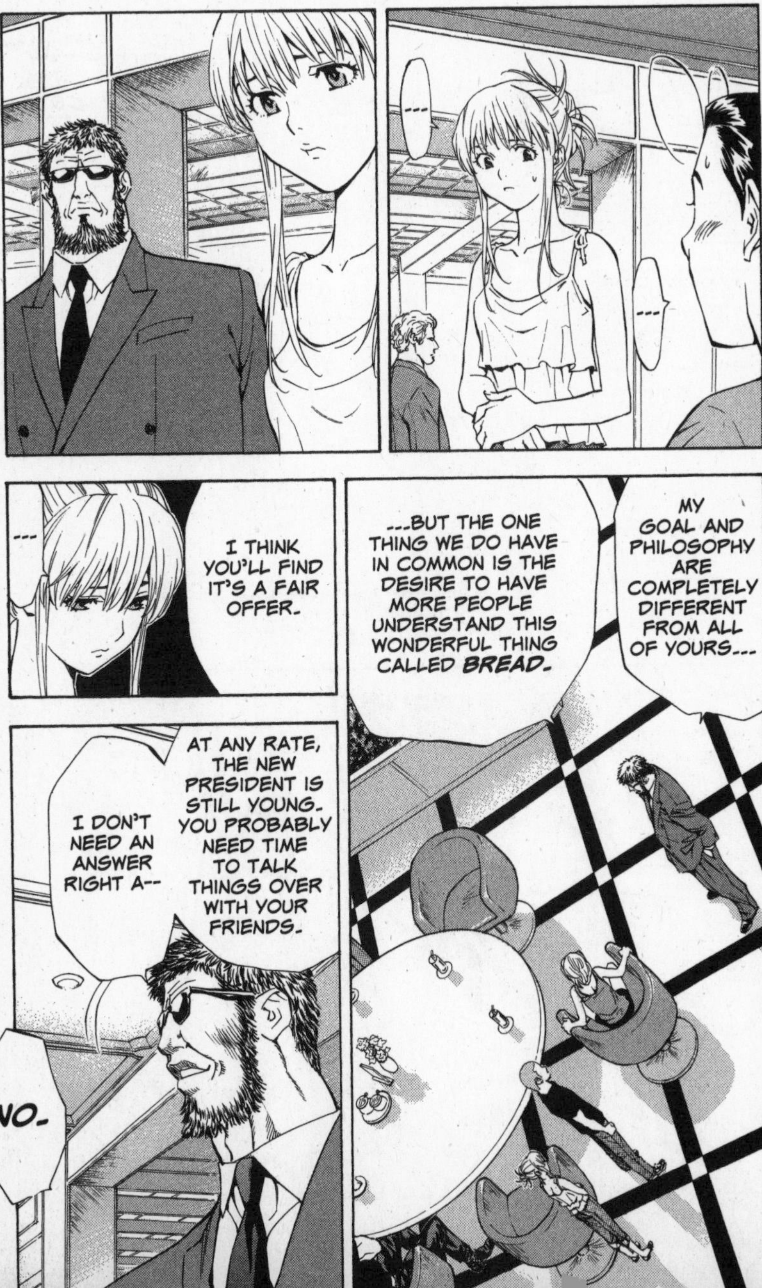
...
...
MY GOAL AND PHILOSOPHY ARE COMPLETELY DIFFERENT FROM ALL OF YOURS...
...BUT THE ONE THING WE DO HAVE IN COMMON IS THE DESIRE TO HAVE MORE PEOPLE UNDERSTAND THIS WONDERFUL THING CALLED BREAD.
I THINK YOU'LL FIND IT'S A FAIR OFFER.
...
AT ANY RATE, THE NEW PRESIDENT IS STILL YOUNG. YOU PROBABLY NEED TIME TO TALK THINGS OVER WITH YOUR FRIENDS.
I DON'T NEED AN ANSWER RIGHT A--
NO.

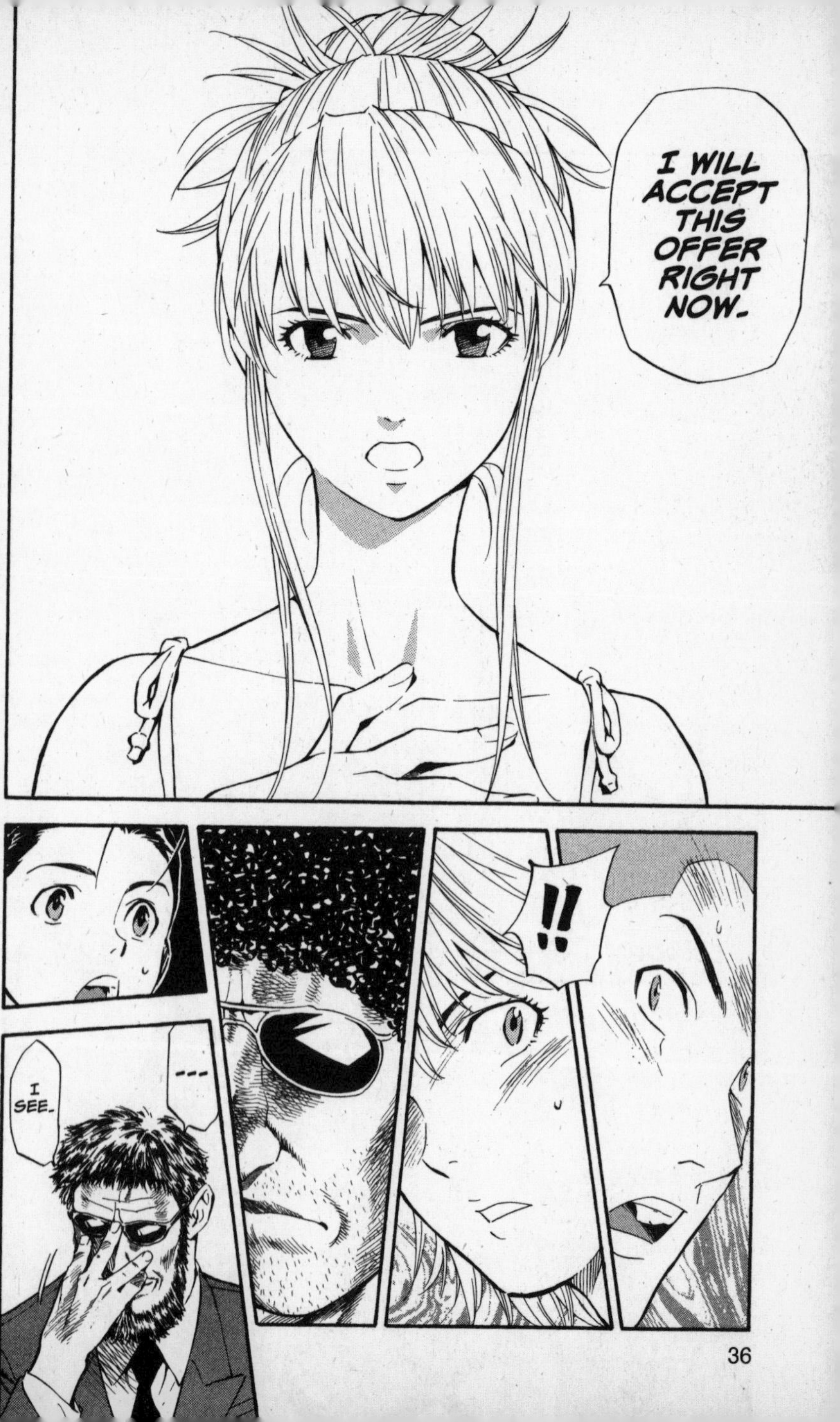
I WILL ACCEPT THIS OFFER RIGHT NOW.
!!
...
I SEE.

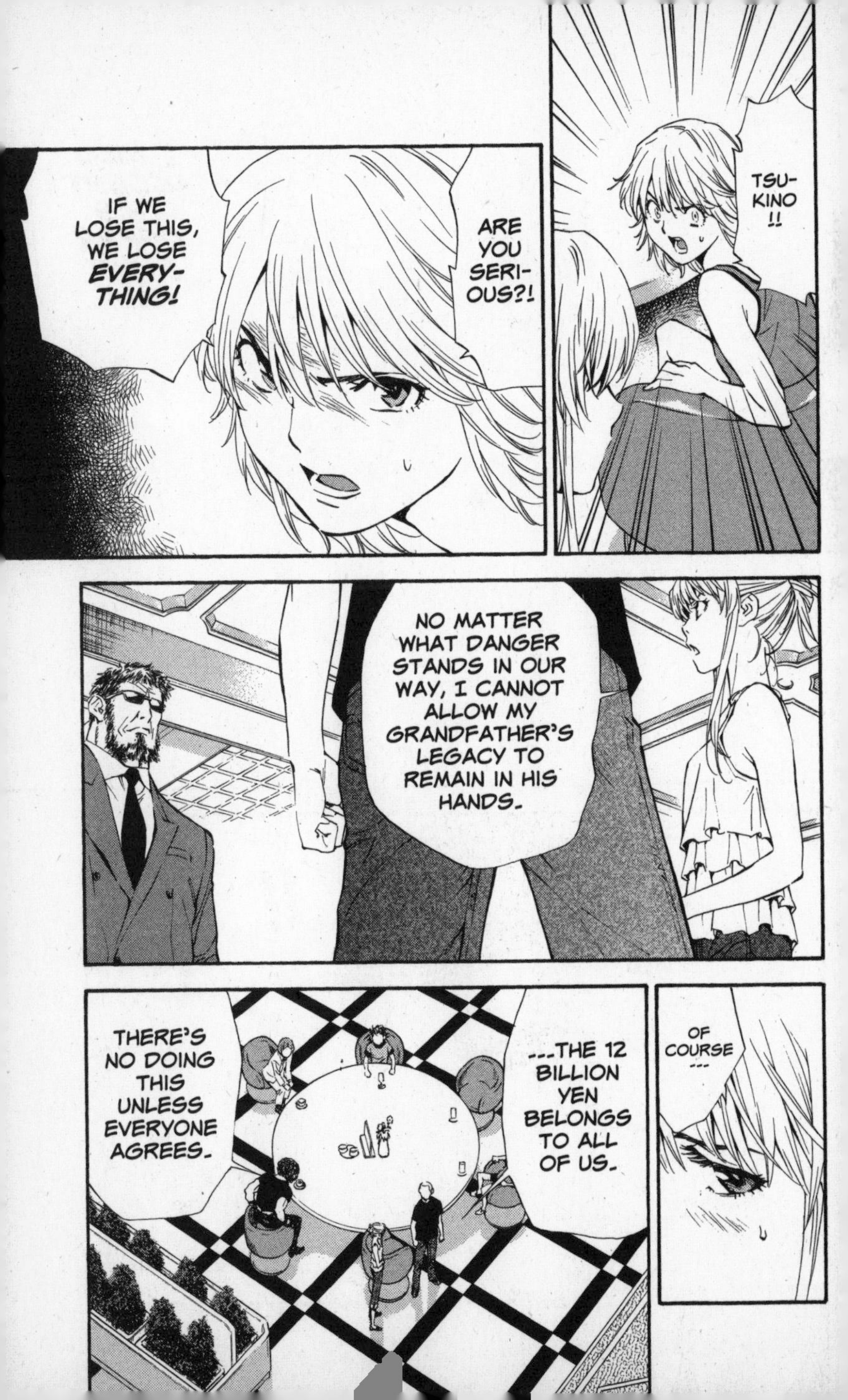
TSU-KINO!!
ARE YOU SERI-OUS?!
IF WE LOSE THIS, WE LOSE EVERY-THING!
NO MATTER WHAT DANGER STANDS IN OUR WAY, I CANNOT ALLOW MY GRANDFATHER'S LEGACY TO REMAIN IN HIS HANDS.
OF COURSE---
---THE 12 BILLION YEN BELONGS TO ALL OF US.
THERE'S NO DOING THIS UNLESS EVERYONE AGREES.

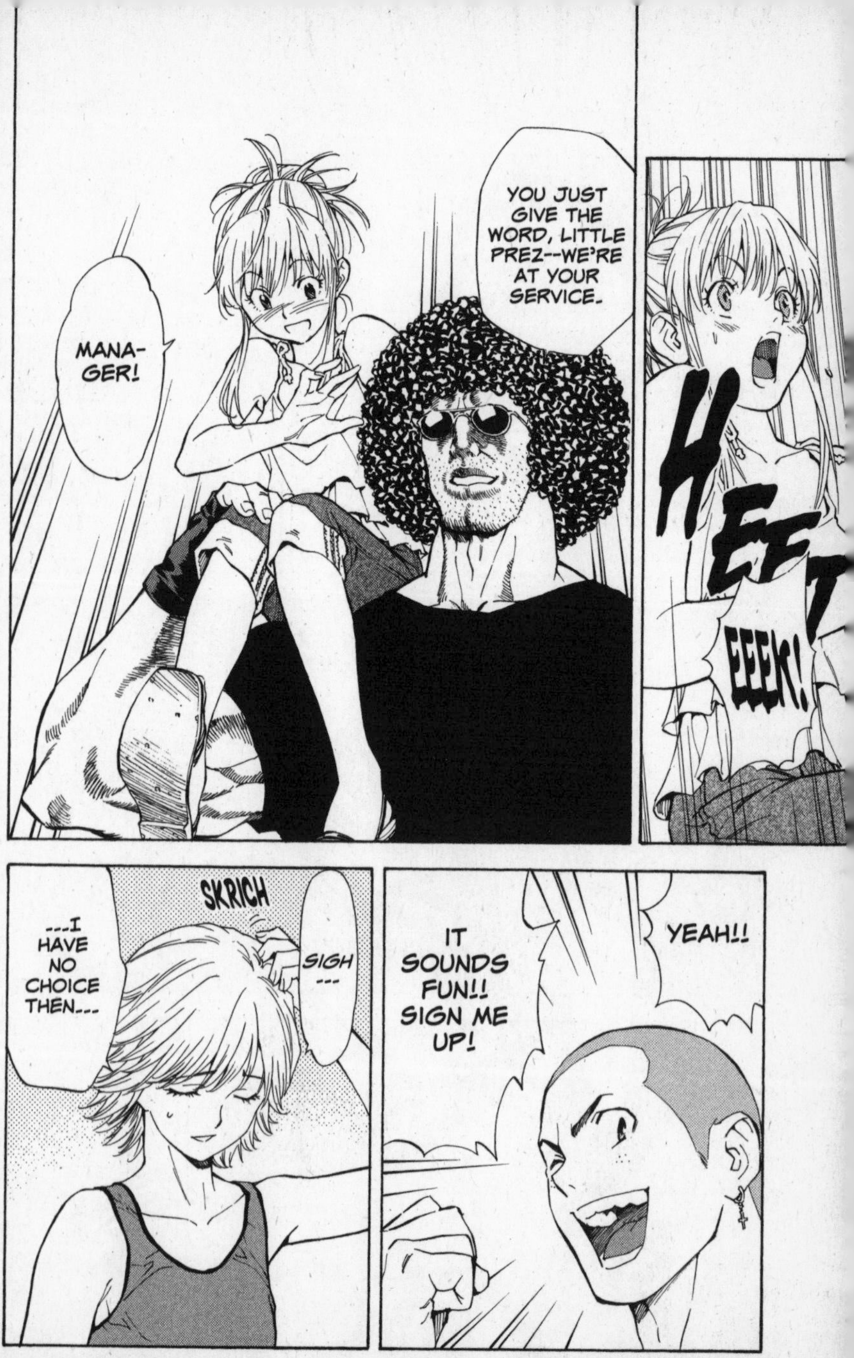
HEE
EEEK!
YOU JUST GIVE THE WORD, LITTLE PREZ--WE'RE AT YOUR SERVICE.
MANA-GER!
YEAH!!
IT SOUNDS FUN!! SIGN ME UP!
SKRICH
SIGH---
---I HAVE NO CHOICE THEN...

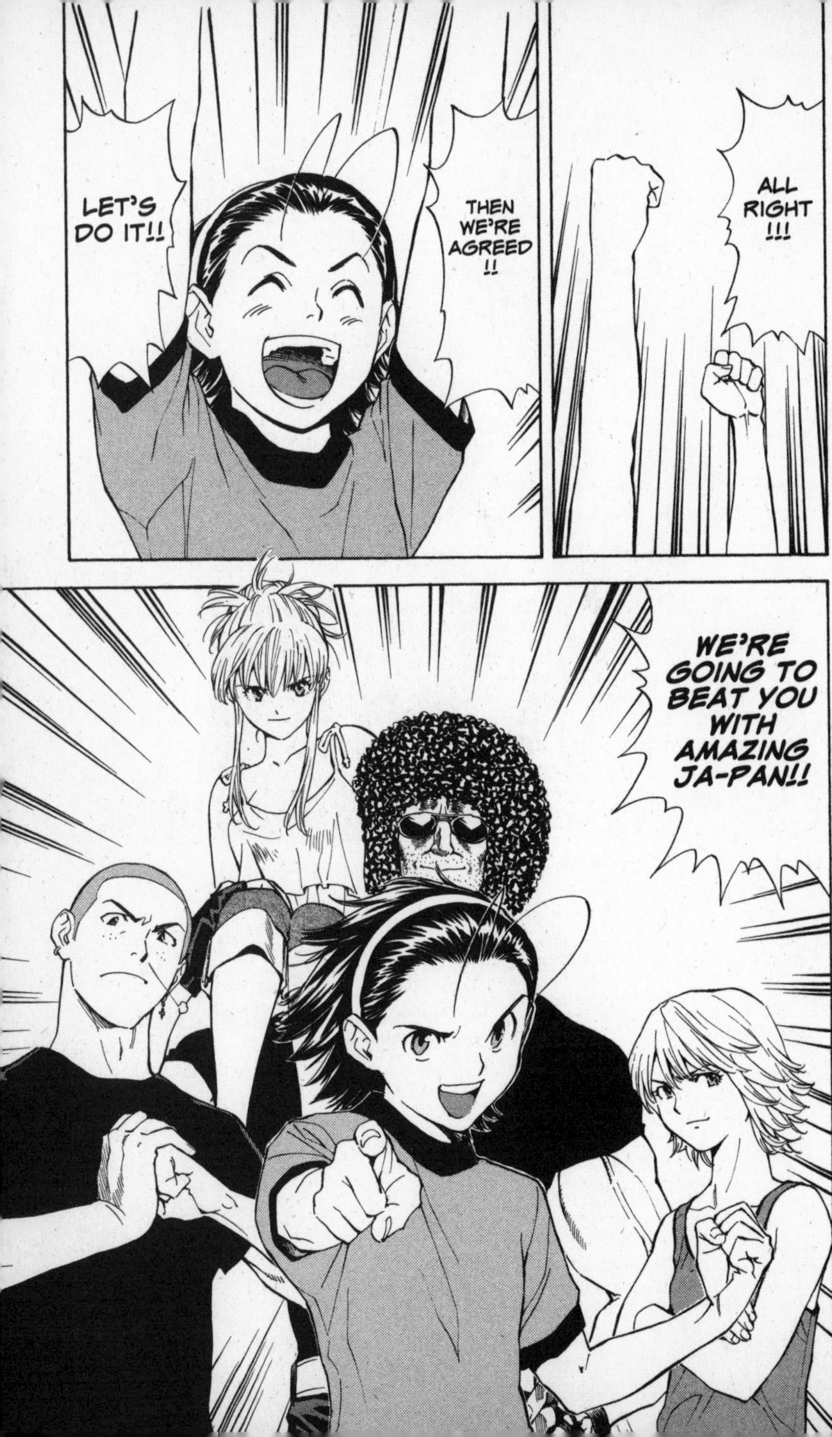
ALL RIGHT!!!
THEN WE'RE AGREED!!
LET'S DO IT!!
WE'RE GOING TO BEAT YOU WITH AMAZING JA-PAN!!

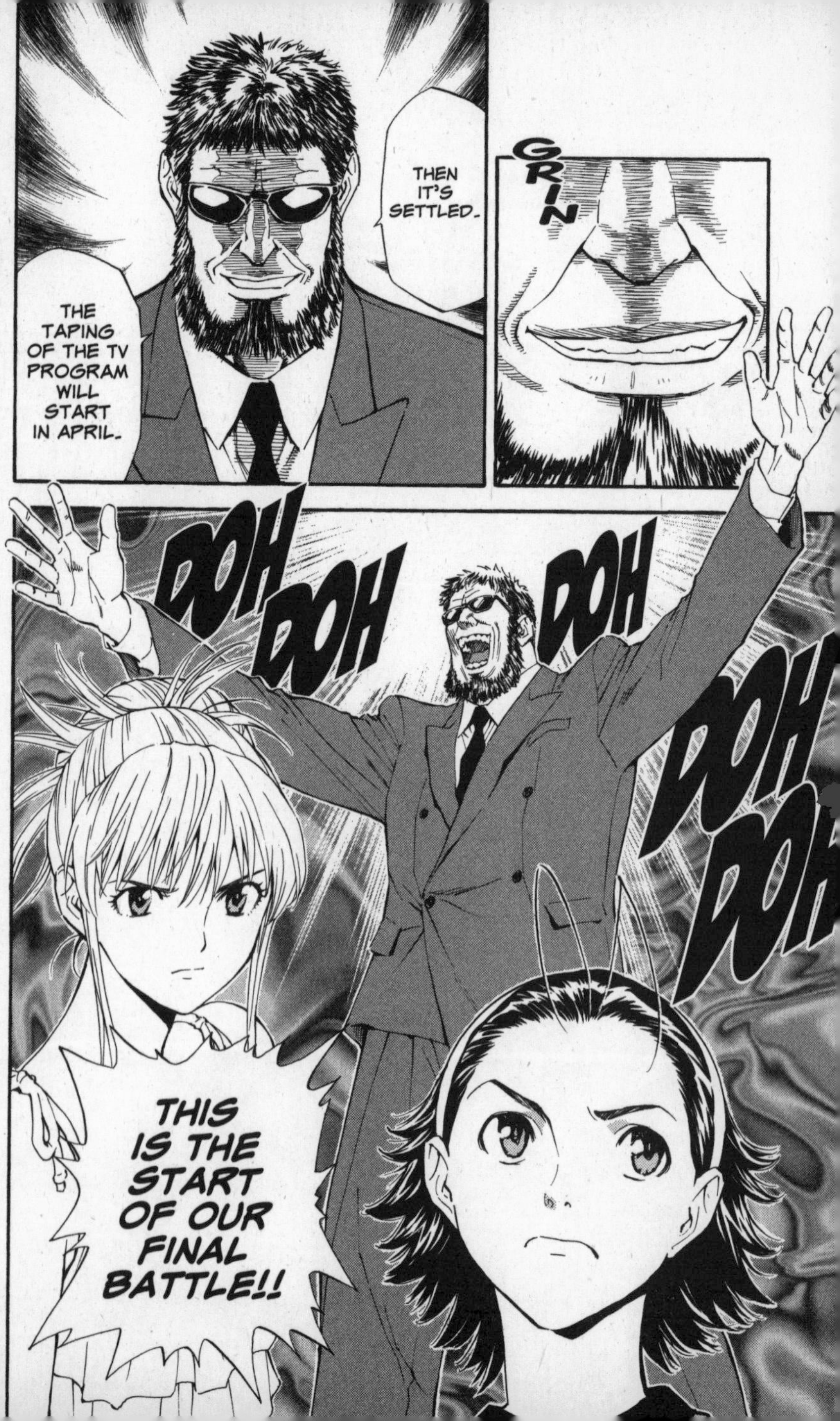
GRIN
THEN IT'S SETTLED.
THE TAPING OF THE TV PROGRAM WILL START IN APRIL.
DOH DOH
DOH
DOH DOH
DOH
THIS IS THE START OF OUR FINAL BATTLE!!

Story 126: First and Last Thing Learned

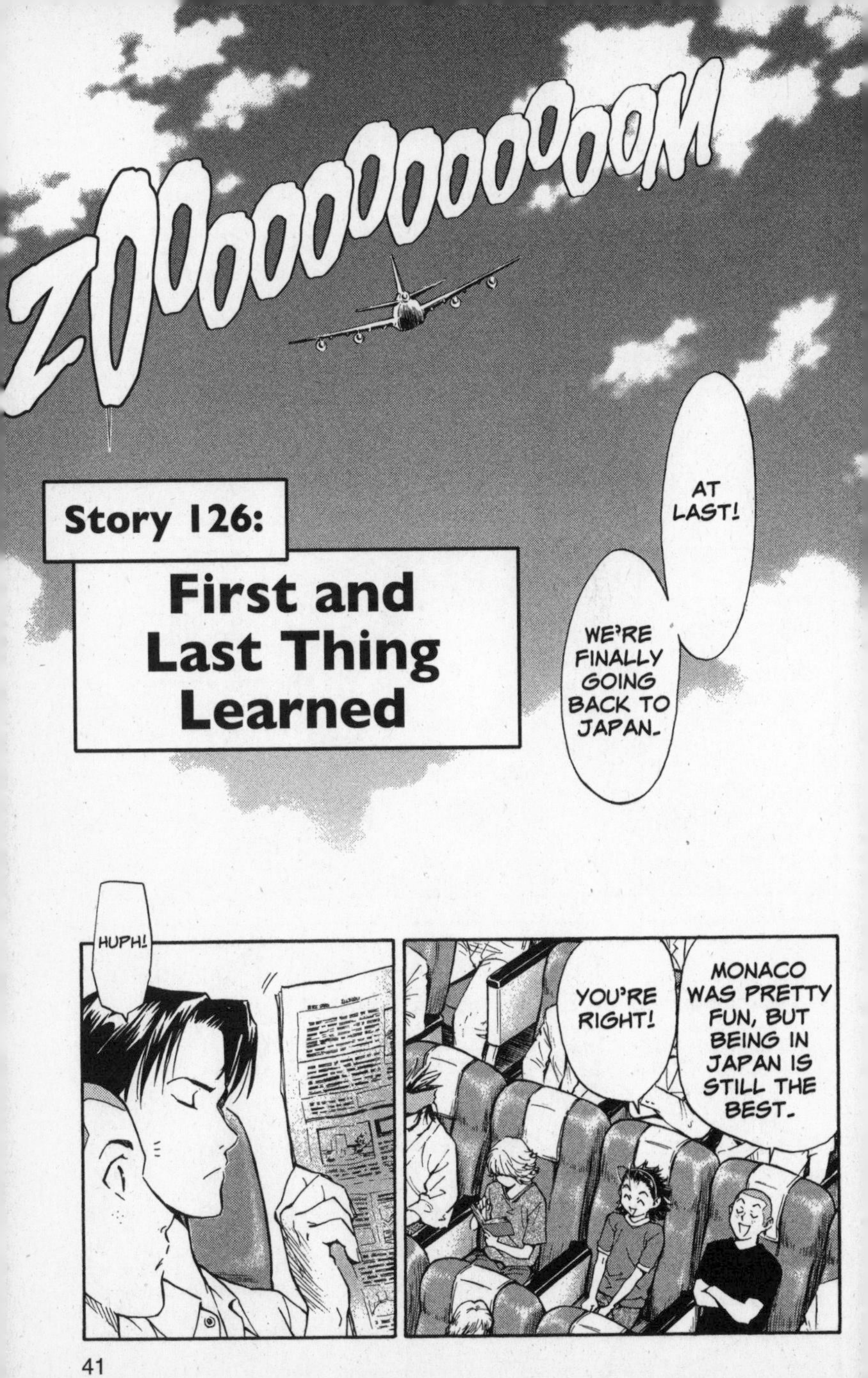
ZOOOOOOOOOOOOOM
AT LAST!
WE'RE FINALLY GOING BACK TO JAPAN.
MONACO WAS PRETTY FUN, BUT BEING IN JAPAN IS STILL THE BEST.
YOU'RE RIGHT!
HUPH!

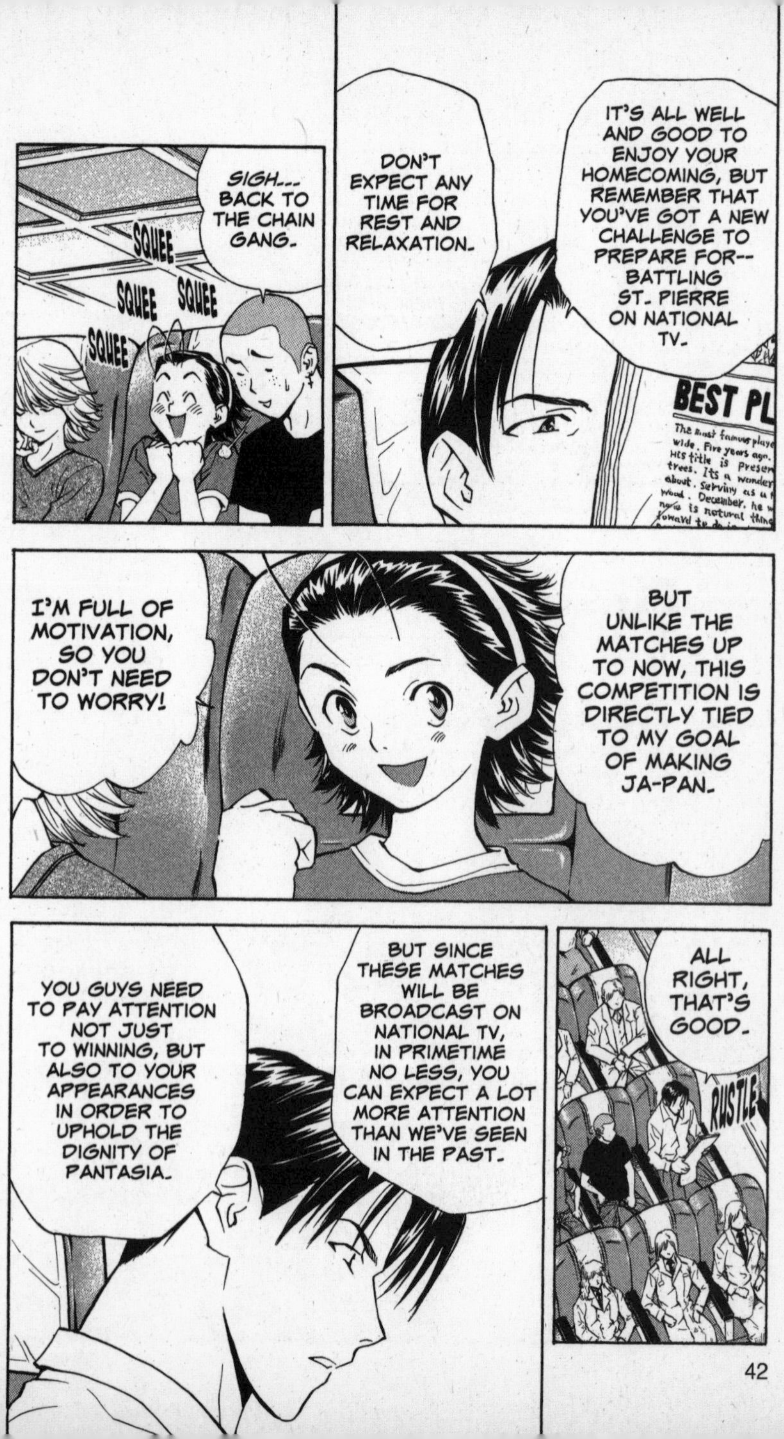
IT'S ALL WELL AND GOOD TO ENJOY YOUR HOMECOMING, BUT REMEMBER THAT YOU'VE GOT A NEW CHALLENGE TO PREPARE FOR-- BATTLING ST. PIERRE ON NATIONAL TV.
DON'T EXPECT ANY TIME FOR REST AND RELAXATION.
SQUEE
SQUEE
SQUEE
SQUEE
SIGH... BACK TO THE CHAIN GANG.
BUT UNLIKE THE MATCHES UP TO NOW, THIS COMPETITION IS DIRECTLY TIED TO MY GOAL OF MAKING JA-PAN.
I'M FULL OF MOTIVATION, SO YOU DON'T NEED TO WORRY!
ALL RIGHT, THAT'S GOOD.
RUSTLE
BUT SINCE THESE MATCHES WILL BE BROADCAST ON NATIONAL TV, IN PRIMETIME NO LESS, YOU CAN EXPECT A LOT MORE ATTENTION THAN WE'VE SEEN IN THE PAST.
YOU GUYS NEED TO PAY ATTENTION NOT JUST TO WINNING, BUT ALSO TO YOUR APPEARANCES IN ORDER TO UPHOLD THE DIGNITY OF PANTASIA.

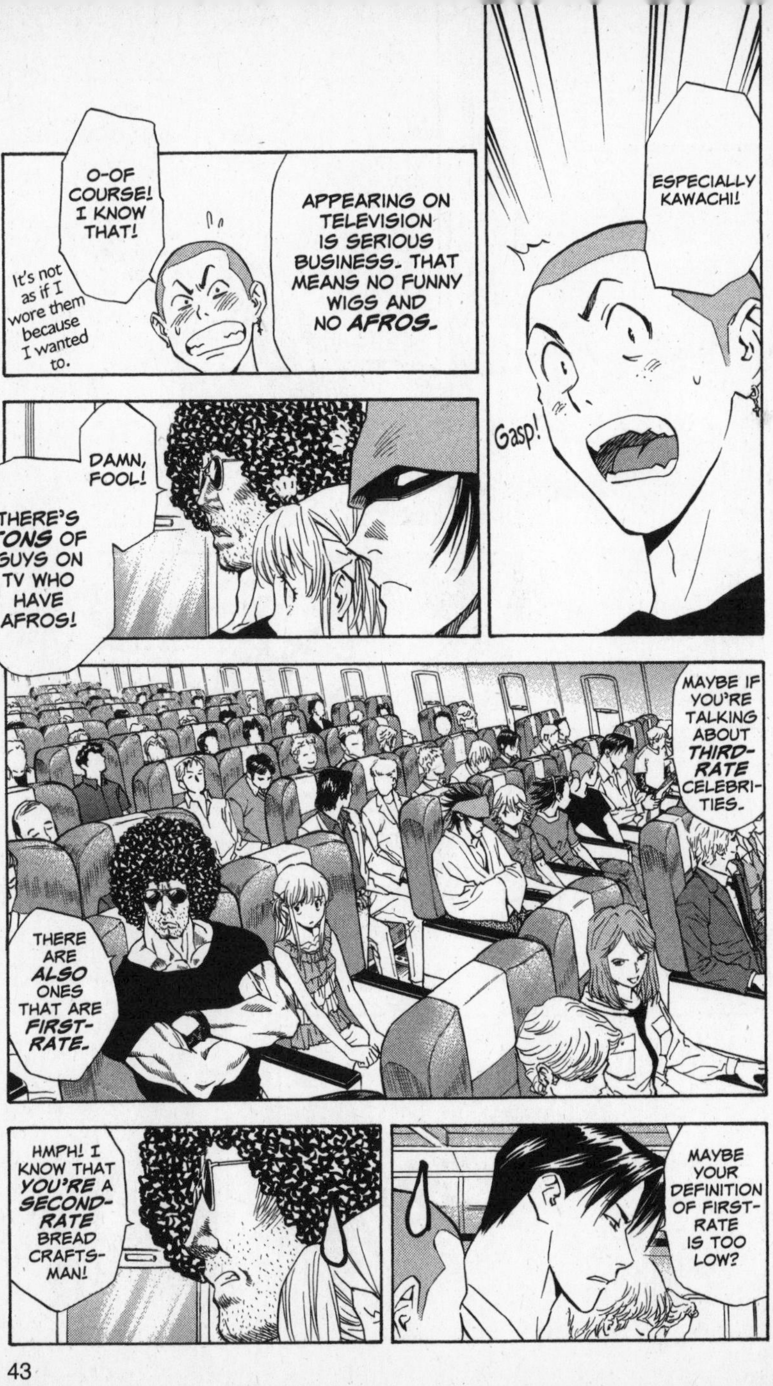

ESPECIALLY KAWACHI!
Gasp!
APPEARING ON TELEVISION IS SERIOUS BUSINESS. THAT MEANS NO FUNNY WIGS AND NO AFROS.
O-OF COURSE! I KNOW THAT!
It's not as if I wore them because I wanted to.
DAMN, FOOL!
THERE'S TONS OF GUYS ON TV WHO HAVE AFROS!
MAYBE IF YOU'RE TALKING ABOUT THIRD-RATE CELEBRITIES.
THERE ARE ALSO ONES THAT ARE FIRST-RATE.
MAYBE YOUR DEFINITION OF FIRST-RATE IS TOO LOW?
HMPH! I KNOW THAT YOU'RE A SECOND-RATE BREAD CRAFTSMAN!

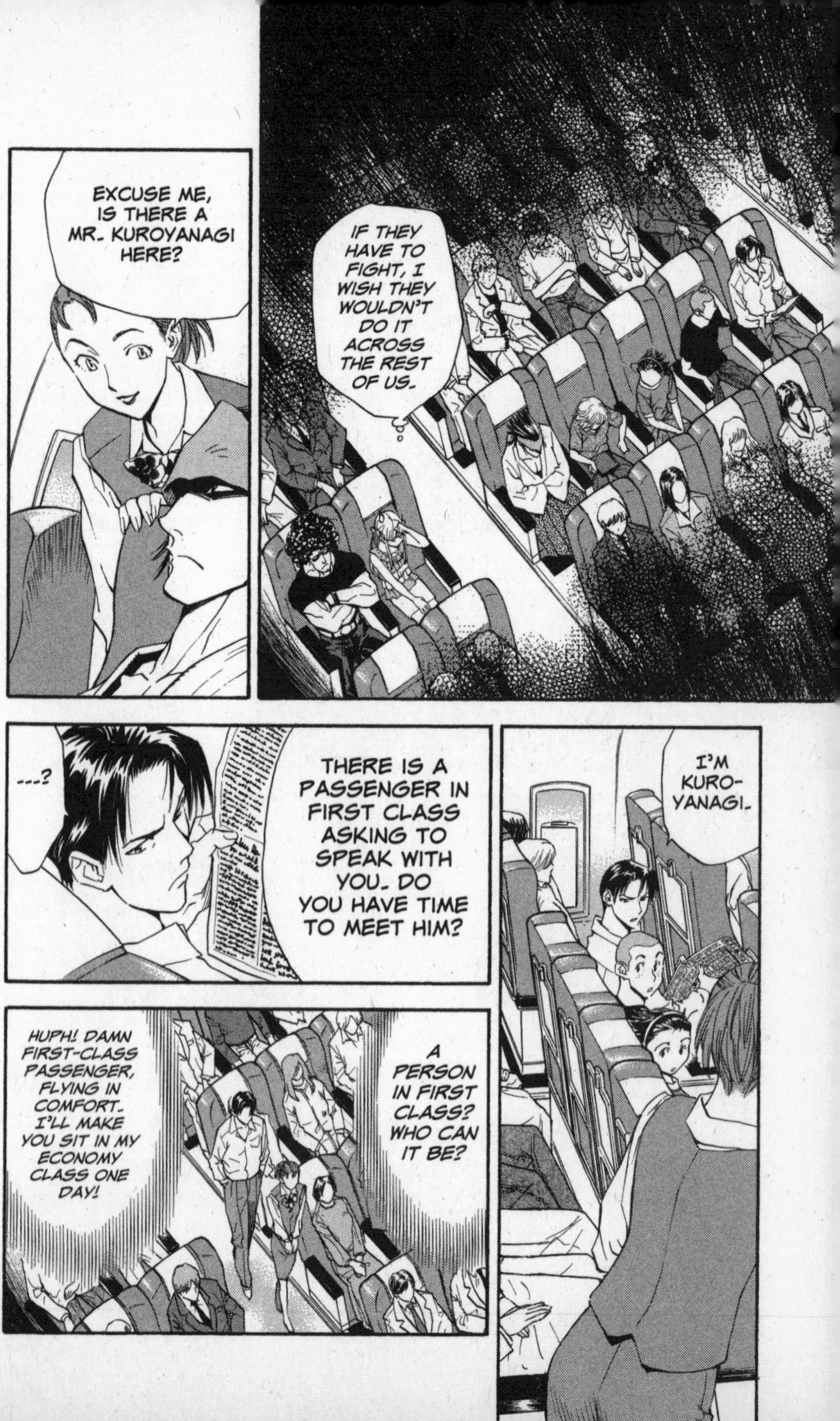
IF THEY HAVE TO FIGHT, I WISH THEY WOULDN'T DO IT ACROSS THE REST OF US.
EXCUSE ME, IS THERE A MR. KUROYANAGI HERE?
I'M KURO-YANAGI.
...?
THERE IS A PASSENGER IN FIRST CLASS ASKING TO SPEAK WITH YOU. DO YOU HAVE TIME TO MEET HIM?
A PERSON IN FIRST CLASS? WHO CAN IT BE?
HUPH! DAMN FIRST-CLASS PASSENGER, FLYING IN COMFORT. I'LL MAKE YOU SIT IN MY ECONOMY CLASS ONE DAY!

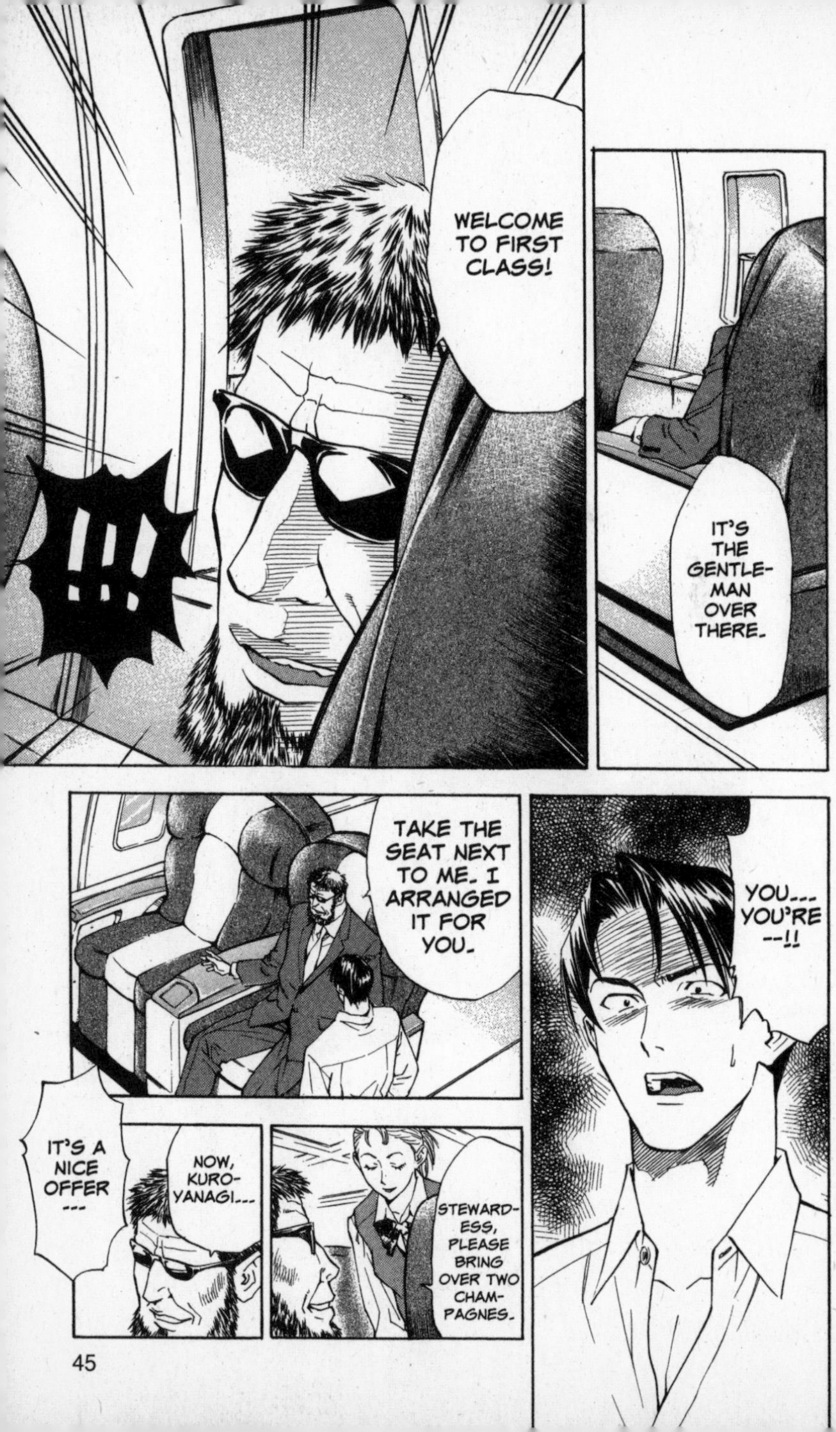
IT'S THE GENTLEMAN OVER THERE.
WELCOME TO FIRST CLASS!
!!
YOU... YOU'RE --!!
TAKE THE SEAT NEXT TO ME. I ARRANGED IT FOR YOU.
STEWARDESS, PLEASE BRING OVER TWO CHAMPAGNES.
NOW, KUROYANAGI...
IT'S A NICE OFFER ---

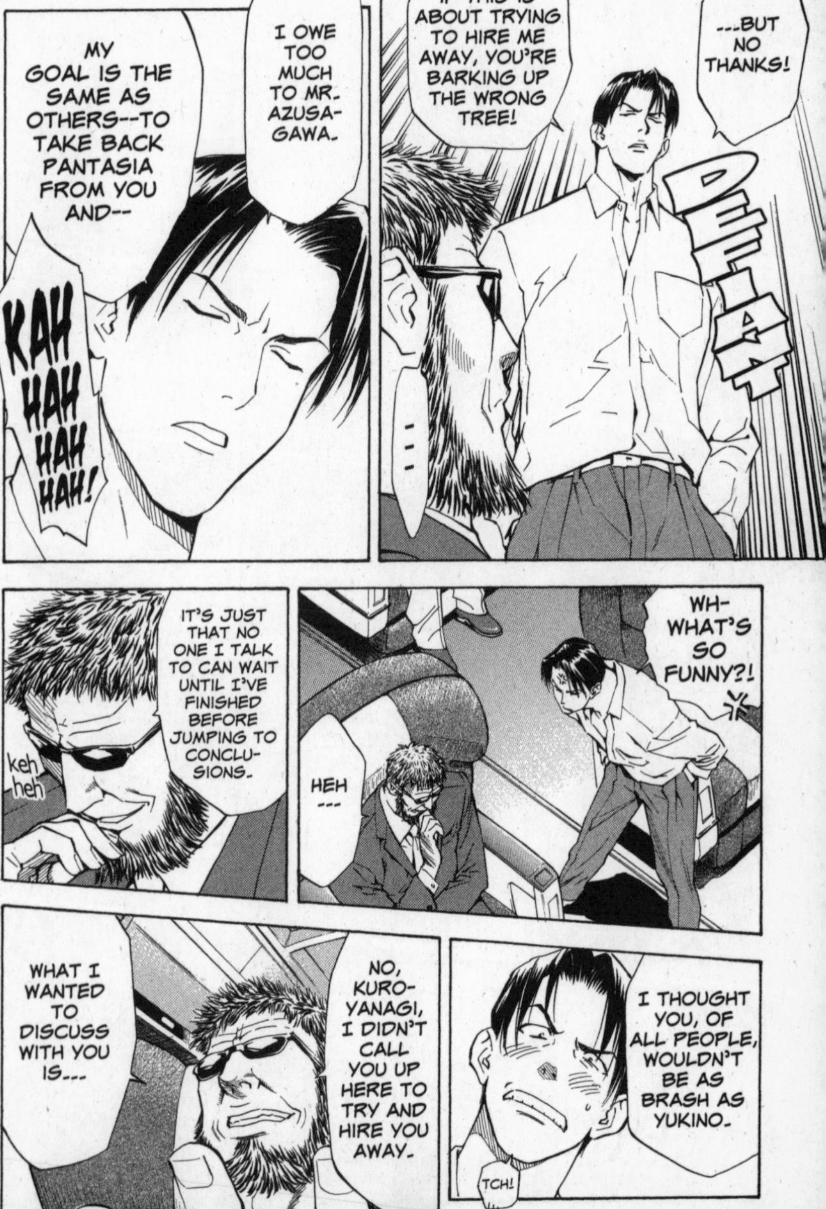

IF THIS IS ABOUT TRYING TO HIRE ME AWAY, YOU'RE BARKING UP THE WRONG TREE!
---BUT NO THANKS!
I OWE TOO MUCH TO MR. AZUSAGAWA.
MY GOAL IS THE SAME AS OTHERS--TO TAKE BACK PANTASIA FROM YOU AND--
KAH HAH HAH HAH!
WH-WHAT'S SO FUNNY?!
HEH---
IT'S JUST THAT NO ONE I TALK TO CAN WAIT UNTIL I'VE FINISHED BEFORE JUMPING TO CONCLUSIONS.
keh heh
I THOUGHT YOU, OF ALL PEOPLE, WOULDN'T BE AS BRASH AS YUKINO.
TCH!
NO, KUROYANAGI, I DIDN'T CALL YOU UP HERE TO TRY AND HIRE YOU AWAY.
WHAT I WANTED TO DISCUSS WITH YOU IS...

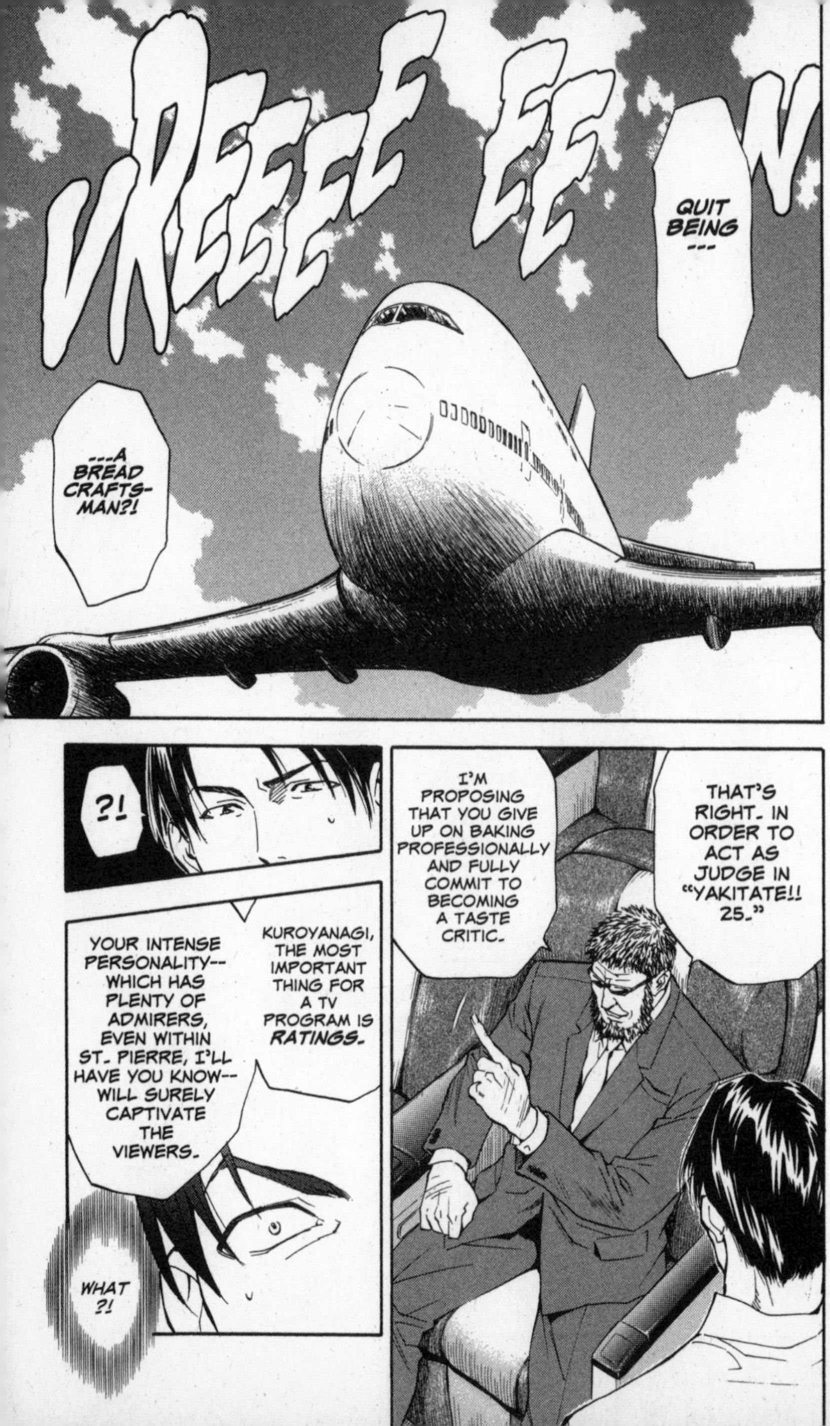
VREEEE EE N
QUIT BEING---
---A BREAD CRAFTSMAN?!
THAT'S RIGHT. IN ORDER TO ACT AS JUDGE IN "YAKITATE!! 25."
I'M PROPOSING THAT YOU GIVE UP ON BAKING PROFESSIONALLY AND FULLY COMMIT TO BECOMING A TASTE CRITIC.
?!
KUROYANAGI, THE MOST IMPORTANT THING FOR A TV PROGRAM IS *RATINGS*.
YOUR INTENSE PERSONALITY--WHICH HAS PLENTY OF ADMIRERS, EVEN WITHIN ST. PIERRE, I'LL HAVE YOU KNOW--WILL SURELY CAPTIVATE THE VIEWERS.
WHAT?!

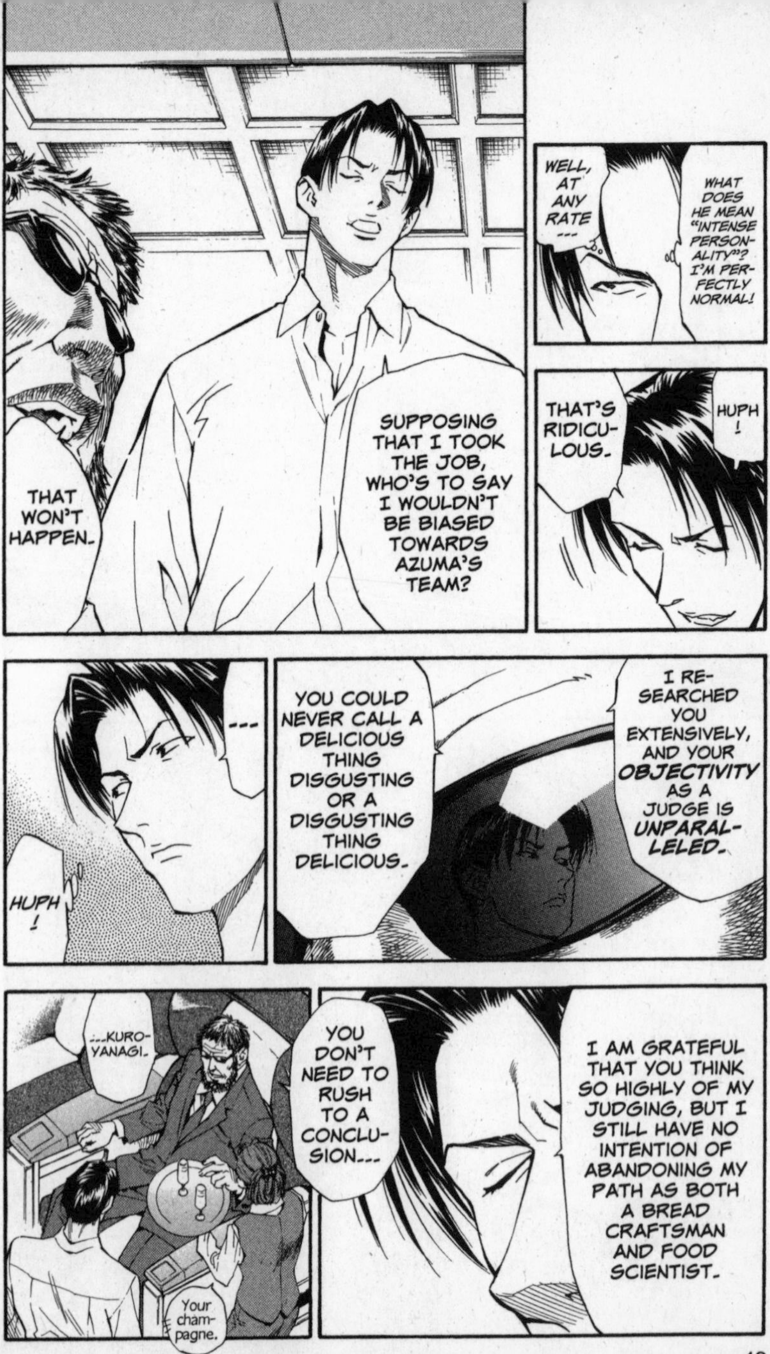
WHAT DOES HE MEAN "INTENSE PERSONALITY"? I'M PERFECTLY NORMAL!
WELL, AT ANY RATE---
HUPH!
THAT'S RIDICULOUS.
SUPPOSING THAT I TOOK THE JOB, WHO'S TO SAY I WOULDN'T BE BIASED TOWARDS AZUMA'S TEAM?
THAT WON'T HAPPEN.
I RESEARCHED YOU EXTENSIVELY, AND YOUR OBJECTIVITY AS A JUDGE IS UNPARALLELED.
YOU COULD NEVER CALL A DELICIOUS THING DISGUSTING OR A DISGUSTING THING DELICIOUS.

HUPH!
I AM GRATEFUL THAT YOU THINK SO HIGHLY OF MY JUDGING, BUT I STILL HAVE NO INTENTION OF ABANDONING MY PATH AS BOTH A BREAD CRAFTSMAN AND FOOD SCIENTIST.
YOU DON'T NEED TO RUSH TO A CONCLUSION---
...KUROYANAGI.
Your champagne.

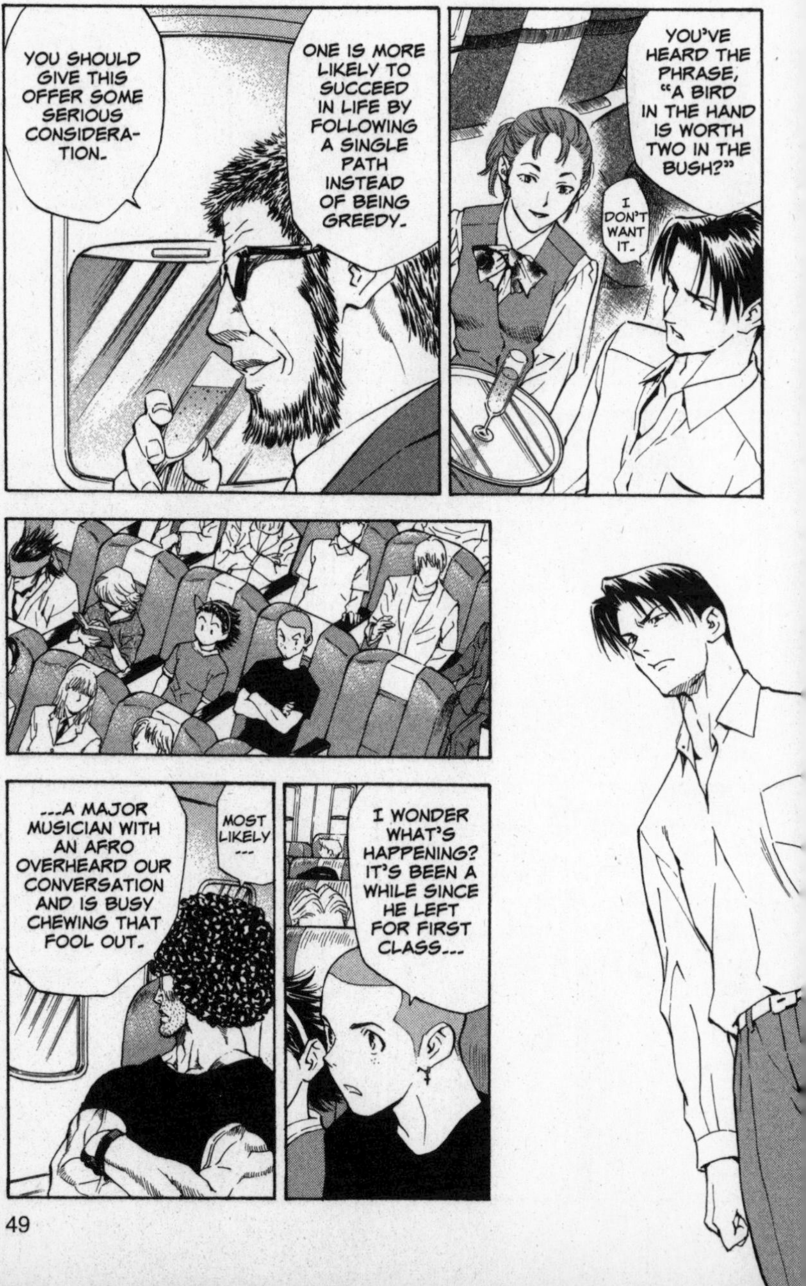
YOU'VE HEARD THE PHRASE, "A BIRD IN THE HAND IS WORTH TWO IN THE BUSH?"
I DON'T WANT IT.
ONE IS MORE LIKELY TO SUCCEED IN LIFE BY FOLLOWING A SINGLE PATH INSTEAD OF BEING GREEDY.
YOU SHOULD GIVE THIS OFFER SOME SERIOUS CONSIDERA-TION.
I WONDER WHAT'S HAPPENING? IT'S BEEN A WHILE SINCE HE LEFT FOR FIRST CLASS...
MOST LIKELY...
...A MAJOR MUSICIAN WITH AN AFRO OVERHEARD OUR CONVERSATION AND IS BUSY CHEWING THAT FOOL OUT.

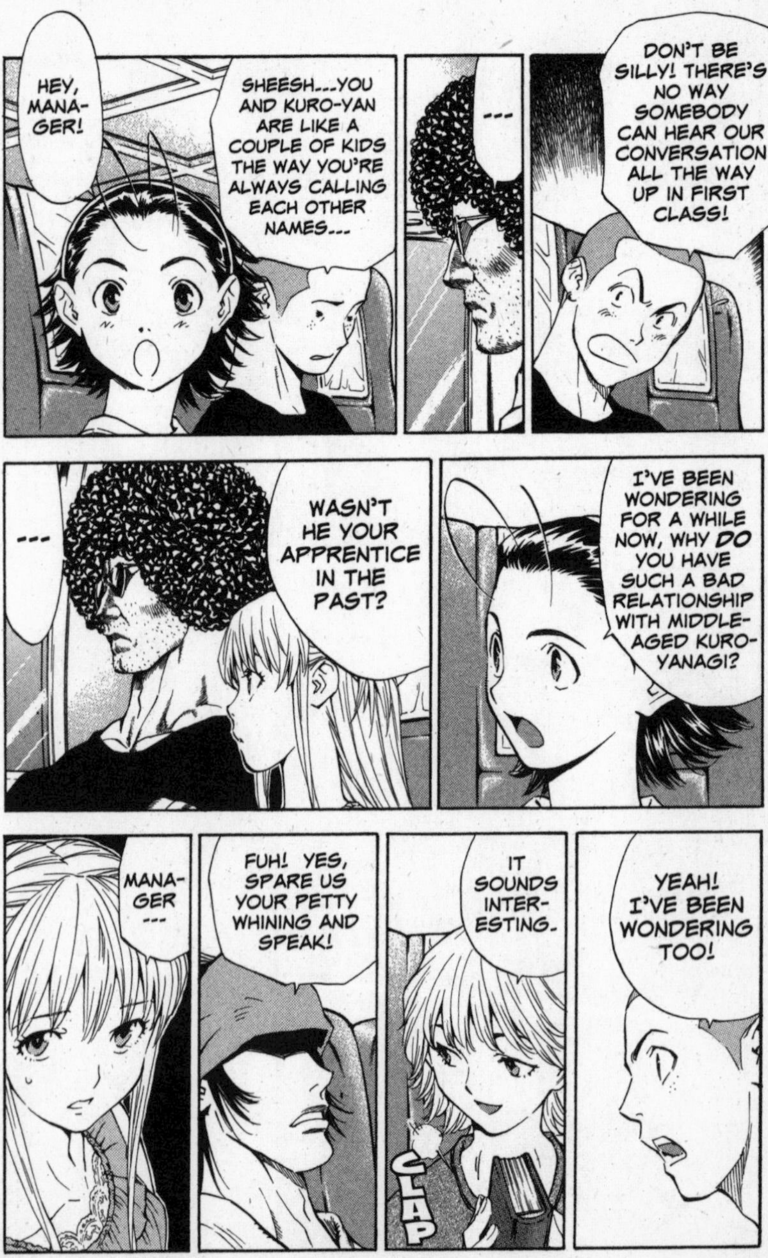
DON'T BE SILLY! THERE'S NO WAY SOMEBODY CAN HEAR OUR CONVERSATION ALL THE WAY UP IN FIRST CLASS!
...
SHEESH...YOU AND KURO-YAN ARE LIKE A COUPLE OF KIDS THE WAY YOU'RE ALWAYS CALLING EACH OTHER NAMES...
HEY, MANAGER!
I'VE BEEN WONDERING FOR A WHILE NOW, WHY *DO* YOU HAVE SUCH A BAD RELATIONSHIP WITH MIDDLE-AGED KURO-YANAGI?
WASN'T HE YOUR APPRENTICE IN THE PAST?
...
YEAH! I'VE BEEN WONDERING TOO!
IT SOUNDS INTERESTING.
CLAP
FUH! YES, SPARE US YOUR PETTY WHINING AND SPEAK!
MANAGER...

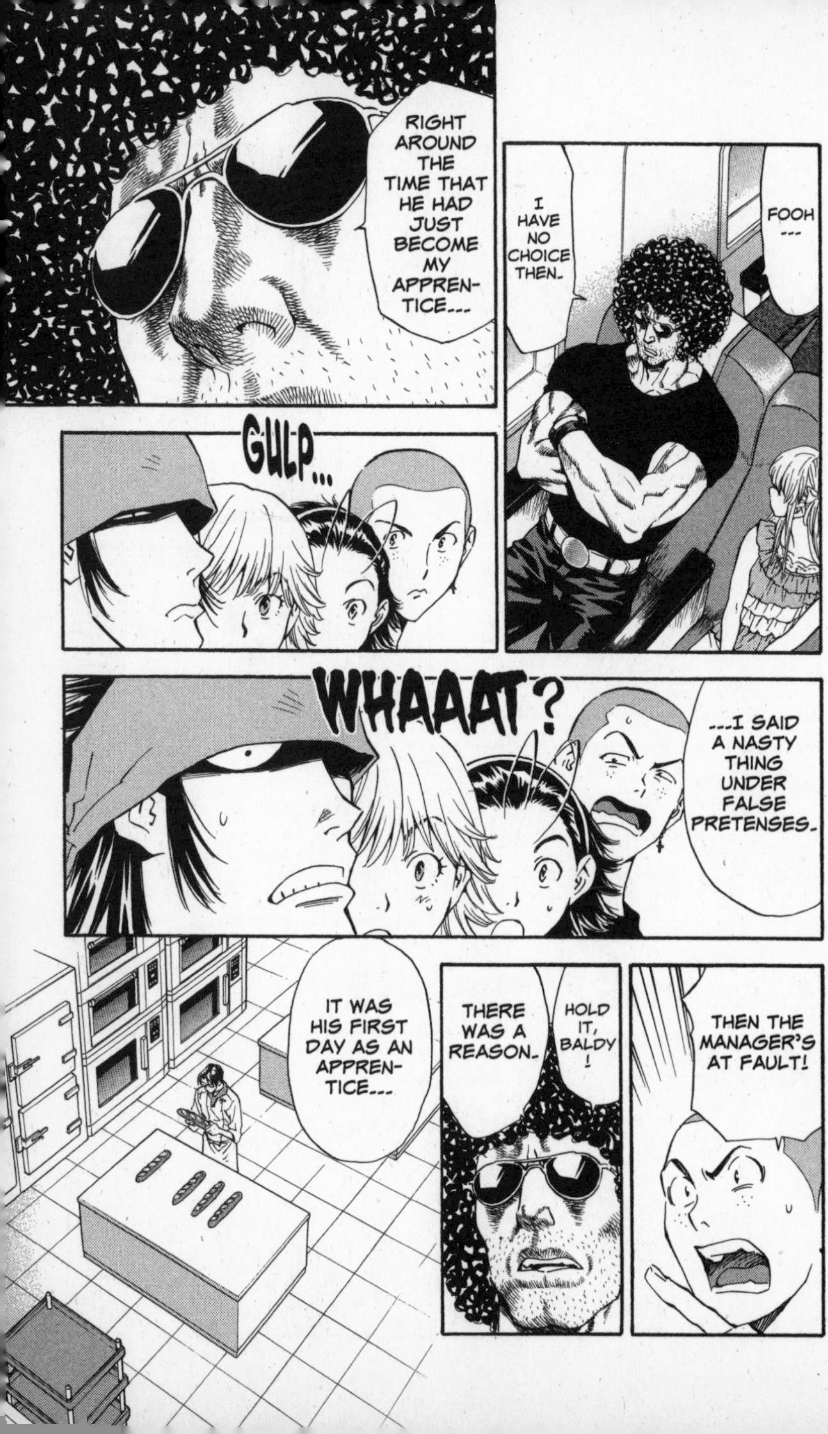
FOOH---
I HAVE NO CHOICE THEN.
RIGHT AROUND THE TIME THAT HE HAD JUST BECOME MY APPREN-TICE---
GULP...
---I SAID A NASTY THING UNDER FALSE PRETENSES.
WHAAAT?
THEN THE MANAGER'S AT FAULT!
HOLD IT, BALDY!
THERE WAS A REASON.
IT WAS HIS FIRST DAY AS AN APPREN-TICE---

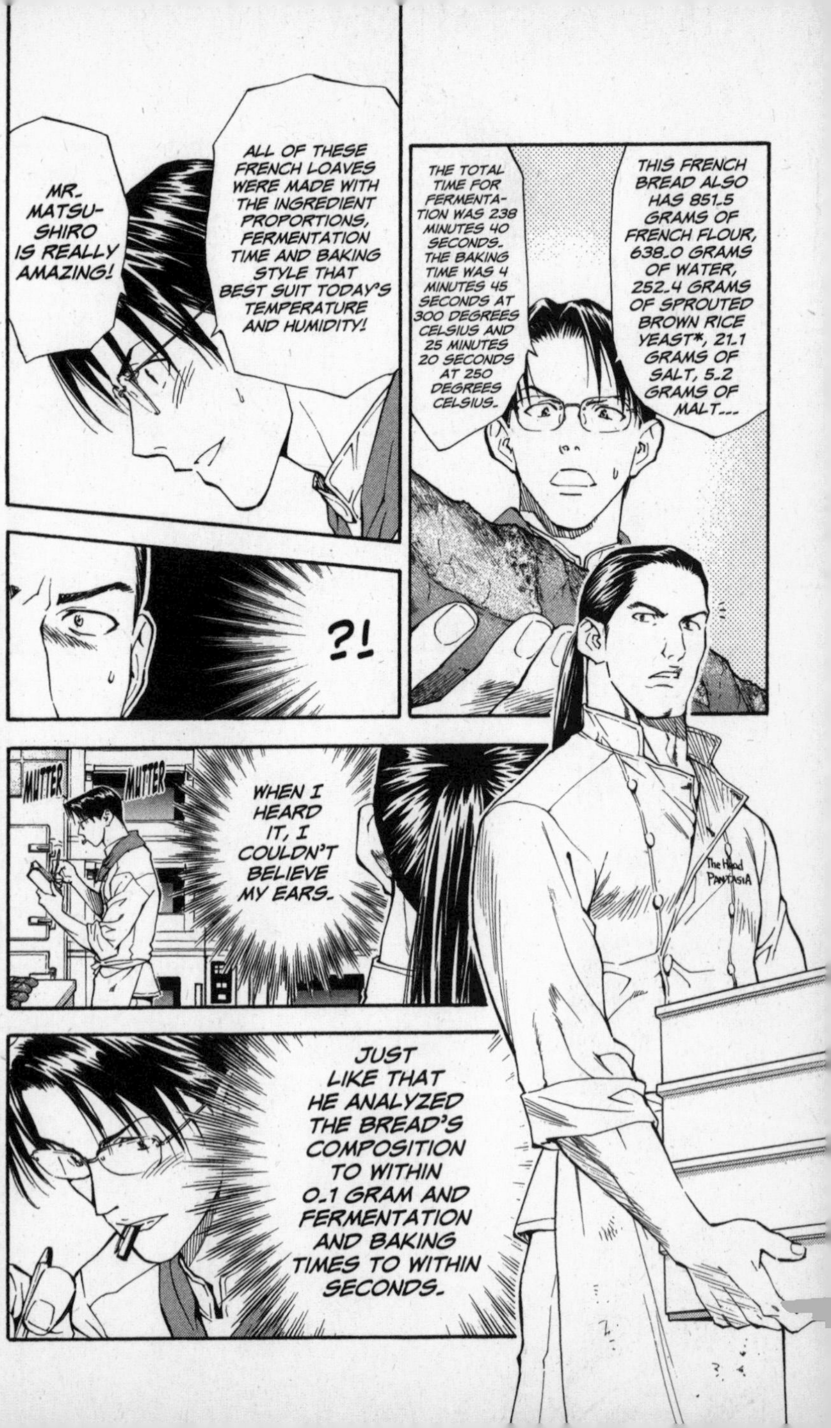
THIS FRENCH BREAD ALSO HAS 851.5 GRAMS OF FRENCH FLOUR, 638.0 GRAMS OF WATER, 252.4 GRAMS OF SPROUTED BROWN RICE YEAST*, 21.1 GRAMS OF SALT, 5.2 GRAMS OF MALT...
THE TOTAL TIME FOR FERMENTATION WAS 238 MINUTES 40 SECONDS. THE BAKING TIME WAS 4 MINUTES 45 SECONDS AT 300 DEGREES CELSIUS AND 25 MINUTES 20 SECONDS AT 250 DEGREES CELSIUS.
ALL OF THESE FRENCH LOAVES WERE MADE WITH THE INGREDIENT PROPORTIONS, FERMENTATION TIME AND BAKING STYLE THAT BEST SUIT TODAY'S TEMPERATURE AND HUMIDITY!
MR. MATSUSHIRO IS REALLY AMAZING!
?!
WHEN I HEARD IT, I COULDN'T BELIEVE MY EARS.
MUTTER
MUTTER
JUST LIKE THAT HE ANALYZED THE BREAD'S COMPOSITION TO WITHIN 0.1 GRAM AND FERMENTATION AND BAKING TIMES TO WITHIN SECONDS.

*NATURAL YEASTS, SUCH AS SPROUTED BROWN RICE YEAST, DON'T COME DRIED, BUT ARE GROWN IN A SLURRY OF FLOUR AND WATER. THE WEIGHT INDICATED REFERS TO THIS MIXTURE, NOT JUST THE YEAST ITSELF.

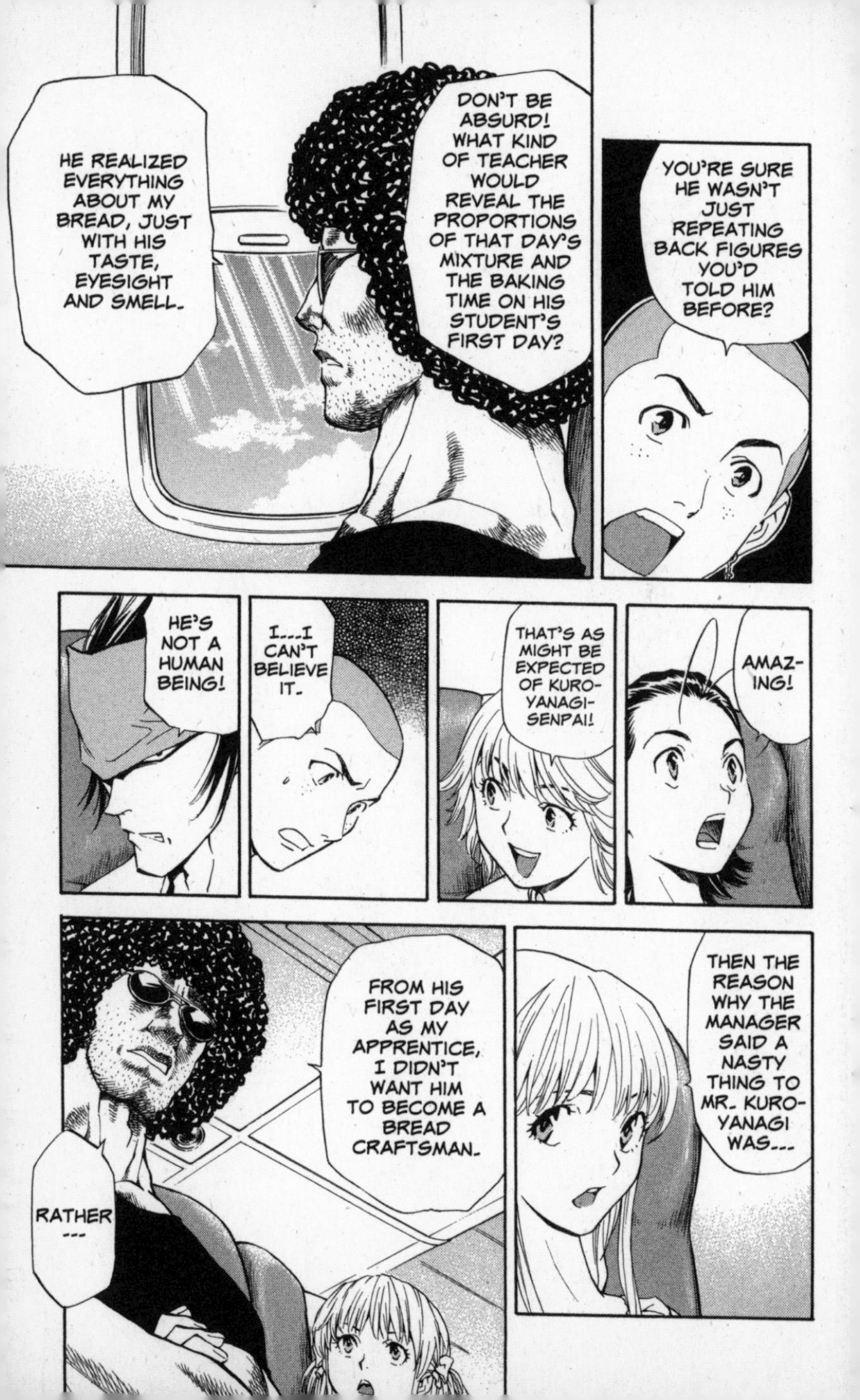
YOU'RE SURE HE WASN'T JUST REPEATING BACK FIGURES YOU'D TOLD HIM BEFORE?
DON'T BE ABSURD! WHAT KIND OF TEACHER WOULD REVEAL THE PROPORTIONS OF THAT DAY'S MIXTURE AND THE BAKING TIME ON HIS STUDENT'S FIRST DAY?
HE REALIZED EVERYTHING ABOUT MY BREAD, JUST WITH HIS TASTE, EYESIGHT AND SMELL.
AMAZ-ING!
THAT'S AS MIGHT BE EXPECTED OF KURO-YANAGI-SENPAI!
I...I CAN'T BELIEVE IT.
HE'S NOT A HUMAN BEING!
THEN THE REASON WHY THE MANAGER SAID A NASTY THING TO MR. KURO-YANAGI WAS...
FROM HIS FIRST DAY AS MY APPRENTICE, I DIDN'T WANT HIM TO BECOME A BREAD CRAFTSMAN.
RATHER ---

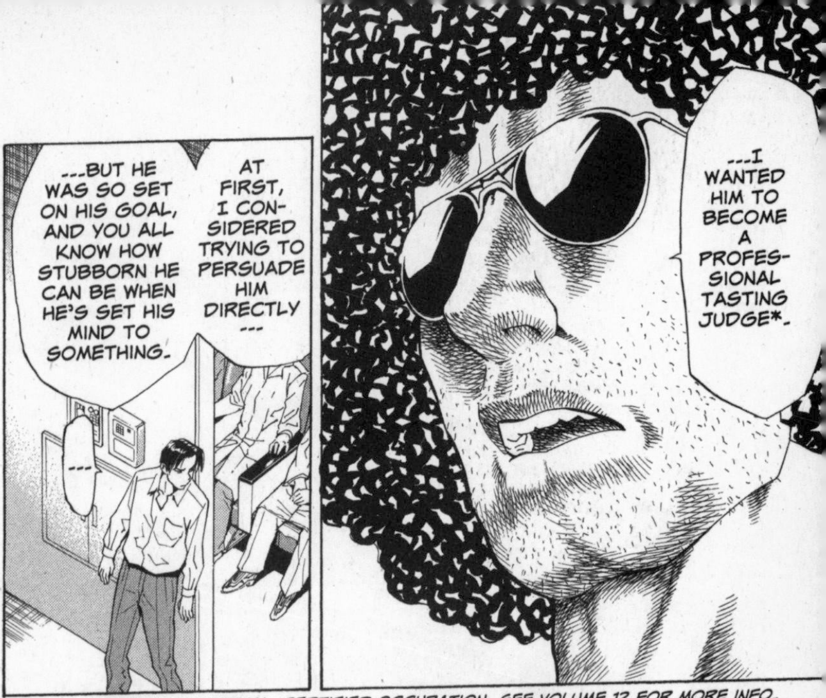
---I WANTED HIM TO BECOME A PROFESSIONAL TASTING JUDGE*.
AT FIRST, I CONSIDERED TRYING TO PERSUADE HIM DIRECTLY---
---BUT HE WAS SO SET ON HIS GOAL, AND YOU ALL KNOW HOW STUBBORN HE CAN BE WHEN HE'S SET HIS MIND TO SOMETHING.
---

*TASTING JUDGE IS AN ACTUAL, CERTIFIED OCCUPATION. SEE VOLUME 12 FOR MORE INFO.

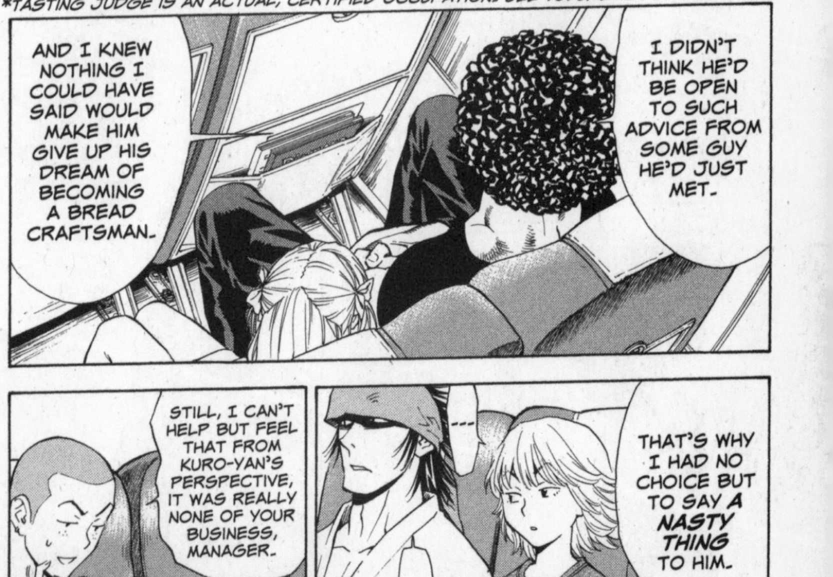
I DIDN'T THINK HE'D BE OPEN TO SUCH ADVICE FROM SOME GUY HE'D JUST MET.
AND I KNEW NOTHING I COULD HAVE SAID WOULD MAKE HIM GIVE UP HIS DREAM OF BECOMING A BREAD CRAFTSMAN.
THAT'S WHY I HAD NO CHOICE BUT TO SAY A *NASTY THING* TO HIM.

STILL, I CAN'T HELP BUT FEEL THAT FROM KURO-YAN'S PERSPECTIVE, IT WAS REALLY NONE OF YOUR BUSINESS, MANAGER.

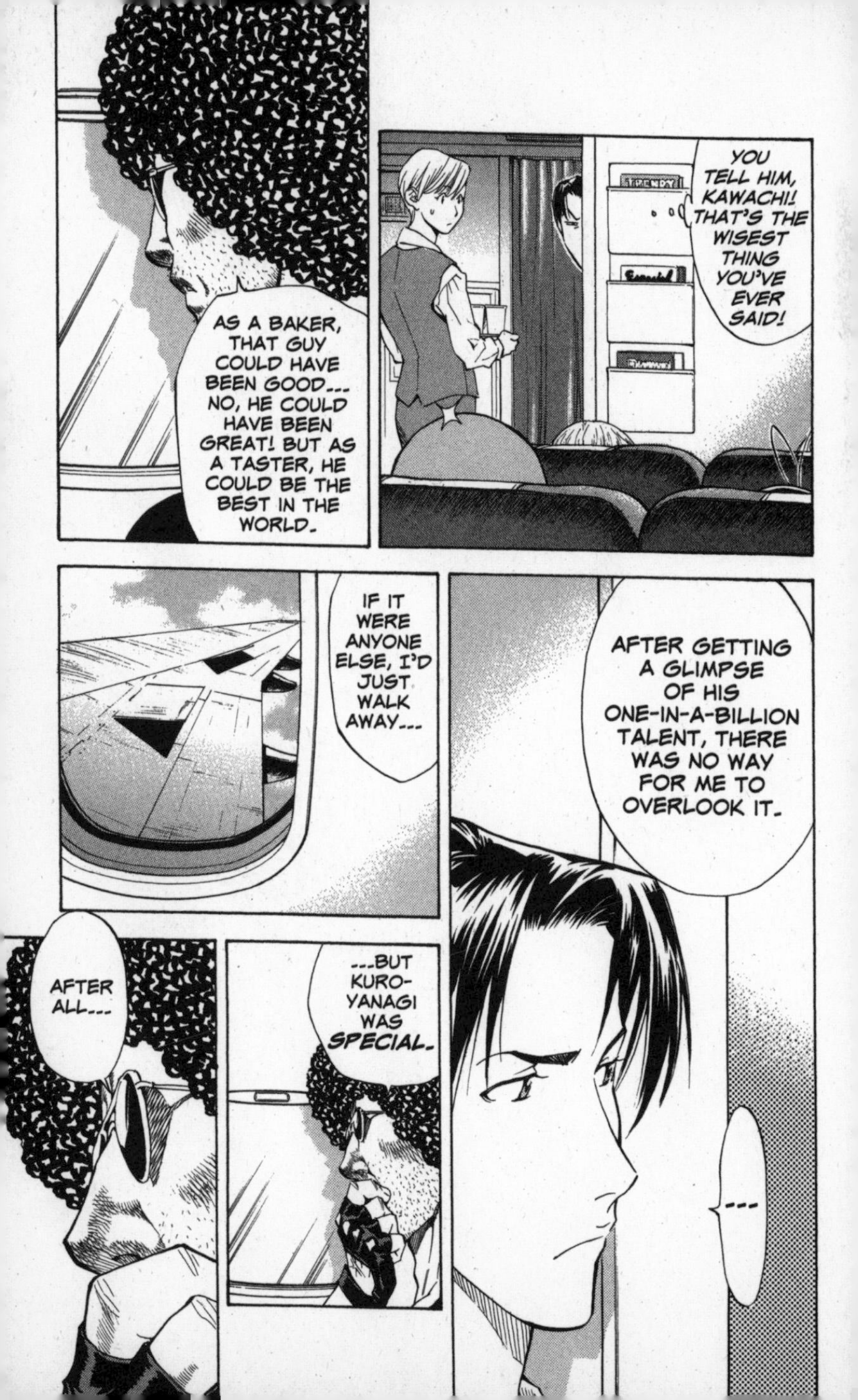
YOU TELL HIM, KAWACHI! THAT'S THE WISEST THING YOU'VE EVER SAID!
AS A BAKER, THAT GUY COULD HAVE BEEN GOOD... NO, HE COULD HAVE BEEN GREAT! BUT AS A TASTER, HE COULD BE THE BEST IN THE WORLD.
AFTER GETTING A GLIMPSE OF HIS ONE-IN-A-BILLION TALENT, THERE WAS NO WAY FOR ME TO OVERLOOK IT.
...
IF IT WERE ANYONE ELSE, I'D JUST WALK AWAY...
...BUT KURO-YANAGI WAS SPECIAL.
AFTER ALL...

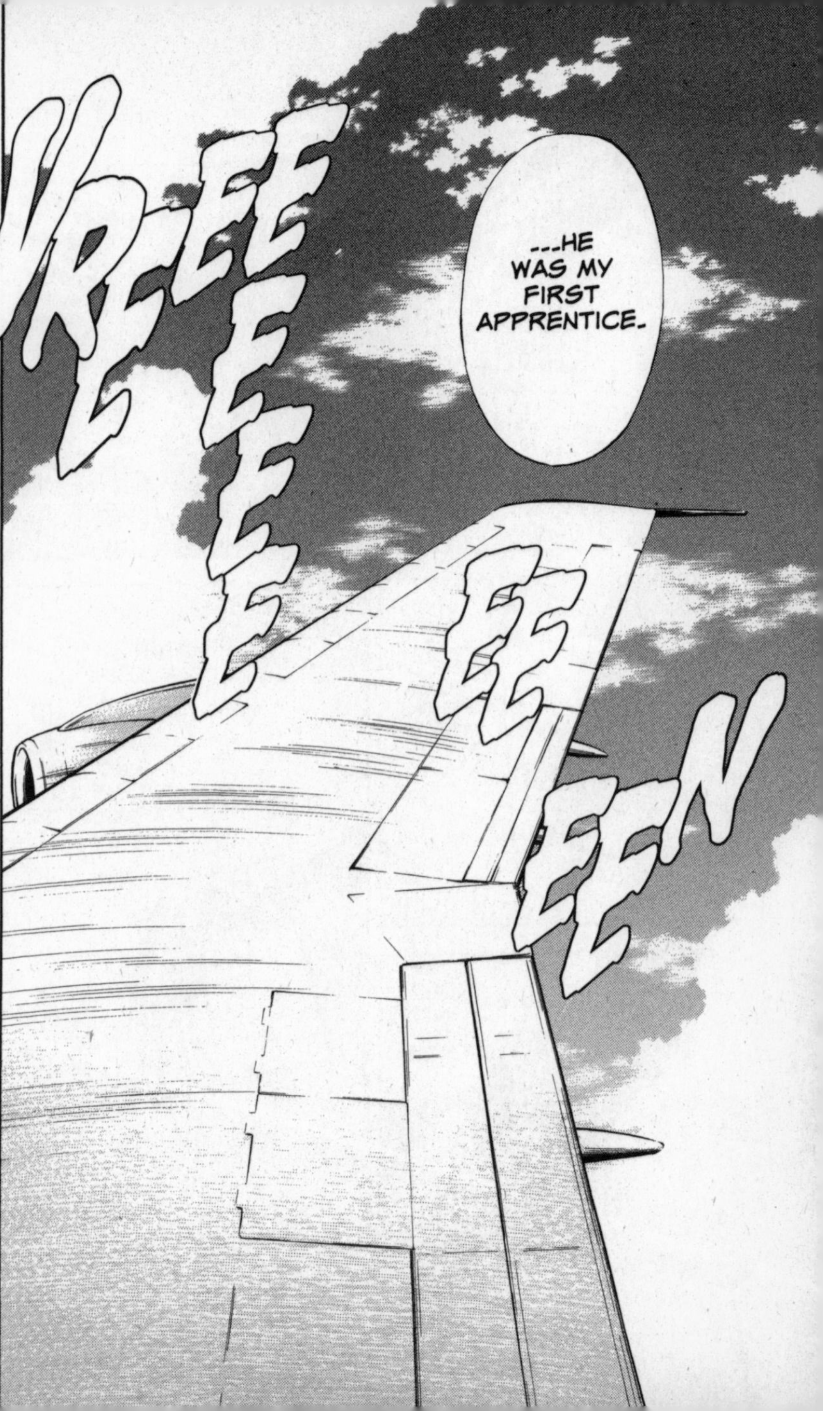
VREEEEEEEEEEEEEN
---HE WAS MY FIRST APPRENTICE.

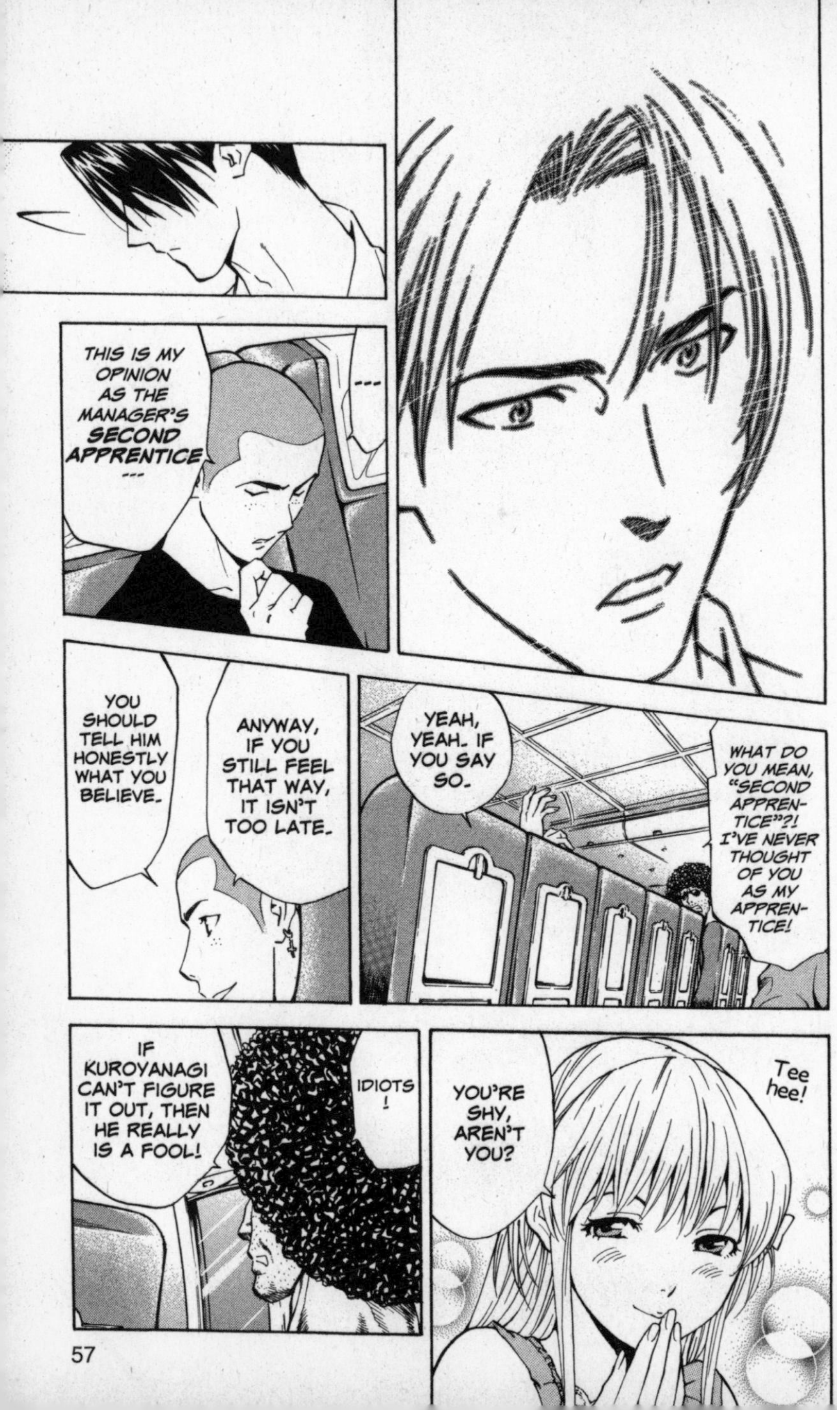

THIS IS MY OPINION AS THE MANAGER'S SECOND APPRENTICE ---
WHAT DO YOU MEAN, "SECOND APPRENTICE"?! I'VE NEVER THOUGHT OF YOU AS MY APPRENTICE!
YEAH, YEAH. IF YOU SAY SO.
ANYWAY, IF YOU STILL FEEL THAT WAY, IT ISN'T TOO LATE.
YOU SHOULD TELL HIM HONESTLY WHAT YOU BELIEVE.
Tee hee!
YOU'RE SHY, AREN'T YOU?
IDIOTS!
IF KUROYANAGI CAN'T FIGURE IT OUT, THEN HE REALLY IS A FOOL!

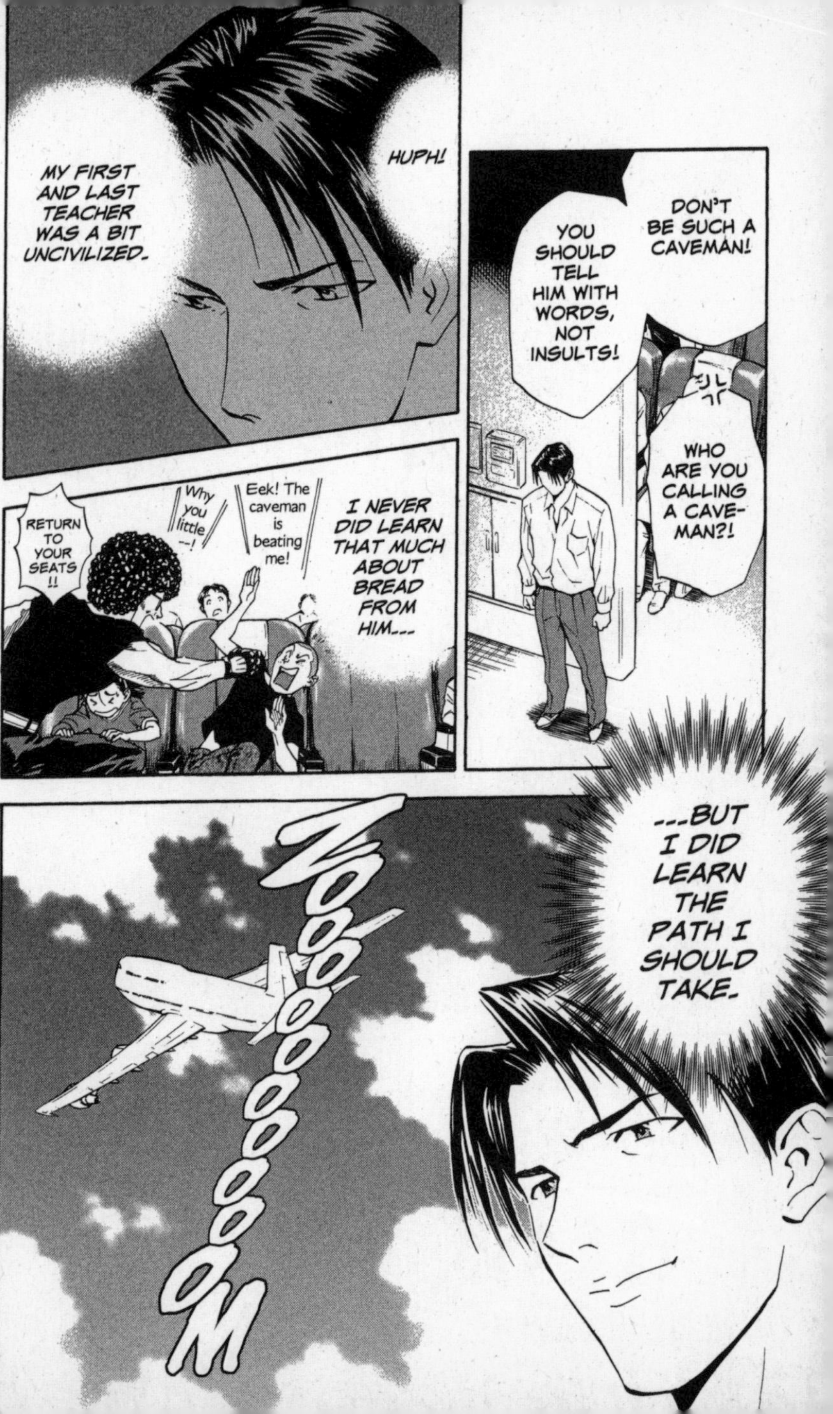
HUPH!
MY FIRST AND LAST TEACHER WAS A BIT UNCIVILIZED.
DON'T BE SUCH A CAVEMAN!
YOU SHOULD TELL HIM WITH WORDS, NOT INSULTS!
WHO ARE YOU CALLING A CAVE-MAN?!
I NEVER DID LEARN THAT MUCH ABOUT BREAD FROM HIM...
Eek! The caveman is beating me!
Why you little--!
RETURN TO YOUR SEATS!!
...BUT I DID LEARN THE PATH I SHOULD TAKE.
NOOOOOOOOOOOOM

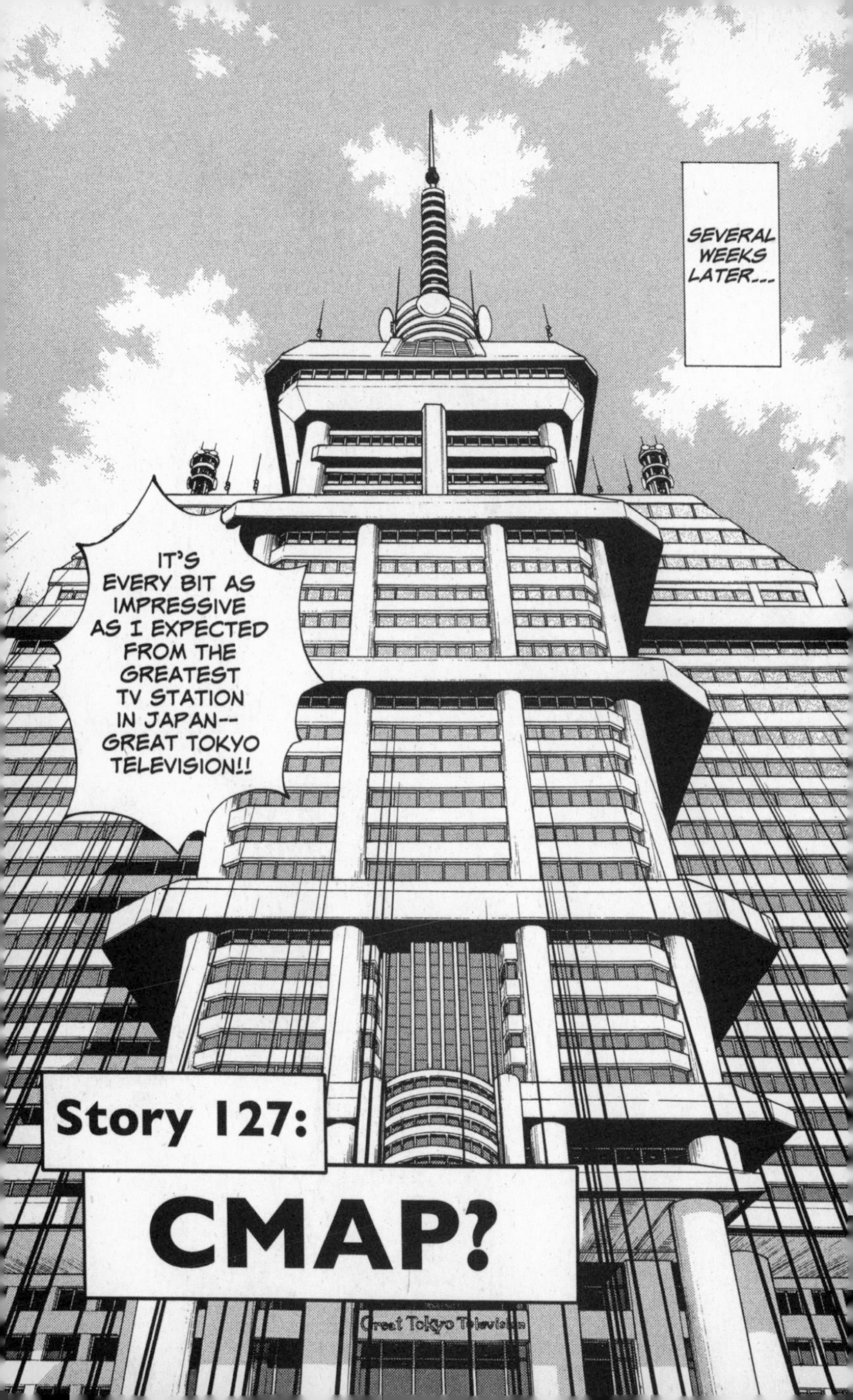
SEVERAL WEEKS LATER...
IT'S EVERY BIT AS IMPRESSIVE AS I EXPECTED FROM THE GREATEST TV STATION IN JAPAN-- GREAT TOKYO TELEVISION!!
Story 127:
CMAP?
Great Tokyo Television

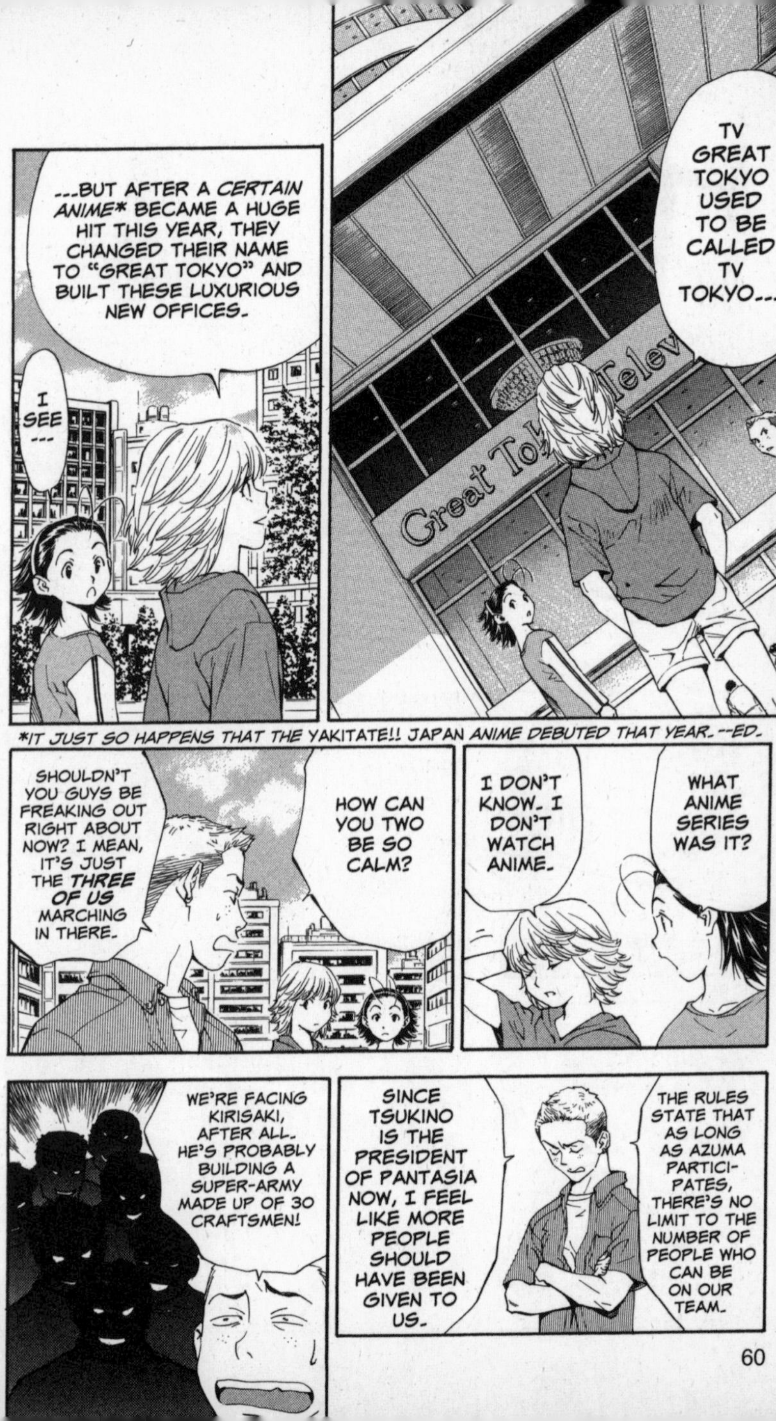
TV GREAT TOKYO USED TO BE CALLED TV TOKYO...
Great Tokyo Telev
...BUT AFTER A CERTAIN ANIME* BECAME A HUGE HIT THIS YEAR, THEY CHANGED THEIR NAME TO "GREAT TOKYO" AND BUILT THESE LUXURIOUS NEW OFFICES.
I SEE...
*IT JUST SO HAPPENS THAT THE YAKITATE!! JAPAN ANIME DEBUTED THAT YEAR. --ED.
WHAT ANIME SERIES WAS IT?
I DON'T KNOW. I DON'T WATCH ANIME.
HOW CAN YOU TWO BE SO CALM?
SHOULDN'T YOU GUYS BE FREAKING OUT RIGHT ABOUT NOW? I MEAN, IT'S JUST THE THREE OF US MARCHING IN THERE.
THE RULES STATE THAT AS LONG AS AZUMA PARTICI-PATES, THERE'S NO LIMIT TO THE NUMBER OF PEOPLE WHO CAN BE ON OUR TEAM.
SINCE TSUKINO IS THE PRESIDENT OF PANTASIA NOW, I FEEL LIKE MORE PEOPLE SHOULD HAVE BEEN GIVEN TO US.
WE'RE FACING KIRISAKI, AFTER ALL. HE'S PROBABLY BUILDING A SUPER-ARMY MADE UP OF 30 CRAFTSMEN!

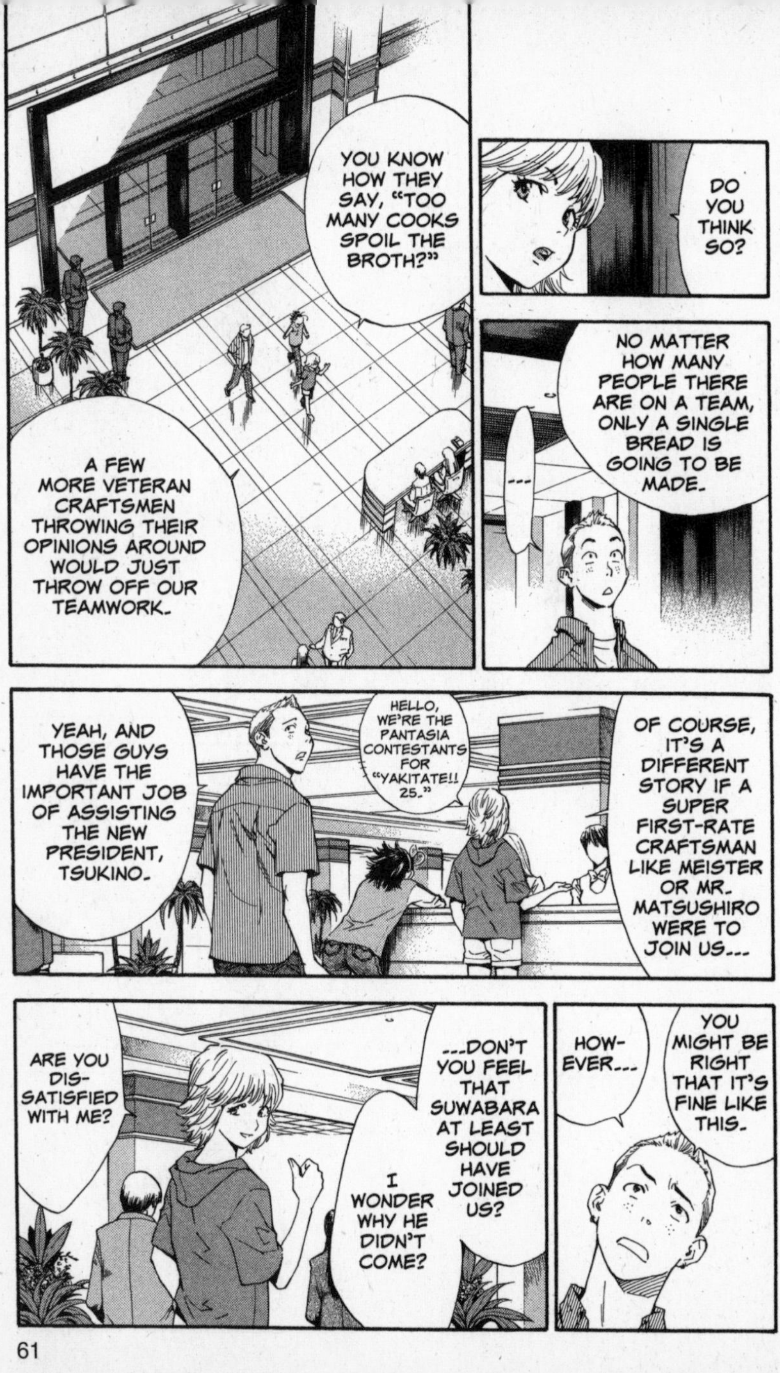
DO YOU THINK SO?
NO MATTER HOW MANY PEOPLE THERE ARE ON A TEAM, ONLY A SINGLE BREAD IS GOING TO BE MADE.
...
YOU KNOW HOW THEY SAY, "TOO MANY COOKS SPOIL THE BROTH?"
A FEW MORE VETERAN CRAFTSMEN THROWING THEIR OPINIONS AROUND WOULD JUST THROW OFF OUR TEAMWORK.
OF COURSE, IT'S A DIFFERENT STORY IF A SUPER FIRST-RATE CRAFTSMAN LIKE MEISTER OR MR. MATSUSHIRO WERE TO JOIN US...
HELLO, WE'RE THE PANTASIA CONTESTANTS FOR "YAKITATE!! 25."
YEAH, AND THOSE GUYS HAVE THE IMPORTANT JOB OF ASSISTING THE NEW PRESIDENT, TSUKINO.
YOU MIGHT BE RIGHT THAT IT'S FINE LIKE THIS.
HOW-EVER...
...DON'T YOU FEEL THAT SUWABARA AT LEAST SHOULD HAVE JOINED US?
I WONDER WHY HE DIDN'T COME?
ARE YOU DIS-SATISFIED WITH ME?

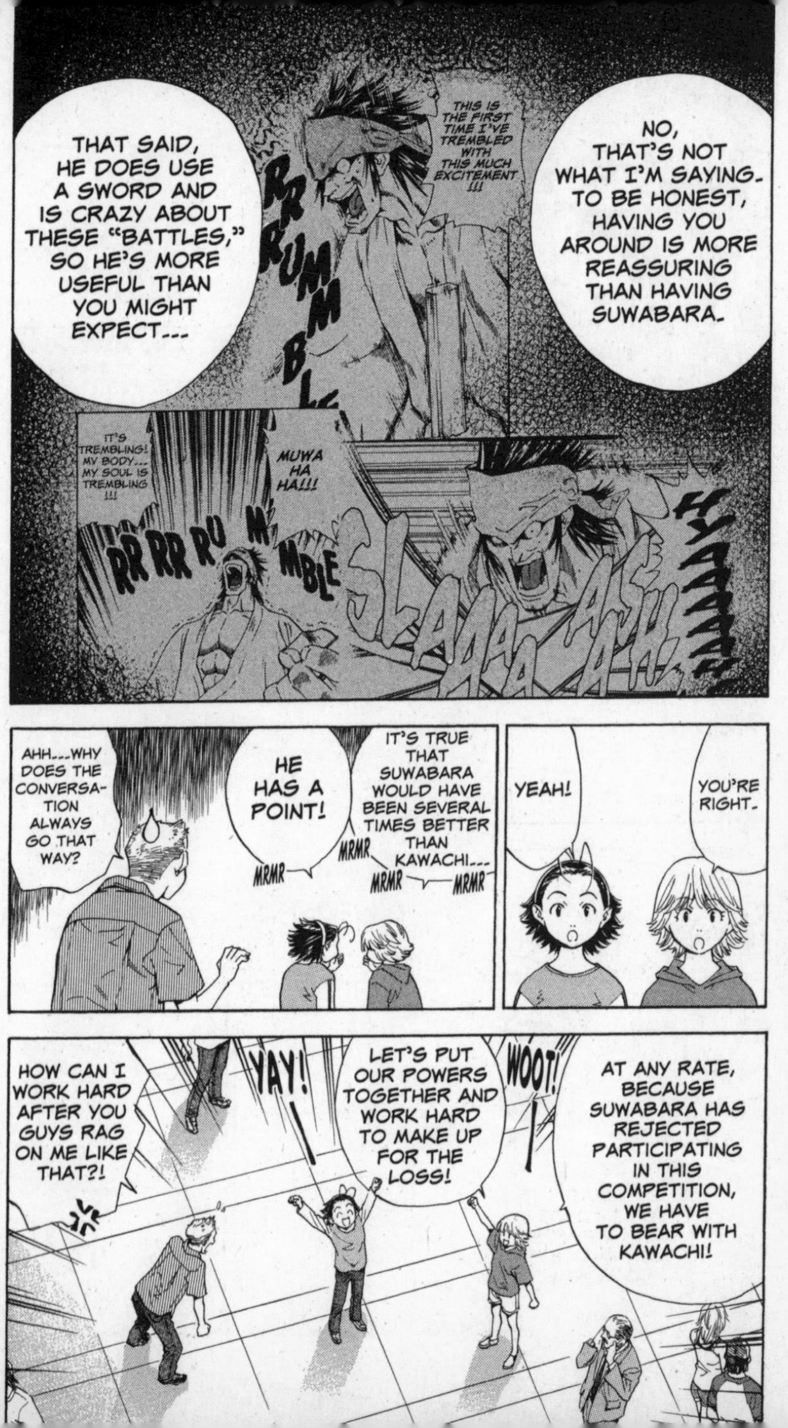
NO, THAT'S NOT WHAT I'M SAYING. TO BE HONEST, HAVING YOU AROUND IS MORE REASSURING THAN HAVING SUWABARA.
THIS IS THE FIRST TIME I'VE TREMBLED WITH THIS MUCH EXCITEMENT!!!
RRRUMMBLE
THAT SAID, HE DOES USE A SWORD AND IS CRAZY ABOUT THESE "BATTLES," SO HE'S MORE USEFUL THAN YOU MIGHT EXPECT...
HYAAAAA
SLAAAAASH
MUWA HA HA!!!
RRRRRUMMBLE
IT'S TREMBLING! MY BODY... MY SOUL IS TREMBLING!!!
YOU'RE RIGHT.
YEAH!
IT'S TRUE THAT SUWABARA WOULD HAVE BEEN SEVERAL TIMES BETTER THAN KAWACHI...
MRMR
MRMR
MRMR
HE HAS A POINT!
MRMR
AHH...WHY DOES THE CONVERSATION ALWAYS GO THAT WAY?
AT ANY RATE, BECAUSE SUWABARA HAS REJECTED PARTICIPATING IN THIS COMPETITION, WE HAVE TO BEAR WITH KAWACHI!
WOOT!
LET'S PUT OUR POWERS TOGETHER AND WORK HARD TO MAKE UP FOR THE LOSS!
YAY!
HOW CAN I WORK HARD AFTER YOU GUYS RAG ON ME LIKE THAT?!

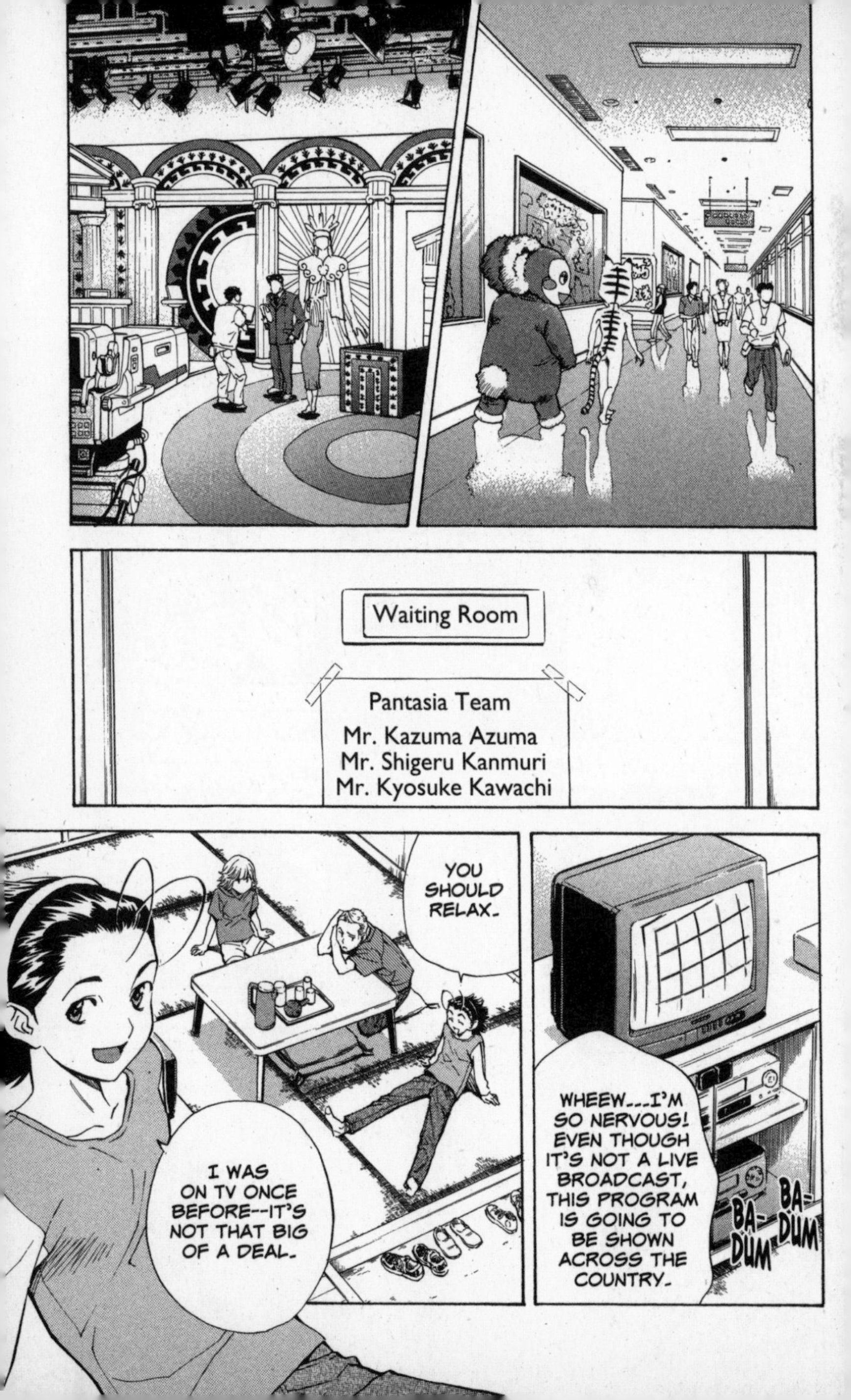
Waiting Room
Pantasia Team
Mr. Kazuma Azuma
Mr. Shigeru Kanmuri
Mr. Kyosuke Kawachi
WHEEW...I'M SO NERVOUS! EVEN THOUGH IT'S NOT A LIVE BROADCAST, THIS PROGRAM IS GOING TO BE SHOWN ACROSS THE COUNTRY.
BA-DUM
BA-DUM
YOU SHOULD RELAX.
I WAS ON TV ONCE BEFORE--IT'S NOT THAT BIG OF A DEAL.

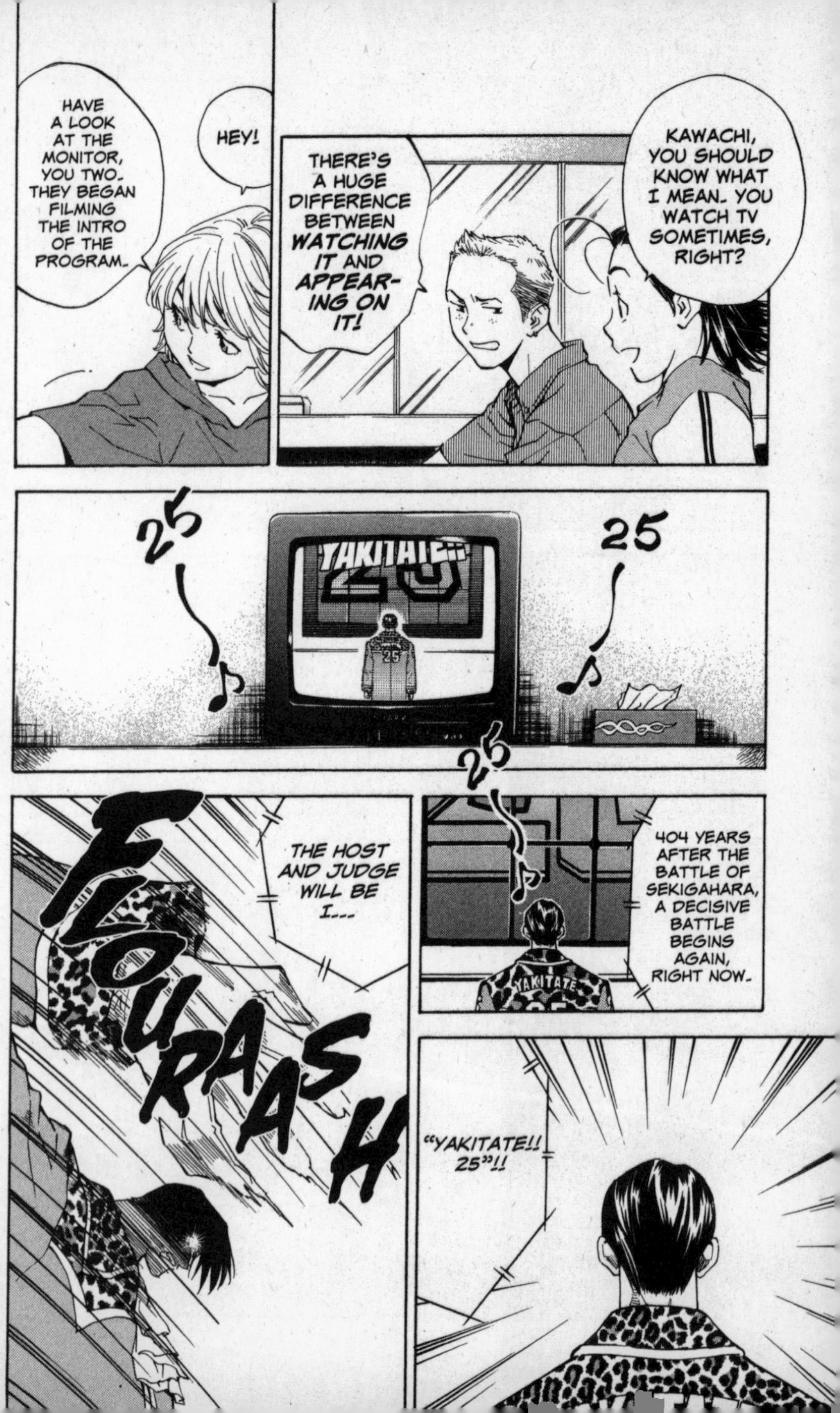
KAWACHI, YOU SHOULD KNOW WHAT I MEAN. YOU WATCH TV SOMETIMES, RIGHT?
THERE'S A HUGE DIFFERENCE BETWEEN *WATCHING* IT AND *APPEARING* ON IT!
HEY!
HAVE A LOOK AT THE MONITOR, YOU TWO. THEY BEGAN FILMING THE INTRO OF THE PROGRAM.
25
25
YAKITATE!!
25
404 YEARS AFTER THE BATTLE OF SEKIGAHARA, A DECISIVE BATTLE BEGINS AGAIN, RIGHT NOW.
YAKITATE
"YAKITATE!! 25"!!
THE HOST AND JUDGE WILL BE I...
FLOURASH

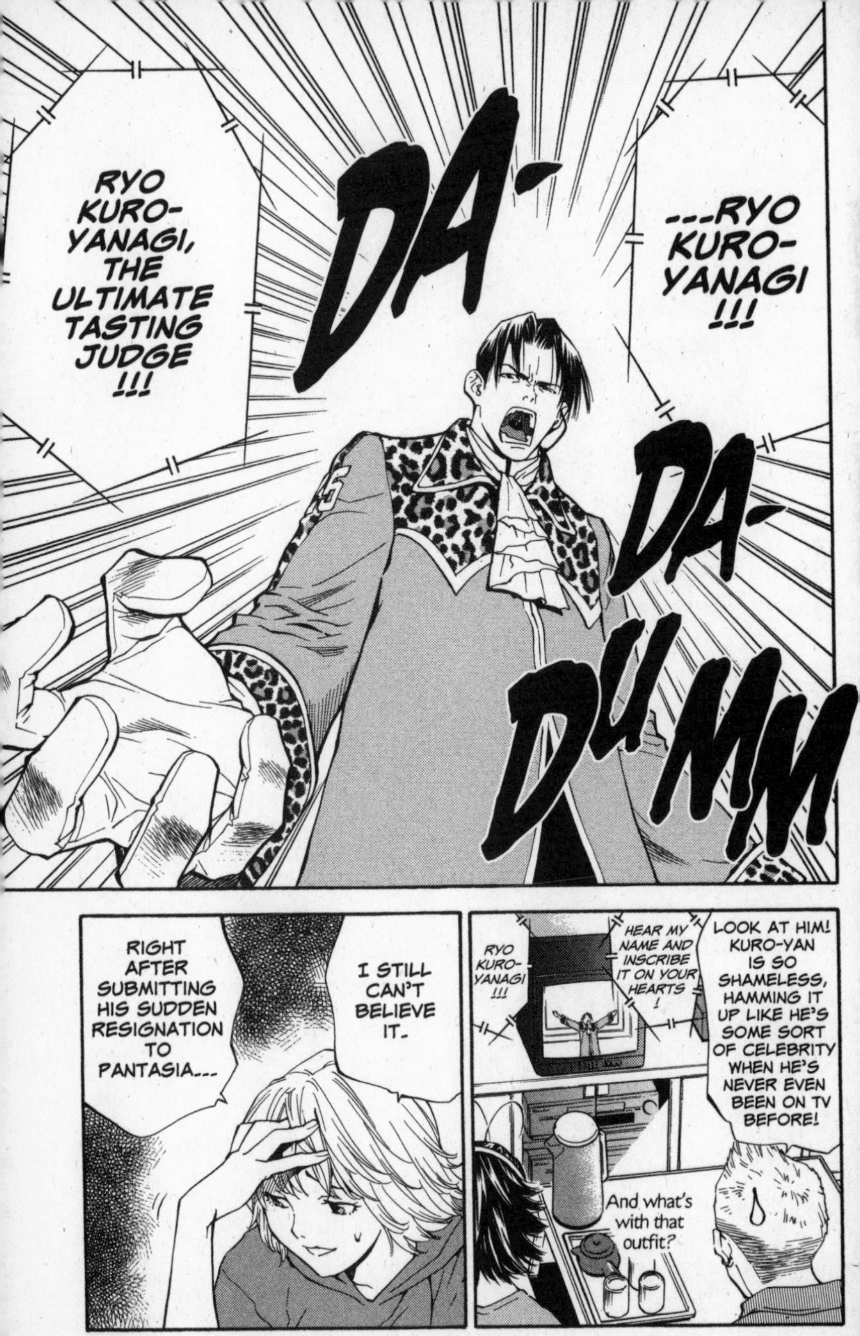
...RYO KURO-YANAGI!!!
DA-
RYO KURO-YANAGI, THE ULTIMATE TASTING JUDGE!!!
DA-DUMM
LOOK AT HIM! KURO-YAN IS SO SHAMELESS, HAMMING IT UP LIKE HE'S SOME SORT OF CELEBRITY WHEN HE'S NEVER EVEN BEEN ON TV BEFORE!
HEAR MY NAME AND INSCRIBE IT ON YOUR HEARTS!
RYO KURO-YANAGI!!!
And what's with that outfit?
I STILL CAN'T BELIEVE IT.
RIGHT AFTER SUBMITTING HIS SUDDEN RESIGNATION TO PANTASIA...

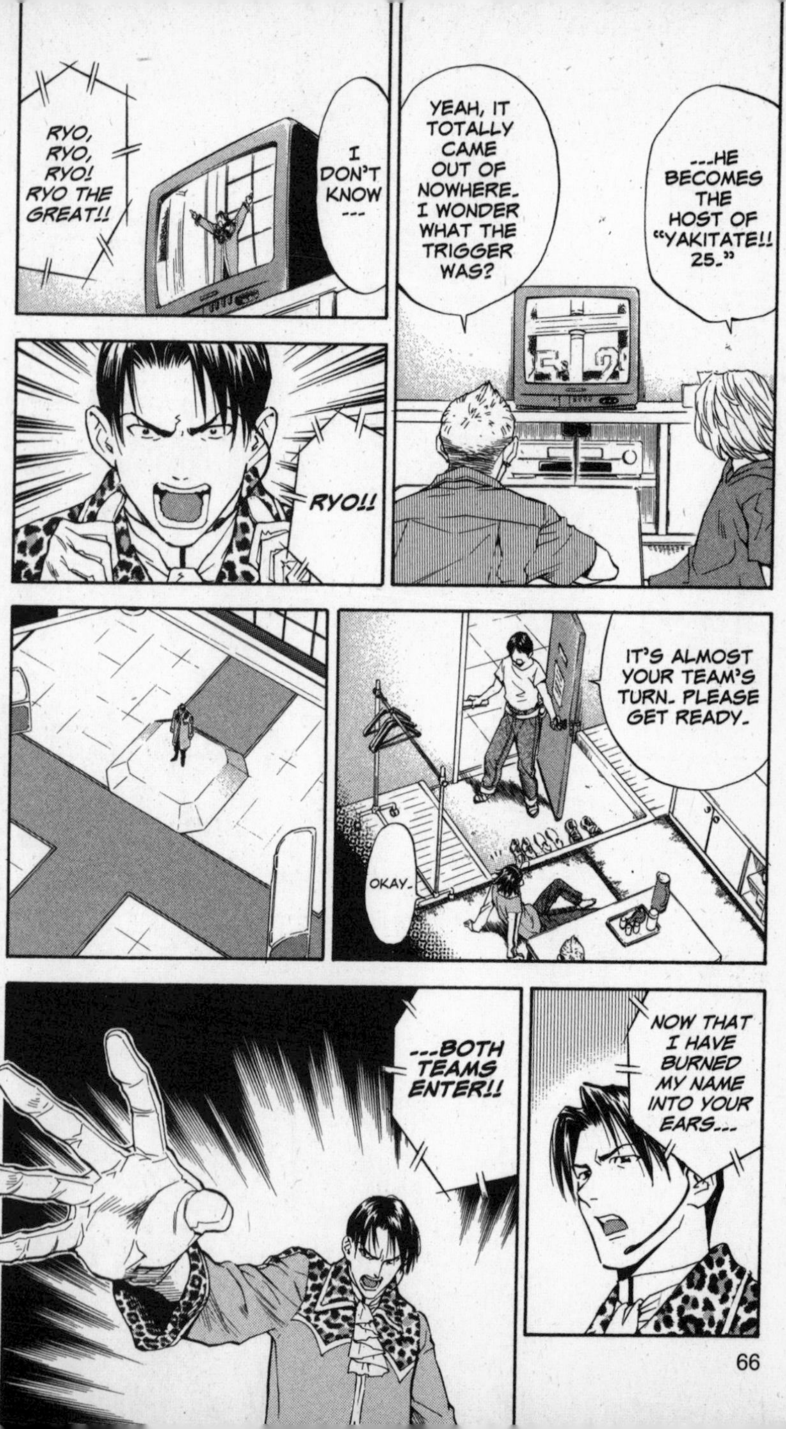
...HE BECOMES THE HOST OF "YAKITATE!! 25."
YEAH, IT TOTALLY CAME OUT OF NOWHERE. I WONDER WHAT THE TRIGGER WAS?
I DON'T KNOW ...
RYO, RYO, RYO! RYO THE GREAT!!
RYO!!
IT'S ALMOST YOUR TEAM'S TURN. PLEASE GET READY.
OKAY.
NOW THAT I HAVE BURNED MY NAME INTO YOUR EARS...
...BOTH TEAMS ENTER!!

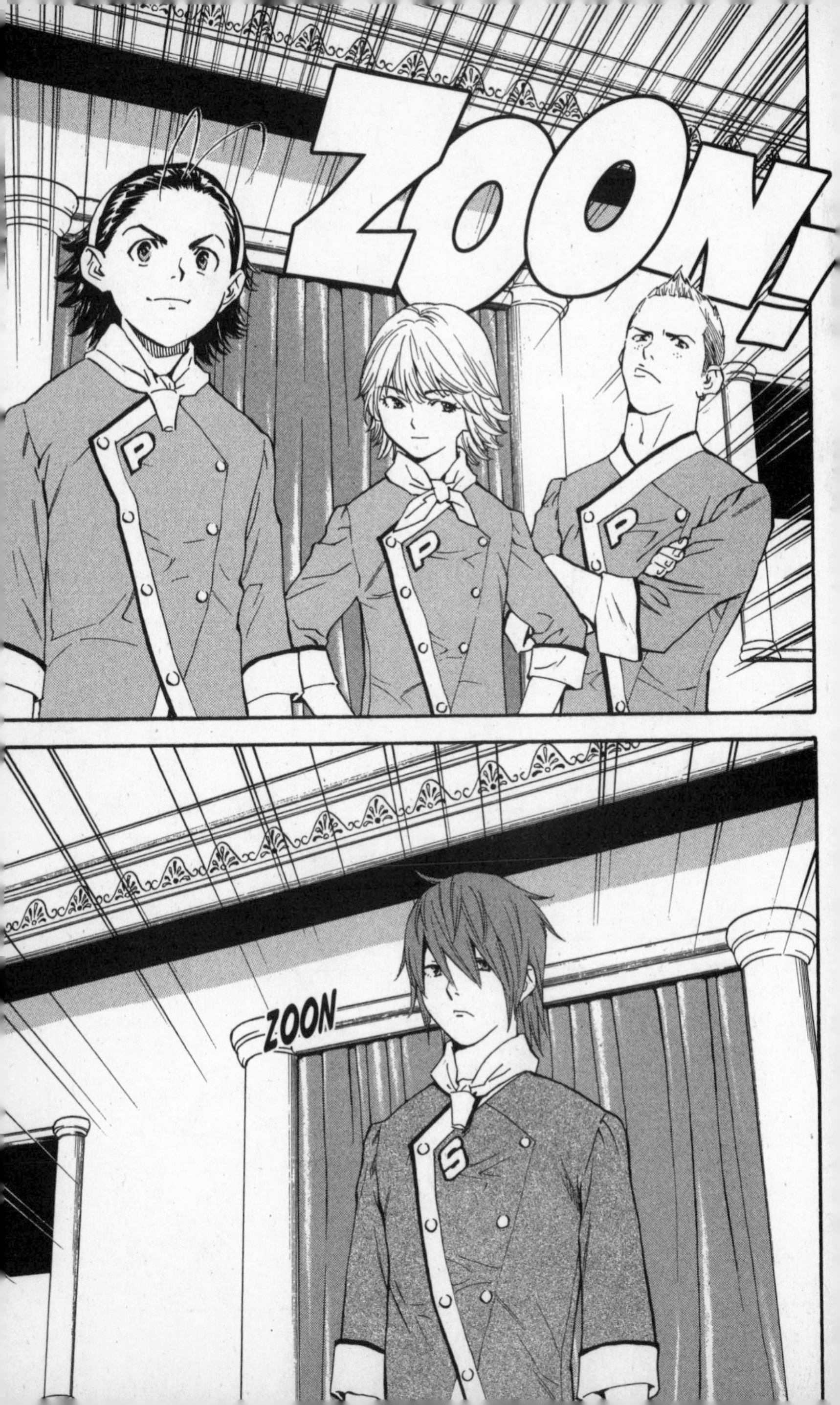
ZOOM!
ZOON

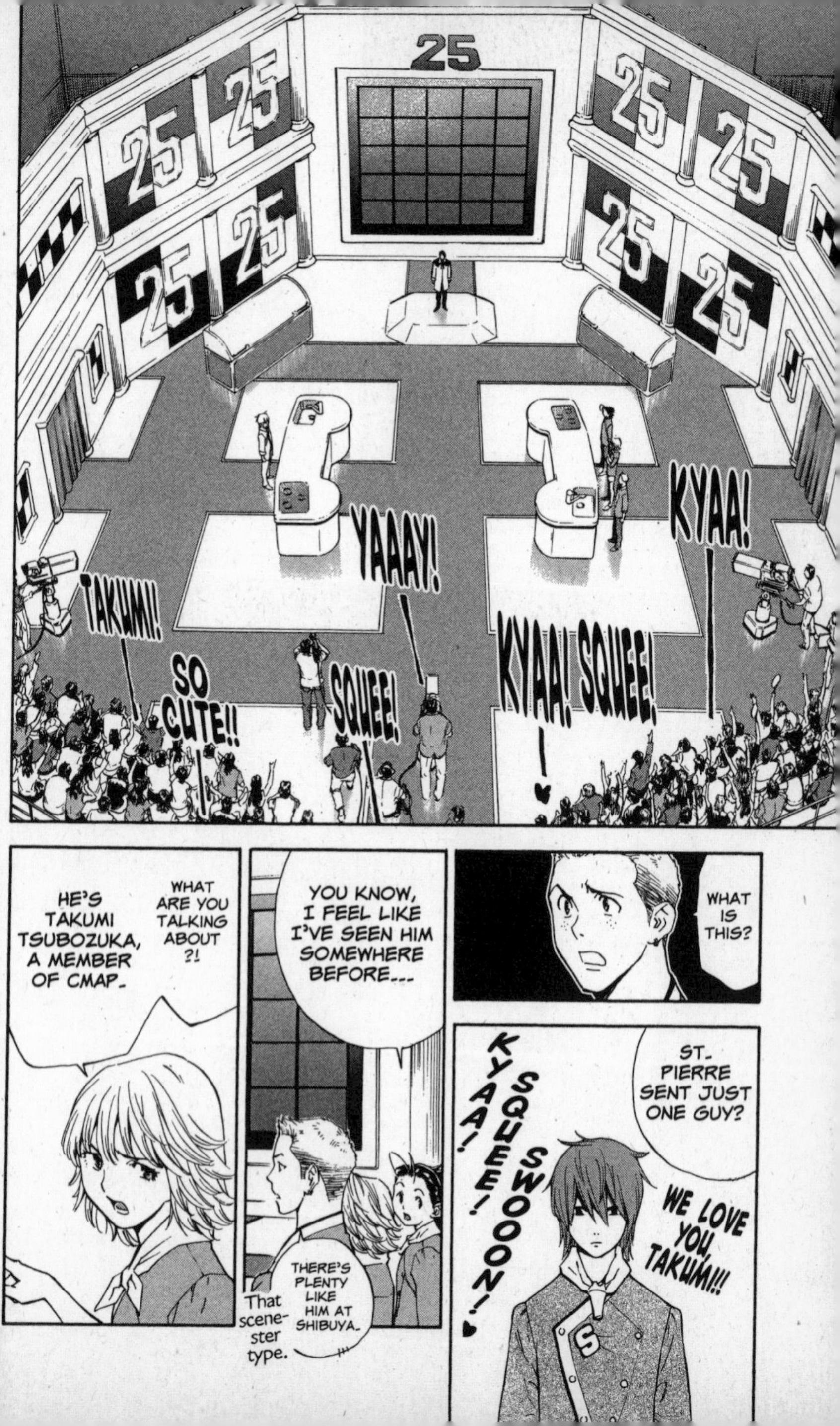

25
KYAA!
YAAAY!
TAKUMI!
KYAA! SQUEE!
SQUEE!
SO CUTE!!
WHAT IS THIS?
ST. PIERRE SENT JUST ONE GUY?
WE LOVE YOU, TAKUMI!!!
SWOOOON!
SQUEEE!
KYAAA!
YOU KNOW, I FEEL LIKE I'VE SEEN HIM SOMEWHERE BEFORE...
THERE'S PLENTY LIKE HIM AT SHIBUYA.
That scenester type.
WHAT ARE YOU TALKING ABOUT?!
HE'S TAKUMI TSUBOZUKA, A MEMBER OF CMAP.

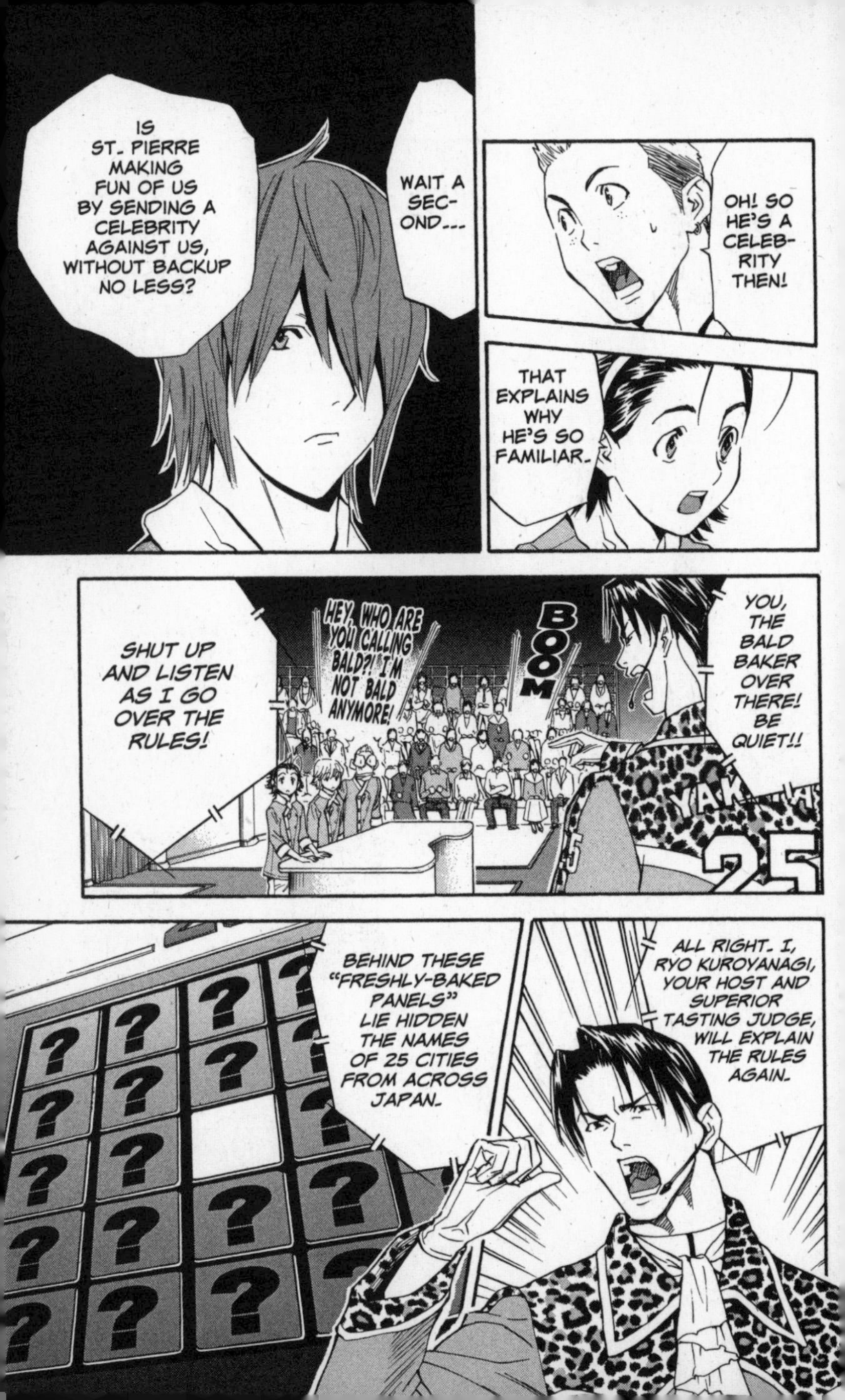
OH! SO HE'S A CELEB-RITY THEN!
THAT EXPLAINS WHY HE'S SO FAMILIAR.
WAIT A SEC-OND...
IS ST. PIERRE MAKING FUN OF US BY SENDING A CELEBRITY AGAINST US, WITHOUT BACKUP NO LESS?
YOU, THE BALD BAKER OVER THERE! BE QUIET!!
BOOOM
HEY, WHO ARE YOU CALLING BALD?! I'M NOT BALD ANYMORE!
SHUT UP AND LISTEN AS I GO OVER THE RULES!
YAK
25
ALL RIGHT. I, RYO KUROYANAGI, YOUR HOST AND SUPERIOR TASTING JUDGE, WILL EXPLAIN THE RULES AGAIN.
BEHIND THESE "FRESHLY-BAKED PANELS" LIE HIDDEN THE NAMES OF 25 CITIES FROM ACROSS JAPAN.

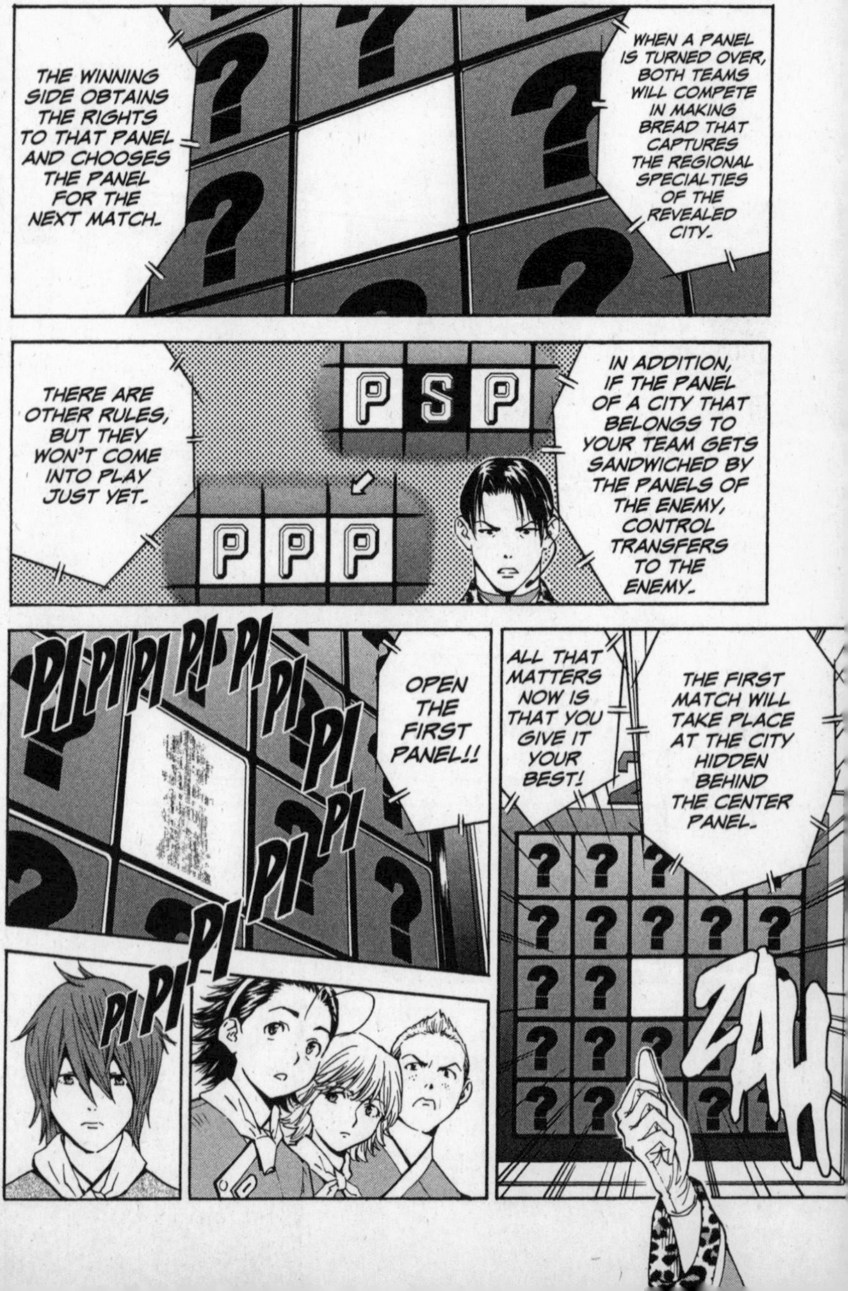
WHEN A PANEL IS TURNED OVER, BOTH TEAMS WILL COMPETE IN MAKING BREAD THAT CAPTURES THE REGIONAL SPECIALTIES OF THE REVEALED CITY.
THE WINNING SIDE OBTAINS THE RIGHTS TO THAT PANEL AND CHOOSES THE PANEL FOR THE NEXT MATCH.
IN ADDITION, IF THE PANEL OF A CITY THAT BELONGS TO YOUR TEAM GETS SANDWICHED BY THE PANELS OF THE ENEMY, CONTROL TRANSFERS TO THE ENEMY.
THERE ARE OTHER RULES, BUT THEY WON'T COME INTO PLAY JUST YET.
THE FIRST MATCH WILL TAKE PLACE AT THE CITY HIDDEN BEHIND THE CENTER PANEL.
ALL THAT MATTERS NOW IS THAT YOU GIVE IT YOUR BEST!
ZAH
OPEN THE FIRST PANEL!!
PI PI PI PI PI PI PI PI PI PI PI PI PI PI

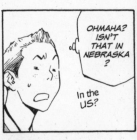

PING
Ohma
OHMAHA? ISN'T THAT IN NEBRASKA?
In the US?
IT'S OHMA...
SO IT'S OHMA...
OHMA IS A TOWN IN SHIMOKITA COUNTY OF AOMORI PREFECTURE!
Ohma
PI PI PI PI PI
OPEN THE MAP VISION!
PIP

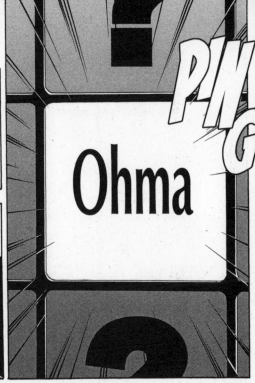

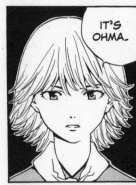

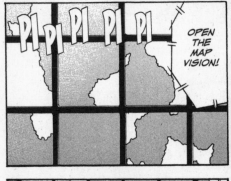

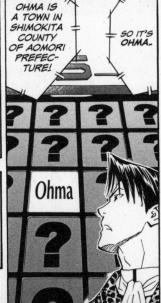

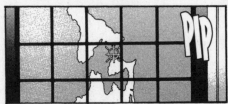

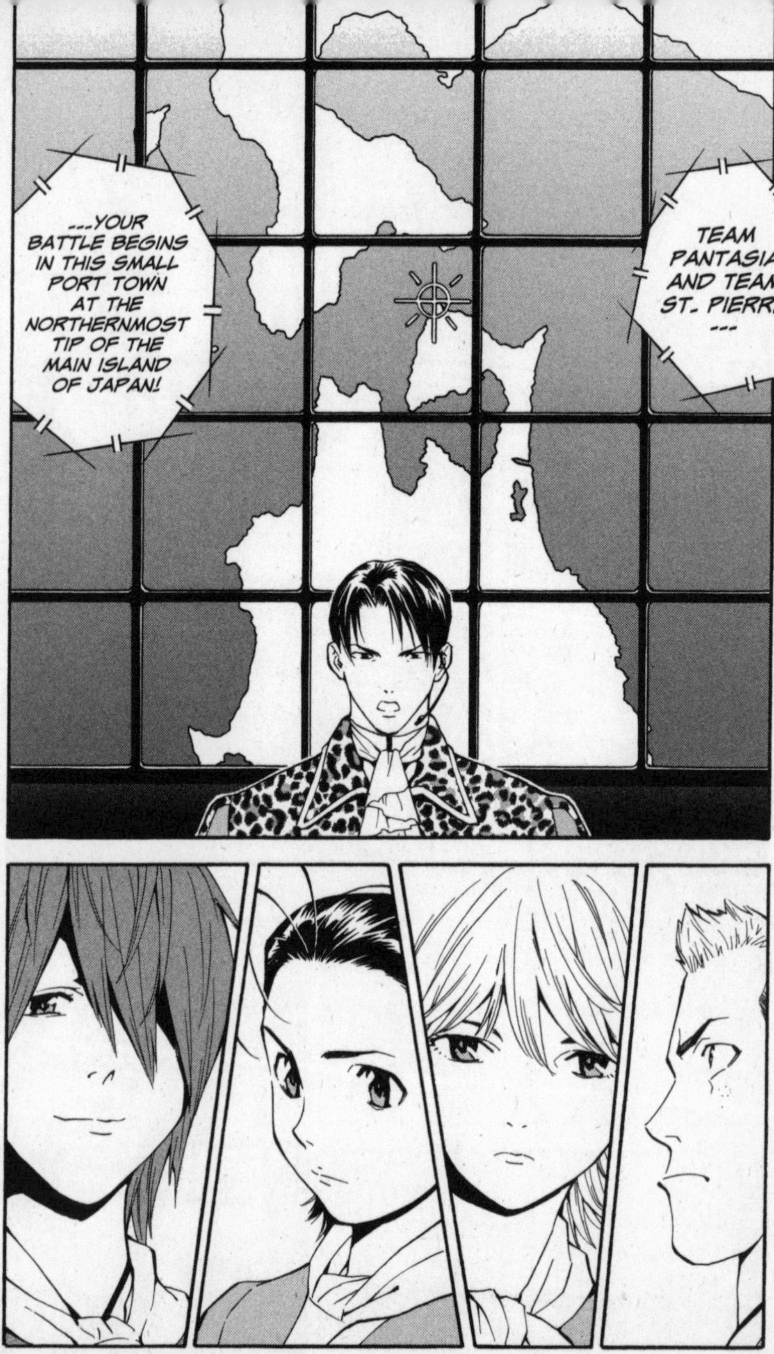
TEAM PANTASIA AND TEAM ST. PIERRE ---
---YOUR BATTLE BEGINS IN THIS SMALL PORT TOWN AT THE NORTHERNMOST TIP OF THE MAIN ISLAND OF JAPAN!

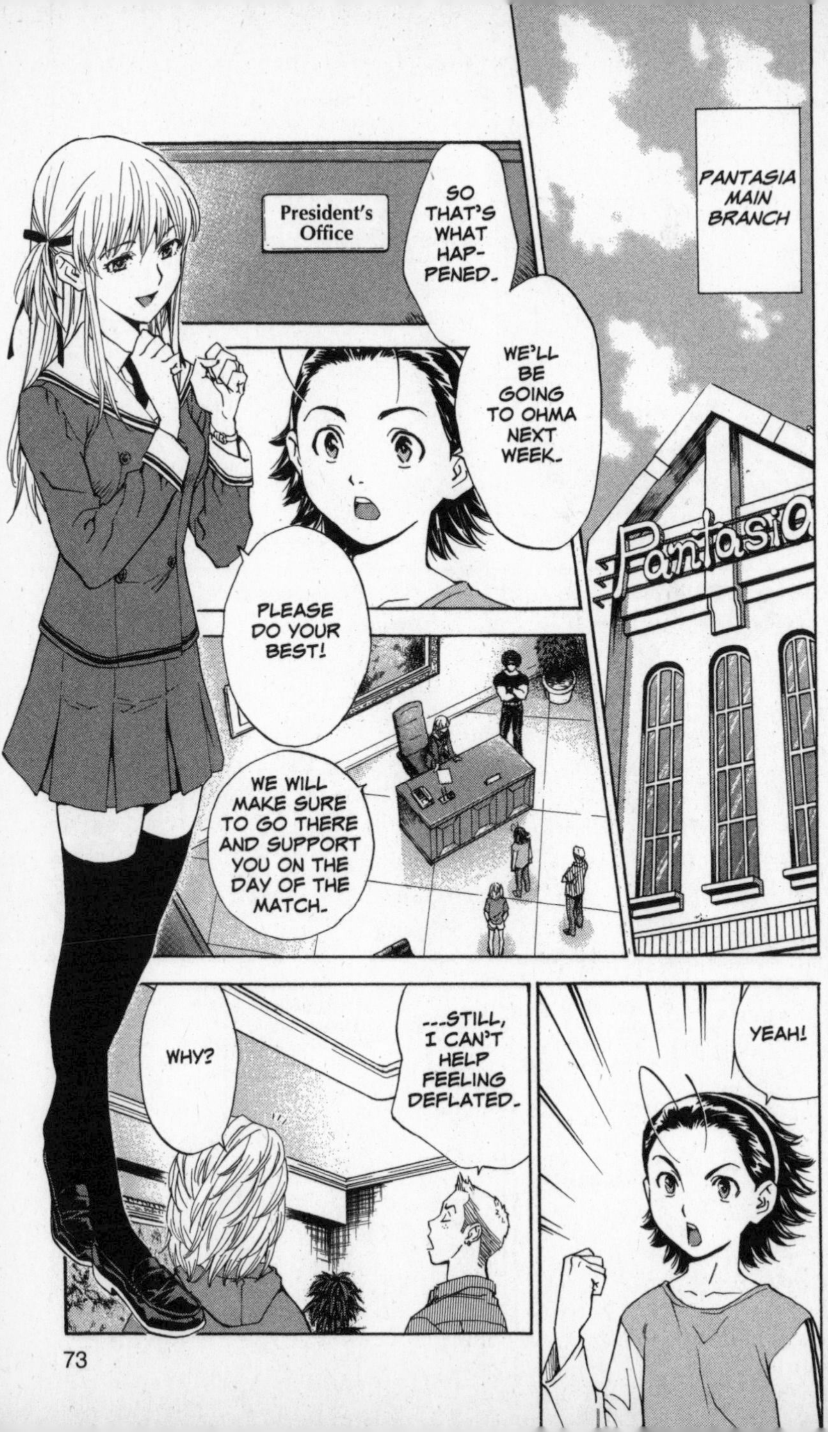
PANTASIA MAIN BRANCH
Pantasia
President's Office
SO THAT'S WHAT HAP-PENED...
WE'LL BE GOING TO OHMA NEXT WEEK...
PLEASE DO YOUR BEST!
WE WILL MAKE SURE TO GO THERE AND SUPPORT YOU ON THE DAY OF THE MATCH...
YEAH!
...STILL, I CAN'T HELP FEELING DEFLATED...
WHY?

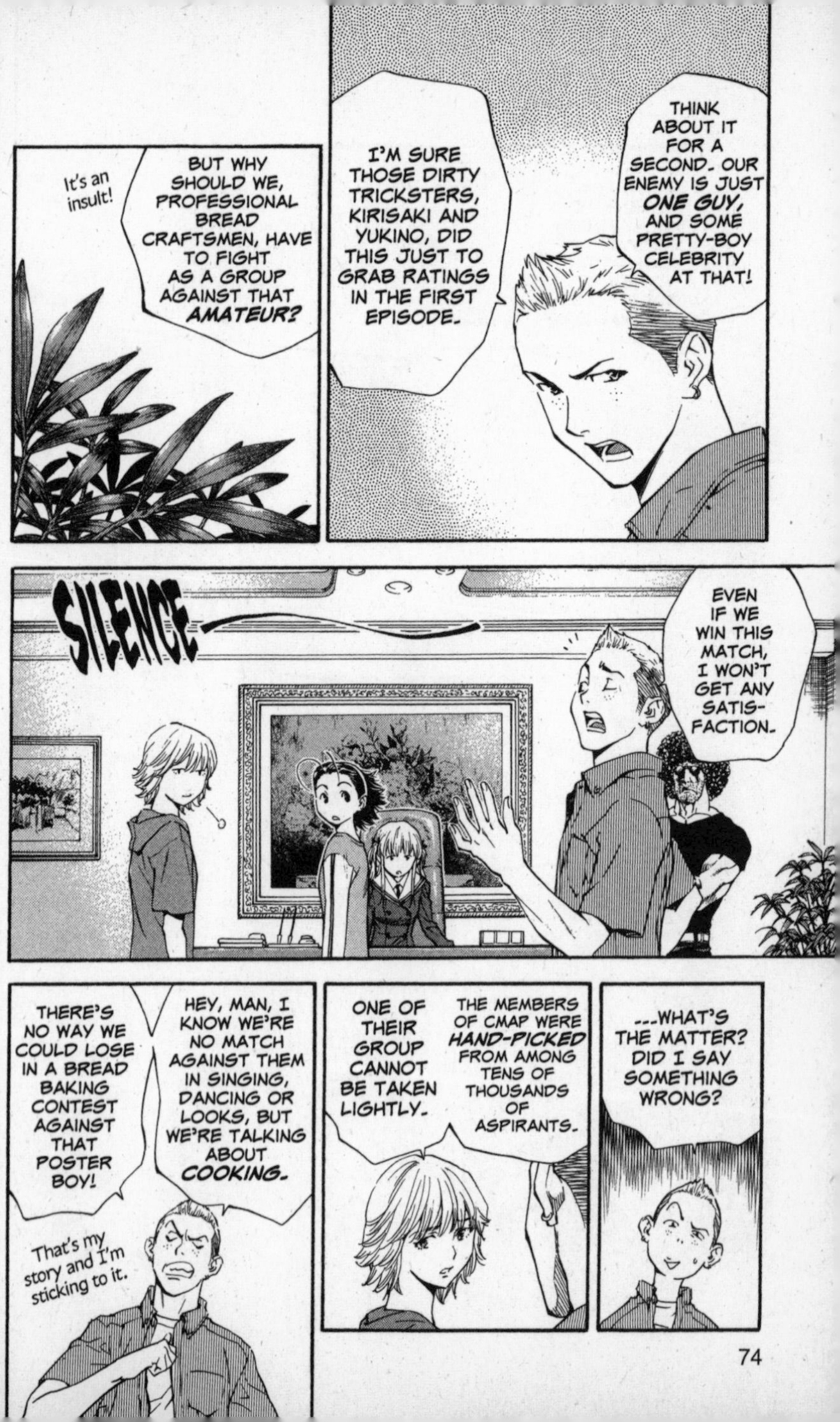

THINK ABOUT IT FOR A SECOND. OUR ENEMY IS JUST ONE GUY, AND SOME PRETTY-BOY CELEBRITY AT THAT!
I'M SURE THOSE DIRTY TRICKSTERS, KIRISAKI AND YUKINO, DID THIS JUST TO GRAB RATINGS IN THE FIRST EPISODE.
BUT WHY SHOULD WE, PROFESSIONAL BREAD CRAFTSMEN, HAVE TO FIGHT AS A GROUP AGAINST THAT AMATEUR?
It's an insult!
EVEN IF WE WIN THIS MATCH, I WON'T GET ANY SATIS-FACTION.
SILENCE
...WHAT'S THE MATTER? DID I SAY SOMETHING WRONG?
THE MEMBERS OF CMAP WERE HAND-PICKED FROM AMONG TENS OF THOUSANDS OF ASPIRANTS.
ONE OF THEIR GROUP CANNOT BE TAKEN LIGHTLY.
HEY, MAN, I KNOW WE'RE NO MATCH AGAINST THEM IN SINGING, DANCING OR LOOKS, BUT WE'RE TALKING ABOUT COOKING.
THERE'S NO WAY WE COULD LOSE IN A BREAD BAKING CONTEST AGAINST THAT POSTER BOY!
That's my story and I'm sticking to it.

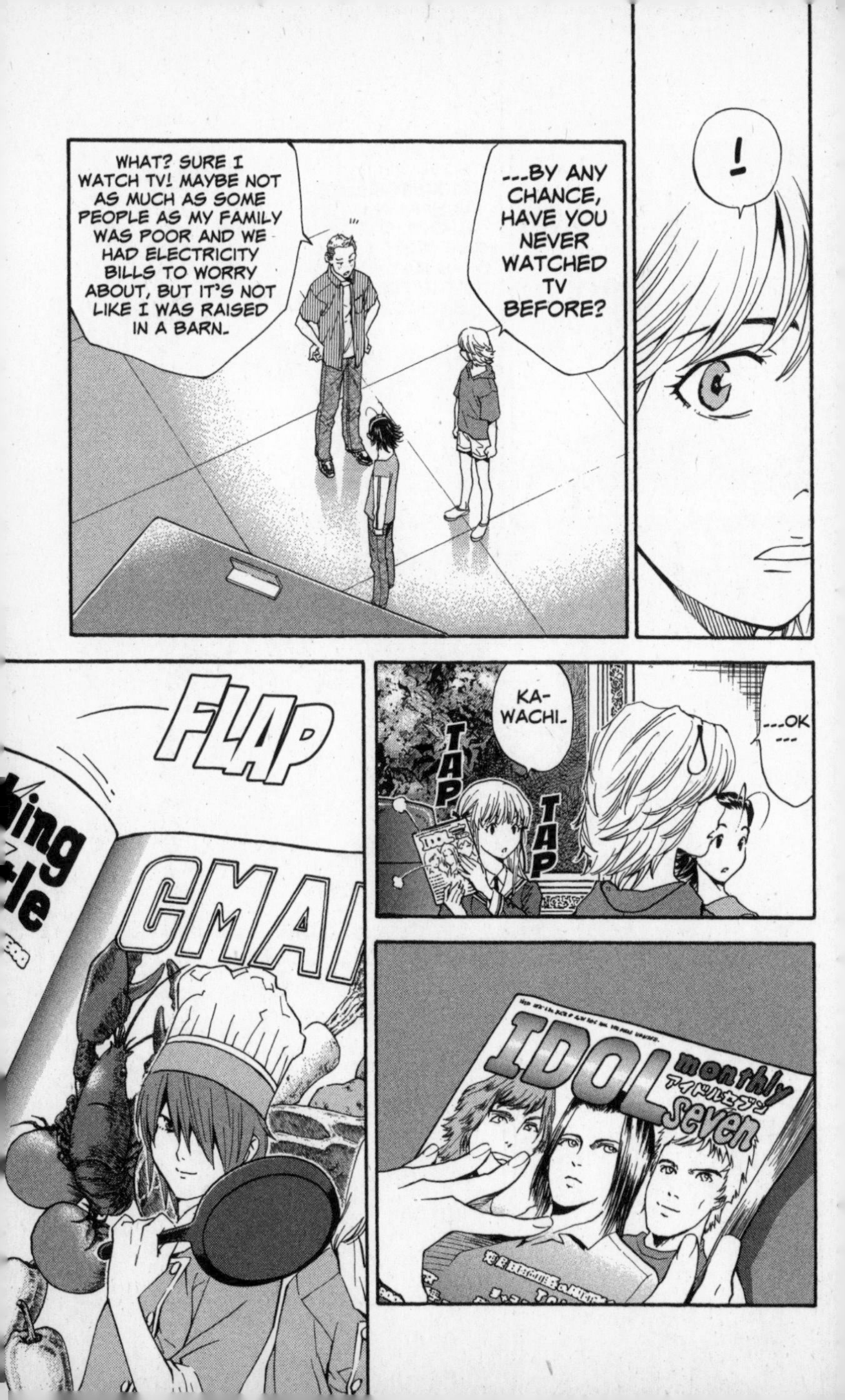
!
...BY ANY CHANCE, HAVE YOU NEVER WATCHED TV BEFORE?
WHAT? SURE I WATCH TV! MAYBE NOT AS MUCH AS SOME PEOPLE AS MY FAMILY WAS POOR AND WE HAD ELECTRICITY BILLS TO WORRY ABOUT, BUT IT'S NOT LIKE I WAS RAISED IN A BARN.
...OK ...
KA-WACHI.
TAP
TAP
IDOL
monthly
アイドルセブン
seven
FLAP

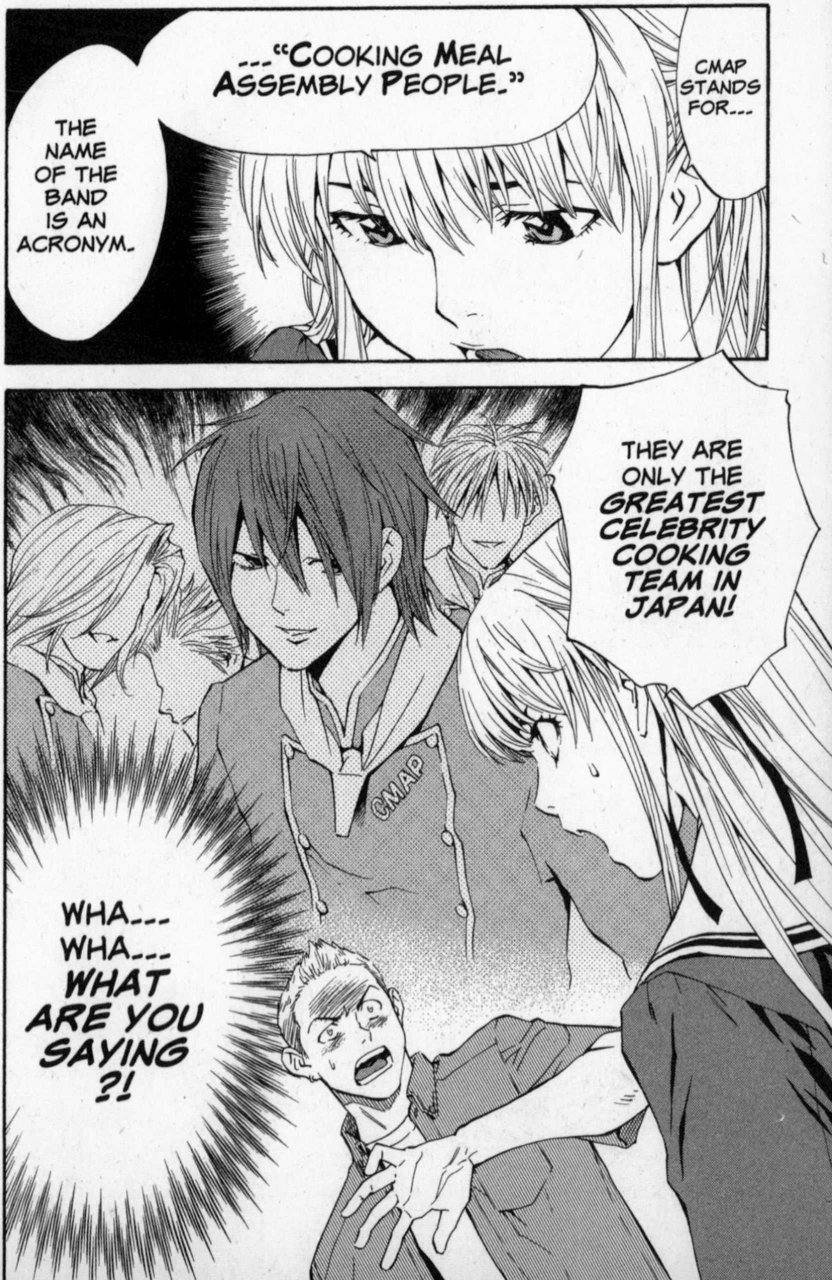
CMAP STANDS FOR...
...“COOKING MEAL ASSEMBLY PEOPLE.”
THE NAME OF THE BAND IS AN ACRONYM.
THEY ARE ONLY THE *GREATEST CELEBRITY COOKING TEAM IN JAPAN!*
CMAP
WHA... WHA... *WHAT ARE YOU SAYING?!*

Story 128:

Super Tuna

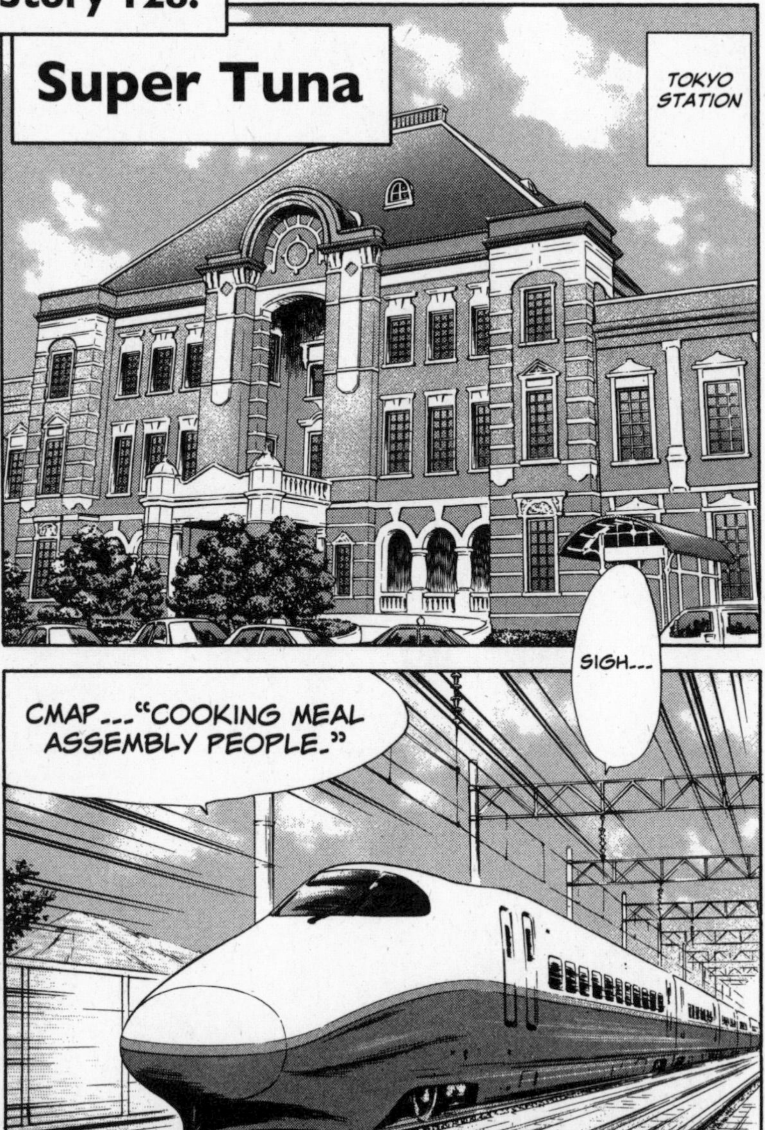
TOKYO STATION
SIGH...
CMAP... "COOKING MEAL ASSEMBLY PEOPLE."

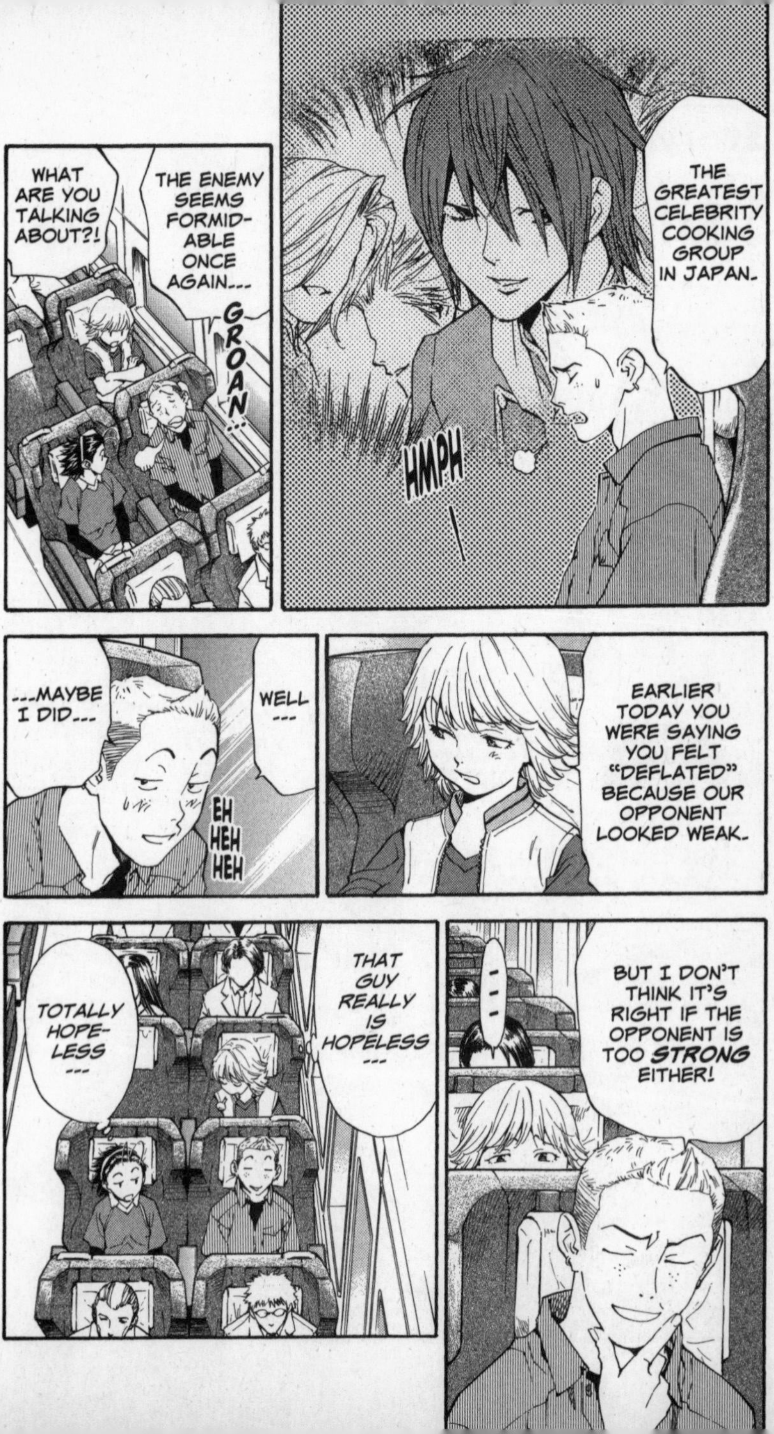
THE GREATEST CELEBRITY COOKING GROUP IN JAPAN.
HMPH
THE ENEMY SEEMS FORMID-ABLE ONCE AGAIN...
GROAN...
WHAT ARE YOU TALKING ABOUT?!
EARLIER TODAY YOU WERE SAYING YOU FELT "DEFLATED" BECAUSE OUR OPPONENT LOOKED WEAK.
WELL...
...MAYBE I DID...
EH HEH HEH
BUT I DON'T THINK IT'S RIGHT IF THE OPPONENT IS TOO STRONG EITHER!
...
THAT GUY REALLY IS HOPELESS...
TOTALLY HOPE-LESS...

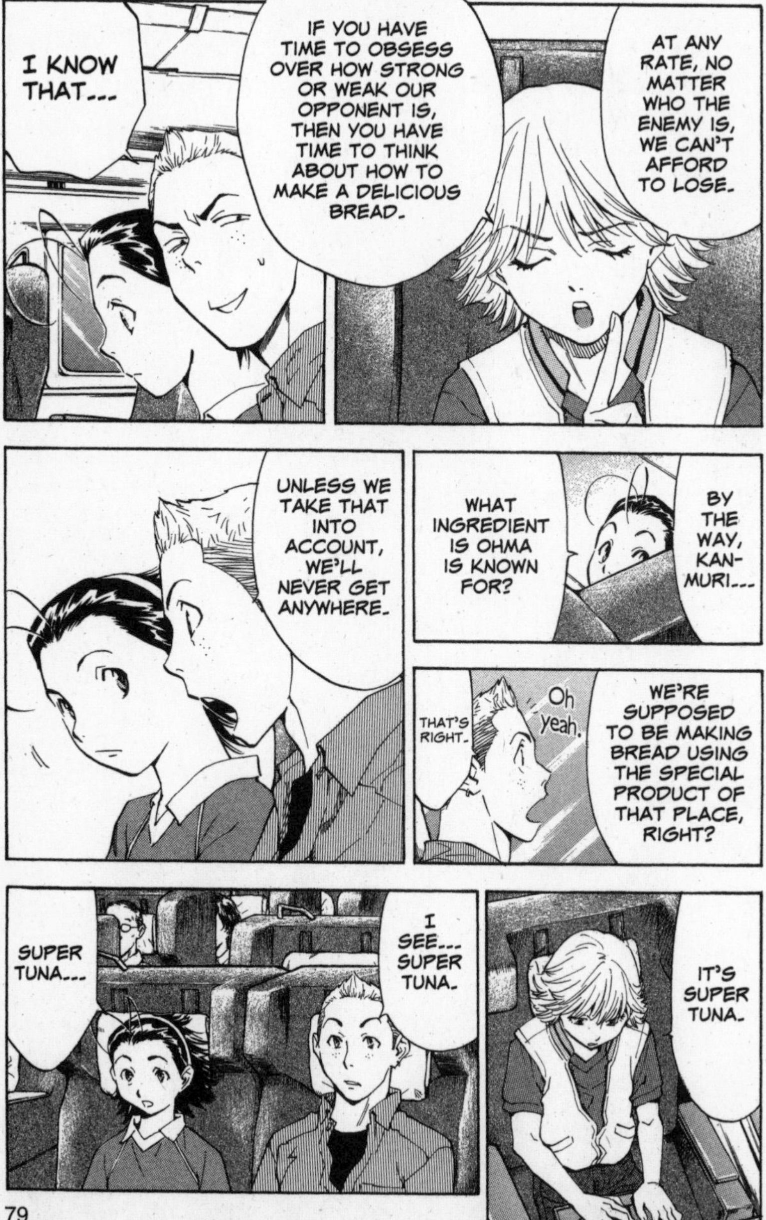
AT ANY RATE, NO MATTER WHO THE ENEMY IS, WE CAN'T AFFORD TO LOSE.
IF YOU HAVE TIME TO OBSESS OVER HOW STRONG OR WEAK OUR OPPONENT IS, THEN YOU HAVE TIME TO THINK ABOUT HOW TO MAKE A DELICIOUS BREAD.
I KNOW THAT...
BY THE WAY, KAN-MURI...
WHAT INGREDIENT IS OHMA IS KNOWN FOR?
WE'RE SUPPOSED TO BE MAKING BREAD USING THE SPECIAL PRODUCT OF THAT PLACE, RIGHT?
Oh yeah.
THAT'S RIGHT.
UNLESS WE TAKE THAT INTO ACCOUNT, WE'LL NEVER GET ANYWHERE.
IT'S SUPER TUNA.
I SEE... SUPER TUNA.
SUPER TUNA...

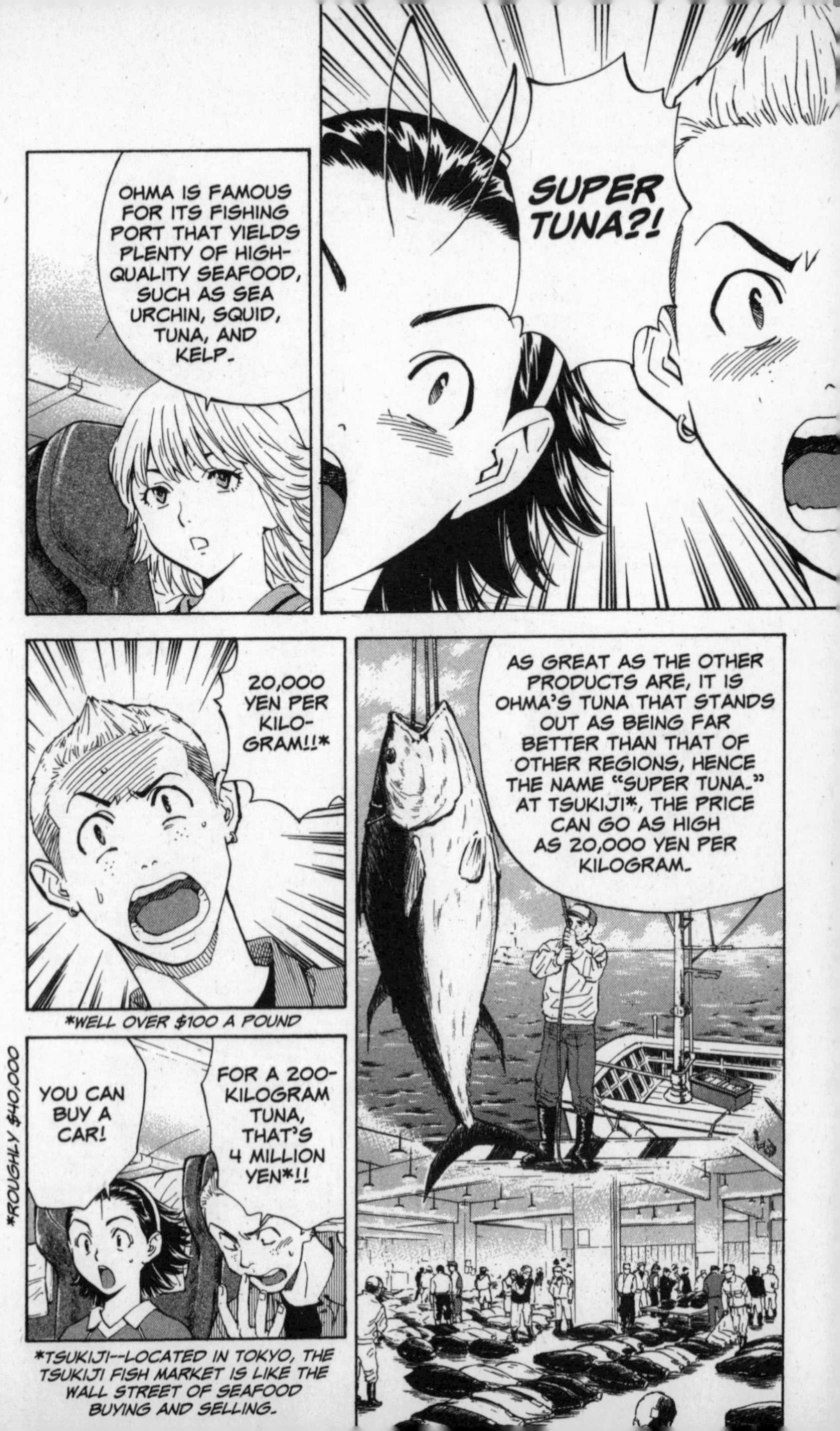
SUPER TUNA?!
OHMA IS FAMOUS FOR ITS FISHING PORT THAT YIELDS PLENTY OF HIGH-QUALITY SEAFOOD, SUCH AS SEA URCHIN, SQUID, TUNA, AND KELP.
AS GREAT AS THE OTHER PRODUCTS ARE, IT IS OHMA'S TUNA THAT STANDS OUT AS BEING FAR BETTER THAN THAT OF OTHER REGIONS, HENCE THE NAME "SUPER TUNA." AT TSUKIJI*, THE PRICE CAN GO AS HIGH AS 20,000 YEN PER KILOGRAM.
20,000 YEN PER KILO-GRAM!!*
*WELL OVER $100 A POUND
FOR A 200-KILOGRAM TUNA, THAT'S 4 MILLION YEN*!!
YOU CAN BUY A CAR!
*ROUGHLY $40,000
*TSUKIJI--LOCATED IN TOKYO, THE TSUKIJI FISH MARKET IS LIKE THE WALL STREET OF SEAFOOD BUYING AND SELLING.

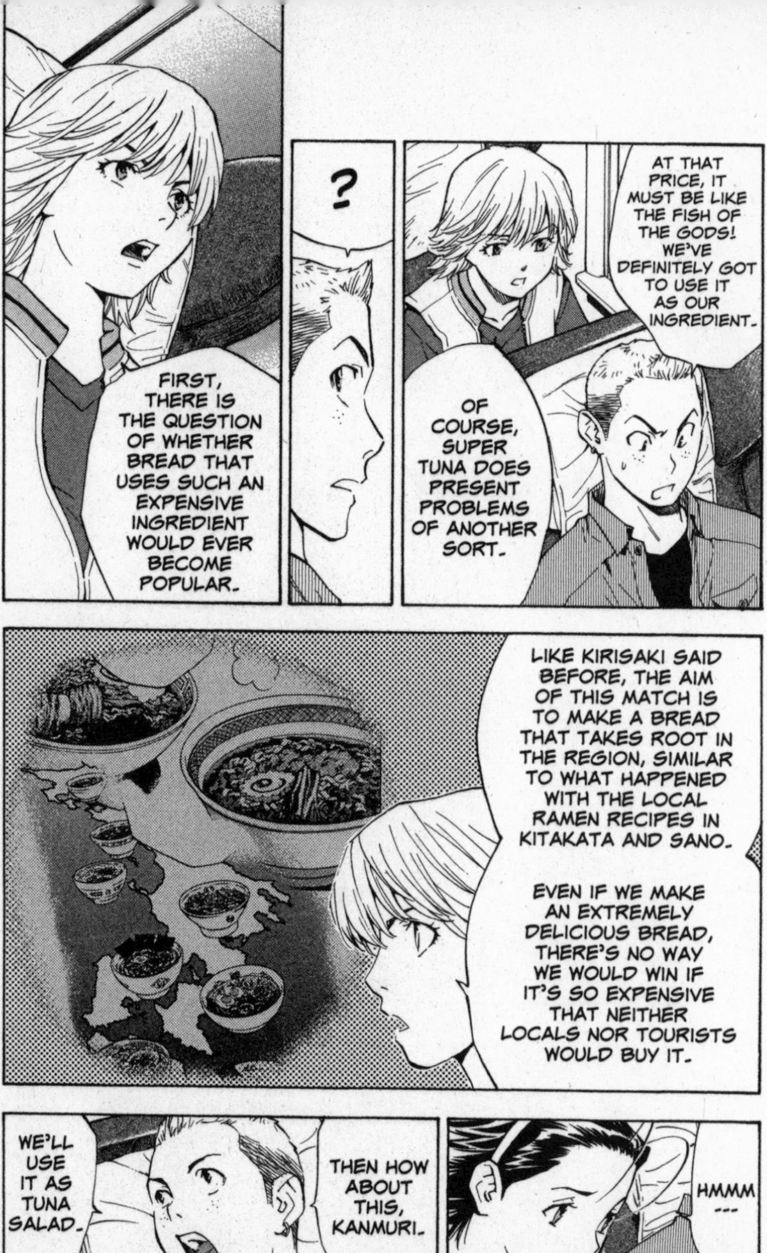
AT THAT PRICE, IT MUST BE LIKE THE FISH OF THE GODS! WE'VE DEFINITELY GOT TO USE IT AS OUR INGREDIENT.
OF COURSE, SUPER TUNA DOES PRESENT PROBLEMS OF ANOTHER SORT.
?
FIRST, THERE IS THE QUESTION OF WHETHER BREAD THAT USES SUCH AN EXPENSIVE INGREDIENT WOULD EVER BECOME POPULAR.
LIKE KIRISAKI SAID BEFORE, THE AIM OF THIS MATCH IS TO MAKE A BREAD THAT TAKES ROOT IN THE REGION, SIMILAR TO WHAT HAPPENED WITH THE LOCAL RAMEN RECIPES IN KITAKATA AND SANO.
EVEN IF WE MAKE AN EXTREMELY DELICIOUS BREAD, THERE'S NO WAY WE WOULD WIN IF IT'S SO EXPENSIVE THAT NEITHER LOCALS NOR TOURISTS WOULD BUY IT.
HMMM...
THEN HOW ABOUT THIS, KANMURI.
WE'LL USE IT AS TUNA SALAD.

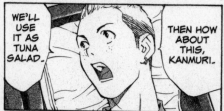

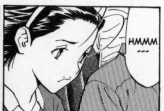

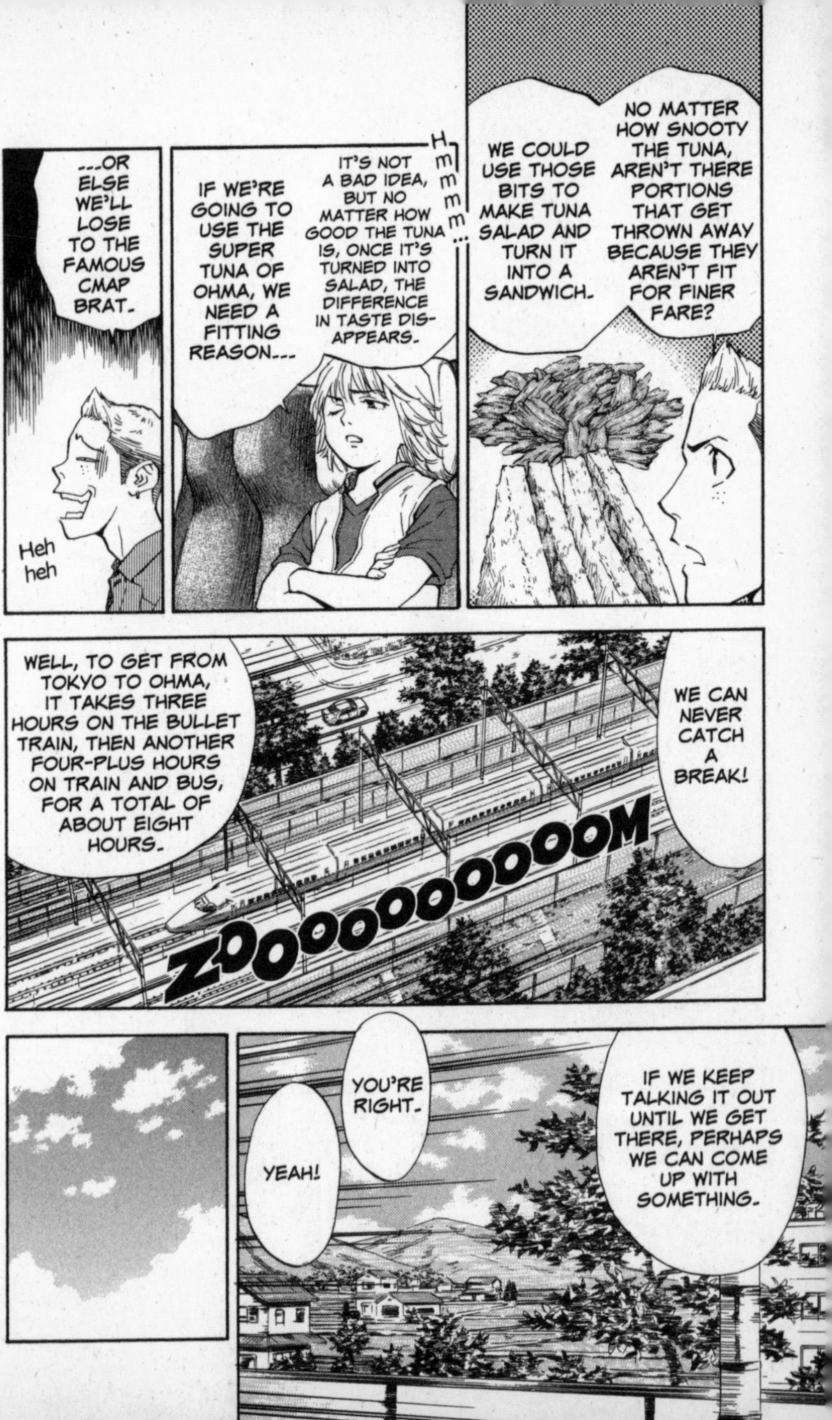
NO MATTER HOW SNOOTY THE TUNA, AREN'T THERE PORTIONS THAT GET THROWN AWAY BECAUSE THEY AREN'T FIT FOR FINER FARE?
WE COULD USE THOSE BITS TO MAKE TUNA SALAD AND TURN IT INTO A SANDWICH.
Hmmmm...
IT'S NOT A BAD IDEA, BUT NO MATTER HOW GOOD THE TUNA IS, ONCE IT'S TURNED INTO SALAD, THE DIFFERENCE IN TASTE DIS-APPEARS.
IF WE'RE GOING TO USE THE SUPER TUNA OF OHMA, WE NEED A FITTING REASON...
...OR ELSE WE'LL LOSE TO THE FAMOUS CMAP BRAT.
Heh heh
WE CAN NEVER CATCH A BREAK!
WELL, TO GET FROM TOKYO TO OHMA, IT TAKES THREE HOURS ON THE BULLET TRAIN, THEN ANOTHER FOUR-PLUS HOURS ON TRAIN AND BUS, FOR A TOTAL OF ABOUT EIGHT HOURS.
ZOOOOOOOOOOOM
IF WE KEEP TALKING IT OUT UNTIL WE GET THERE, PERHAPS WE CAN COME UP WITH SOMETHING.
YOU'RE RIGHT.
YEAH!

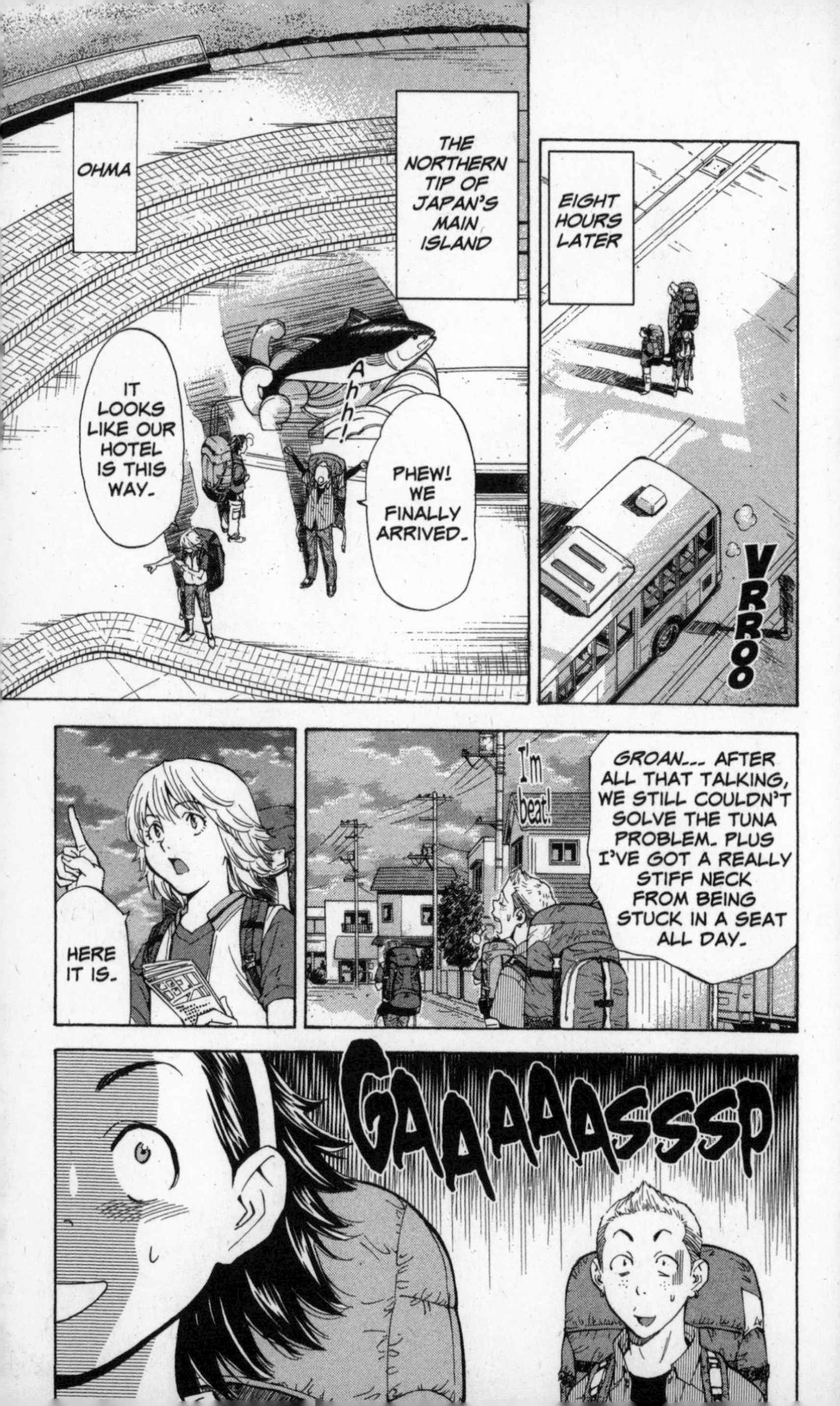
EIGHT HOURS LATER
VRROO
THE NORTHERN TIP OF JAPAN'S MAIN ISLAND
OHMA
Ahh!
PHEW! WE FINALLY ARRIVED.
IT LOOKS LIKE OUR HOTEL IS THIS WAY.
GROAN... AFTER ALL THAT TALKING, WE STILL COULDN'T SOLVE THE TUNA PROBLEM. PLUS I'VE GOT A REALLY STIFF NECK FROM BEING STUCK IN A SEAT ALL DAY.
I'm beat!
HERE IT IS.
GAAAAASSSP

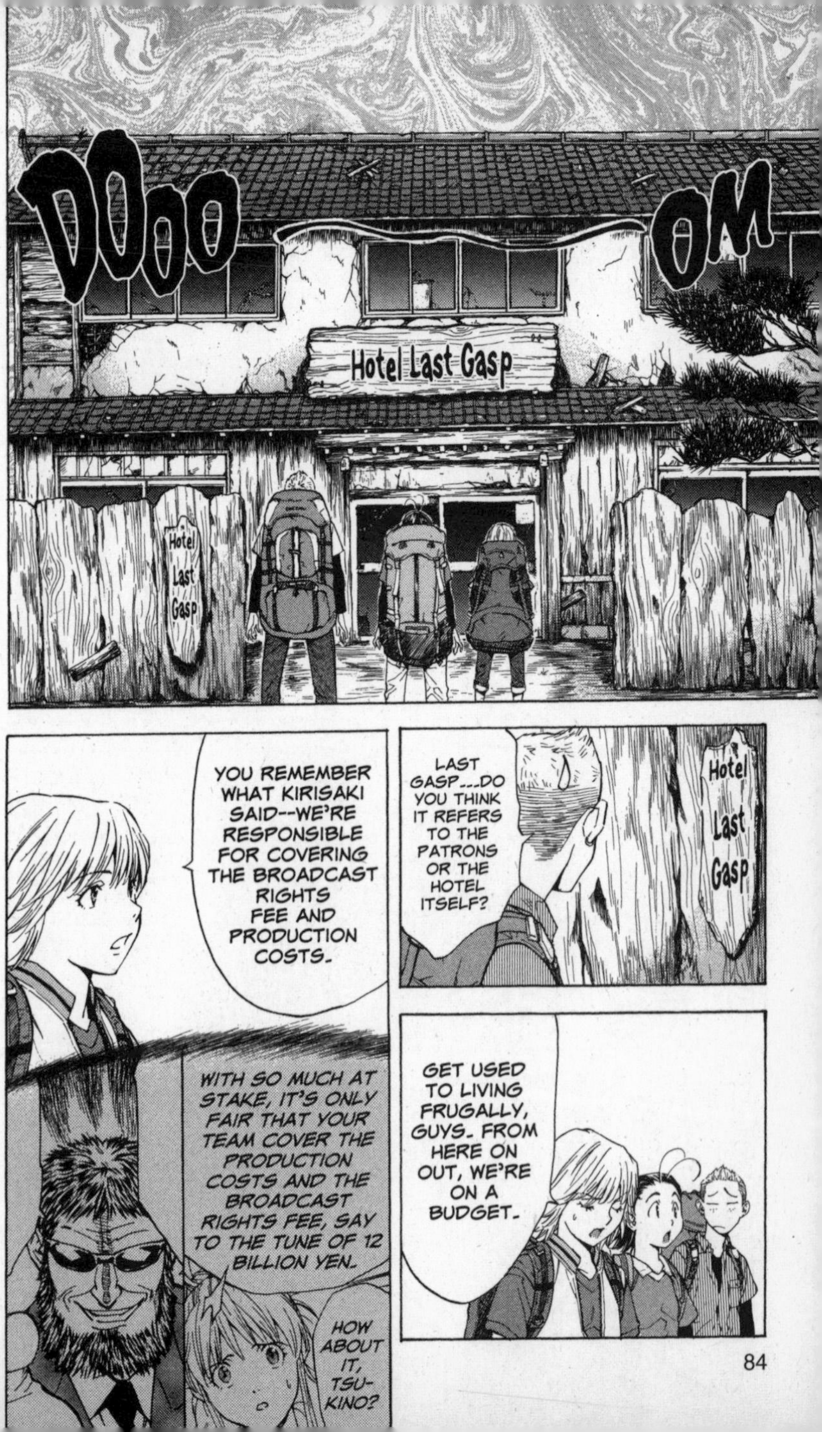
DOOO
OM
Hotel Last Gasp
Hotel Last Gasp
LAST GASP...DO YOU THINK IT REFERS TO THE PATRONS OR THE HOTEL ITSELF?
Hotel Last Gasp
YOU REMEMBER WHAT KIRISAKI SAID--WE'RE RESPONSIBLE FOR COVERING THE BROADCAST RIGHTS FEE AND PRODUCTION COSTS.
GET USED TO LIVING FRUGALLY, GUYS. FROM HERE ON OUT, WE'RE ON A BUDGET.
WITH SO MUCH AT STAKE, IT'S ONLY FAIR THAT YOUR TEAM COVER THE PRODUCTION COSTS AND THE BROADCAST RIGHTS FEE, SAY TO THE TUNE OF 12 BILLION YEN.
HOW ABOUT IT, TSU-KINO?

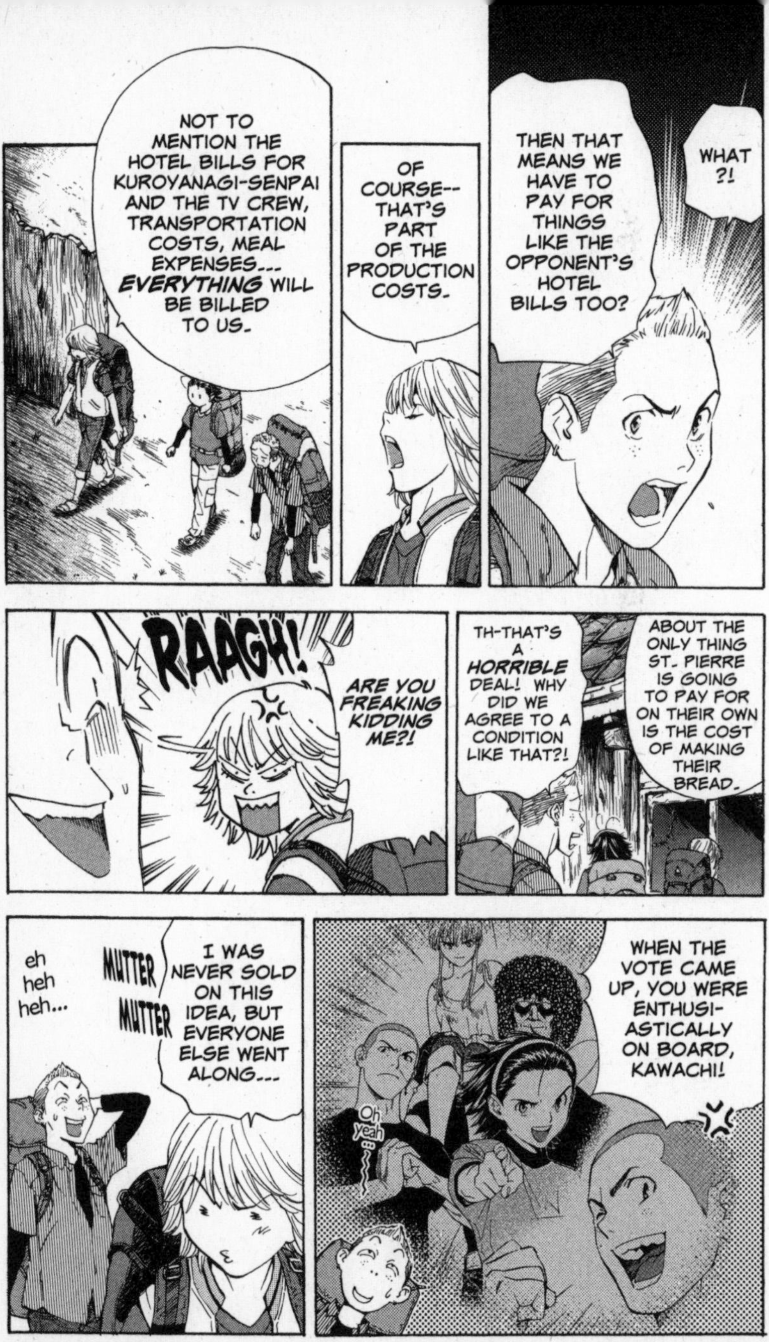
WHAT ?!
THEN THAT MEANS WE HAVE TO PAY FOR THINGS LIKE THE OPPONENT'S HOTEL BILLS TOO?
OF COURSE-- THAT'S PART OF THE PRODUCTION COSTS.
NOT TO MENTION THE HOTEL BILLS FOR KUROYANAGI-SENPAI AND THE TV CREW, TRANSPORTATION COSTS, MEAL EXPENSES... EVERYTHING WILL BE BILLED TO US.
ABOUT THE ONLY THING ST. PIERRE IS GOING TO PAY FOR ON THEIR OWN IS THE COST OF MAKING THEIR BREAD.
TH-THAT'S A HORRIBLE DEAL! WHY DID WE AGREE TO A CONDITION LIKE THAT?!
RAAGH!
ARE YOU FREAKING KIDDING ME?!
WHEN THE VOTE CAME UP, YOU WERE ENTHUSI-ASTICALLY ON BOARD, KAWACHI!
Oh yeah...
I WAS NEVER SOLD ON THIS IDEA, BUT EVERYONE ELSE WENT ALONG...
MUTTER MUTTER
eh heh heh...

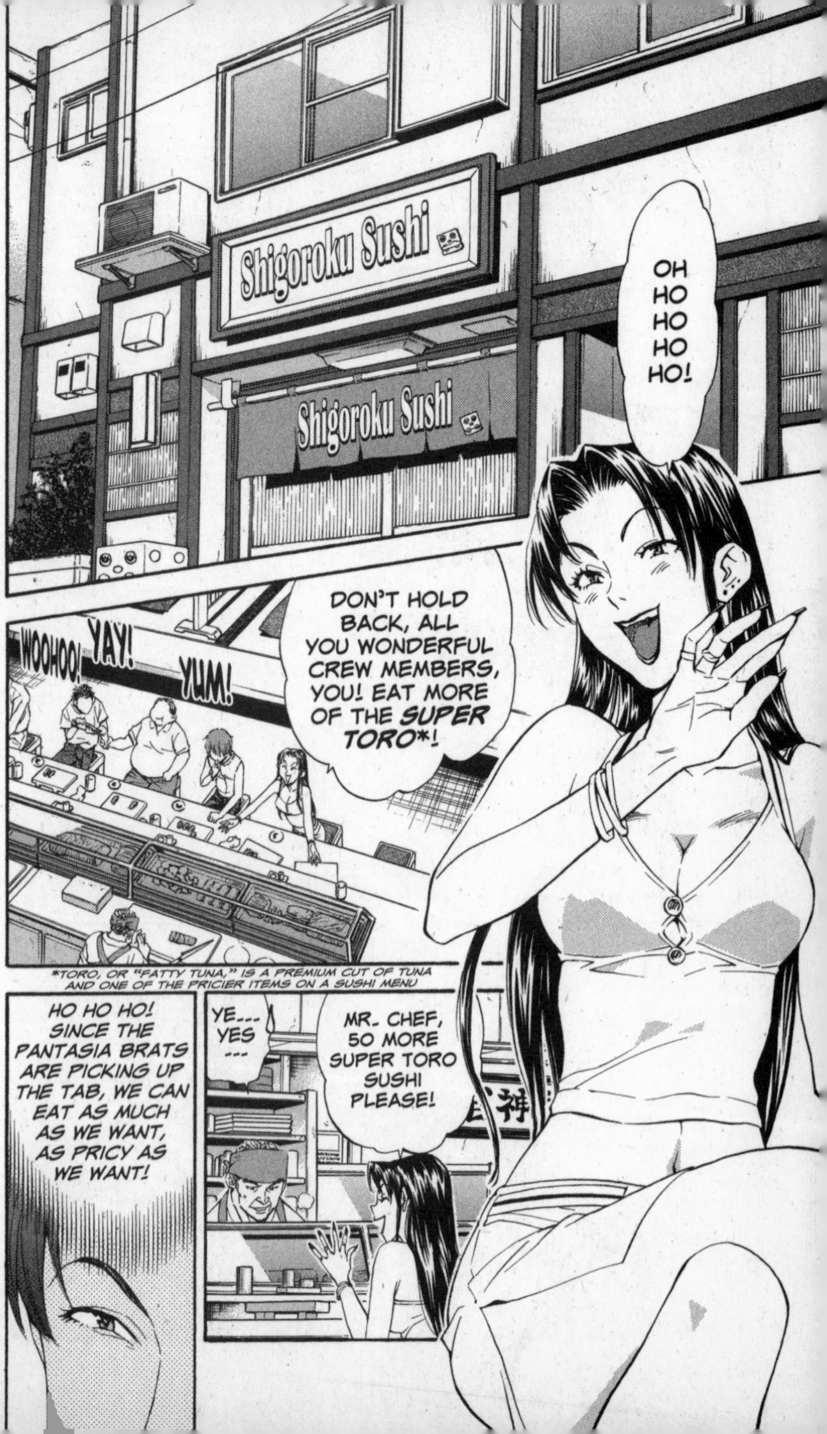
Shigoroku Sushi
Shigoroku Sushi
OH HO HO HO HO!
DON'T HOLD BACK, ALL YOU WONDERFUL CREW MEMBERS, YOU! EAT MORE OF THE *SUPER TORO**!
YUM!
YAY!
WOOHOO!
MR. CHEF, 50 MORE SUPER TORO SUSHI PLEASE!
YE... YES ---
HO HO HO! SINCE THE PANTASIA BRATS ARE PICKING UP THE TAB, WE CAN EAT AS MUCH AS WE WANT, AS PRICY AS WE WANT!

*TORO, OR "FATTY TUNA," IS A PREMIUM CUT OF TUNA AND ONE OF THE PRICIER ITEMS ON A SUSHI MENU

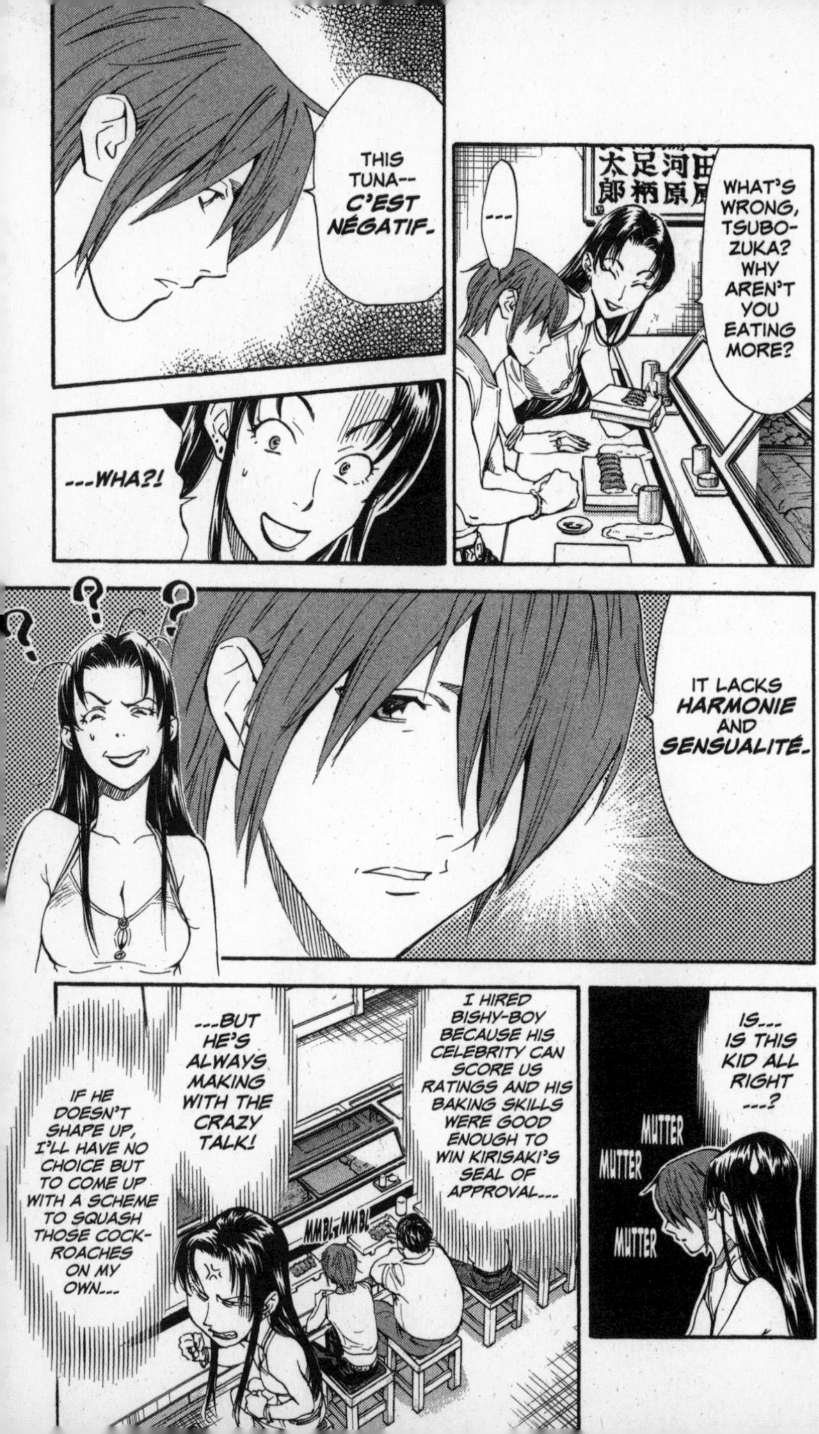
WHAT'S WRONG, TSUBOZUKA? WHY AREN'T YOU EATING MORE?

太郎 足柄 河原 田
THIS TUNA-- C'EST NÉGATIF.
---WHA?!
IT LACKS HARMONIE AND SENSUALITÉ.
IS--- IS THIS KID ALL RIGHT---?
MUTTER
MUTTER
MUTTER
I HIRED BISHY-BOY BECAUSE HIS CELEBRITY CAN SCORE US RATINGS AND HIS BAKING SKILLS WERE GOOD ENOUGH TO WIN KIRISAKI'S SEAL OF APPROVAL---
---BUT HE'S ALWAYS MAKING WITH THE CRAZY TALK!
IF HE DOESN'T SHAPE UP, I'LL HAVE NO CHOICE BUT TO COME UP WITH A SCHEME TO SQUASH THOSE COCKROACHES ON MY OWN---
MMBL MMBL

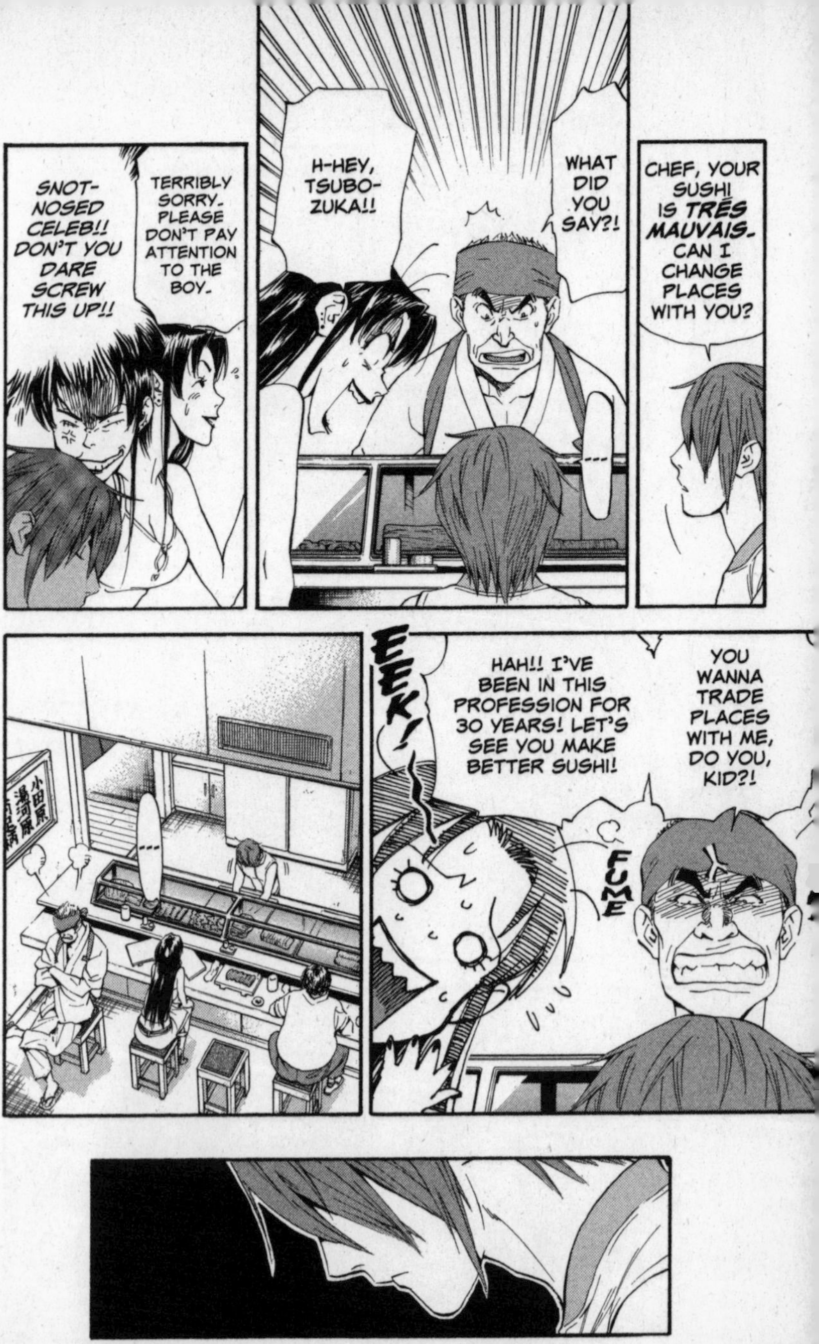
CHEF, YOUR SUSHI IS *TRÉS MAUVAIS*. CAN I CHANGE PLACES WITH YOU?
WHAT DID YOU SAY?!
H-HEY, TSUBOZUKA!!
...
TERRIBLY SORRY. PLEASE DON'T PAY ATTENTION TO THE BOY.
SNOT-NOSED CELEB!! DON'T YOU DARE SCREW THIS UP!!
YOU WANNA TRADE PLACES WITH ME, DO YOU, KID?!
FUME
HAH!! I'VE BEEN IN THIS PROFESSION FOR 30 YEARS! LET'S SEE YOU MAKE BETTER SUSHI!
EEK!
小田原
湯河原
...

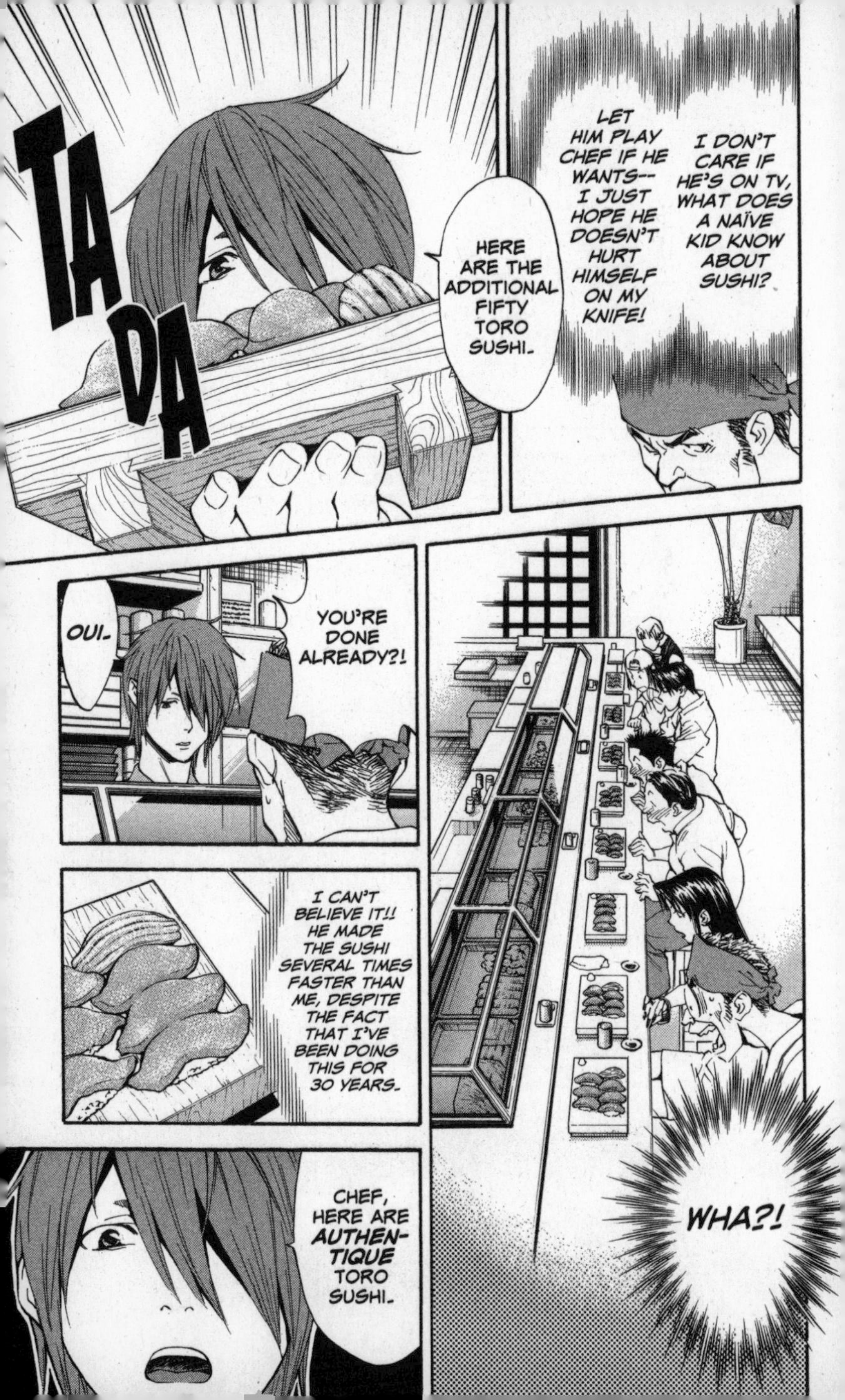

I DON'T CARE IF HE'S ON TV, WHAT DOES A NAÏVE KID KNOW ABOUT SUSHI?
LET HIM PLAY CHEF IF HE WANTS-- I JUST HOPE HE DOESN'T HURT HIMSELF ON MY KNIFE!
TA DA
HERE ARE THE ADDITIONAL FIFTY TORO SUSHI.
WHA?!
YOU'RE DONE ALREADY?!
OUI.
I CAN'T BELIEVE IT!! HE MADE THE SUSHI SEVERAL TIMES FASTER THAN ME, DESPITE THE FACT THAT I'VE BEEN DOING THIS FOR 30 YEARS.
CHEF, HERE ARE AUTHENTIQUE TORO SUSHI.

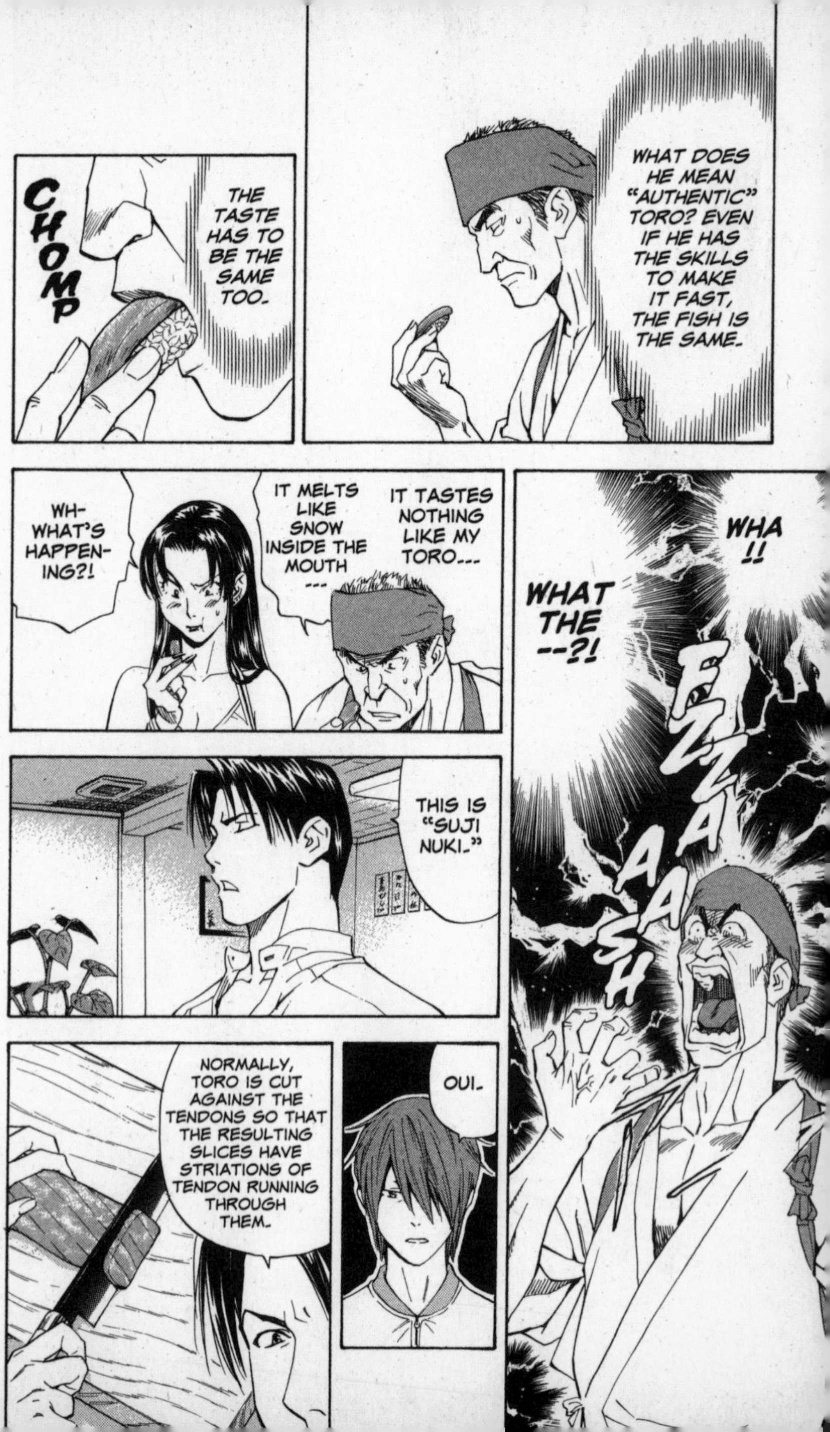
WHAT DOES HE MEAN "AUTHENTIC" TORO? EVEN IF HE HAS THE SKILLS TO MAKE IT FAST, THE FISH IS THE SAME.
CHOMP
THE TASTE HAS TO BE THE SAME TOO.
WHA !!
WHAT THE --?!
FZZAAAASH
IT TASTES NOTHING LIKE MY TORO...
IT MELTS LIKE SNOW INSIDE THE MOUTH ...
WH-WHAT'S HAPPENING?!
THIS IS "SUJI NUKI."
OUI.
NORMALLY, TORO IS CUT AGAINST THE TENDONS SO THAT THE RESULTING SLICES HAVE STRIATIONS OF TENDON RUNNING THROUGH THEM.

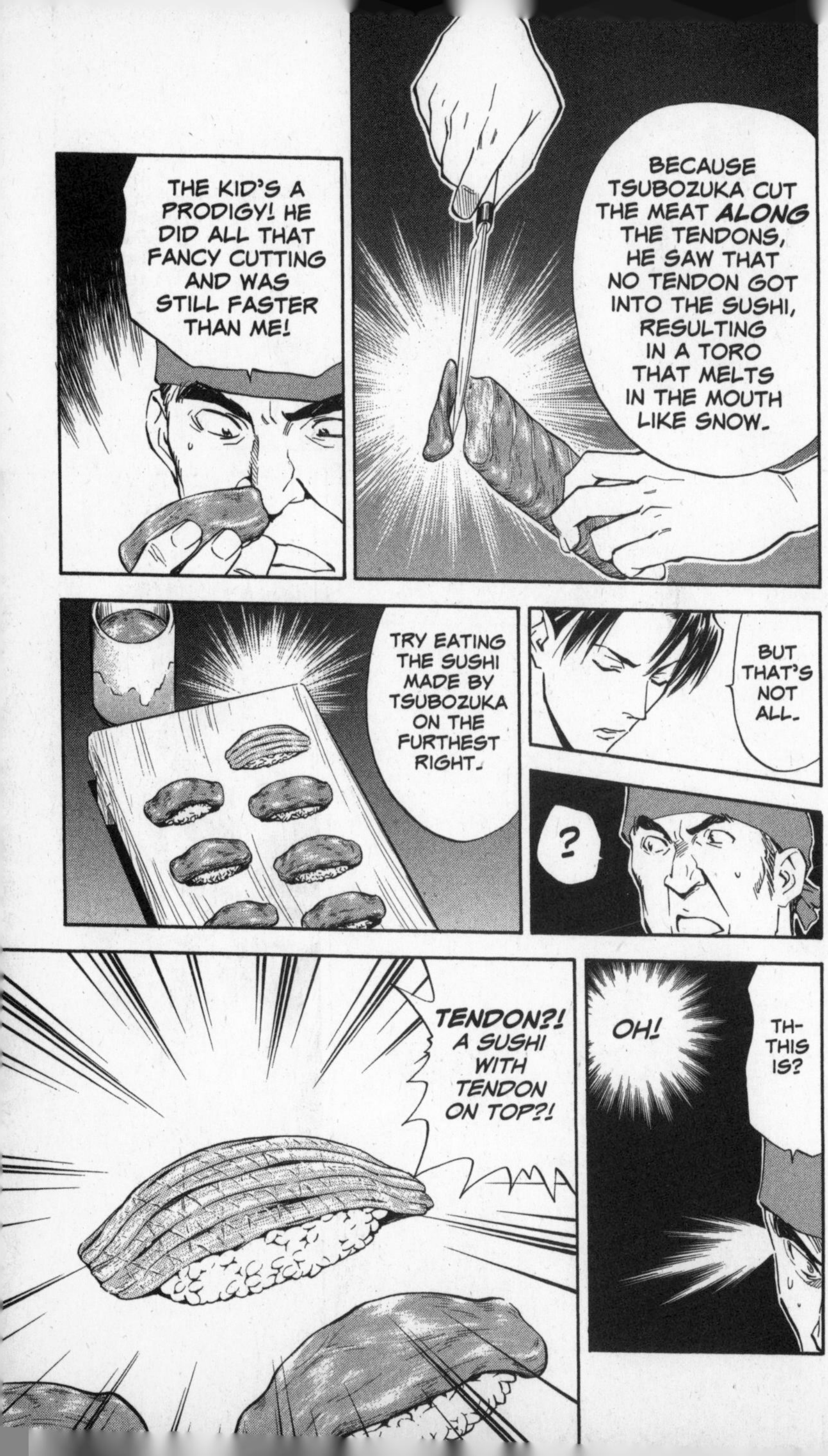
BECAUSE TSUBOZUKA CUT THE MEAT ALONG THE TENDONS, HE SAW THAT NO TENDON GOT INTO THE SUSHI, RESULTING IN A TORO THAT MELTS IN THE MOUTH LIKE SNOW.
THE KID'S A PRODIGY! HE DID ALL THAT FANCY CUTTING AND WAS STILL FASTER THAN ME!
BUT THAT'S NOT ALL.
?
TRY EATING THE SUSHI MADE BY TSUBOZUKA ON THE FURTHEST RIGHT.
TH- THIS IS?
OH!
TENDON?! A SUSHI WITH TENDON ON TOP?!

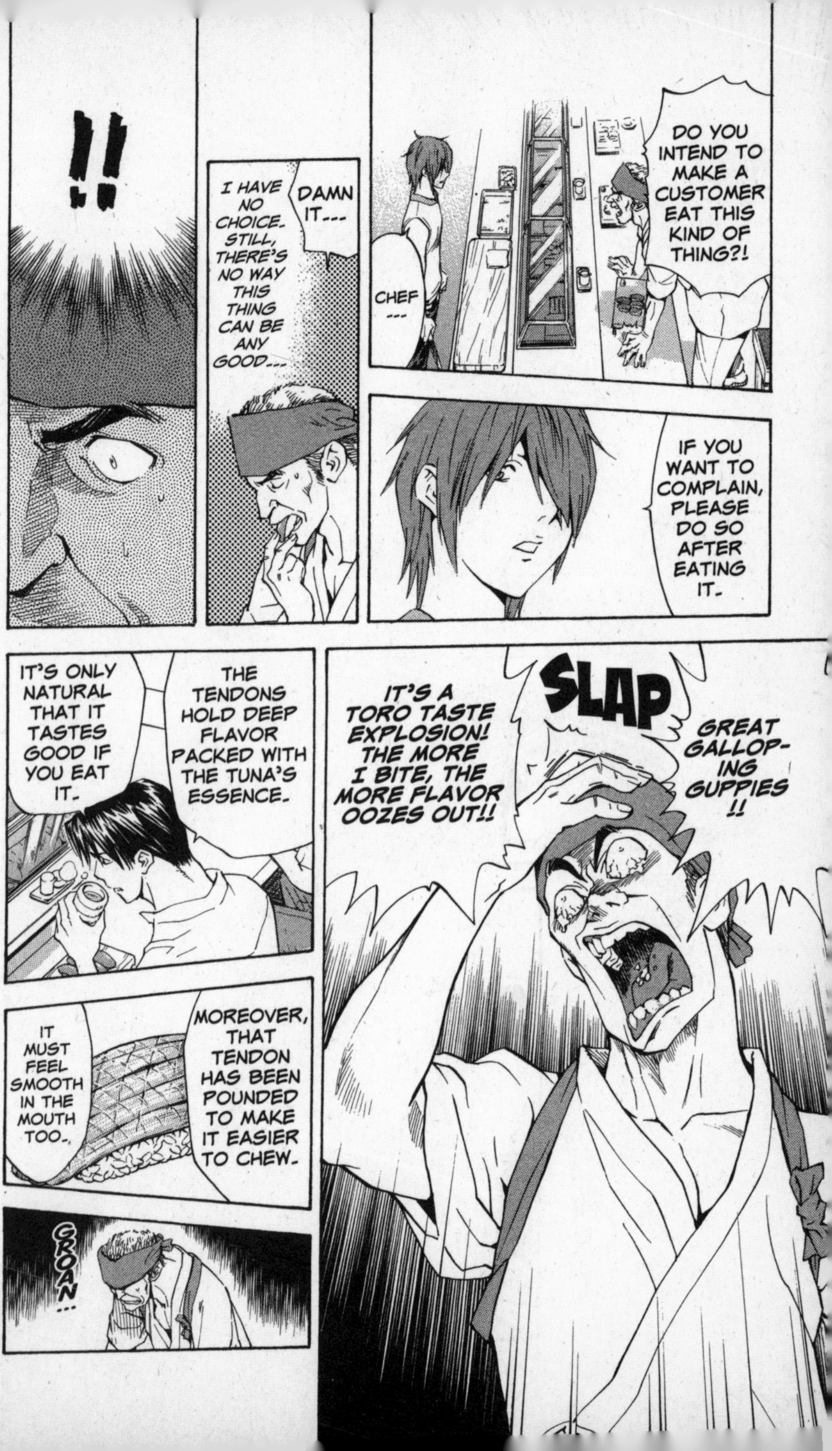
DO YOU INTEND TO MAKE A CUSTOMER EAT THIS KIND OF THING?!
CHEF...
IF YOU WANT TO COMPLAIN, PLEASE DO SO AFTER EATING IT.
DAMN IT...
I HAVE NO CHOICE. STILL, THERE'S NO WAY THIS THING CAN BE ANY GOOD...
!!
SLAP
GREAT GALLOP-ING GUPPIES!!
IT'S A TORO TASTE EXPLOSION! THE MORE I BITE, THE MORE FLAVOR OOZES OUT!!
THE TENDONS HOLD DEEP FLAVOR PACKED WITH THE TUNA'S ESSENCE.
IT'S ONLY NATURAL THAT IT TASTES GOOD IF YOU EAT IT.
MOREOVER, THAT TENDON HAS BEEN POUNDED TO MAKE IT EASIER TO CHEW.
IT MUST FEEL SMOOTH IN THE MOUTH TOO.
GROAN...

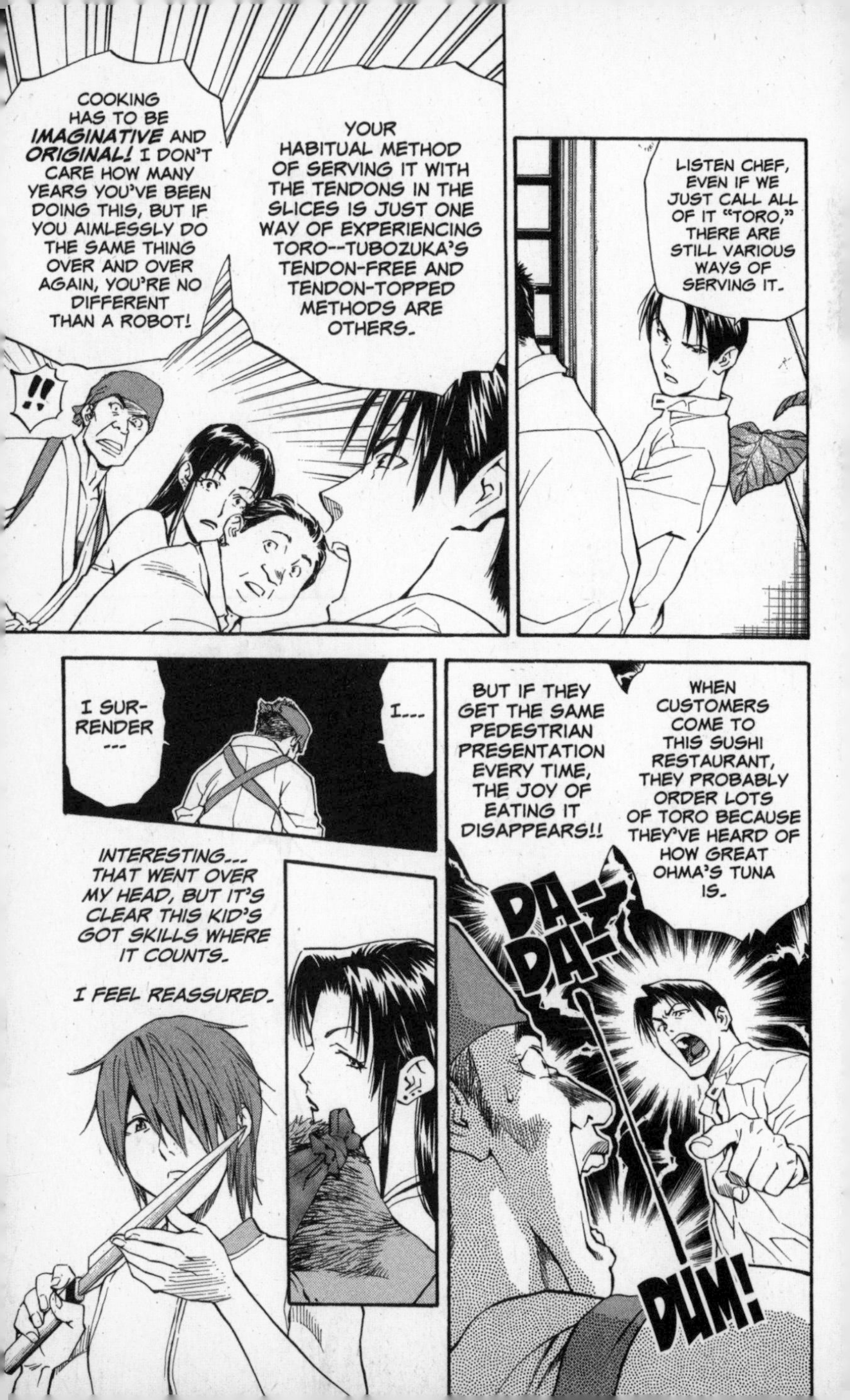
LISTEN CHEF, EVEN IF WE JUST CALL ALL OF IT "TORO," THERE ARE STILL VARIOUS WAYS OF SERVING IT.
YOUR HABITUAL METHOD OF SERVING IT WITH THE TENDONS IN THE SLICES IS JUST ONE WAY OF EXPERIENCING TORO--TUBOZUKA'S TENDON-FREE AND TENDON-TOPPED METHODS ARE OTHERS.
COOKING HAS TO BE IMAGINATIVE AND ORIGINAL! I DON'T CARE HOW MANY YEARS YOU'VE BEEN DOING THIS, BUT IF YOU AIMLESSLY DO THE SAME THING OVER AND OVER AGAIN, YOU'RE NO DIFFERENT THAN A ROBOT!
!!
WHEN CUSTOMERS COME TO THIS SUSHI RESTAURANT, THEY PROBABLY ORDER LOTS OF TORO BECAUSE THEY'VE HEARD OF HOW GREAT OHMA'S TUNA IS.
BUT IF THEY GET THE SAME PEDESTRIAN PRESENTATION EVERY TIME, THE JOY OF EATING IT DISAPPEARS!!
DA-DA-DUM!
I...
I SUR-RENDER---
INTERESTING... THAT WENT OVER MY HEAD, BUT IT'S CLEAR THIS KID'S GOT SKILLS WHERE IT COUNTS.
I FEEL REASSURED.

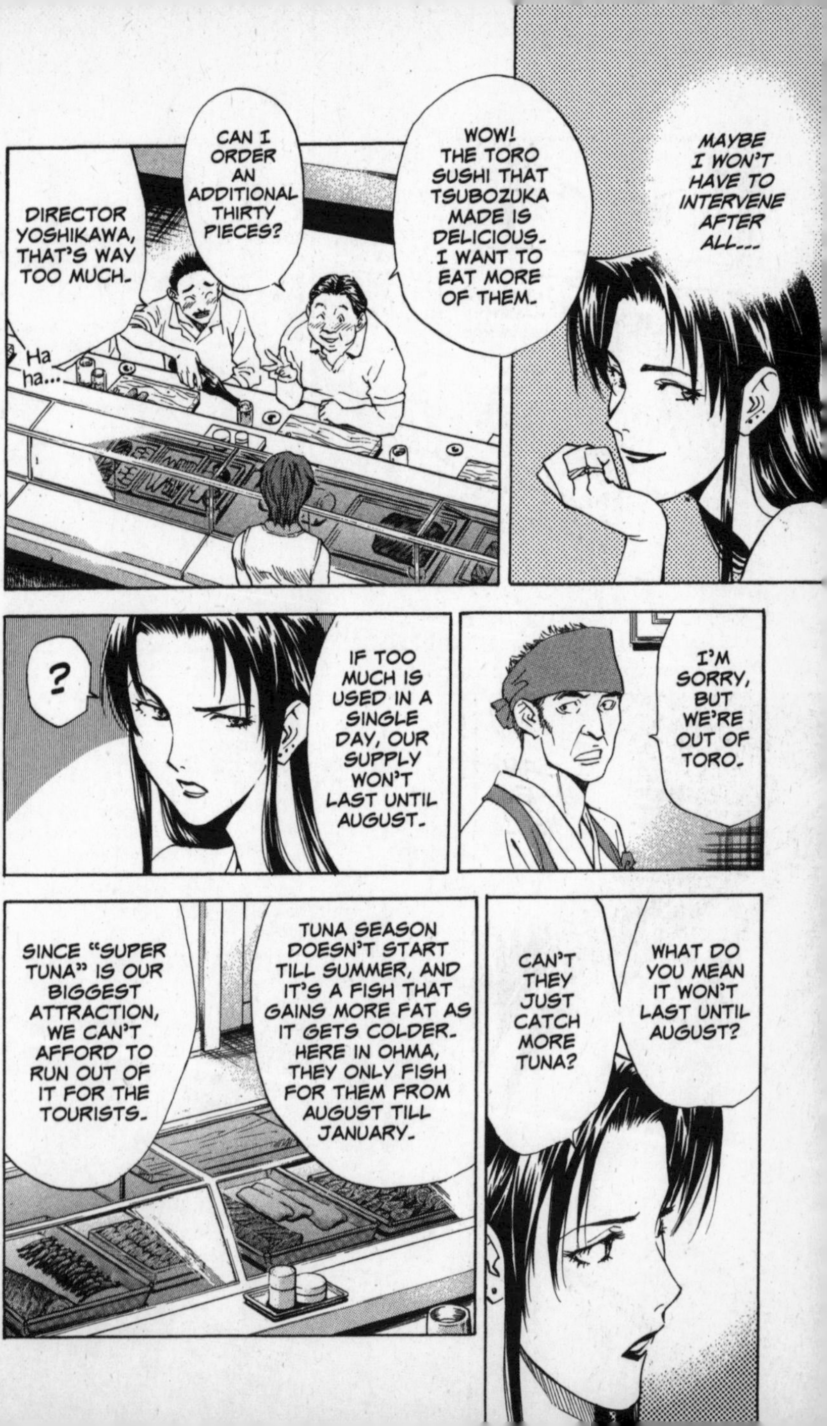
MAYBE I WON'T HAVE TO INTERVENE AFTER ALL...
WOW! THE TORO SUSHI THAT TSUBOZUKA MADE IS DELICIOUS. I WANT TO EAT MORE OF THEM.
CAN I ORDER AN ADDITIONAL THIRTY PIECES?
DIRECTOR YOSHIKAWA, THAT'S WAY TOO MUCH.
Ha ha...
I'M SORRY, BUT WE'RE OUT OF TORO.
IF TOO MUCH IS USED IN A SINGLE DAY, OUR SUPPLY WON'T LAST UNTIL AUGUST.
?
WHAT DO YOU MEAN IT WON'T LAST UNTIL AUGUST?
CAN'T THEY JUST CATCH MORE TUNA?
TUNA SEASON DOESN'T START TILL SUMMER, AND IT'S A FISH THAT GAINS MORE FAT AS IT GETS COLDER. HERE IN OHMA, THEY ONLY FISH FOR THEM FROM AUGUST TILL JANUARY.
SINCE "SUPER TUNA" IS OUR BIGGEST ATTRACTION, WE CAN'T AFFORD TO RUN OUT OF IT FOR THE TOURISTS.

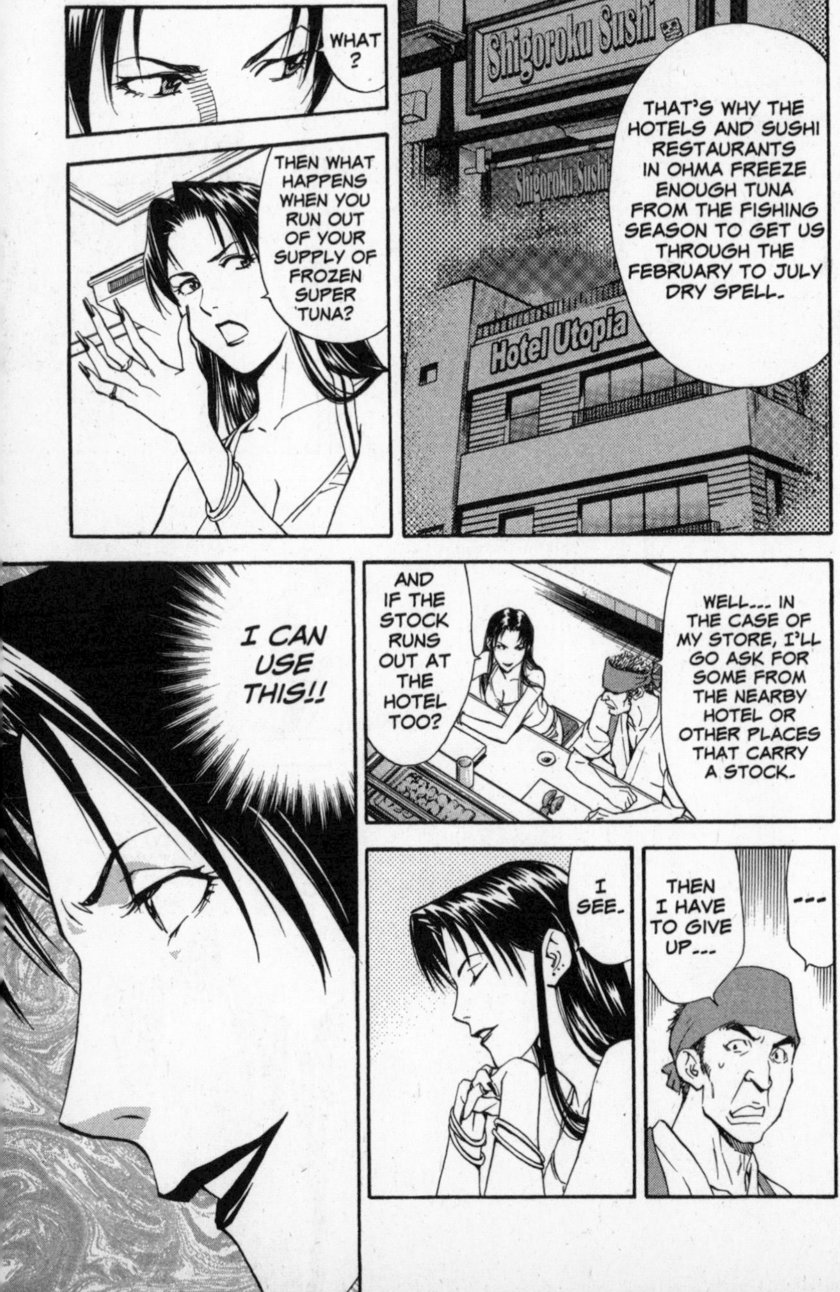
Shigoroku Sushi
Shigoroku Sushi
Hotel Utopia
THAT'S WHY THE HOTELS AND SUSHI RESTAURANTS IN OHMA FREEZE ENOUGH TUNA FROM THE FISHING SEASON TO GET US THROUGH THE FEBRUARY TO JULY DRY SPELL.
WHAT ?
THEN WHAT HAPPENS WHEN YOU RUN OUT OF YOUR SUPPLY OF FROZEN SUPER TUNA?
WELL... IN THE CASE OF MY STORE, I'LL GO ASK FOR SOME FROM THE NEARBY HOTEL OR OTHER PLACES THAT CARRY A STOCK.
AND IF THE STOCK RUNS OUT AT THE HOTEL TOO?
...
THEN I HAVE TO GIVE UP...
I SEE.
I CAN USE THIS!!

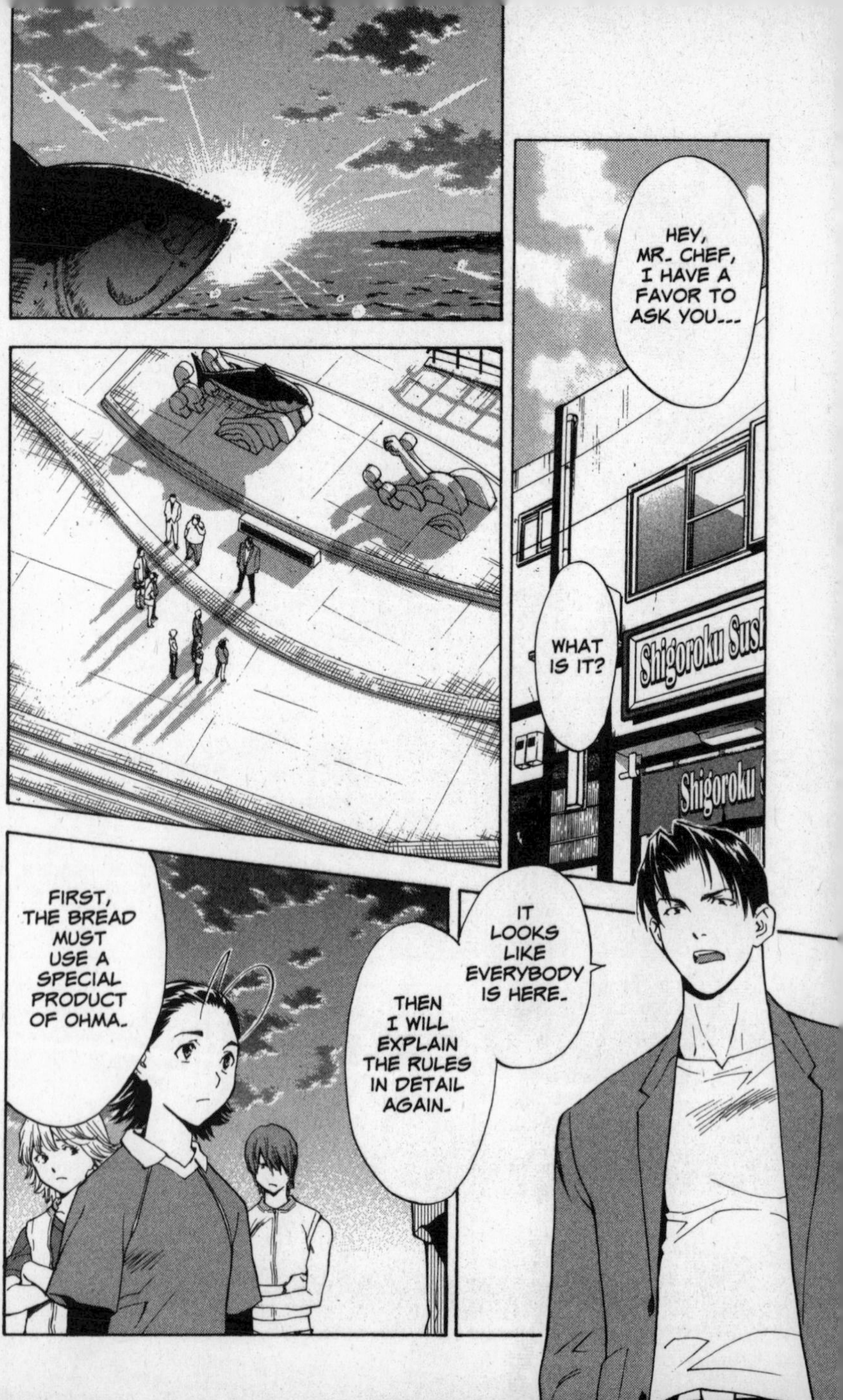
HEY, MR. CHEF, I HAVE A FAVOR TO ASK YOU...
WHAT IS IT?
IT LOOKS LIKE EVERYBODY IS HERE.
THEN I WILL EXPLAIN THE RULES IN DETAIL AGAIN.
FIRST, THE BREAD MUST USE A SPECIAL PRODUCT OF OHMA.

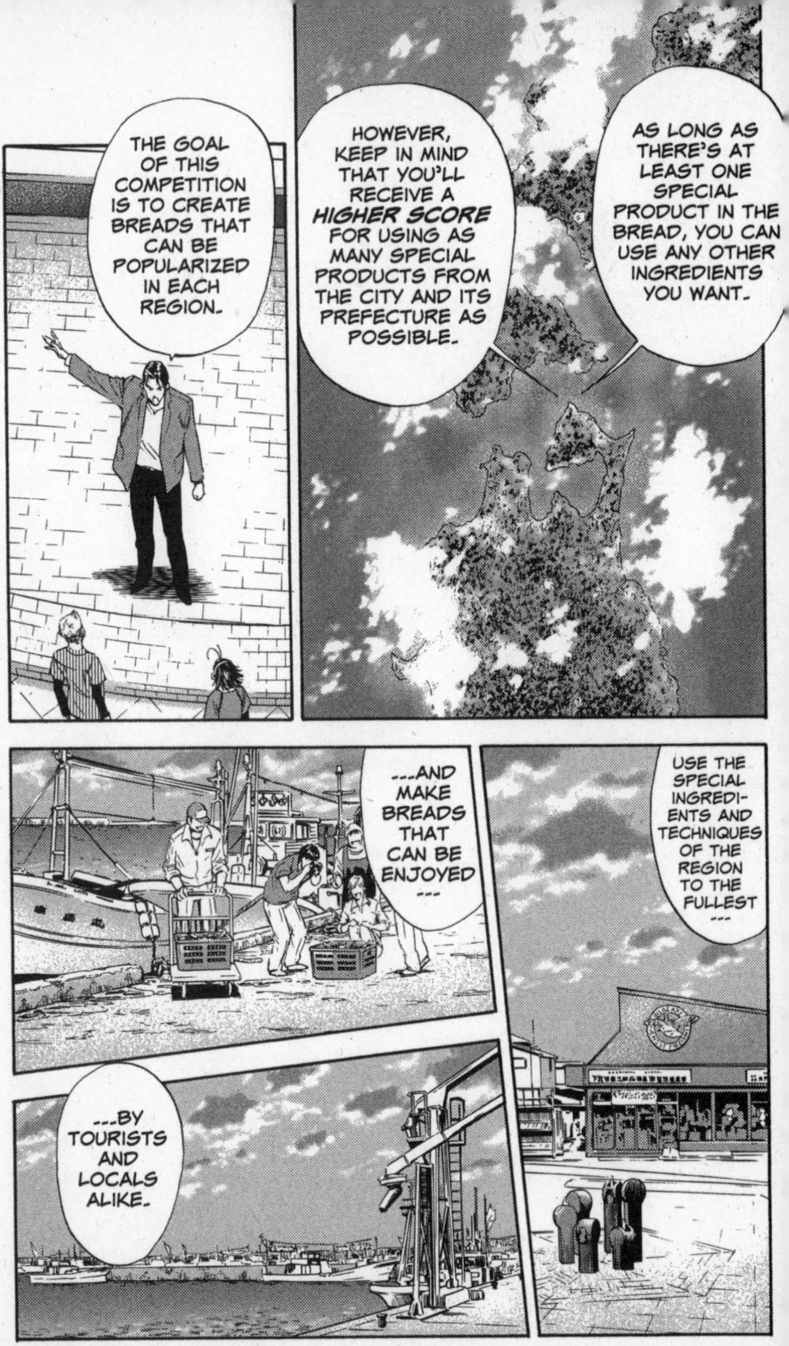
AS LONG AS THERE'S AT LEAST ONE SPECIAL PRODUCT IN THE BREAD, YOU CAN USE ANY OTHER INGREDIENTS YOU WANT.
HOWEVER, KEEP IN MIND THAT YOU'LL RECEIVE A HIGHER SCORE FOR USING AS MANY SPECIAL PRODUCTS FROM THE CITY AND ITS PREFECTURE AS POSSIBLE.
THE GOAL OF THIS COMPETITION IS TO CREATE BREADS THAT CAN BE POPULARIZED IN EACH REGION.
USE THE SPECIAL INGREDI-ENTS AND TECHNIQUES OF THE REGION TO THE FULLEST...
...AND MAKE BREADS THAT CAN BE ENJOYED...
...BY TOURISTS AND LOCALS ALIKE.

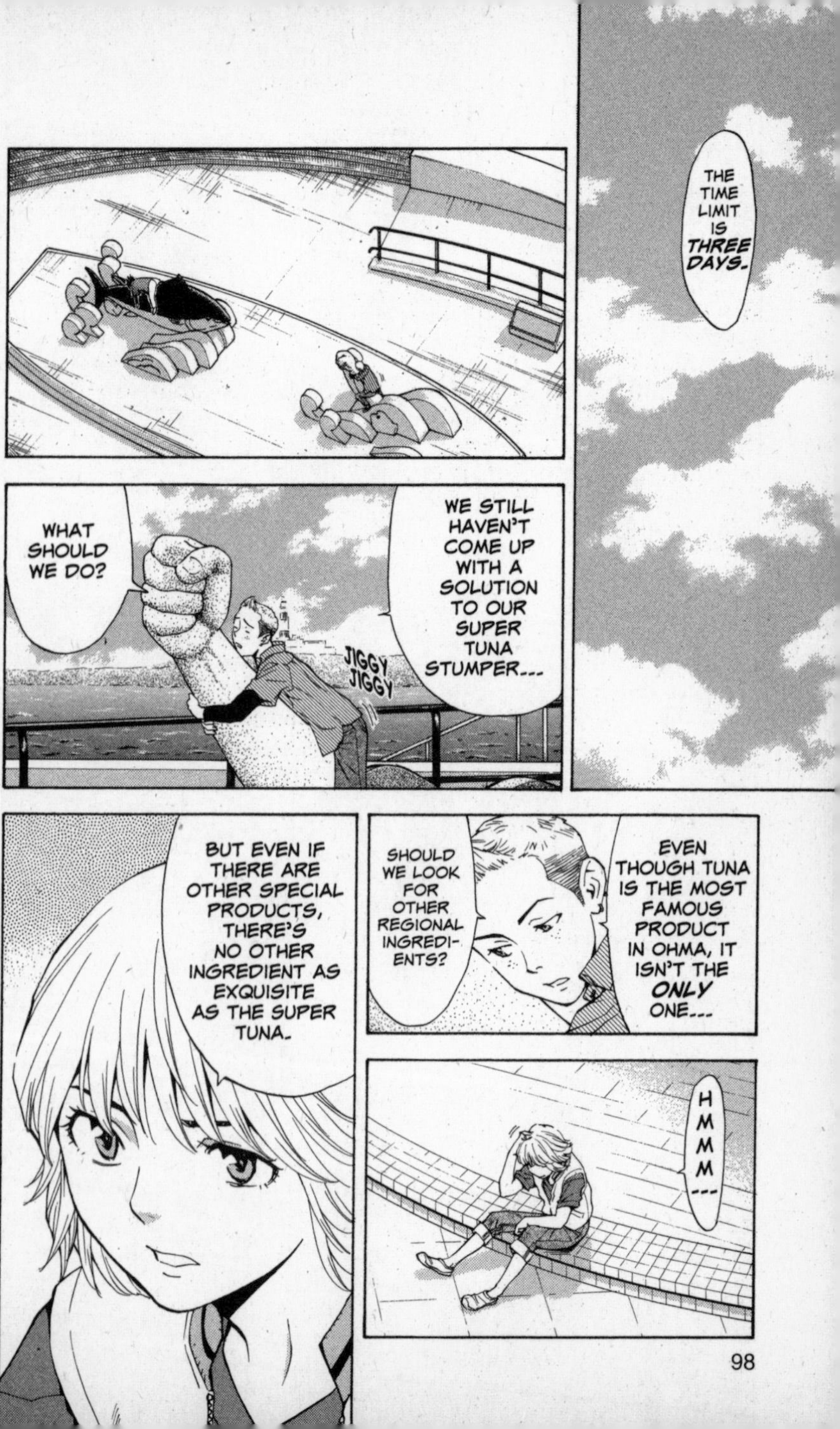
THE TIME LIMIT IS THREE DAYS.
WE STILL HAVEN'T COME UP WITH A SOLUTION TO OUR SUPER TUNA STUMPER...
JIGGY JIGGY
WHAT SHOULD WE DO?
EVEN THOUGH TUNA IS THE MOST FAMOUS PRODUCT IN OHMA, IT ISN'T THE ONLY ONE...
SHOULD WE LOOK FOR OTHER REGIONAL INGREDI-ENTS?
HMMM...
BUT EVEN IF THERE ARE OTHER SPECIAL PRODUCTS, THERE'S NO OTHER INGREDIENT AS EXQUISITE AS THE SUPER TUNA.

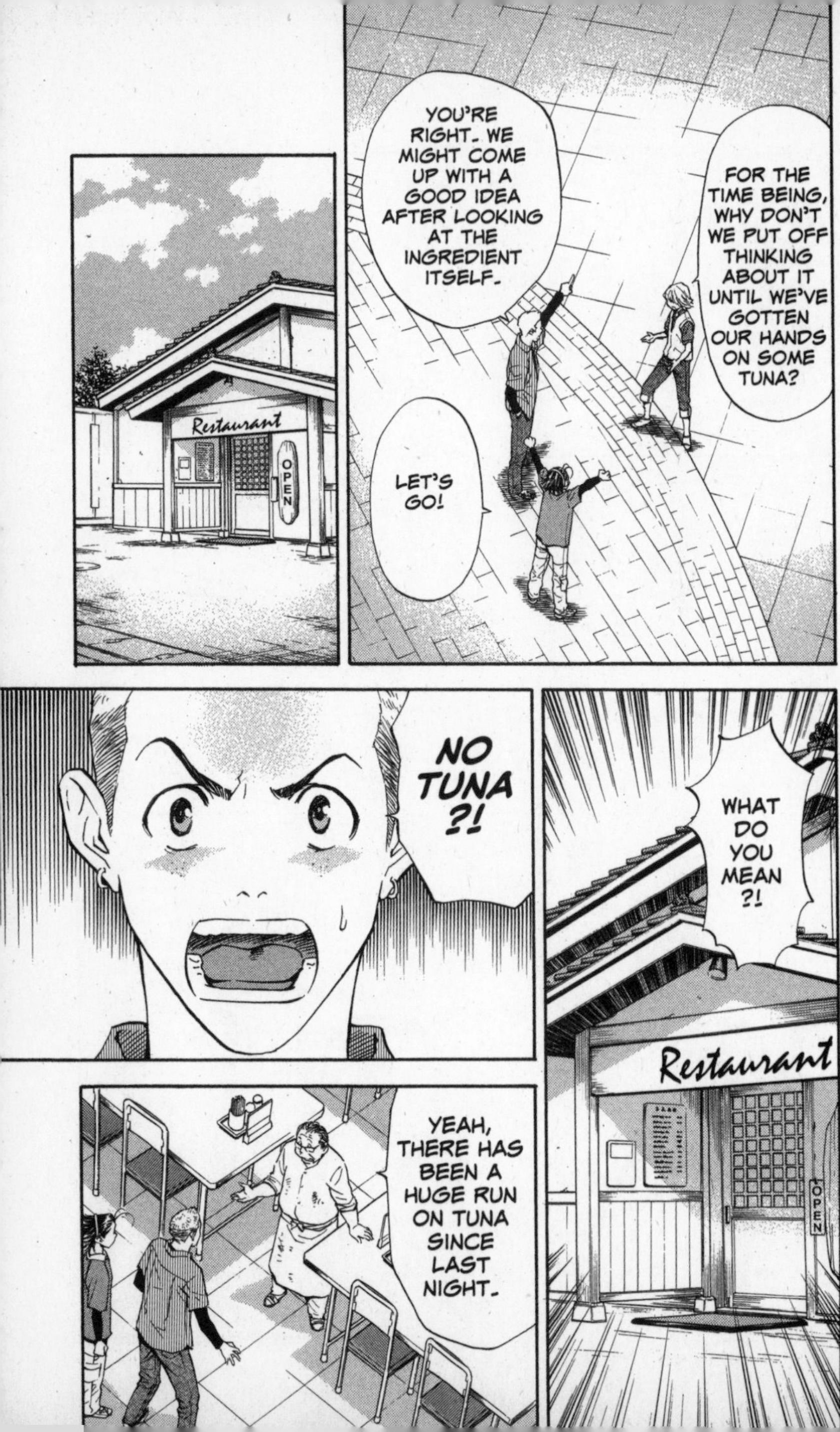
FOR THE TIME BEING, WHY DON'T WE PUT OFF THINKING ABOUT IT UNTIL WE'VE GOTTEN OUR HANDS ON SOME TUNA?
YOU'RE RIGHT... WE MIGHT COME UP WITH A GOOD IDEA AFTER LOOKING AT THE INGREDIENT ITSELF...
LET'S GO!
Restaurant
OPEN
WHAT DO YOU MEAN ?!
Restaurant
OPEN
NO TUNA ?!
YEAH, THERE HAS BEEN A HUGE RUN ON TUNA SINCE LAST NIGHT...

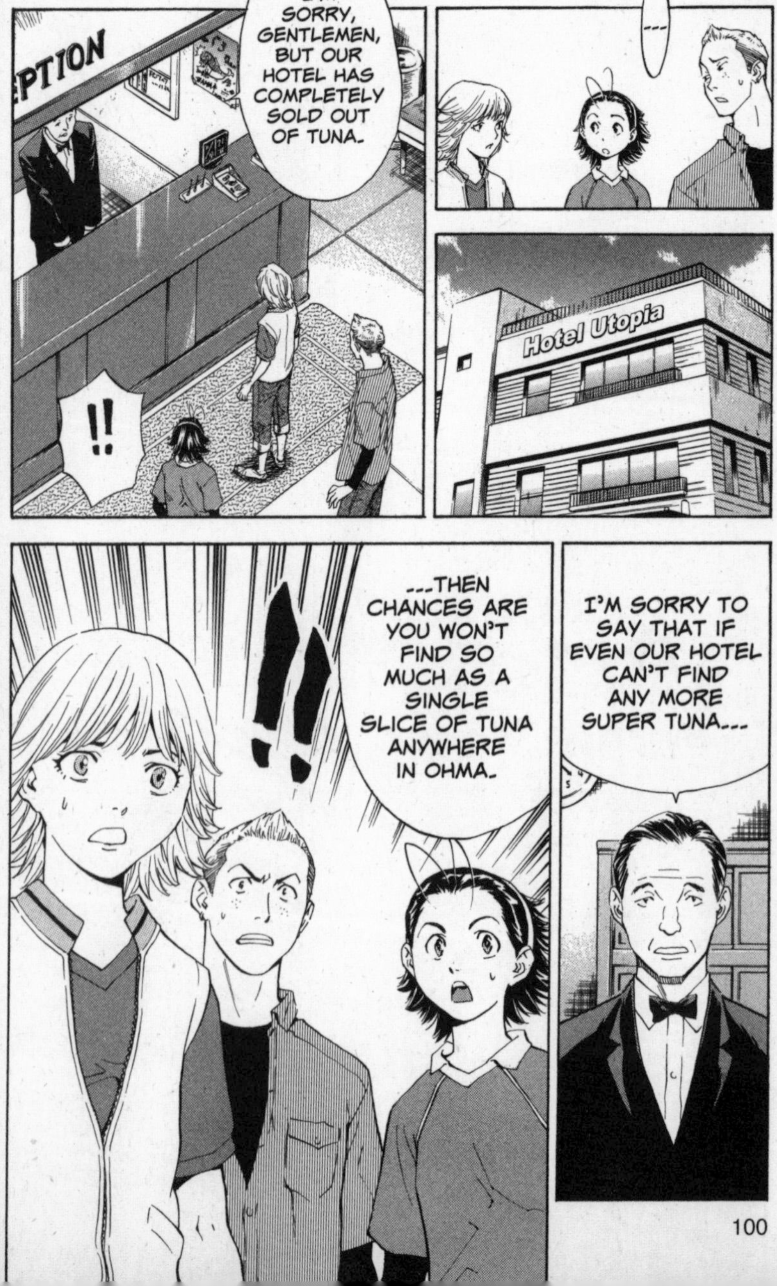
...
Hotel Utopia
I'M SORRY, GENTLEMEN, BUT OUR HOTEL HAS COMPLETELY SOLD OUT OF TUNA.
EPTION
!!
I'M SORRY TO SAY THAT IF EVEN OUR HOTEL CAN'T FIND ANY MORE SUPER TUNA...
...THEN CHANCES ARE YOU WON'T FIND SO MUCH AS A SINGLE SLICE OF TUNA ANYWHERE IN OHMA.
!!

Story 129: Purple Spines, White Meat

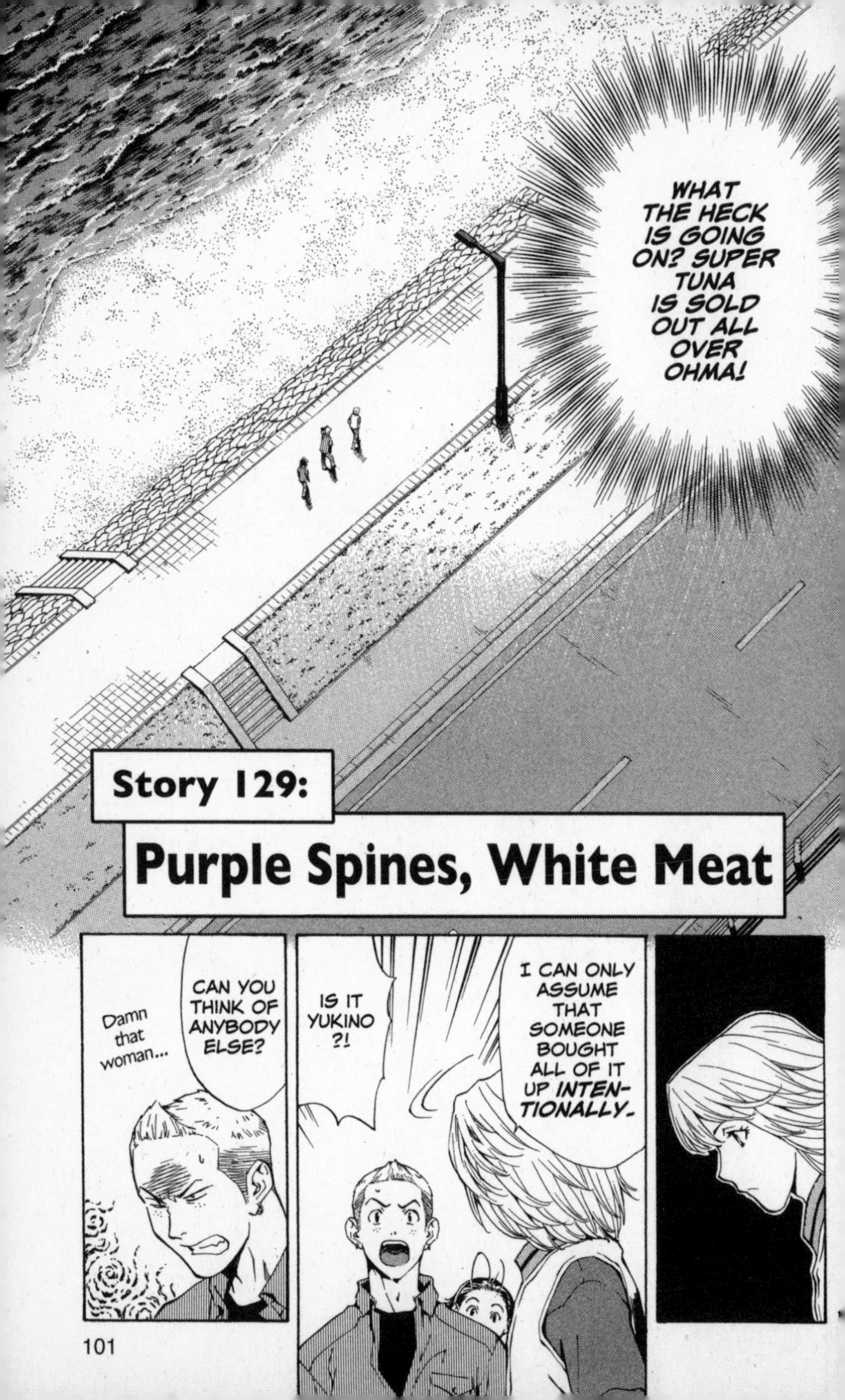
WHAT THE HECK IS GOING ON? SUPER TUNA IS SOLD OUT ALL OVER OHMA!
I CAN ONLY ASSUME THAT SOMEONE BOUGHT ALL OF IT UP INTENTIONALLY.
IS IT YUKINO ?!
CAN YOU THINK OF ANYBODY ELSE?
Damn that woman...

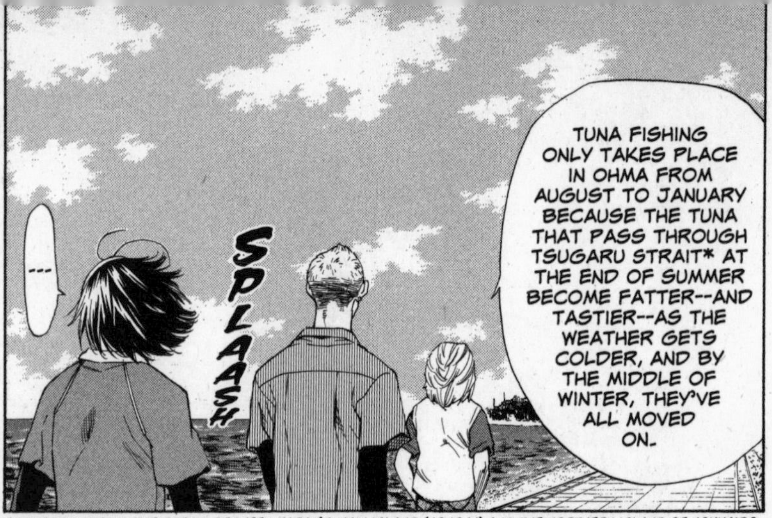
TUNA FISHING ONLY TAKES PLACE IN OHMA FROM AUGUST TO JANUARY BECAUSE THE TUNA THAT PASS THROUGH TSUGARU STRAIT* AT THE END OF SUMMER BECOME FATTER--AND TASTIER--AS THE WEATHER GETS COLDER, AND BY THE MIDDLE OF WINTER, THEY'VE ALL MOVED ON.
SPLAASH
...

*TSUGARU STRAIT: THE STRAIT BETWEEN JAPAN'S MAIN ISLAND (HONSHU) AND THE NORTHERN ISLAND OF HOKKAIDO.

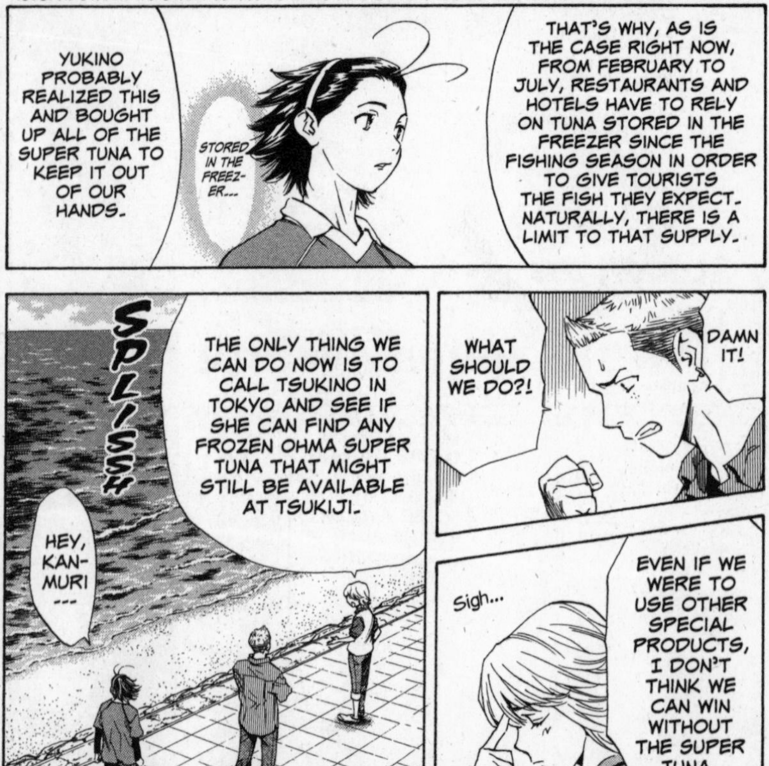
THAT'S WHY, AS IS THE CASE RIGHT NOW, FROM FEBRUARY TO JULY, RESTAURANTS AND HOTELS HAVE TO RELY ON TUNA STORED IN THE FREEZER SINCE THE FISHING SEASON IN ORDER TO GIVE TOURISTS THE FISH THEY EXPECT. NATURALLY, THERE IS A LIMIT TO THAT SUPPLY.
STORED IN THE FREEZER...
YUKINO PROBABLY REALIZED THIS AND BOUGHT UP ALL OF THE SUPER TUNA TO KEEP IT OUT OF OUR HANDS.
DAMN IT!
WHAT SHOULD WE DO?!
EVEN IF WE WERE TO USE OTHER SPECIAL PRODUCTS, I DON'T THINK WE CAN WIN WITHOUT THE SUPER TUNA.
Sigh...
THE ONLY THING WE CAN DO NOW IS TO CALL TSUKINO IN TOKYO AND SEE IF SHE CAN FIND ANY FROZEN OHMA SUPER TUNA THAT MIGHT STILL BE AVAILABLE AT TSUKIJI.
SPLISSH
HEY, KANMURI...

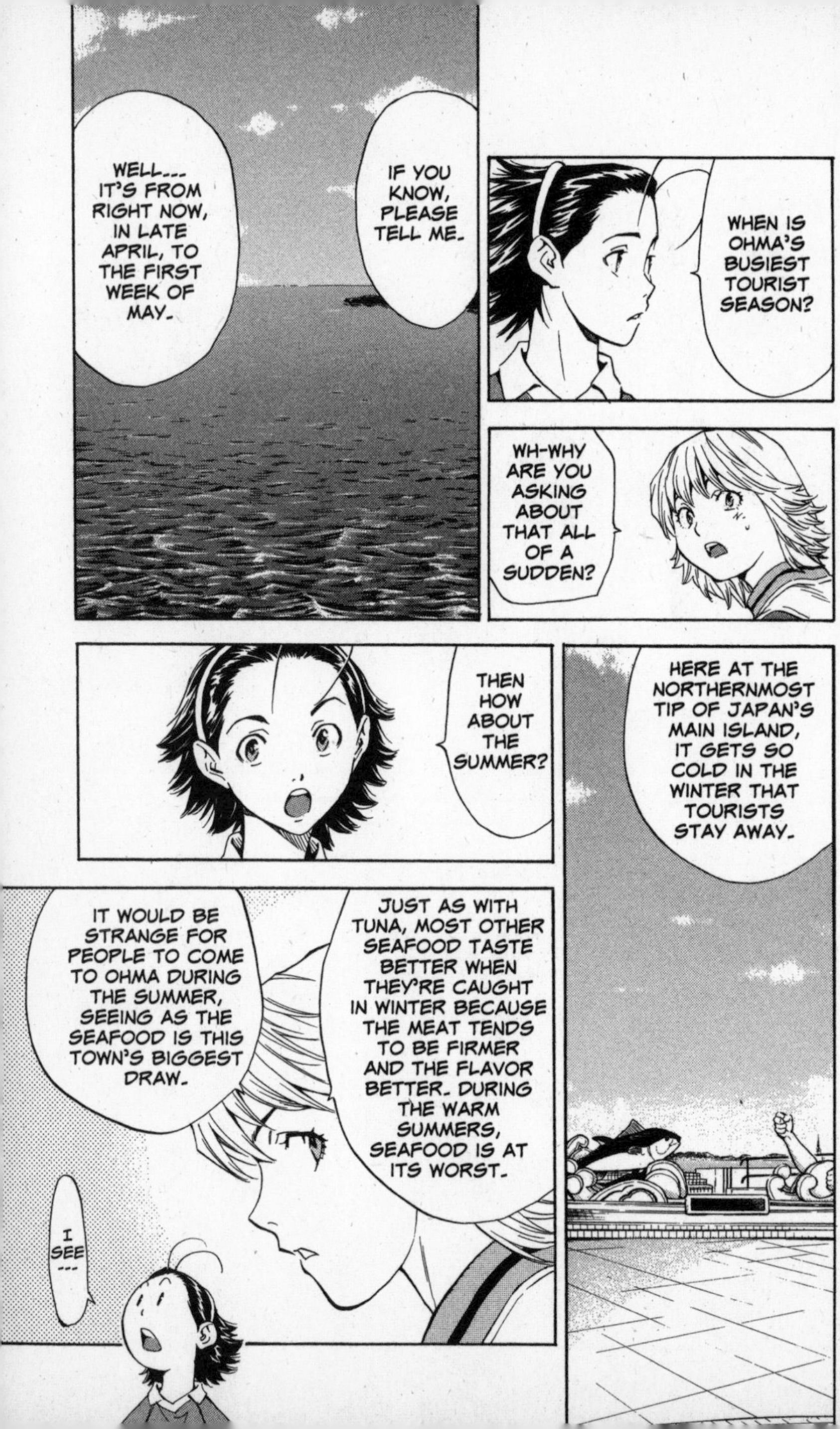
WHEN IS OHMA'S BUSIEST TOURIST SEASON?
WH-WHY ARE YOU ASKING ABOUT THAT ALL OF A SUDDEN?
IF YOU KNOW, PLEASE TELL ME.
WELL... IT'S FROM RIGHT NOW, IN LATE APRIL, TO THE FIRST WEEK OF MAY.
HERE AT THE NORTHERNMOST TIP OF JAPAN'S MAIN ISLAND, IT GETS SO COLD IN THE WINTER THAT TOURISTS STAY AWAY.
THEN HOW ABOUT THE SUMMER?
JUST AS WITH TUNA, MOST OTHER SEAFOOD TASTE BETTER WHEN THEY'RE CAUGHT IN WINTER BECAUSE THE MEAT TENDS TO BE FIRMER AND THE FLAVOR BETTER. DURING THE WARM SUMMERS, SEAFOOD IS AT ITS WORST.
IT WOULD BE STRANGE FOR PEOPLE TO COME TO OHMA DURING THE SUMMER, SEEING AS THE SEAFOOD IS THIS TOWN'S BIGGEST DRAW.
I SEE...

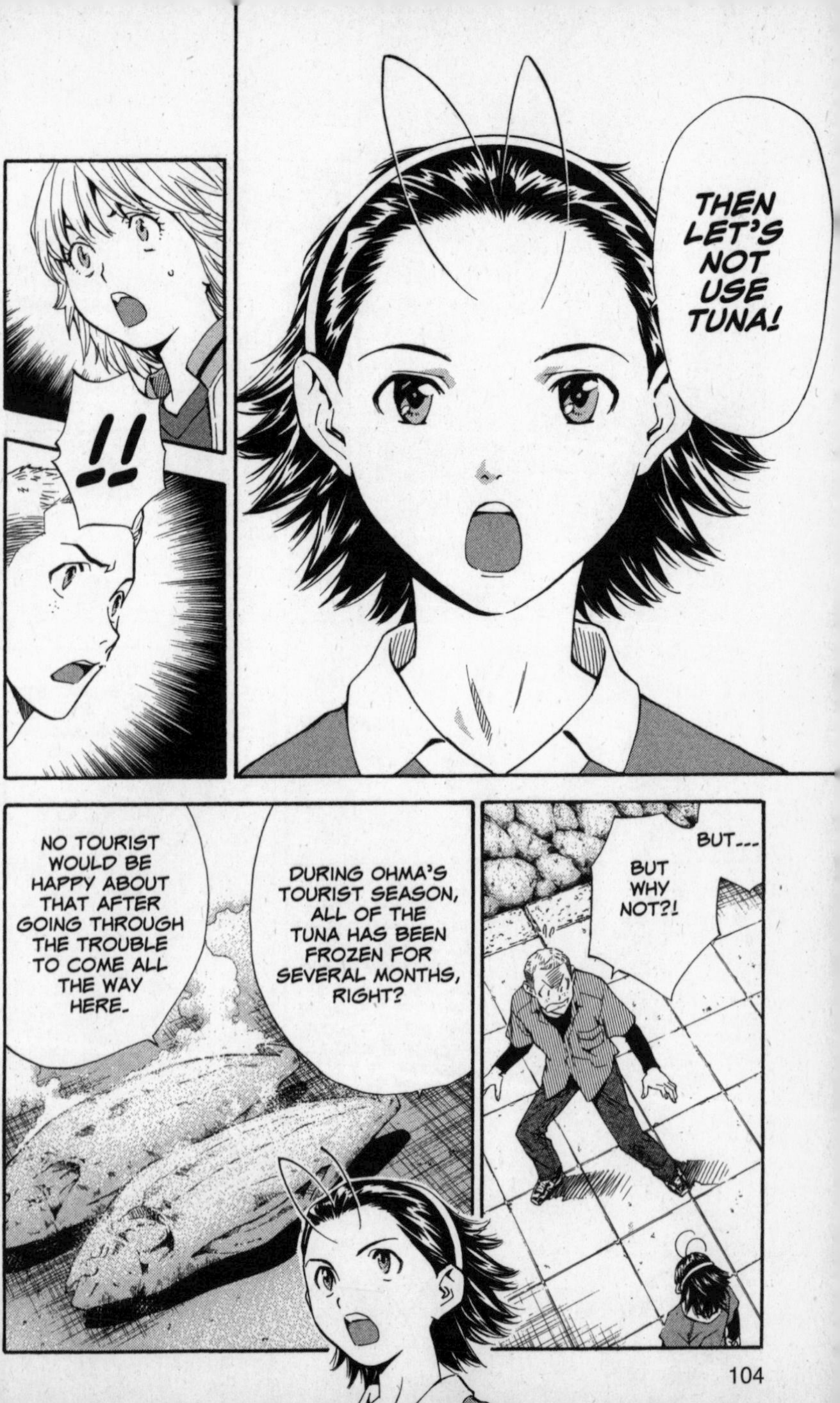
THEN LET'S NOT USE TUNA!
!!
BUT...
BUT WHY NOT?!
DURING OHMA'S TOURIST SEASON, ALL OF THE TUNA HAS BEEN FROZEN FOR SEVERAL MONTHS, RIGHT?
NO TOURIST WOULD BE HAPPY ABOUT THAT AFTER GOING THROUGH THE TROUBLE TO COME ALL THE WAY HERE.

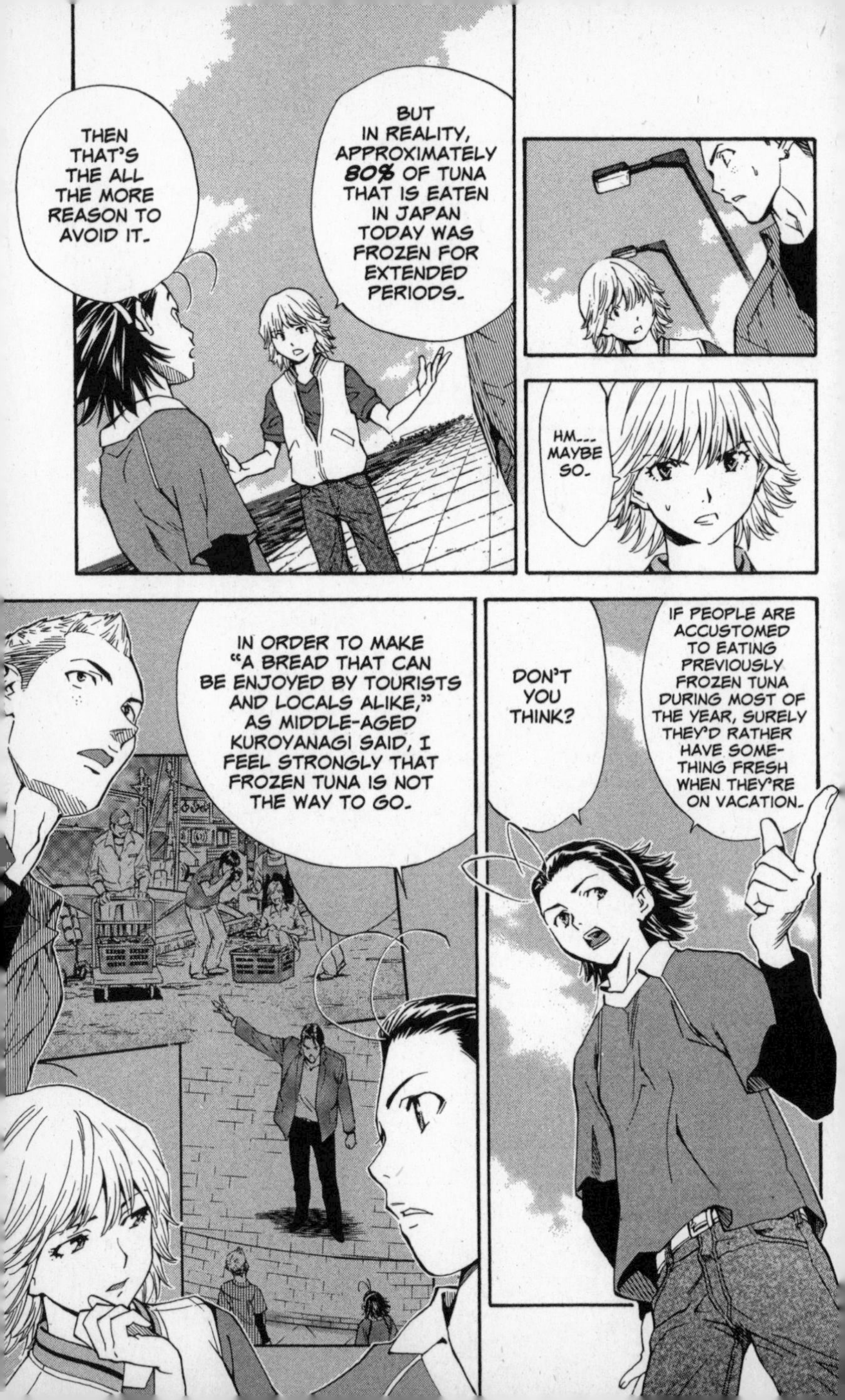
HM... MAYBE SO.
BUT IN REALITY, APPROXIMATELY 80% OF TUNA THAT IS EATEN IN JAPAN TODAY WAS FROZEN FOR EXTENDED PERIODS.
THEN THAT'S THE ALL THE MORE REASON TO AVOID IT.
IF PEOPLE ARE ACCUSTOMED TO EATING PREVIOUSLY FROZEN TUNA DURING MOST OF THE YEAR, SURELY THEY'D RATHER HAVE SOME-THING FRESH WHEN THEY'RE ON VACATION.
DON'T YOU THINK?
IN ORDER TO MAKE "A BREAD THAT CAN BE ENJOYED BY TOURISTS AND LOCALS ALIKE," AS MIDDLE-AGED KUROYANAGI SAID, I FEEL STRONGLY THAT FROZEN TUNA IS NOT THE WAY TO GO.

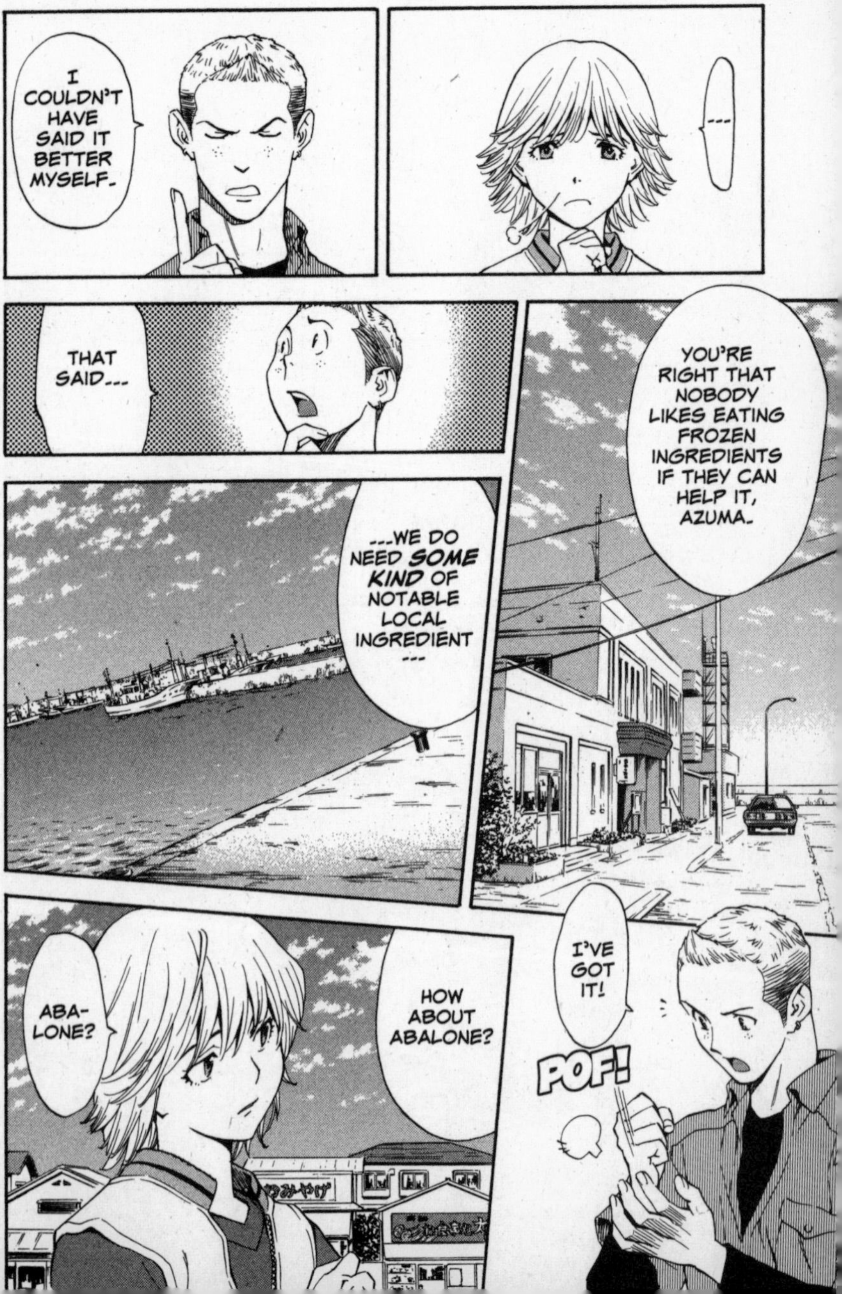
...
I COULDN'T HAVE SAID IT BETTER MYSELF.
YOU'RE RIGHT THAT NOBODY LIKES EATING FROZEN INGREDIENTS IF THEY CAN HELP IT, AZUMA.
THAT SAID...
...WE DO NEED *SOME KIND* OF NOTABLE LOCAL INGREDIENT...
I'VE GOT IT!
POF!
HOW ABOUT ABALONE?
ABA-LONE?

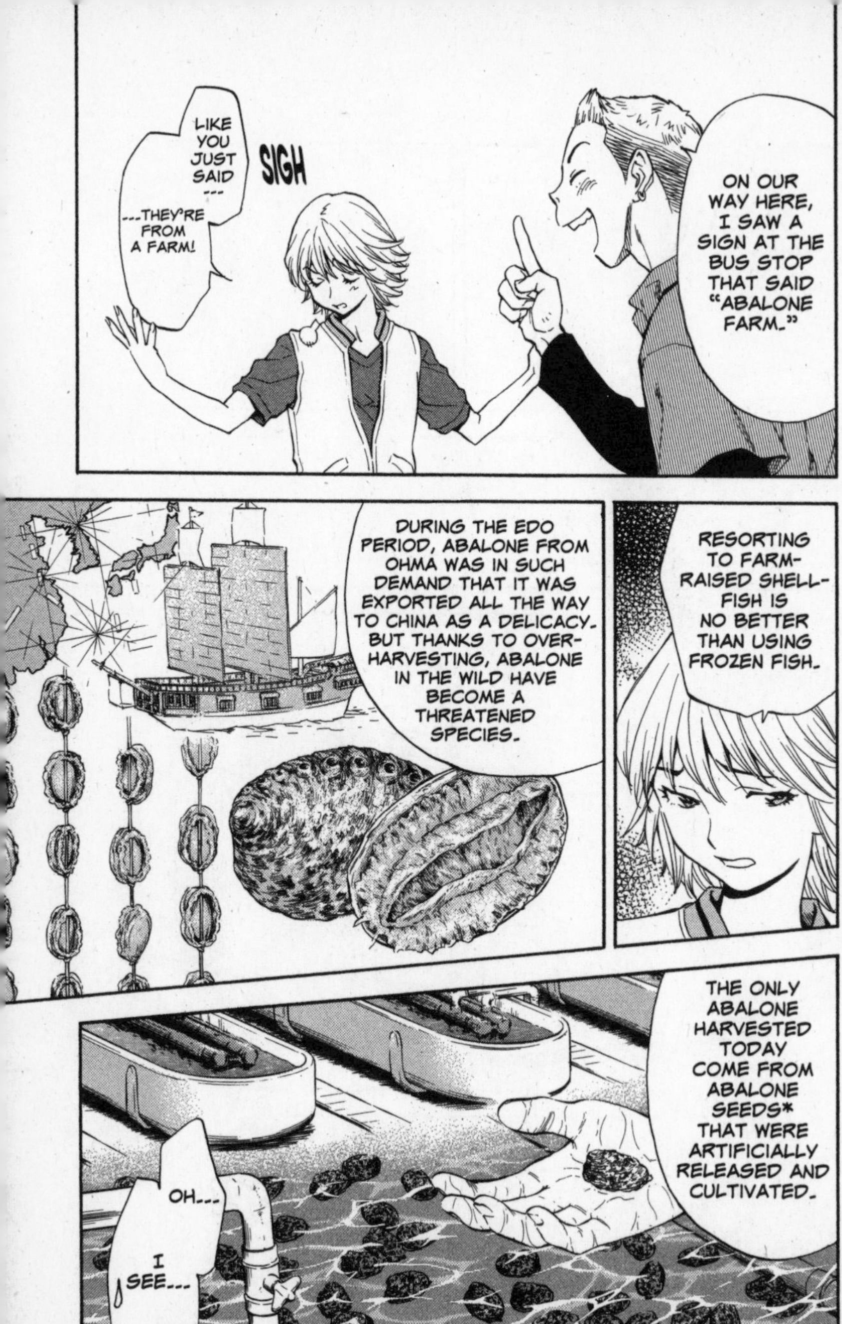
ON OUR WAY HERE, I SAW A SIGN AT THE BUS STOP THAT SAID "ABALONE FARM."
SIGH
LIKE YOU JUST SAID ...
...THEY'RE FROM A FARM!
RESORTING TO FARM-RAISED SHELL-FISH IS NO BETTER THAN USING FROZEN FISH.
DURING THE EDO PERIOD, ABALONE FROM OHMA WAS IN SUCH DEMAND THAT IT WAS EXPORTED ALL THE WAY TO CHINA AS A DELICACY. BUT THANKS TO OVER-HARVESTING, ABALONE IN THE WILD HAVE BECOME A THREATENED SPECIES.
THE ONLY ABALONE HARVESTED TODAY COME FROM ABALONE SEEDS* THAT WERE ARTIFICIALLY RELEASED AND CULTIVATED.
OH... I SEE...

*SEEDS: JUVENILE SHELLFISH USED IN FISH FARMING, SIMILAR TO FISH "FRY."

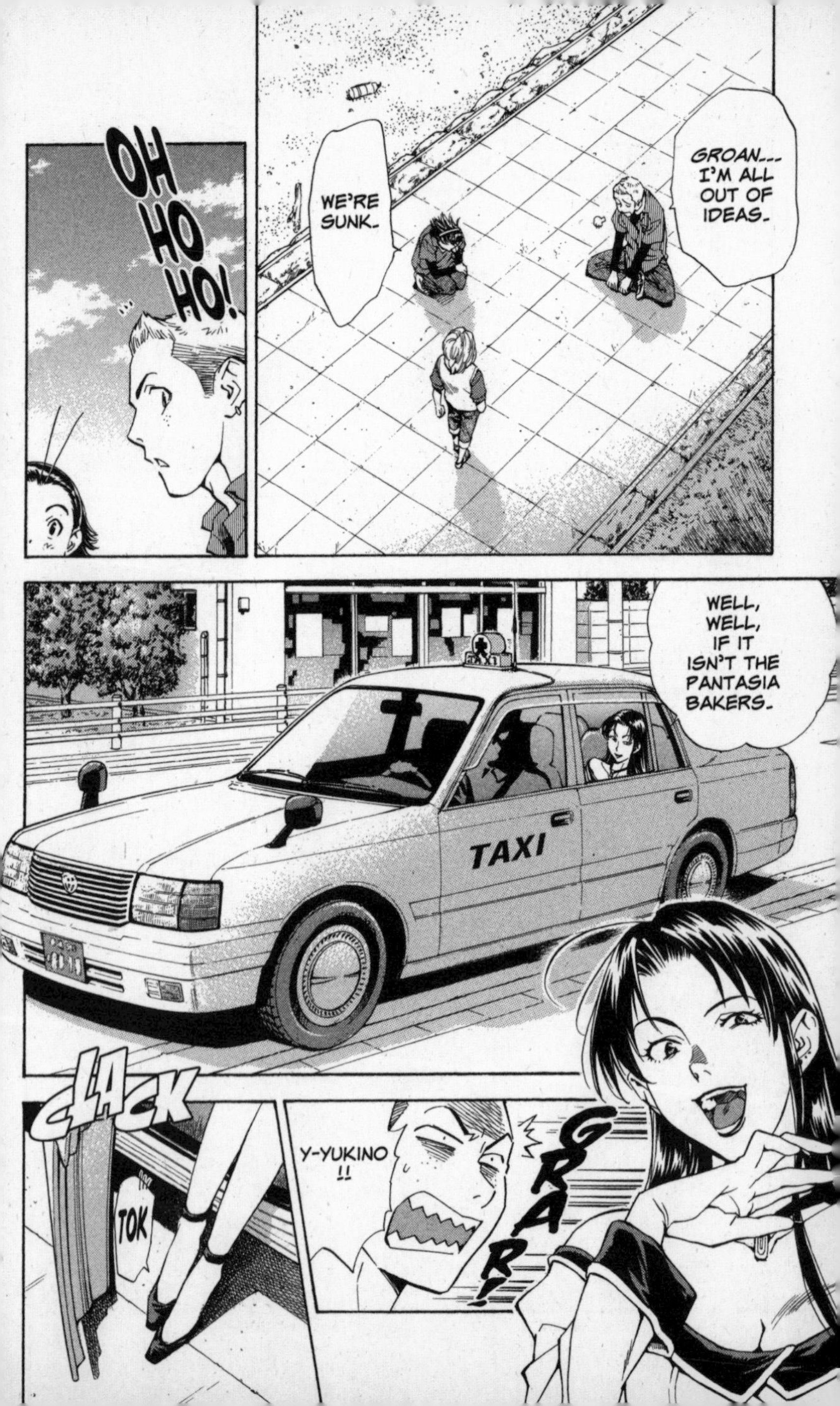
GROAN... I'M ALL OUT OF IDEAS.
WE'RE SUNK.
OH HO HO HO!
WELL, WELL, IF IT ISN'T THE PANTASIA BAKERS.
TAXI
GRAR!
Y-YUKINO !!
CLACK
TOK

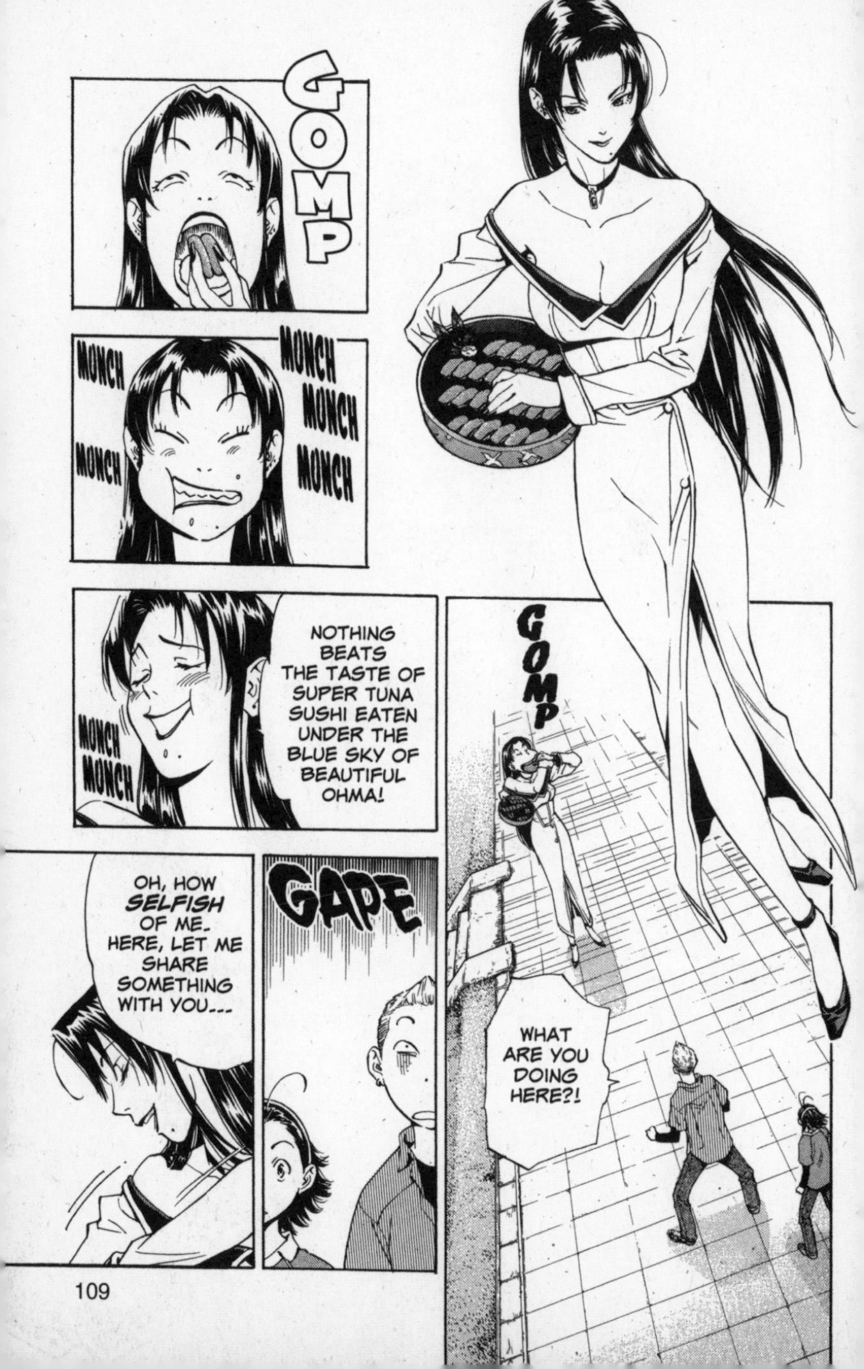
GOMP
WHAT ARE YOU DOING HERE?!
GOMP
MUNCH MUNCH MUNCH MUNCH MUNCH
NOTHING BEATS THE TASTE OF SUPER TUNA SUSHI EATEN UNDER THE BLUE SKY OF BEAUTIFUL OHMA!
MUNCH MUNCH
GAPE
OH, HOW *SELFISH* OF ME. HERE, LET ME SHARE SOMETHING WITH YOU...

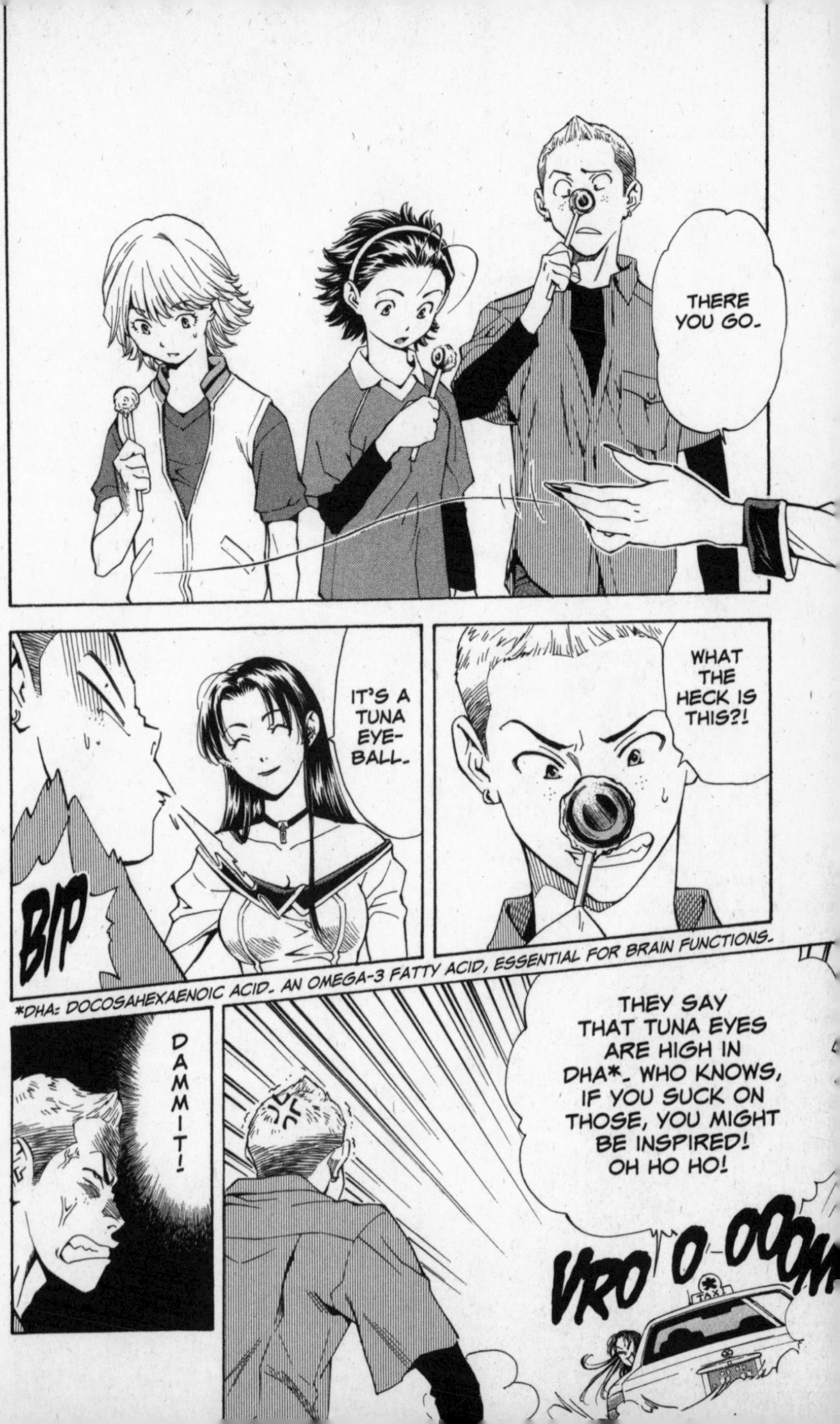
THERE YOU GO.
WHAT THE HECK IS THIS?!
IT'S A TUNA EYEBALL.
BIP
*DHA: DOCOSAHEXAENOIC ACID. AN OMEGA-3 FATTY ACID, ESSENTIAL FOR BRAIN FUNCTIONS.
THEY SAY THAT TUNA EYES ARE HIGH IN DHA*. WHO KNOWS, IF YOU SUCK ON THOSE, YOU MIGHT BE INSPIRED! OH HO HO!
VRO O-OOOM
DAMMIT!

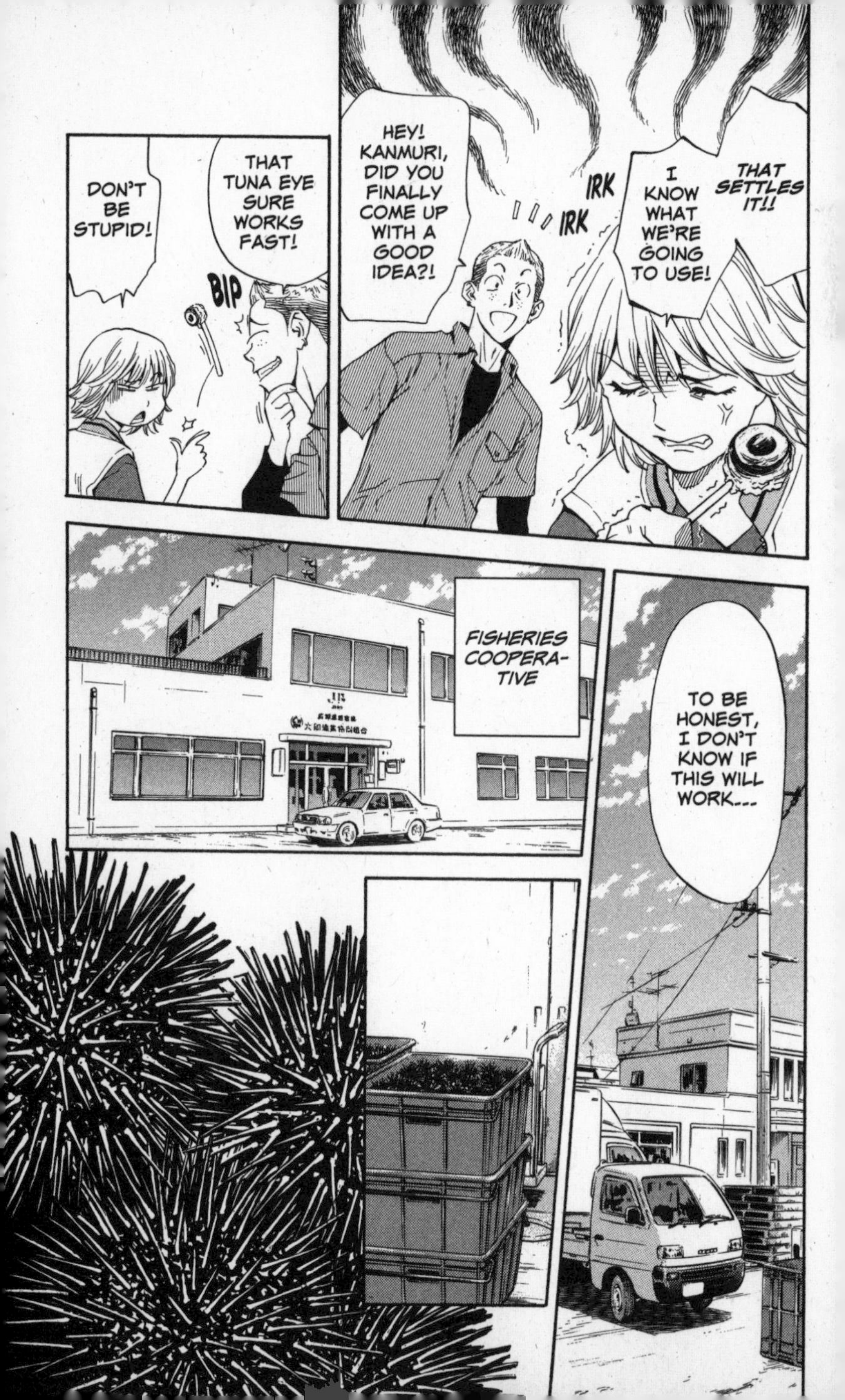
THAT SETTLES IT!!
I KNOW WHAT WE'RE GOING TO USE!
IRK
IRK
HEY! KANMURI, DID YOU FINALLY COME UP WITH A GOOD IDEA?!
THAT TUNA EYE SURE WORKS FAST!
BIP
DON'T BE STUPID!
TO BE HONEST, I DON'T KNOW IF THIS WILL WORK...
FISHERIES COOPERATIVE

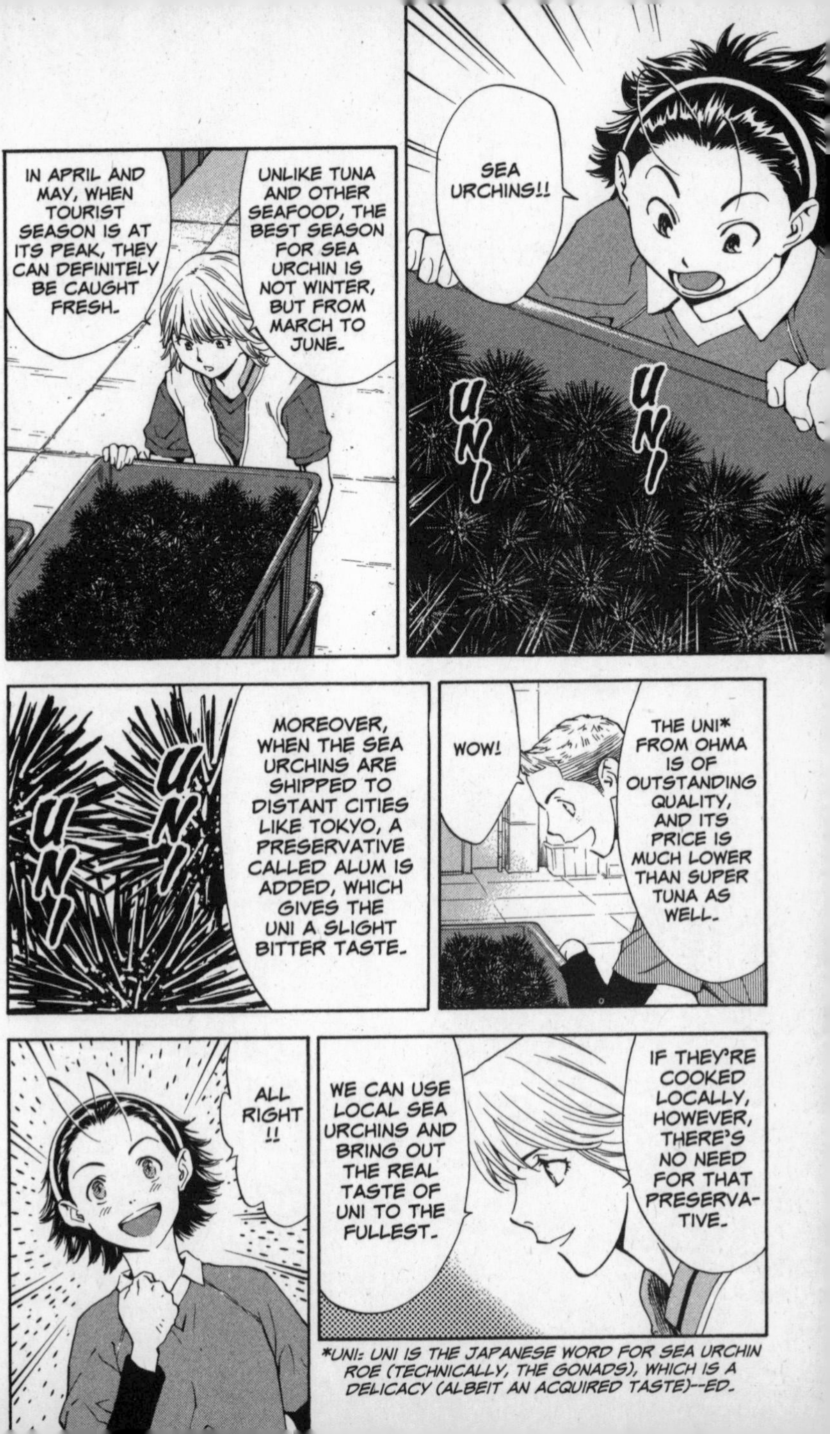
SEA URCHINS!!
UNI
UNI
UNLIKE TUNA AND OTHER SEAFOOD, THE BEST SEASON FOR SEA URCHIN IS NOT WINTER, BUT FROM MARCH TO JUNE.
IN APRIL AND MAY, WHEN TOURIST SEASON IS AT ITS PEAK, THEY CAN DEFINITELY BE CAUGHT FRESH.
THE UNI* FROM OHMA IS OF OUTSTANDING QUALITY, AND ITS PRICE IS MUCH LOWER THAN SUPER TUNA AS WELL.
WOW!
MOREOVER, WHEN THE SEA URCHINS ARE SHIPPED TO DISTANT CITIES LIKE TOKYO, A PRESERVATIVE CALLED ALUM IS ADDED, WHICH GIVES THE UNI A SLIGHT BITTER TASTE.
UNI
UNI
IF THEY'RE COOKED LOCALLY, HOWEVER, THERE'S NO NEED FOR THAT PRESERVA-TIVE.
WE CAN USE LOCAL SEA URCHINS AND BRING OUT THE REAL TASTE OF UNI TO THE FULLEST.
ALL RIGHT!!

*UNI: UNI IS THE JAPANESE WORD FOR SEA URCHIN ROE (TECHNICALLY, THE GONADS), WHICH IS A DELICACY (ALBEIT AN ACQUIRED TASTE)--ED.

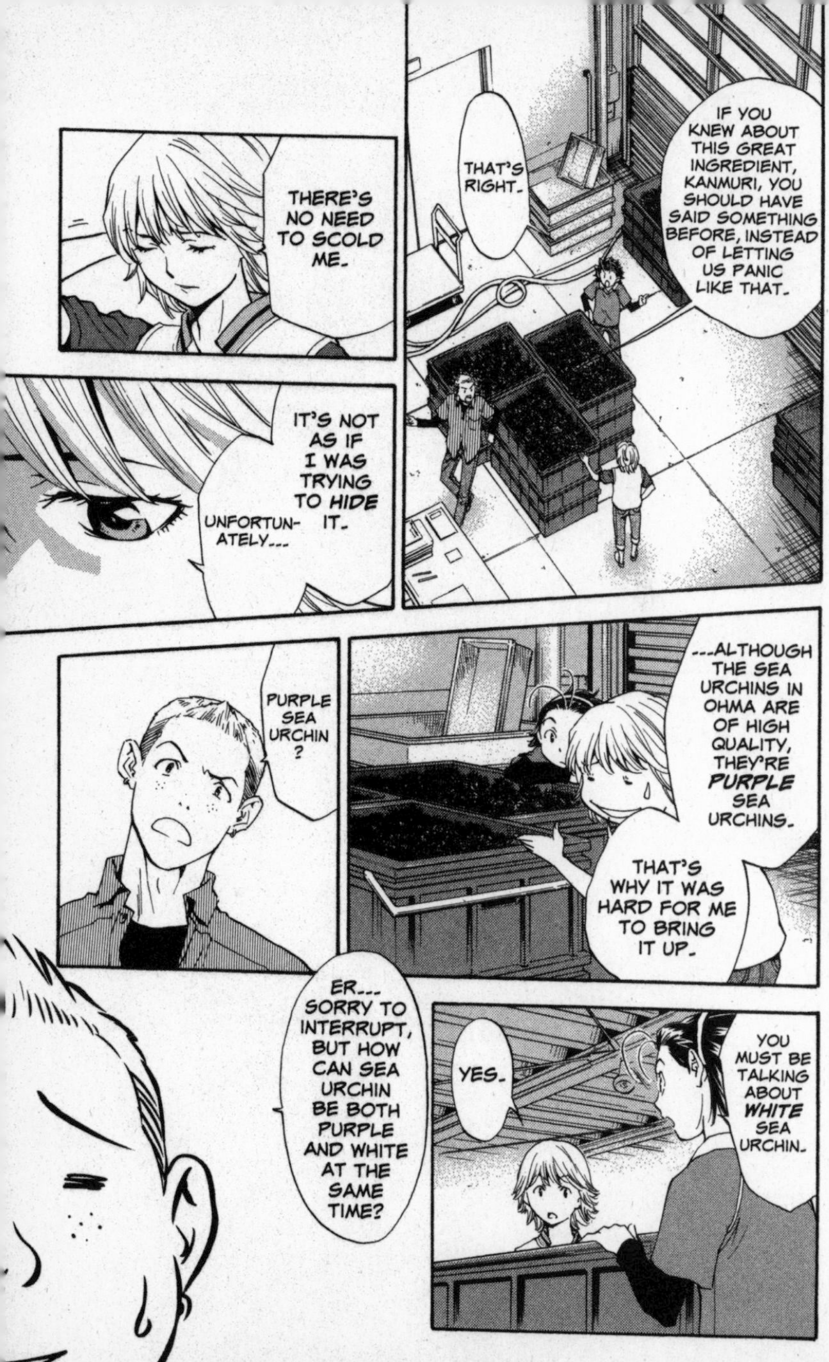
IF YOU KNEW ABOUT THIS GREAT INGREDIENT, KANMURI, YOU SHOULD HAVE SAID SOMETHING BEFORE, INSTEAD OF LETTING US PANIC LIKE THAT.
THAT'S RIGHT.
THERE'S NO NEED TO SCOLD ME.
IT'S NOT AS IF I WAS TRYING TO *HIDE* IT.
UNFORTUN-ATELY...
...ALTHOUGH THE SEA URCHINS IN OHMA ARE OF HIGH QUALITY, THEY'RE *PURPLE* SEA URCHINS.
THAT'S WHY IT WAS HARD FOR ME TO BRING IT UP.
PURPLE SEA URCHIN?
YOU MUST BE TALKING ABOUT *WHITE* SEA URCHIN.
YES.
ER... SORRY TO INTERRUPT, BUT HOW CAN SEA URCHIN BE BOTH PURPLE AND WHITE AT THE SAME TIME?

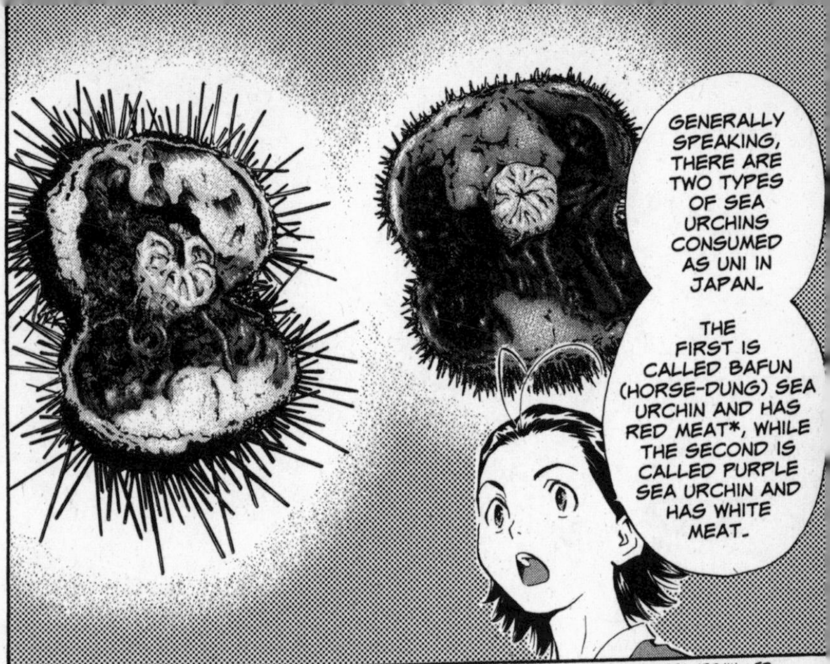
GENERALLY SPEAKING, THERE ARE TWO TYPES OF SEA URCHINS CONSUMED AS UNI IN JAPAN.
THE FIRST IS CALLED BAFUN (HORSE-DUNG) SEA URCHIN AND HAS RED MEAT*, WHILE THE SECOND IS CALLED PURPLE SEA URCHIN AND HAS WHITE MEAT.

*BY MEAT, AZUMA MEANS THE ROE (TECHNICALLY GONADS), AS THAT'S THE ONLY EDIBLE PART OF A SEA URCHIN.--ED.

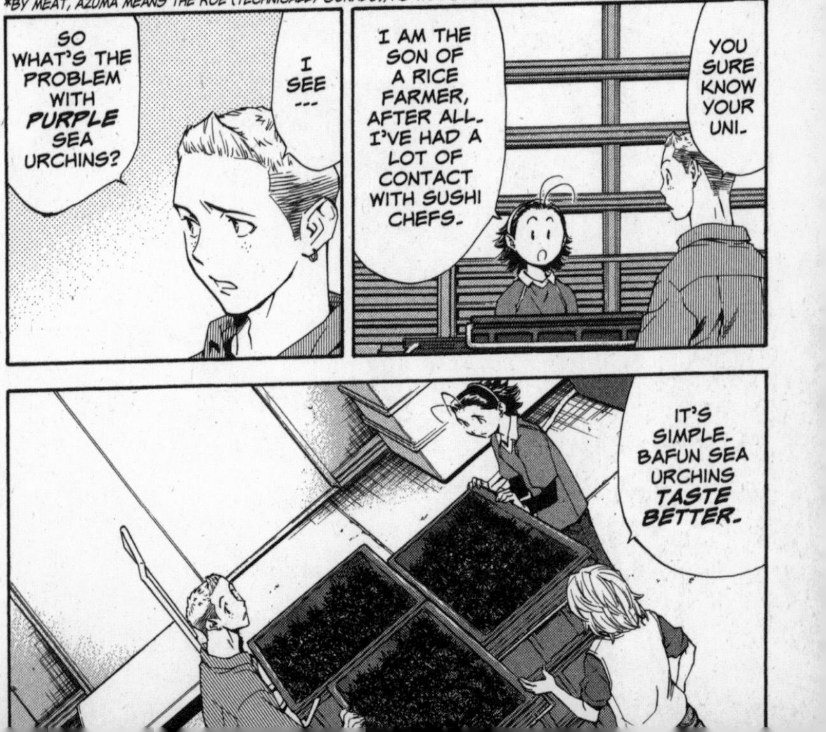
YOU SURE KNOW YOUR UNI.
I AM THE SON OF A RICE FARMER, AFTER ALL. I'VE HAD A LOT OF CONTACT WITH SUSHI CHEFS.
I SEE ---
SO WHAT'S THE PROBLEM WITH *PURPLE* SEA URCHINS?
IT'S SIMPLE. BAFUN SEA URCHINS *TASTE BETTER*.

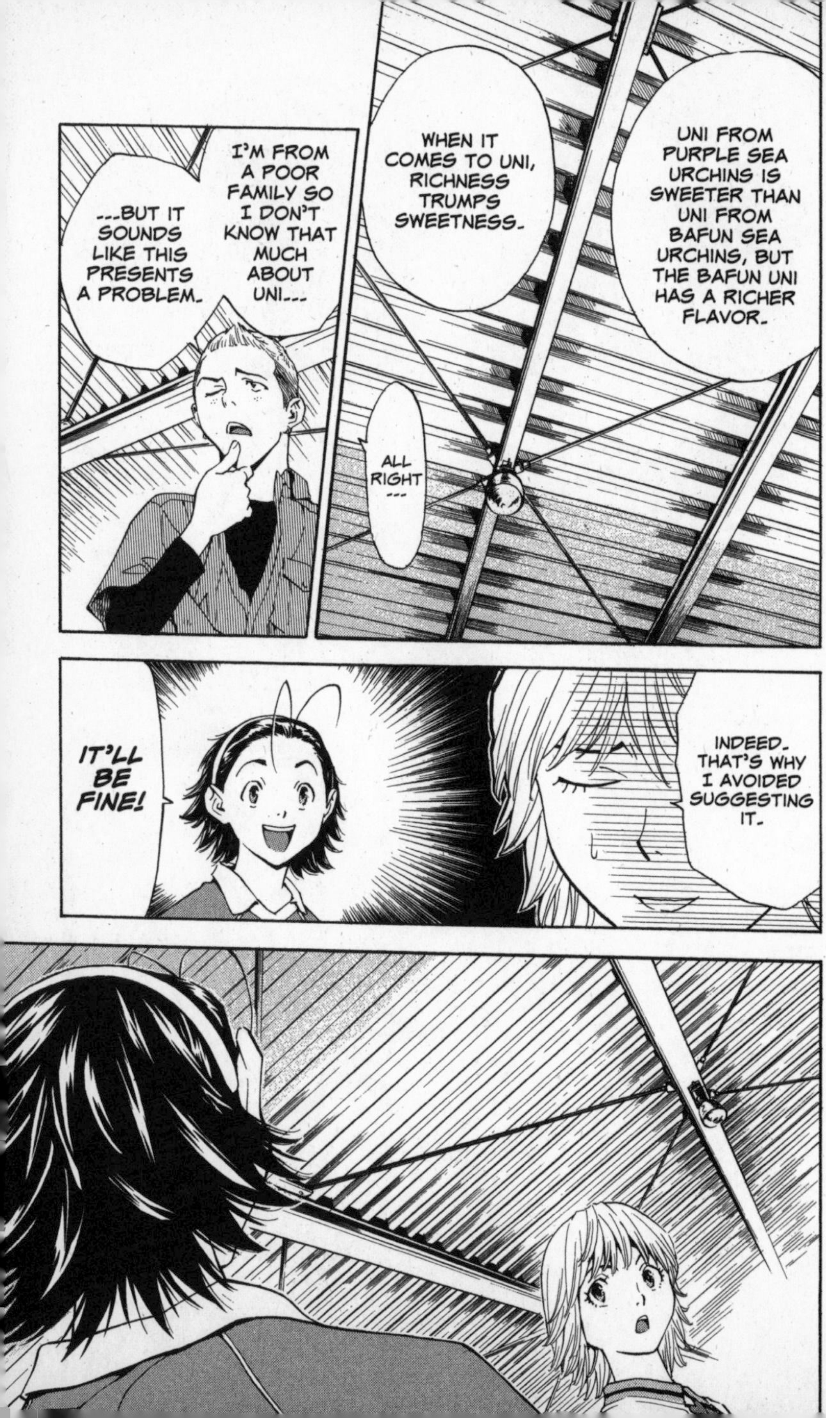
UNI FROM PURPLE SEA URCHINS IS SWEETER THAN UNI FROM BAFUN SEA URCHINS, BUT THE BAFUN UNI HAS A RICHER FLAVOR.
WHEN IT COMES TO UNI, RICHNESS TRUMPS SWEETNESS.
ALL RIGHT...
I'M FROM A POOR FAMILY SO I DON'T KNOW THAT MUCH ABOUT UNI...
...BUT IT SOUNDS LIKE THIS PRESENTS A PROBLEM.
INDEED. THAT'S WHY I AVOIDED SUGGESTING IT.
IT'LL BE FINE!

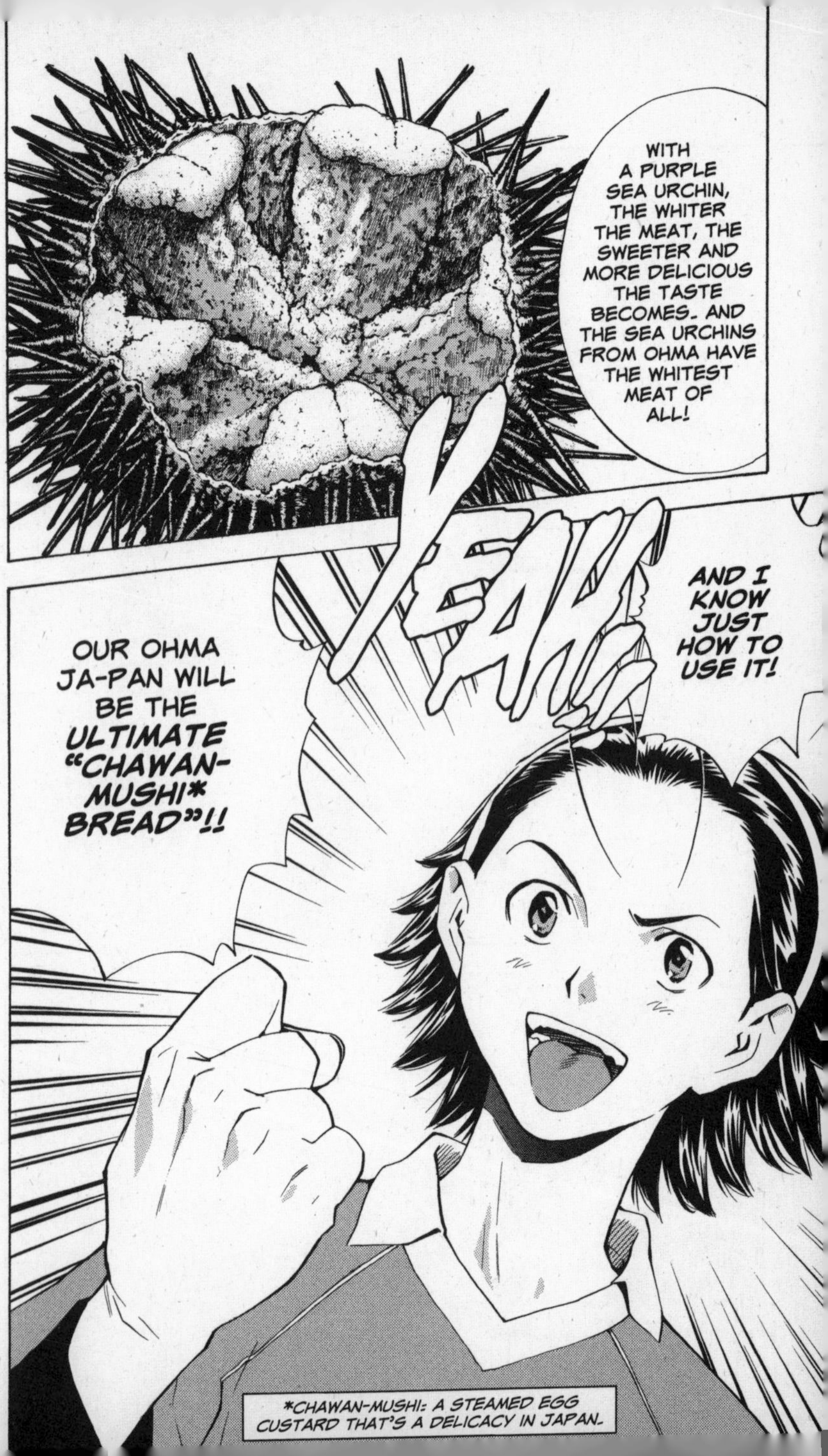
WITH A PURPLE SEA URCHIN, THE WHITER THE MEAT, THE SWEETER AND MORE DELICIOUS THE TASTE BECOMES. AND THE SEA URCHINS FROM OHMA HAVE THE WHITEST MEAT OF ALL!
YEAH!
AND I KNOW JUST HOW TO USE IT!
OUR OHMA JA-PAN WILL BE THE ULTIMATE "CHAWAN-MUSHI* BREAD"!!

*CHAWAN-MUSHI: A STEAMED EGG CUSTARD THAT'S A DELICACY IN JAPAN.

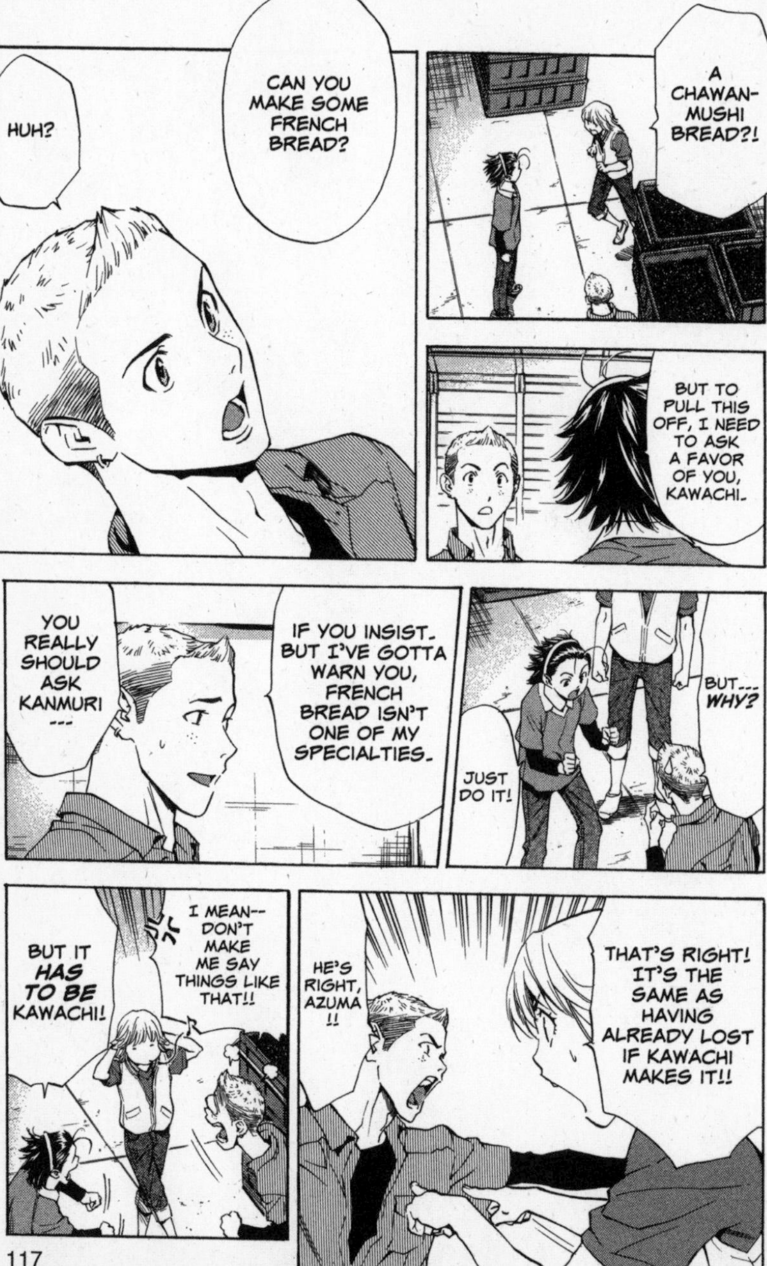
A CHAWAN-MUSHI BREAD?!
BUT TO PULL THIS OFF, I NEED TO ASK A FAVOR OF YOU, KAWACHI.
CAN YOU MAKE SOME FRENCH BREAD?
HUH?
BUT... *WHY?*
JUST DO IT!
IF YOU INSIST. BUT I'VE GOTTA WARN YOU, FRENCH BREAD ISN'T ONE OF MY SPECIALTIES.
YOU REALLY SHOULD ASK KANMURI...
THAT'S RIGHT! IT'S THE SAME AS HAVING ALREADY LOST IF KAWACHI MAKES IT!!
HE'S RIGHT, AZUMA!!
I MEAN-- DON'T MAKE ME SAY THINGS LIKE THAT!!
BUT IT *HAS TO BE* KAWACHI!

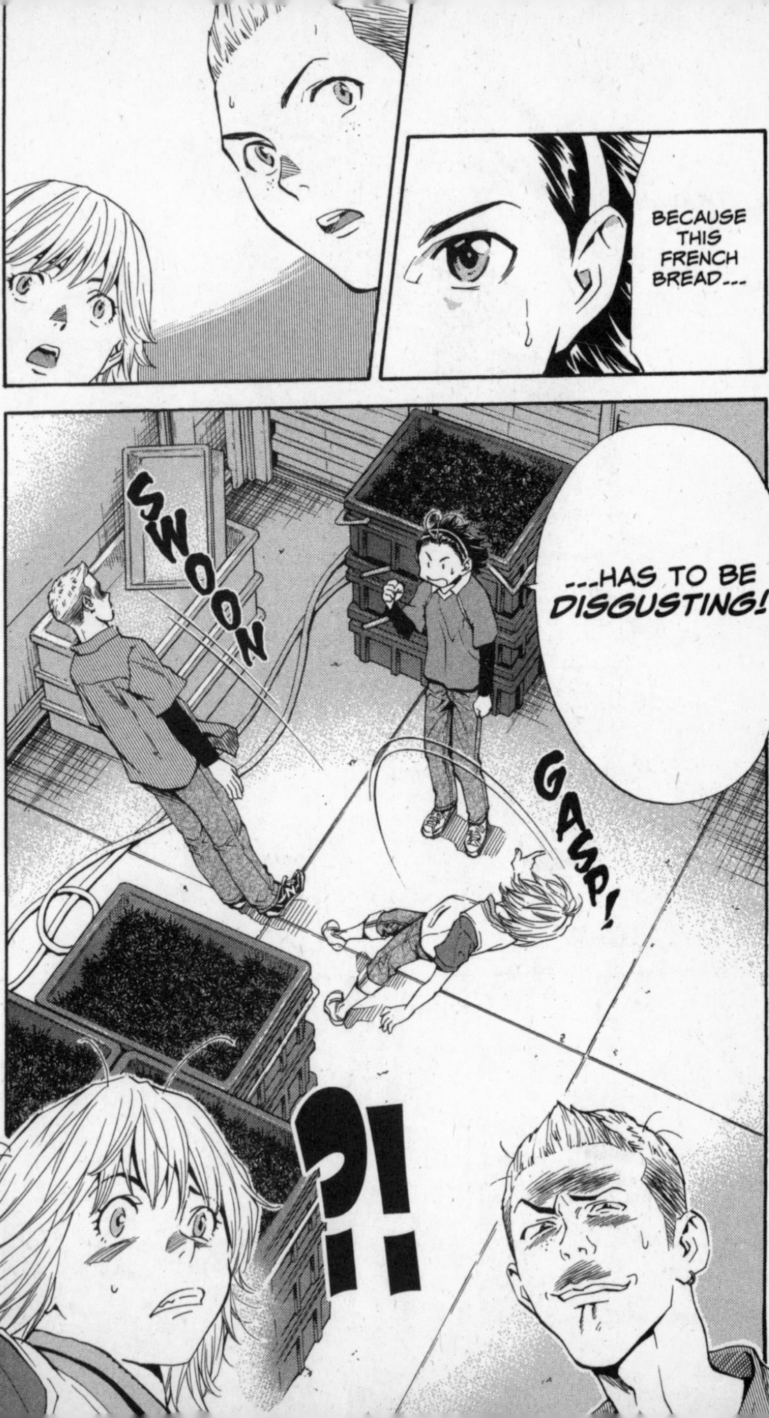
BECAUSE THIS FRENCH BREAD...
...HAS TO BE DISGUSTING!
SWOON
GASP!
?!

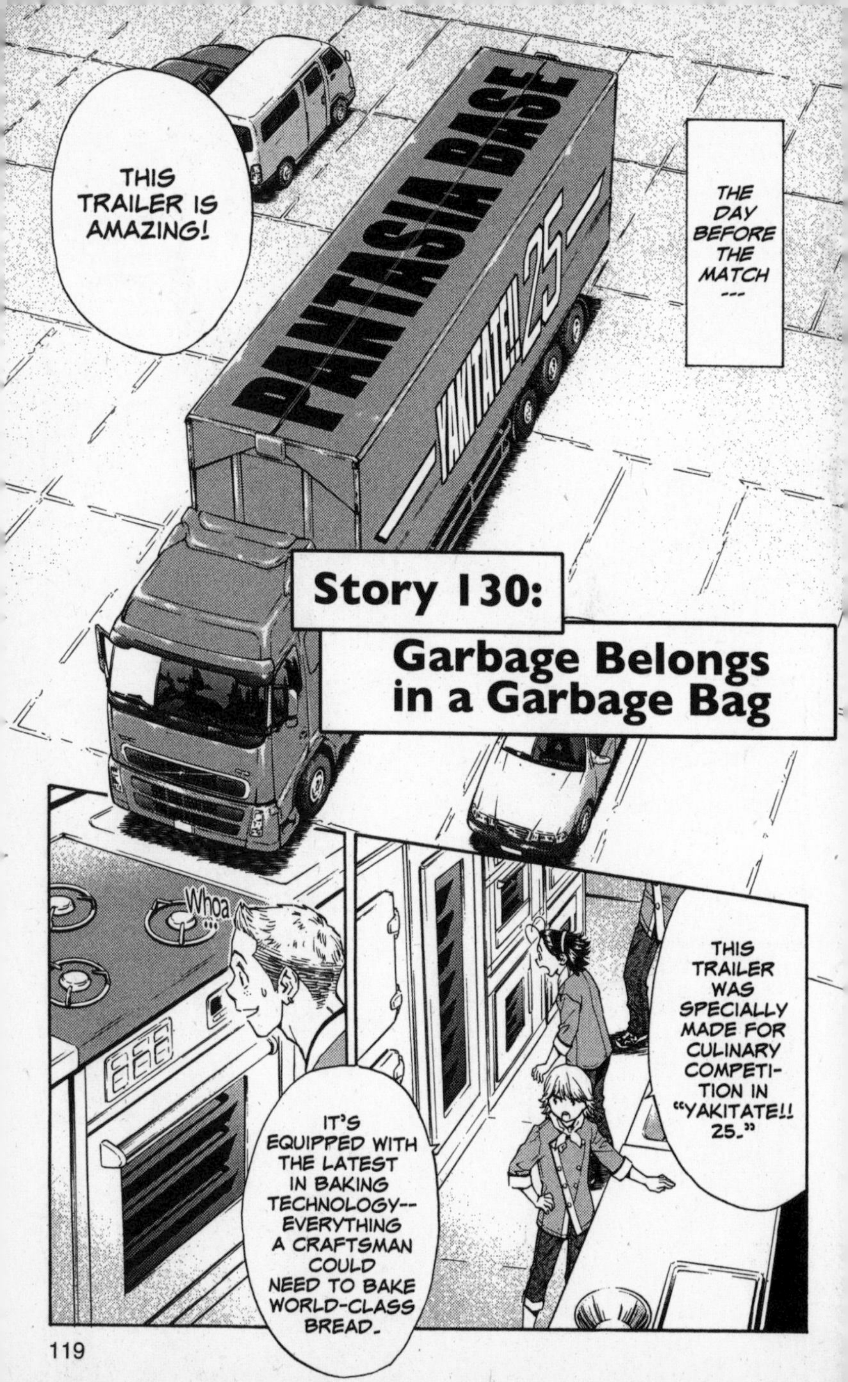

THE DAY BEFORE THE MATCH ---
THIS TRAILER IS AMAZING!
PANTASIA BASE
YAKITATE!! 25
Story 130:
Garbage Belongs in a Garbage Bag
THIS TRAILER WAS SPECIALLY MADE FOR CULINARY COMPETITION IN "YAKITATE!! 25."
IT'S EQUIPPED WITH THE LATEST IN BAKING TECHNOLOGY--EVERYTHING A CRAFTSMAN COULD NEED TO BAKE WORLD-CLASS BREAD.
Whoa...

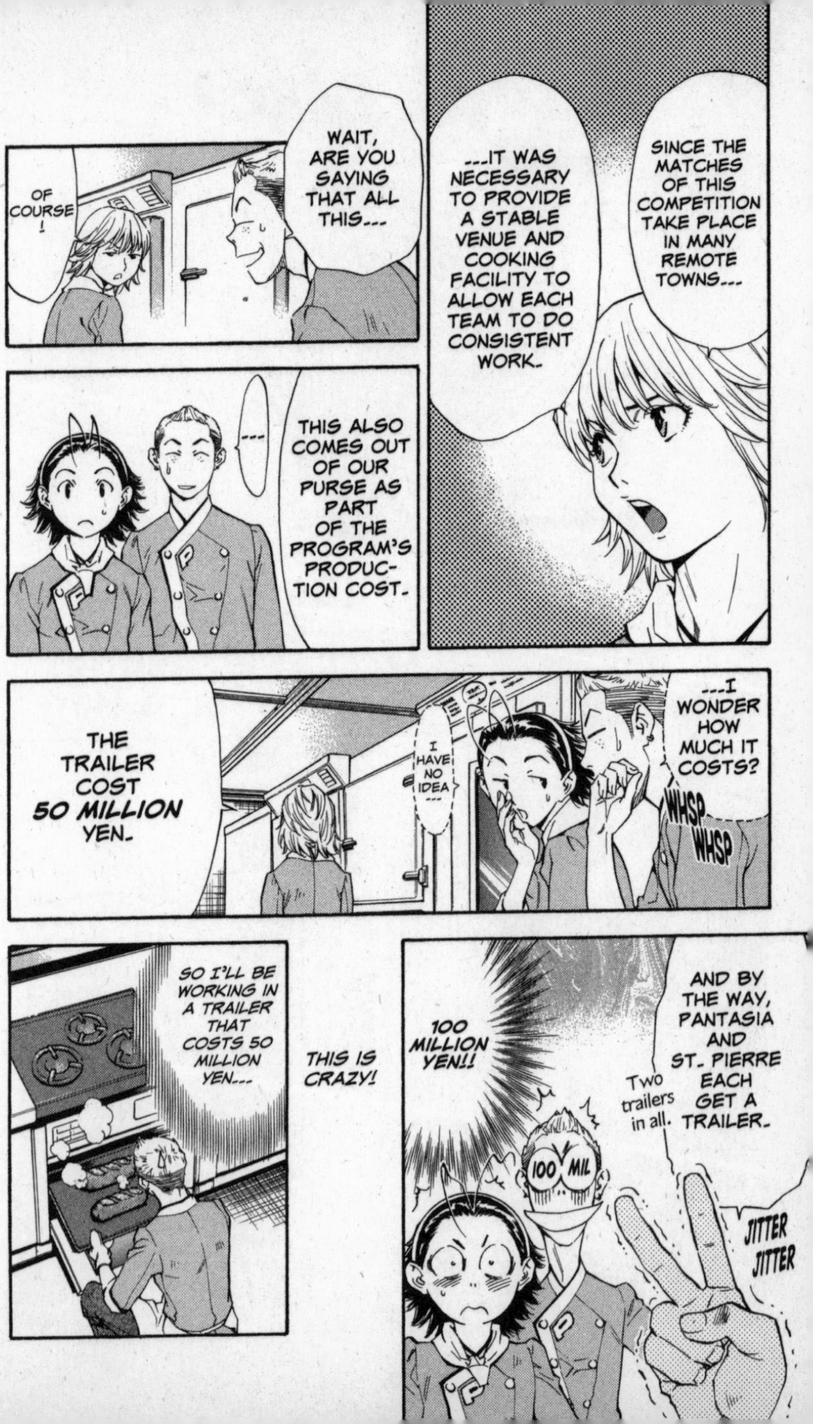

SINCE THE MATCHES OF THIS COMPETITION TAKE PLACE IN MANY REMOTE TOWNS...
...IT WAS NECESSARY TO PROVIDE A STABLE VENUE AND COOKING FACILITY TO ALLOW EACH TEAM TO DO CONSISTENT WORK.
WAIT, ARE YOU SAYING THAT ALL THIS...
OF COURSE!
THIS ALSO COMES OUT OF OUR PURSE AS PART OF THE PROGRAM'S PRODUCTION COST.
...
...I WONDER HOW MUCH IT COSTS?
WHSP WHSP
I HAVE NO IDEA...
THE TRAILER COST 50 MILLION YEN.
AND BY THE WAY, PANTASIA AND ST. PIERRE EACH GET A TRAILER.
Two trailers in all.
100 MILLION YEN!!
THIS IS CRAZY!
100 MIL
JITTER JITTER
SO I'LL BE WORKING IN A TRAILER THAT COSTS 50 MILLION YEN...

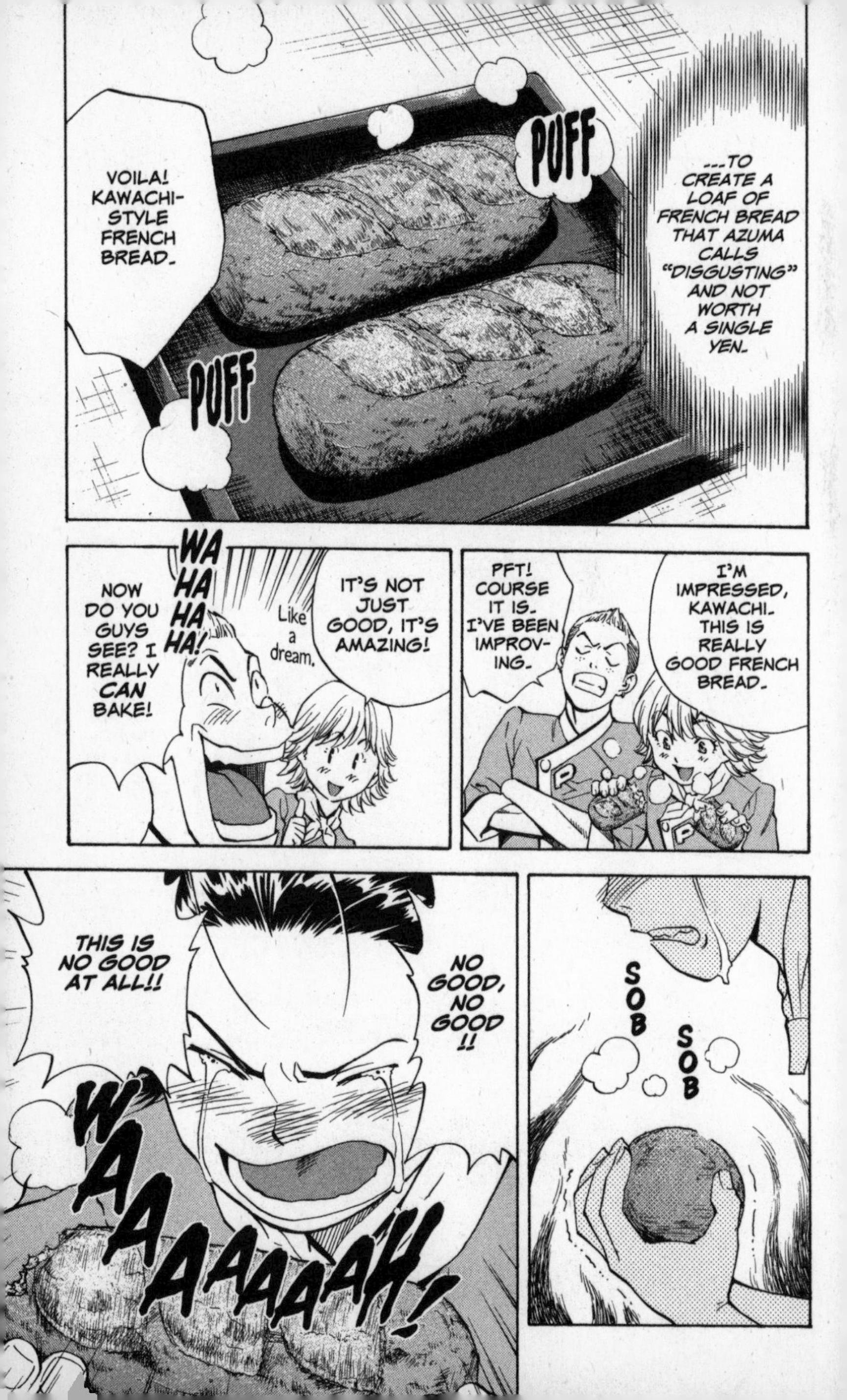
...TO CREATE A LOAF OF FRENCH BREAD THAT AZUMA CALLS "DISGUSTING" AND NOT WORTH A SINGLE YEN.
PUFF
VOILA! KAWACHI-STYLE FRENCH BREAD.
PUFF
I'M IMPRESSED, KAWACHI. THIS IS REALLY GOOD FRENCH BREAD.
PFT! COURSE IT IS. I'VE BEEN IMPROVING.
IT'S NOT JUST GOOD, IT'S AMAZING!
Like a dream.
WA HA HA HA!
NOW DO YOU GUYS SEE? I REALLY CAN BAKE!
SOB SOB
NO GOOD, NO GOOD!!
THIS IS NO GOOD AT ALL!!
WAAAAAAAH!

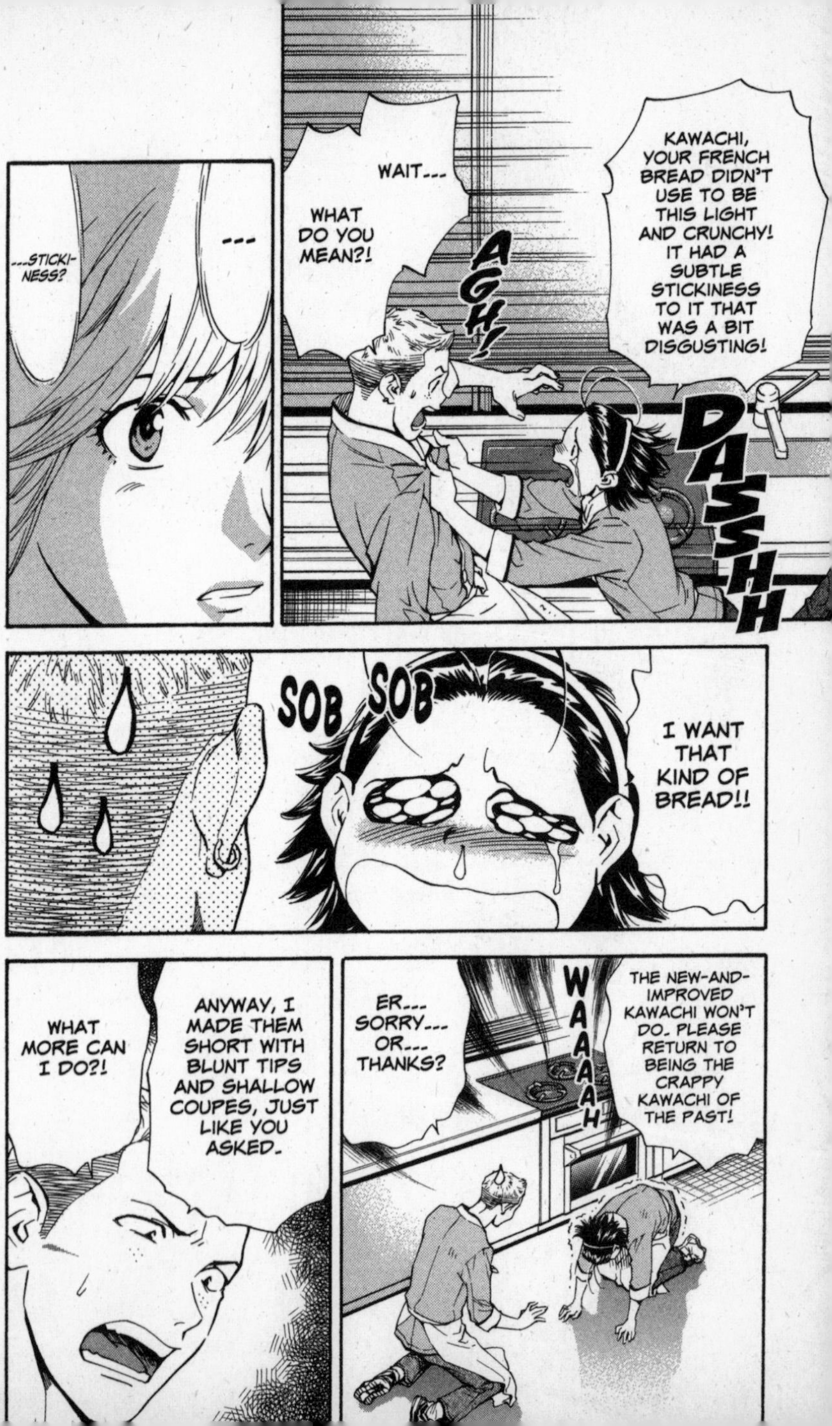
KAWACHI, YOUR FRENCH BREAD DIDN'T USE TO BE THIS LIGHT AND CRUNCHY! IT HAD A SUBTLE STICKINESS TO IT THAT WAS A BIT DISGUSTING!
WAIT...
WHAT DO YOU MEAN?!
AGH!
DASSHH
...
...STICKINESS?
I WANT THAT KIND OF BREAD!!
SOB SOB
THE NEW-AND-IMPROVED KAWACHI WON'T DO. PLEASE RETURN TO BEING THE CRAPPY KAWACHI OF THE PAST!
WAAAAAH
ER... SORRY... OR... THANKS?
ANYWAY, I MADE THEM SHORT WITH BLUNT TIPS AND SHALLOW COUPES, JUST LIKE YOU ASKED.
WHAT MORE CAN I DO?!

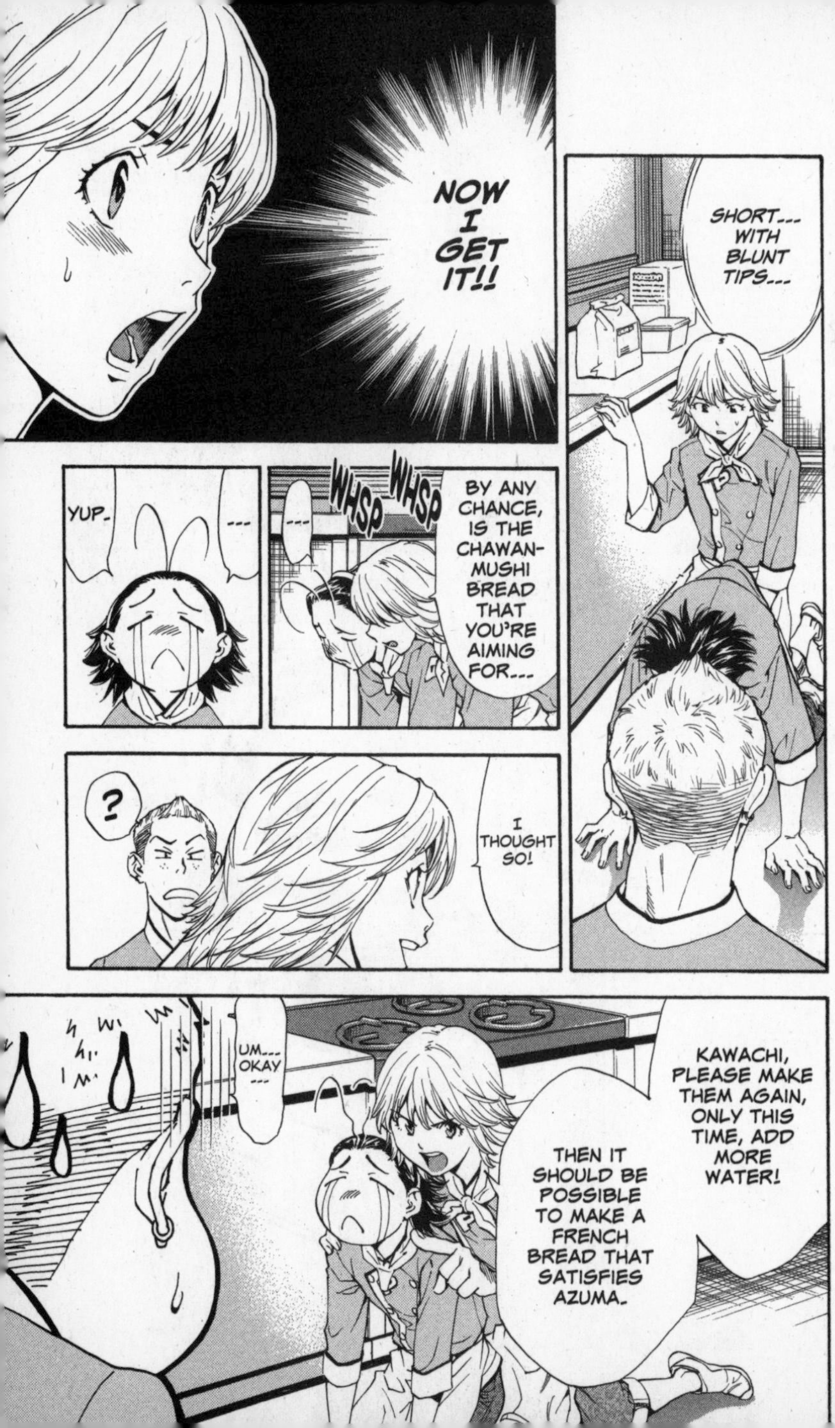
SHORT... WITH BLUNT TIPS...
NOW I GET IT!!
WHSP WHSP
BY ANY CHANCE, IS THE CHAWAN-MUSHI BREAD THAT YOU'RE AIMING FOR...
...
...
YUP.
I THOUGHT SO!
?
KAWACHI, PLEASE MAKE THEM AGAIN, ONLY THIS TIME, ADD MORE WATER!
THEN IT SHOULD BE POSSIBLE TO MAKE A FRENCH BREAD THAT SATISFIES AZUMA.
UM... OKAY...

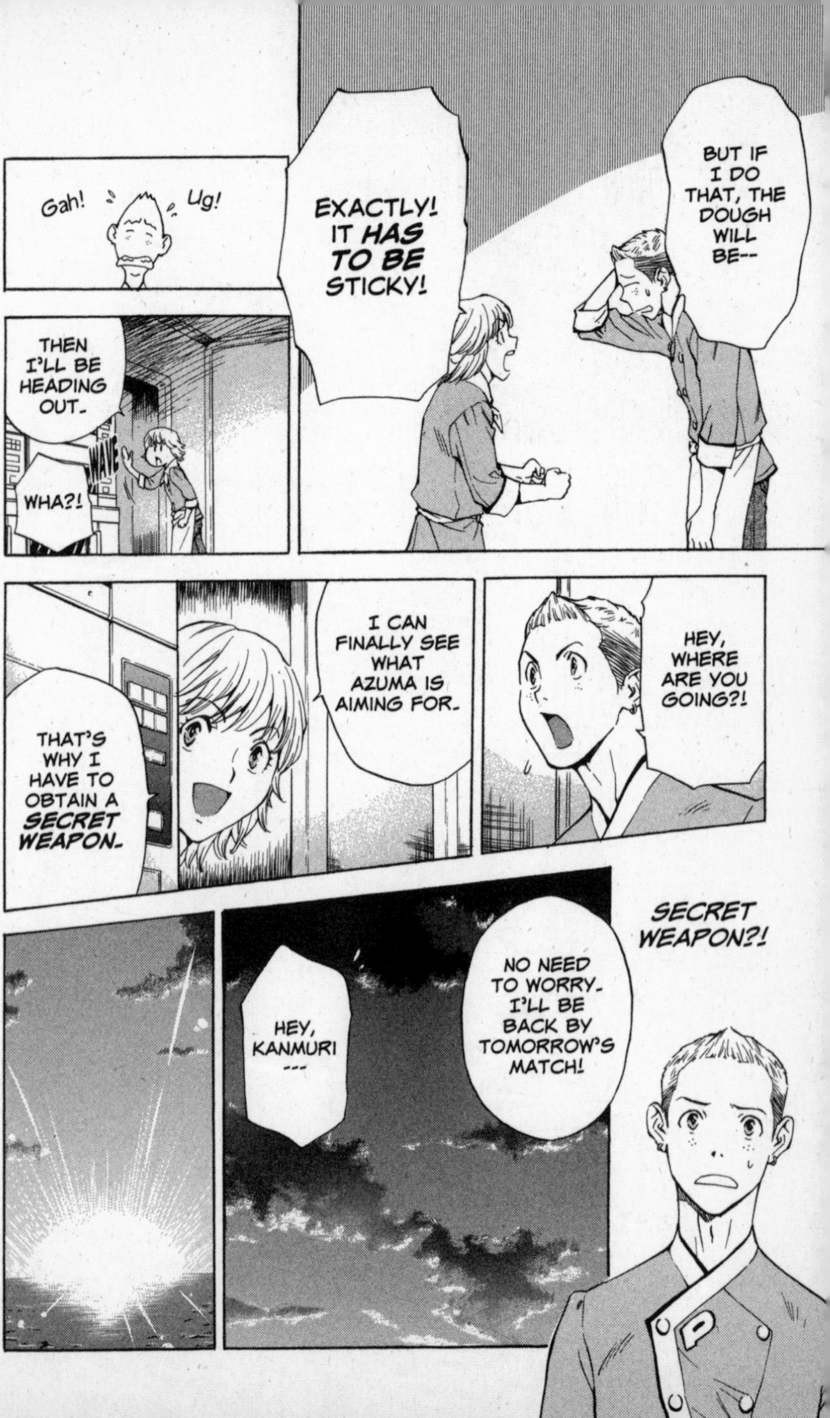
BUT IF I DO THAT, THE DOUGH WILL BE--
EXACTLY! IT HAS TO BE STICKY!
Gah!
Ug!
THEN I'LL BE HEADING OUT.
WAVE
WHA?!
HEY, WHERE ARE YOU GOING?!
I CAN FINALLY SEE WHAT AZUMA IS AIMING FOR.
THAT'S WHY I HAVE TO OBTAIN A SECRET WEAPON.
SECRET WEAPON?!
NO NEED TO WORRY. I'LL BE BACK BY TOMORROW'S MATCH!
HEY, KANMURI---

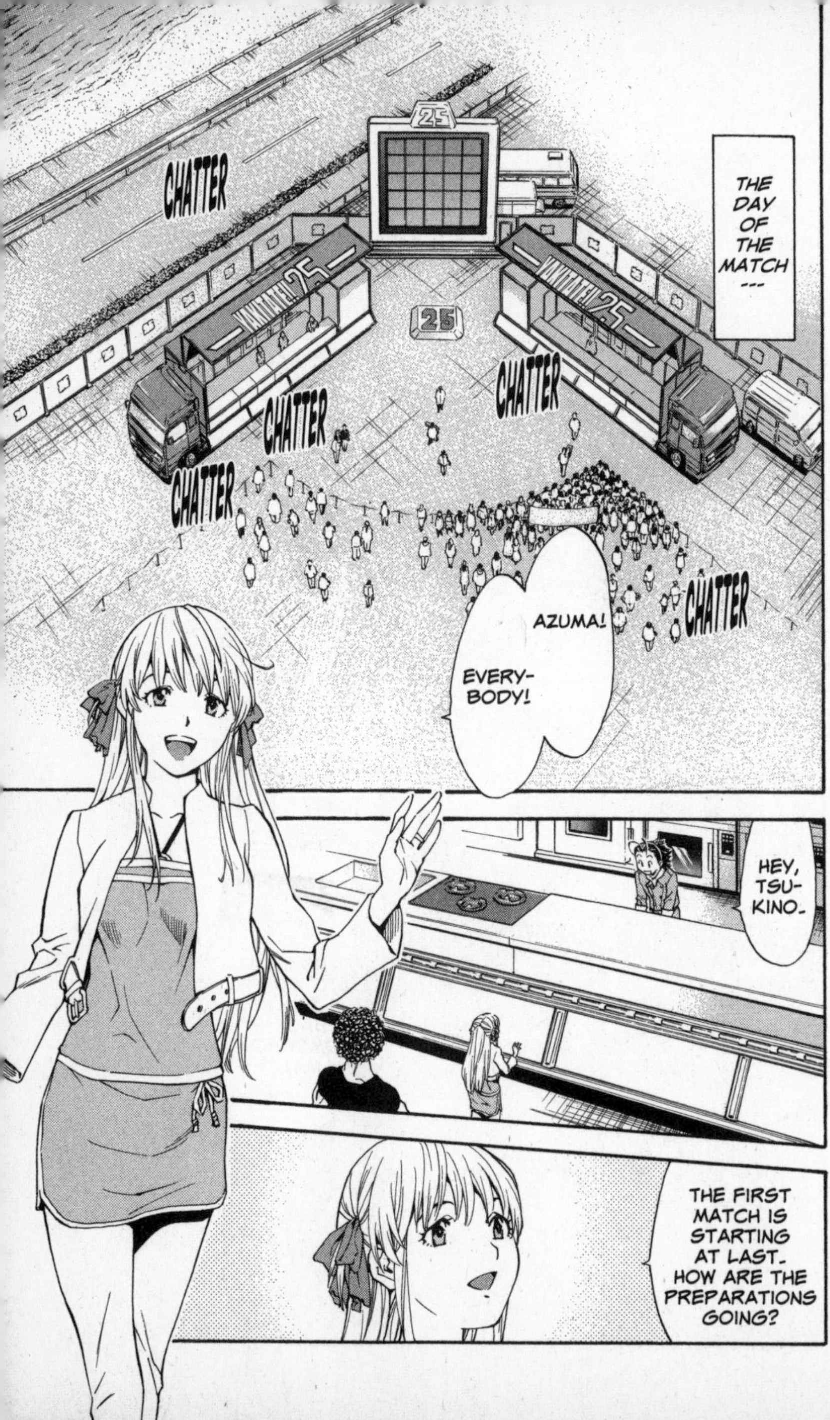
THE DAY OF THE MATCH ---
CHATTER
CHATTER
CHATTER
CHATTER
CHATTER
AZUMA! EVERYBODY!
HEY, TSUKINO.
THE FIRST MATCH IS STARTING AT LAST. HOW ARE THE PREPARATIONS GOING?

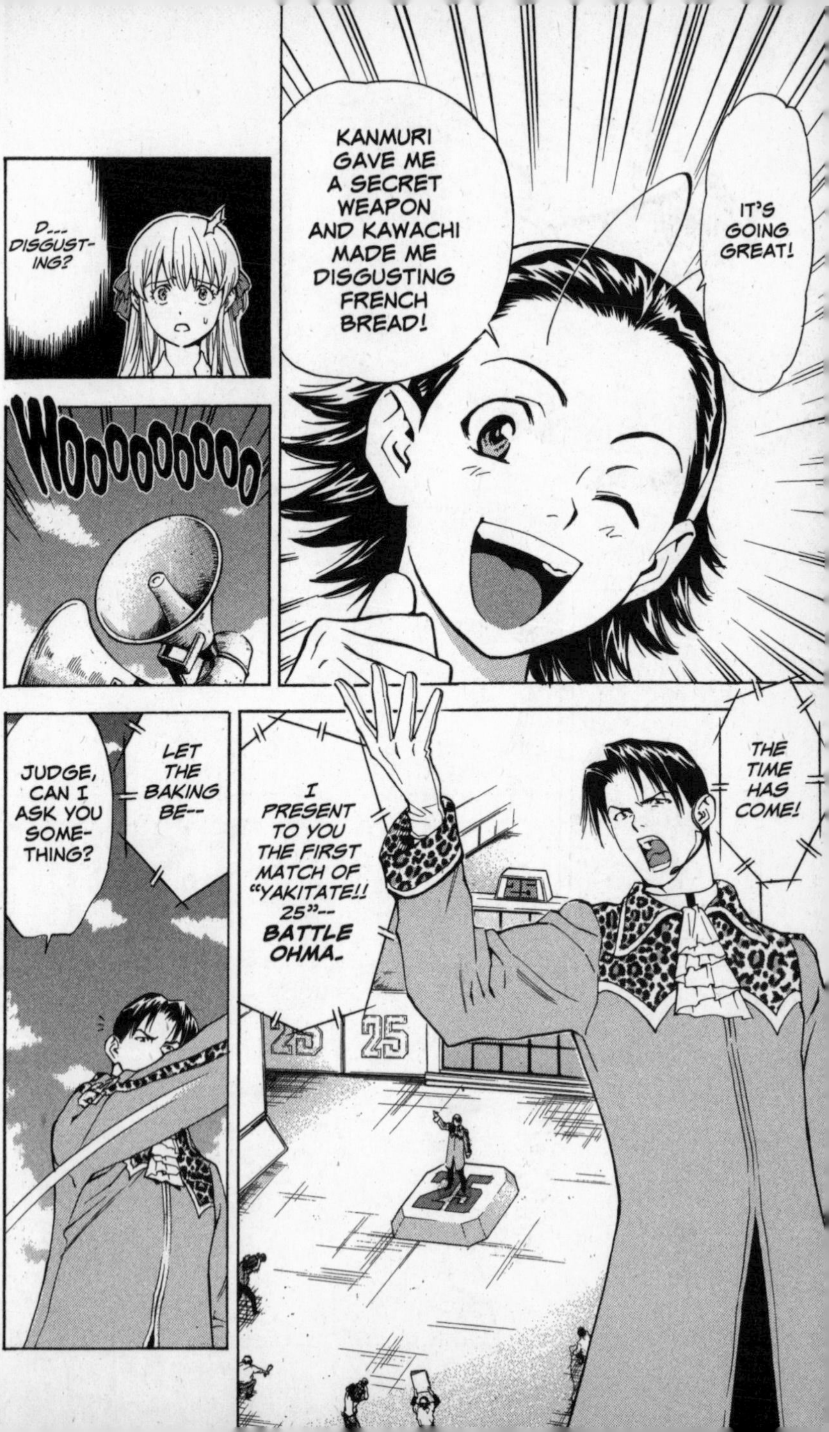
IT'S GOING GREAT!
KANMURI GAVE ME A SECRET WEAPON AND KAWACHI MADE ME DISGUSTING FRENCH BREAD!
D... DISGUSTING?
WOOOOOOOOO
THE TIME HAS COME!
I PRESENT TO YOU THE FIRST MATCH OF "YAKITATE!! 25"-- BATTLE OHMA.
LET THE BAKING BE--
JUDGE, CAN I ASK YOU SOMETHING?

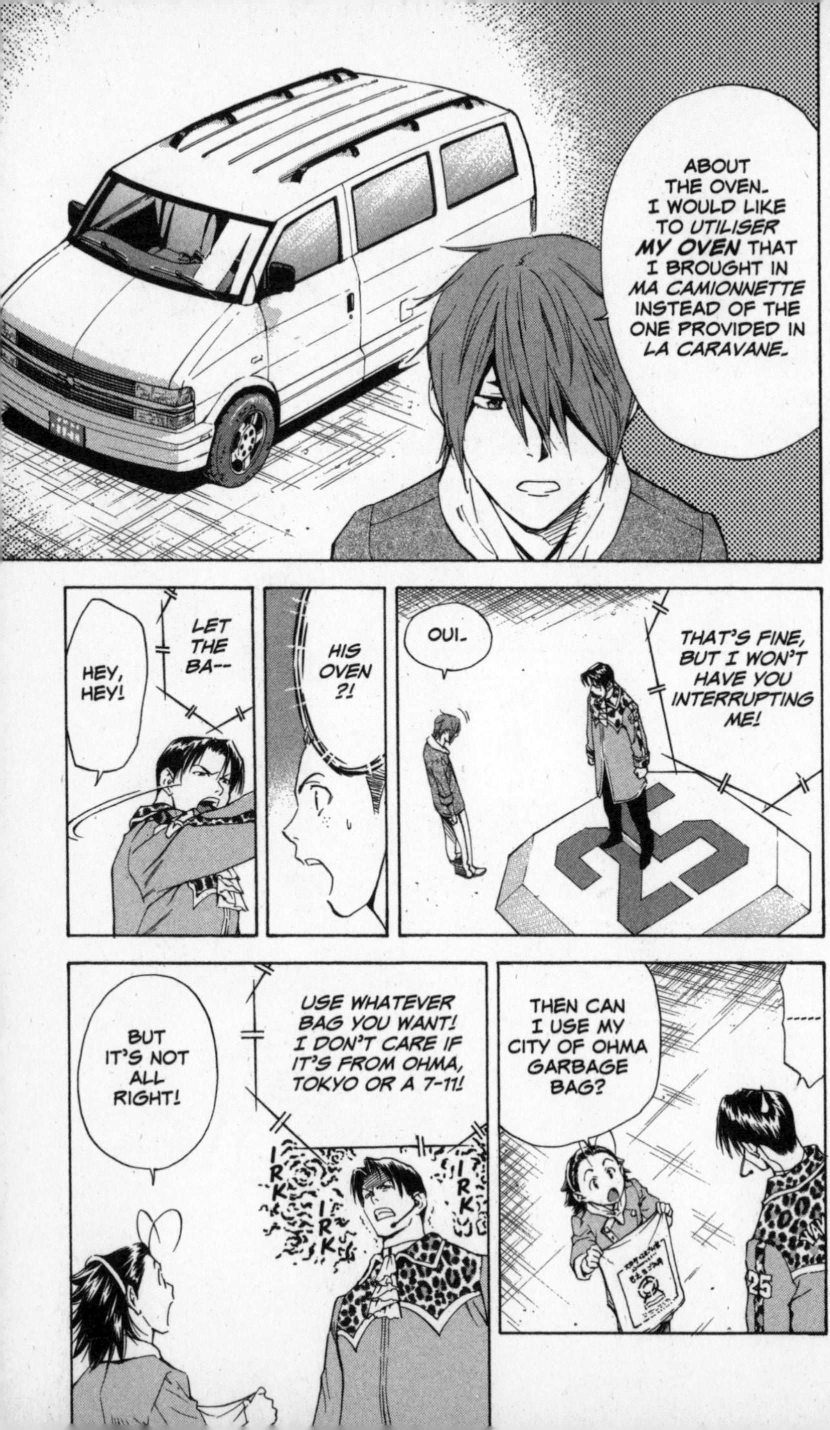
ABOUT THE OVEN. I WOULD LIKE TO UTILISER MY OVEN THAT I BROUGHT IN MA CAMIONNETTE INSTEAD OF THE ONE PROVIDED IN LA CARAVANE.
THAT'S FINE, BUT I WON'T HAVE YOU INTERRUPTING ME!
OUI.
HIS OVEN ?!
LET THE BA--
HEY, HEY!

THEN CAN I USE MY CITY OF OHMA GARBAGE BAG?
USE WHATEVER BAG YOU WANT! I DON'T CARE IF IT'S FROM OHMA, TOKYO OR A 7-11!
IRK
IRK
IRK
BUT IT'S NOT ALL RIGHT!

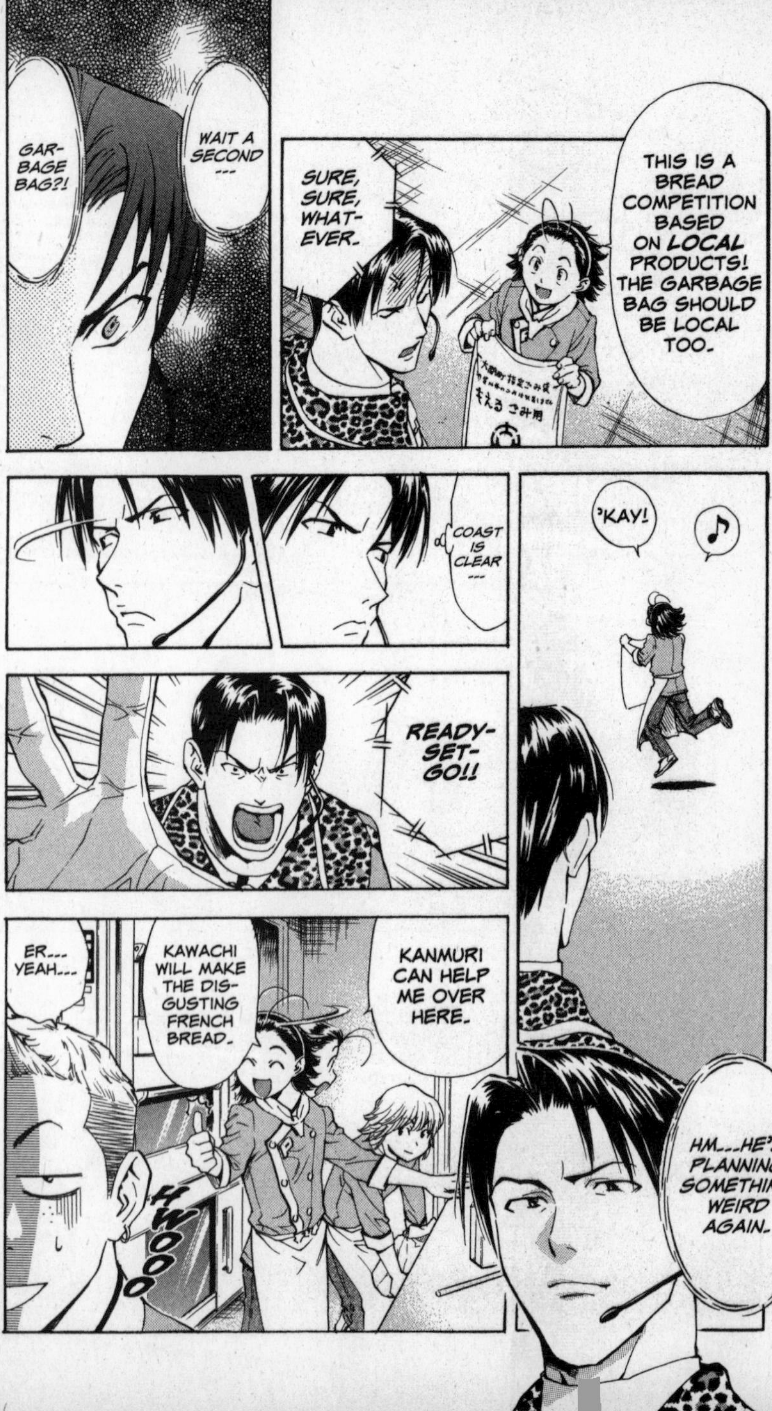

THIS IS A BREAD COMPETITION BASED ON *LOCAL* PRODUCTS! THE GARBAGE BAG SHOULD BE LOCAL TOO.
もえる ごみ用
SURE, SURE, WHATEVER.
WAIT A SECOND---
GAR-BAGE BAG?!
'KAY!
♪
HM...HE'S PLANNING SOMETHING WEIRD AGAIN.
COAST IS CLEAR---
READY-SET-GO!!
KANMURI CAN HELP ME OVER HERE.
KAWACHI WILL MAKE THE DIS-GUSTING FRENCH BREAD.
ER... YEAH...
HWOOO

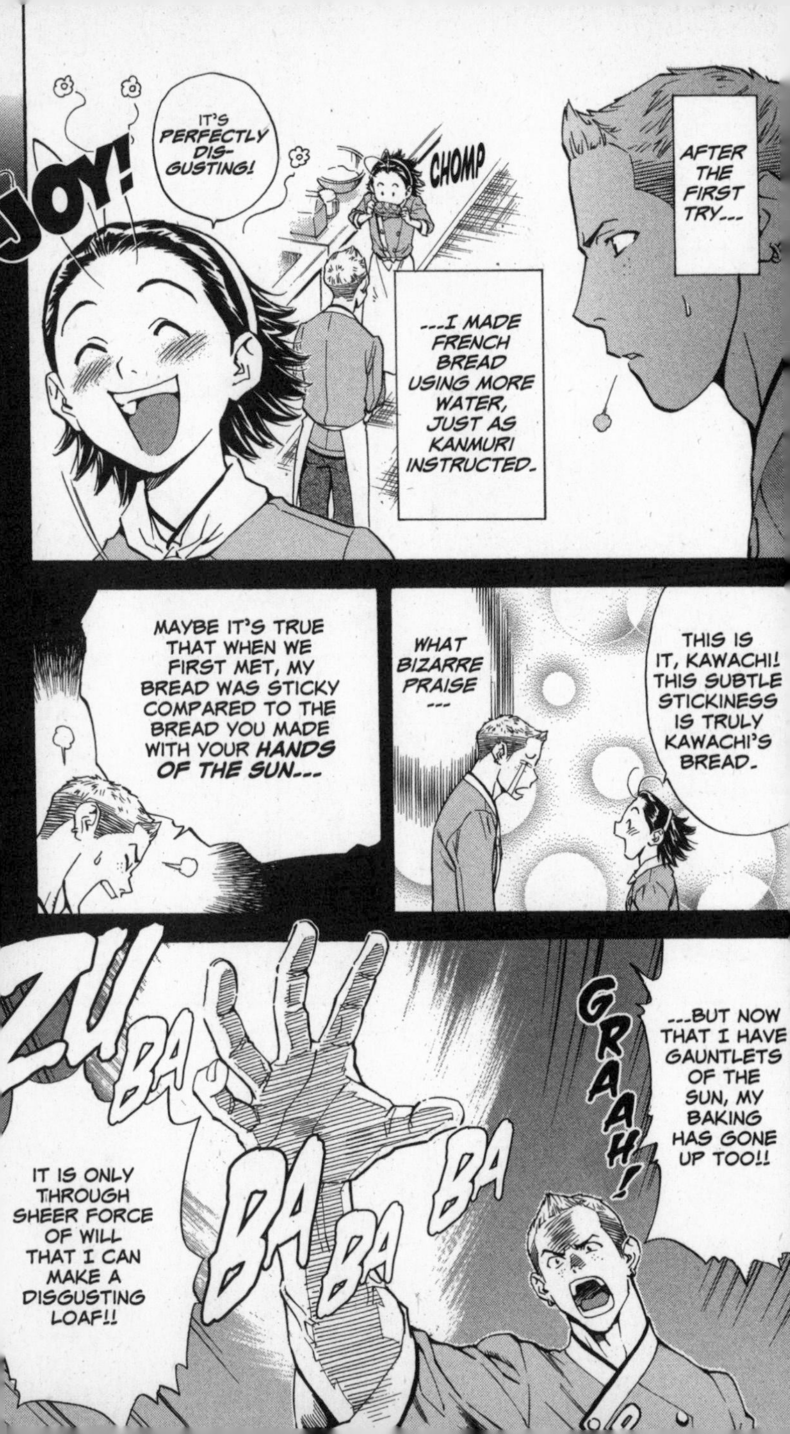
AFTER THE FIRST TRY...
...I MADE FRENCH BREAD USING MORE WATER, JUST AS KANMURI INSTRUCTED.
CHOMP
IT'S PERFECTLY DIS-GUSTING!
JOY!
THIS IS IT, KAWACHI! THIS SUBTLE STICKINESS IS TRULY KAWACHI'S BREAD.
WHAT BIZARRE PRAISE...
MAYBE IT'S TRUE THAT WHEN WE FIRST MET, MY BREAD WAS STICKY COMPARED TO THE BREAD YOU MADE WITH YOUR *HANDS OF THE SUN...*
...BUT NOW THAT I HAVE GAUNTLETS OF THE SUN, MY BAKING HAS GONE UP TOO!!
GRAAH!
BA
BA
BA
BA
ZU BA
IT IS ONLY THROUGH SHEER FORCE OF WILL THAT I CAN MAKE A DISGUSTING LOAF!!

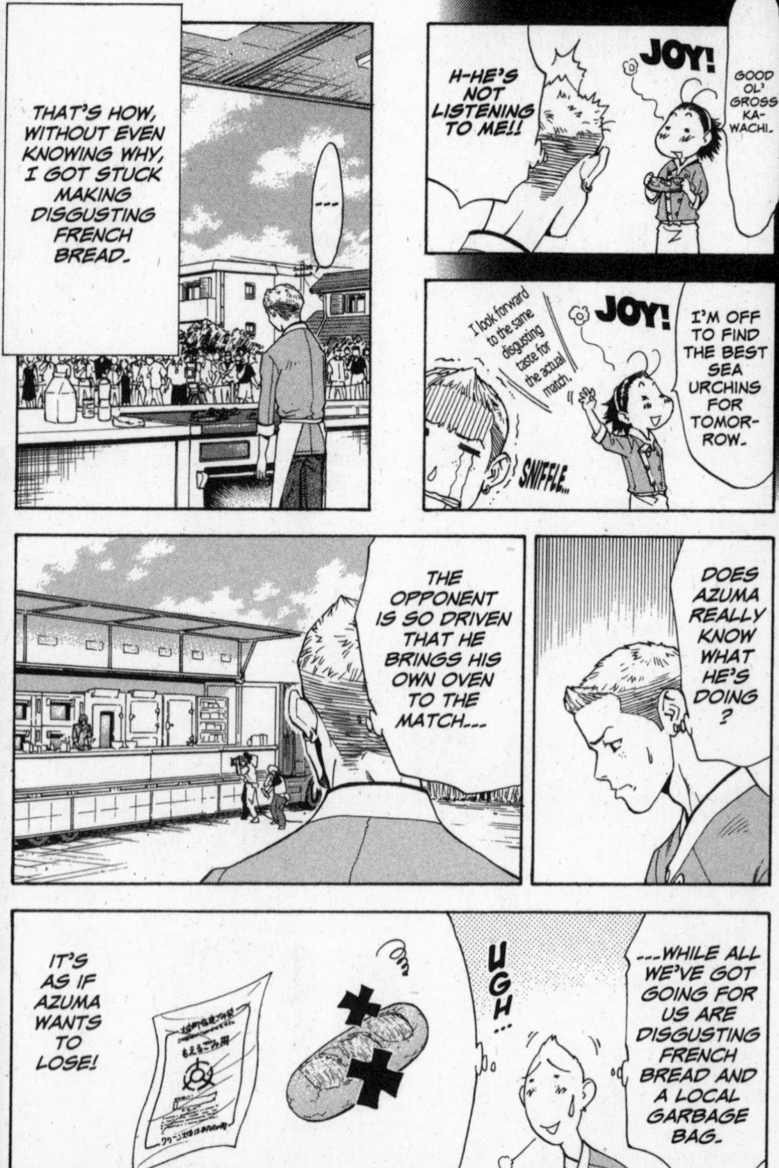
GOOD OL' GROSS KAWACHI.
JOY!
H-HE'S NOT LISTENING TO ME!!
I'M OFF TO FIND THE BEST SEA URCHINS FOR TOMORROW.
JOY!
I look forward to the same disgusting taste for the actual match.
SNIFFLE...
THAT'S HOW, WITHOUT EVEN KNOWING WHY, I GOT STUCK MAKING DISGUSTING FRENCH BREAD.
...
DOES AZUMA REALLY KNOW WHAT HE'S DOING?
THE OPPONENT IS SO DRIVEN THAT HE BRINGS HIS OWN OVEN TO THE MATCH...
...WHILE ALL WE'VE GOT GOING FOR US ARE DISGUSTING FRENCH BREAD AND A LOCAL GARBAGE BAG.
UGH...
IT'S AS IF AZUMA WANTS TO LOSE!

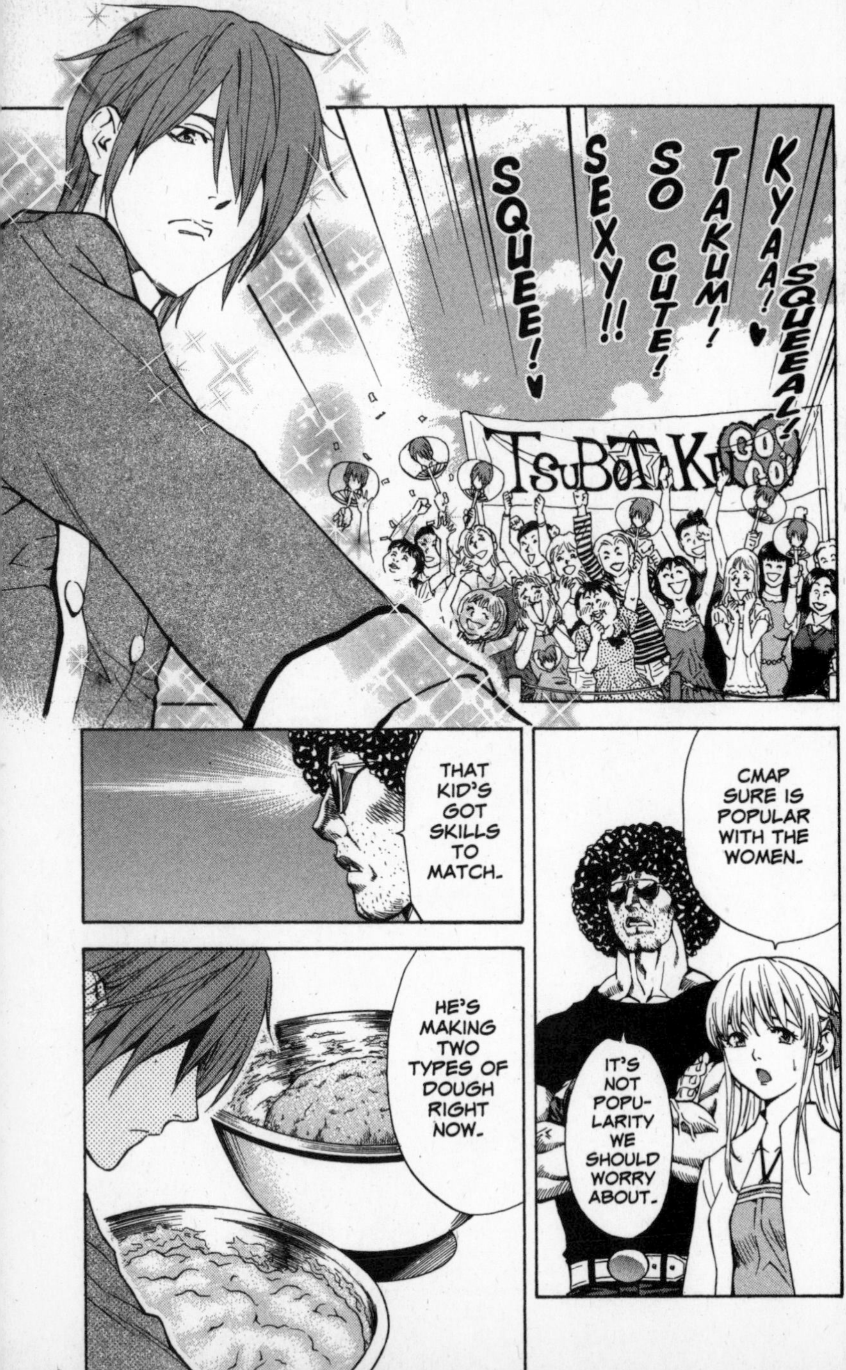
SQUEEEAL!
KYAAA! ♥
TAKUMI!
SO CUTE!
SEXY!!
SQUEEE! ♥
TSUBOTAKU
GO GO
CMAP SURE IS POPULAR WITH THE WOMEN.
IT'S NOT POPULARITY WE SHOULD WORRY ABOUT.
THAT KID'S GOT SKILLS TO MATCH.
HE'S MAKING TWO TYPES OF DOUGH RIGHT NOW.

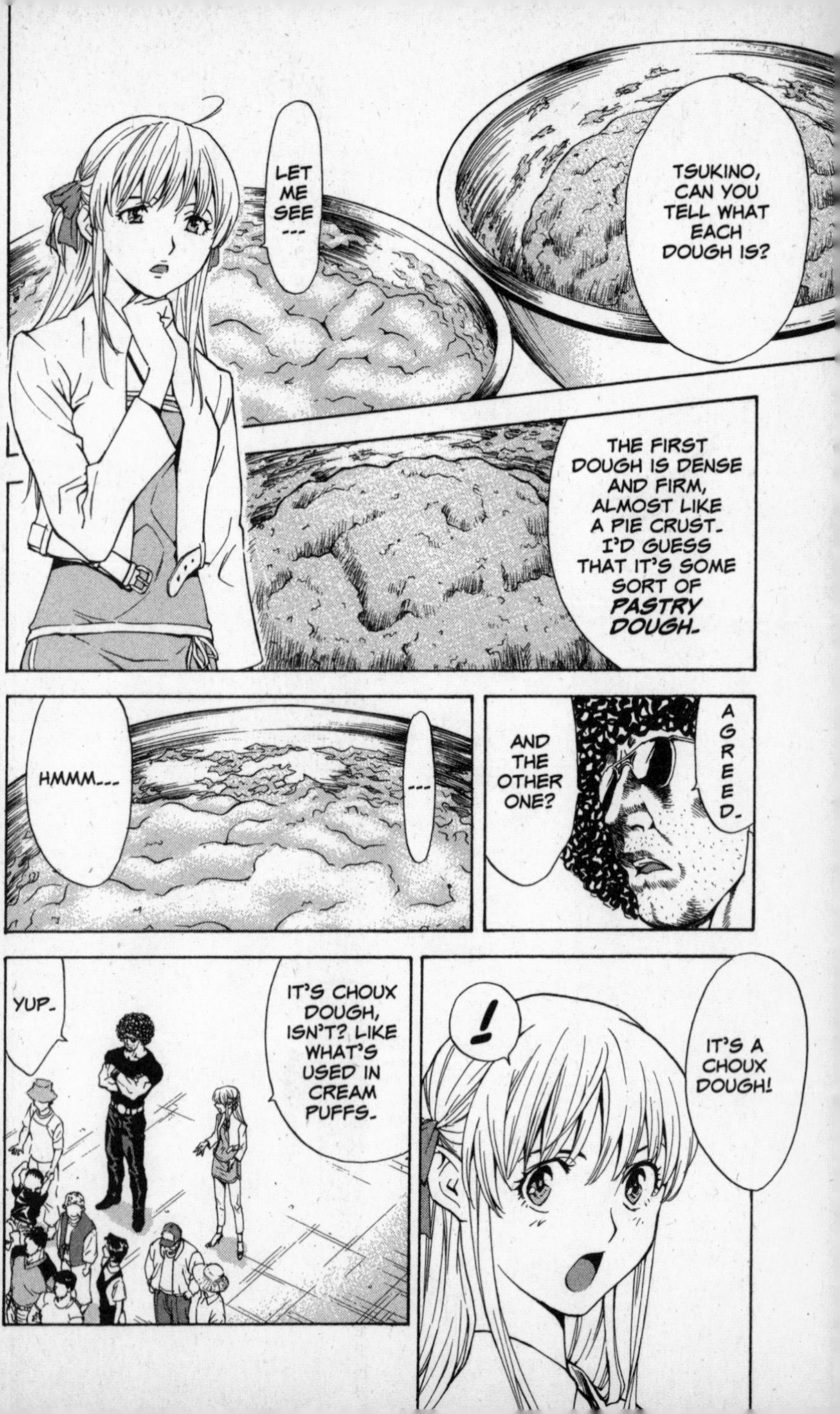
TSUKINO, CAN YOU TELL WHAT EACH DOUGH IS?
LET ME SEE ---
THE FIRST DOUGH IS DENSE AND FIRM, ALMOST LIKE A PIE CRUST. I'D GUESS THAT IT'S SOME SORT OF *PASTRY DOUGH.*
AGREED.
AND THE OTHER ONE?

HMMM...
!
IT'S A CHOUX DOUGH!
IT'S CHOUX DOUGH, ISN'T? LIKE WHAT'S USED IN CREAM PUFFS.
YUP.

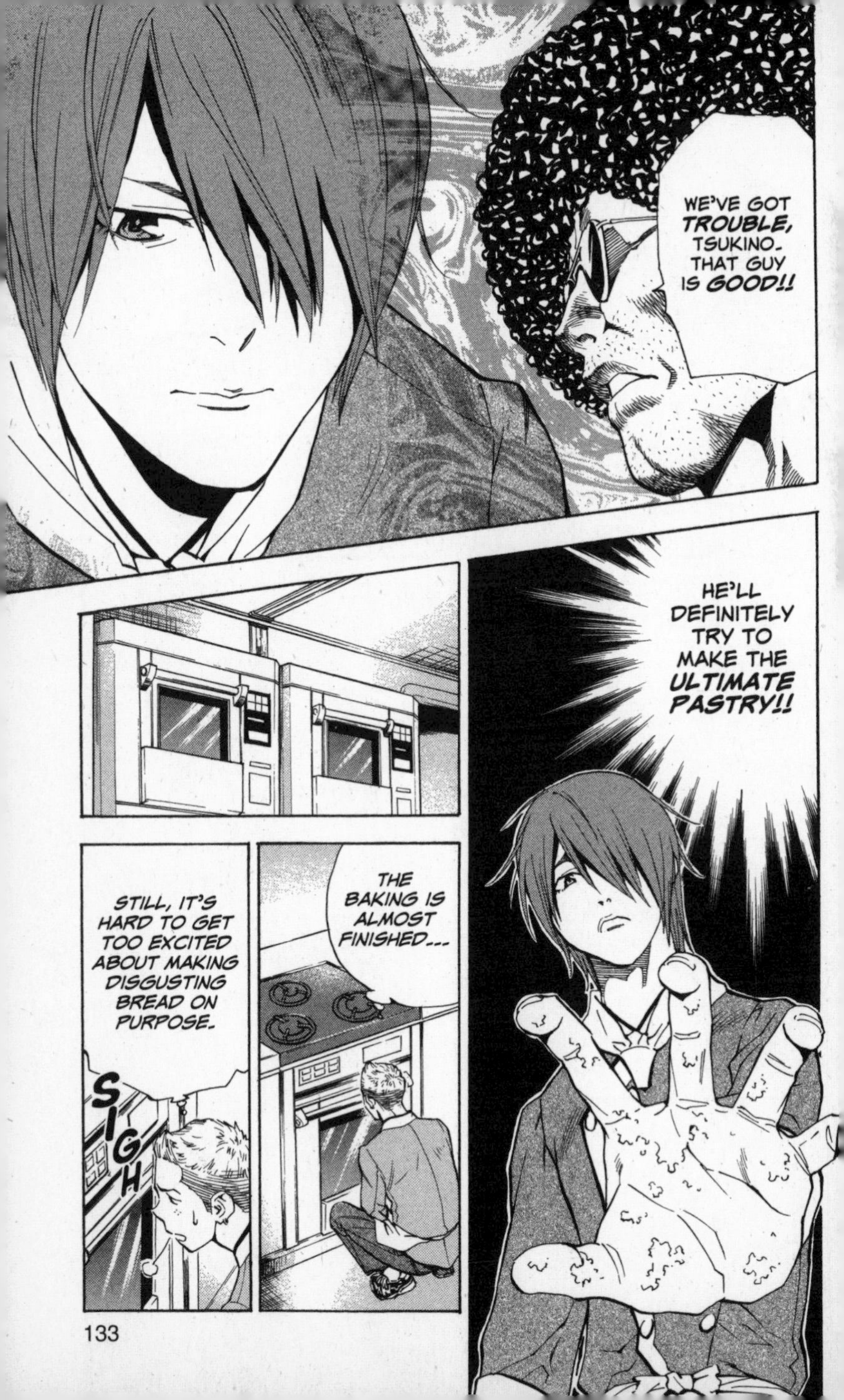
WE'VE GOT TROUBLE, TSUKINO. THAT GUY IS GOOD!!
HE'LL DEFINITELY TRY TO MAKE THE ULTIMATE PASTRY!!
THE BAKING IS ALMOST FINISHED...
STILL, IT'S HARD TO GET TOO EXCITED ABOUT MAKING DISGUSTING BREAD ON PURPOSE.
SIGH

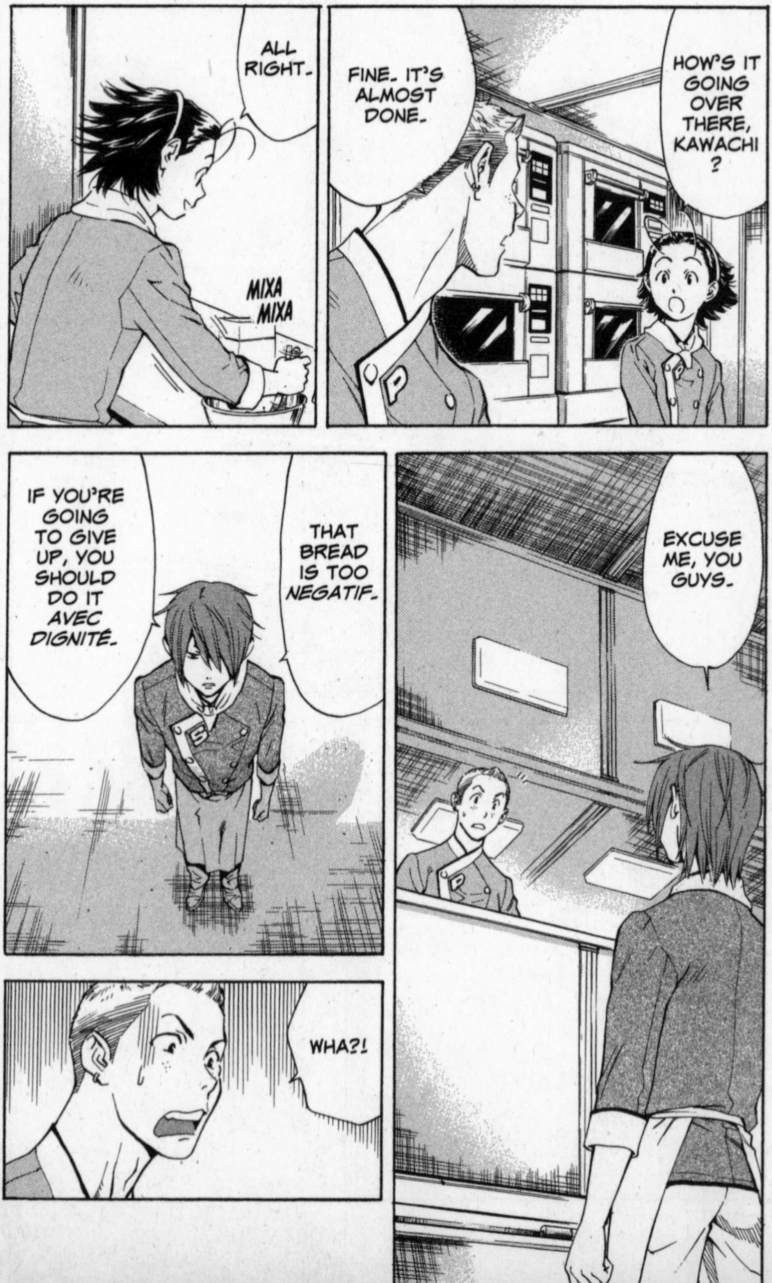
HOW'S IT GOING OVER THERE, KAWACHI?
FINE. IT'S ALMOST DONE.
ALL RIGHT.
MIXA MIXA
EXCUSE ME, YOU GUYS.
THAT BREAD IS TOO *NEGATIF*.
IF YOU'RE GOING TO GIVE UP, YOU SHOULD DO IT *AVEC DIGNITÉ*.
WHA?!

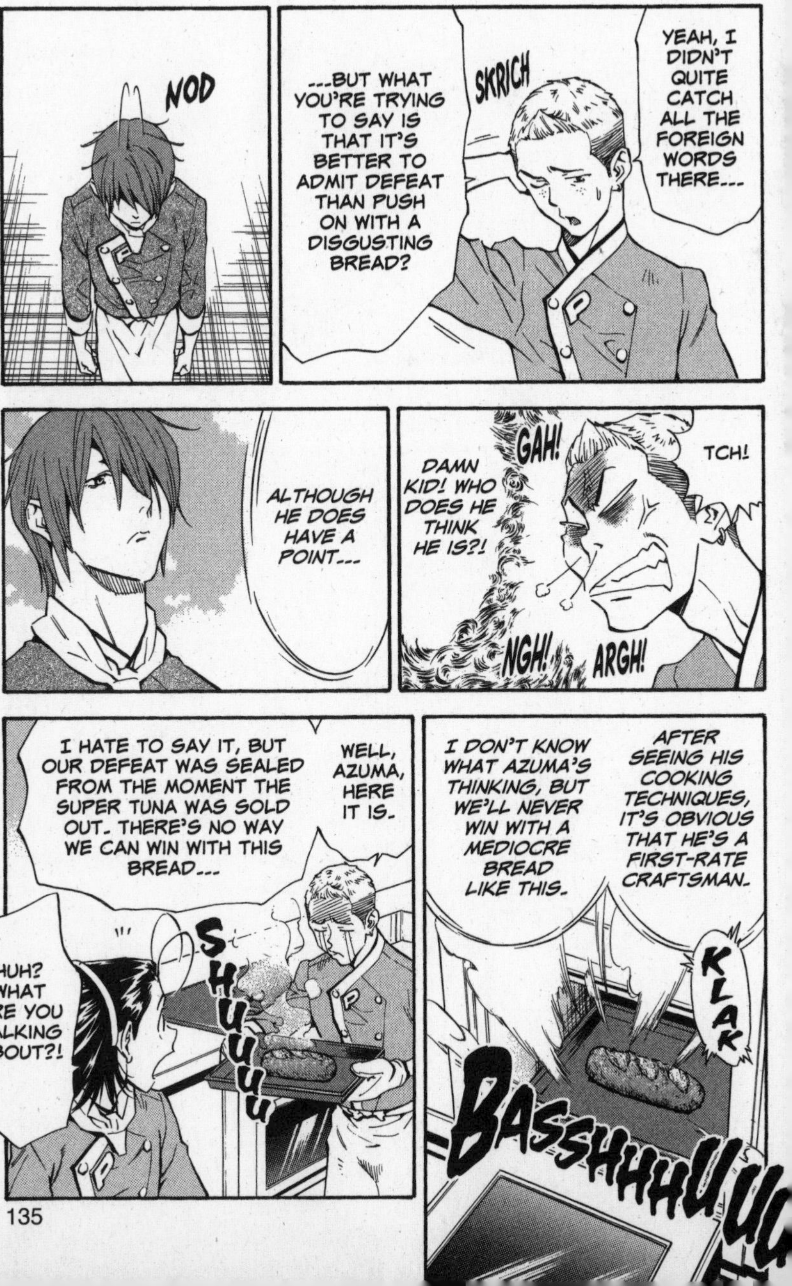
YEAH, I DIDN'T QUITE CATCH ALL THE FOREIGN WORDS THERE...
SKRICH
...BUT WHAT YOU'RE TRYING TO SAY IS THAT IT'S BETTER TO ADMIT DEFEAT THAN PUSH ON WITH A DISGUSTING BREAD?
NOD
TCH!
GAH!
DAMN KID! WHO DOES HE THINK HE IS?!
NGH!
ARGH!
ALTHOUGH HE DOES HAVE A POINT...
AFTER SEEING HIS COOKING TECHNIQUES, IT'S OBVIOUS THAT HE'S A FIRST-RATE CRAFTSMAN.
I DON'T KNOW WHAT AZUMA'S THINKING, BUT WE'LL NEVER WIN WITH A MEDIOCRE BREAD LIKE THIS.
KLAK
BASSHHHUUUU
WELL, AZUMA, HERE IT IS.
I HATE TO SAY IT, BUT OUR DEFEAT WAS SEALED FROM THE MOMENT THE SUPER TUNA WAS SOLD OUT. THERE'S NO WAY WE CAN WIN WITH THIS BREAD...
SHUUUU
HUH? WHAT ARE YOU TALKING ABOUT?!

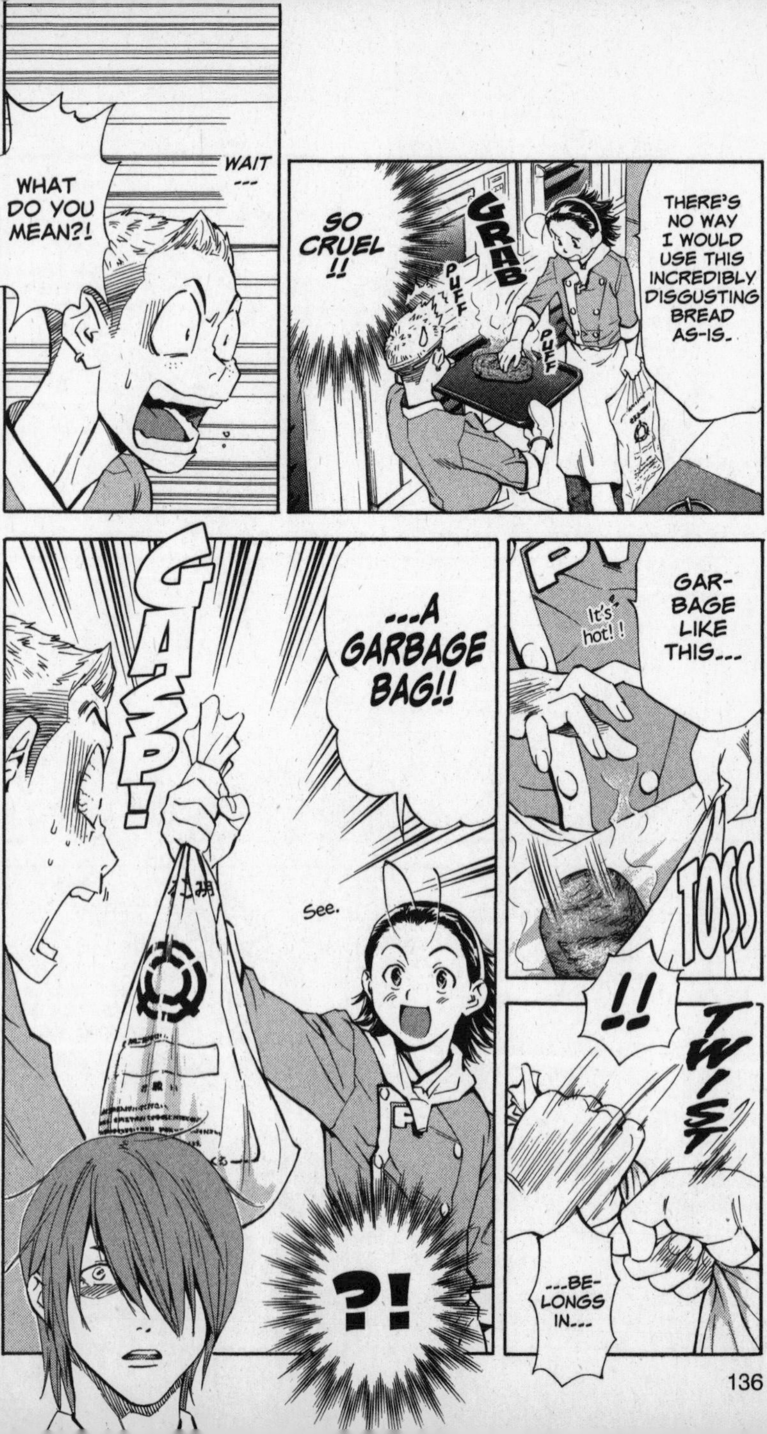
THERE'S NO WAY I WOULD USE THIS INCREDIBLY DISGUSTING BREAD AS-IS.
GRAB
PUFF
PUFF
SO CRUEL!!
WAIT---
WHAT DO YOU MEAN?!
GAR-BAGE LIKE THIS...
It's hot!!
TOSS
!!
TWIST
...BE-LONGS IN...
...A GARBAGE BAG!!
See.
GASP!
?!

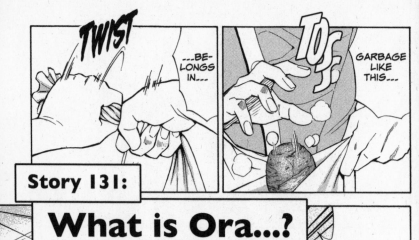

TWIST

...BE-
LONGS
IN...

TOSS

GARBAGE
LIKE
THIS...

Story 131:

What is Ora...?

...A
GARBAGE
BAG!!

GASP!

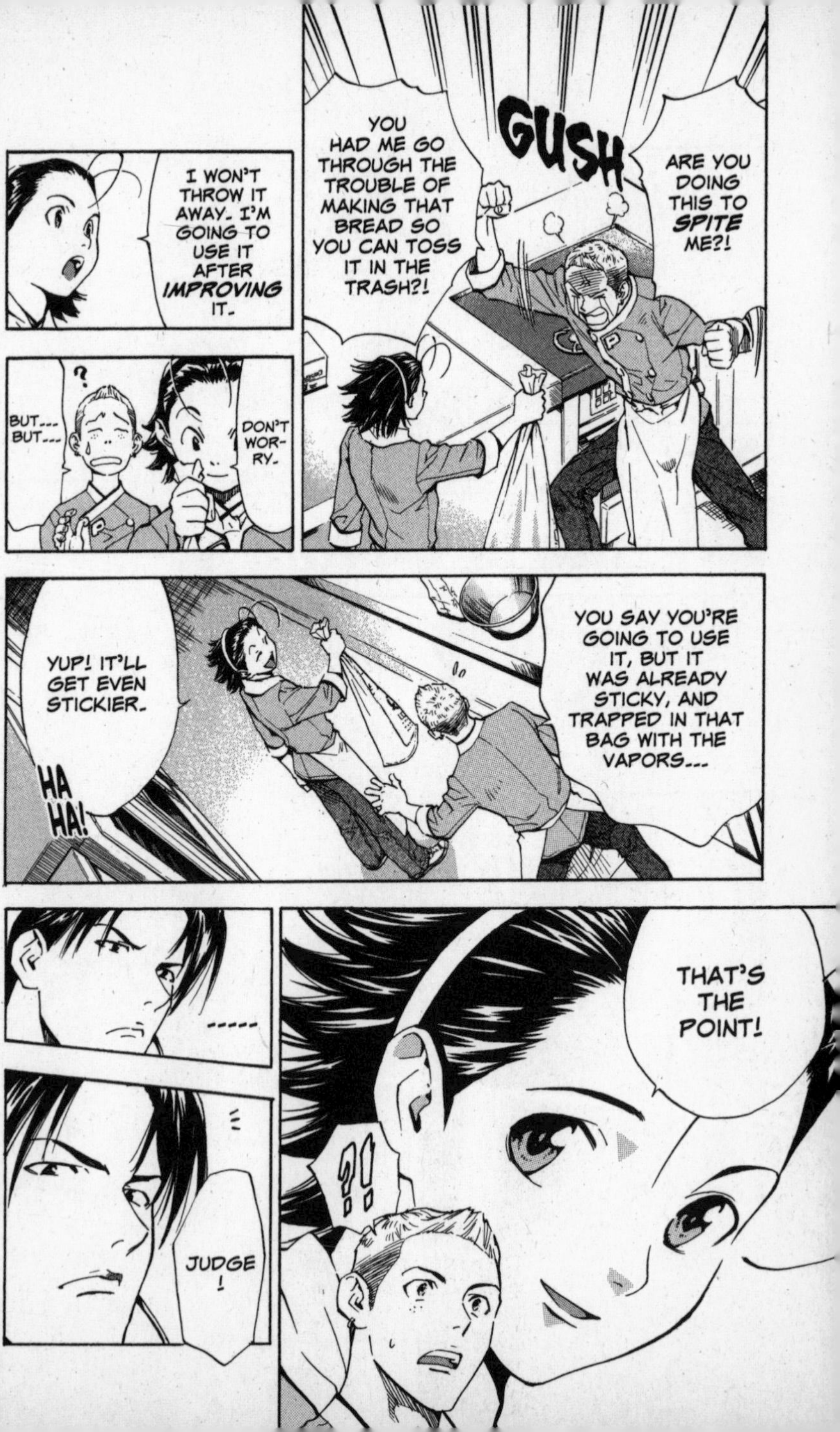
GUSH
ARE YOU DOING THIS TO SPITE ME?!
YOU HAD ME GO THROUGH THE TROUBLE OF MAKING THAT BREAD SO YOU CAN TOSS IT IN THE TRASH?!
I WON'T THROW IT AWAY. I'M GOING TO USE IT AFTER IMPROVING IT.
DON'T WORRY.
?
BUT... BUT...
YOU SAY YOU'RE GOING TO USE IT, BUT IT WAS ALREADY STICKY, AND TRAPPED IN THAT BAG WITH THE VAPORS...
YUP! IT'LL GET EVEN STICKIER.
HA HA!
THAT'S THE POINT!
?!
.....
JUDGE!

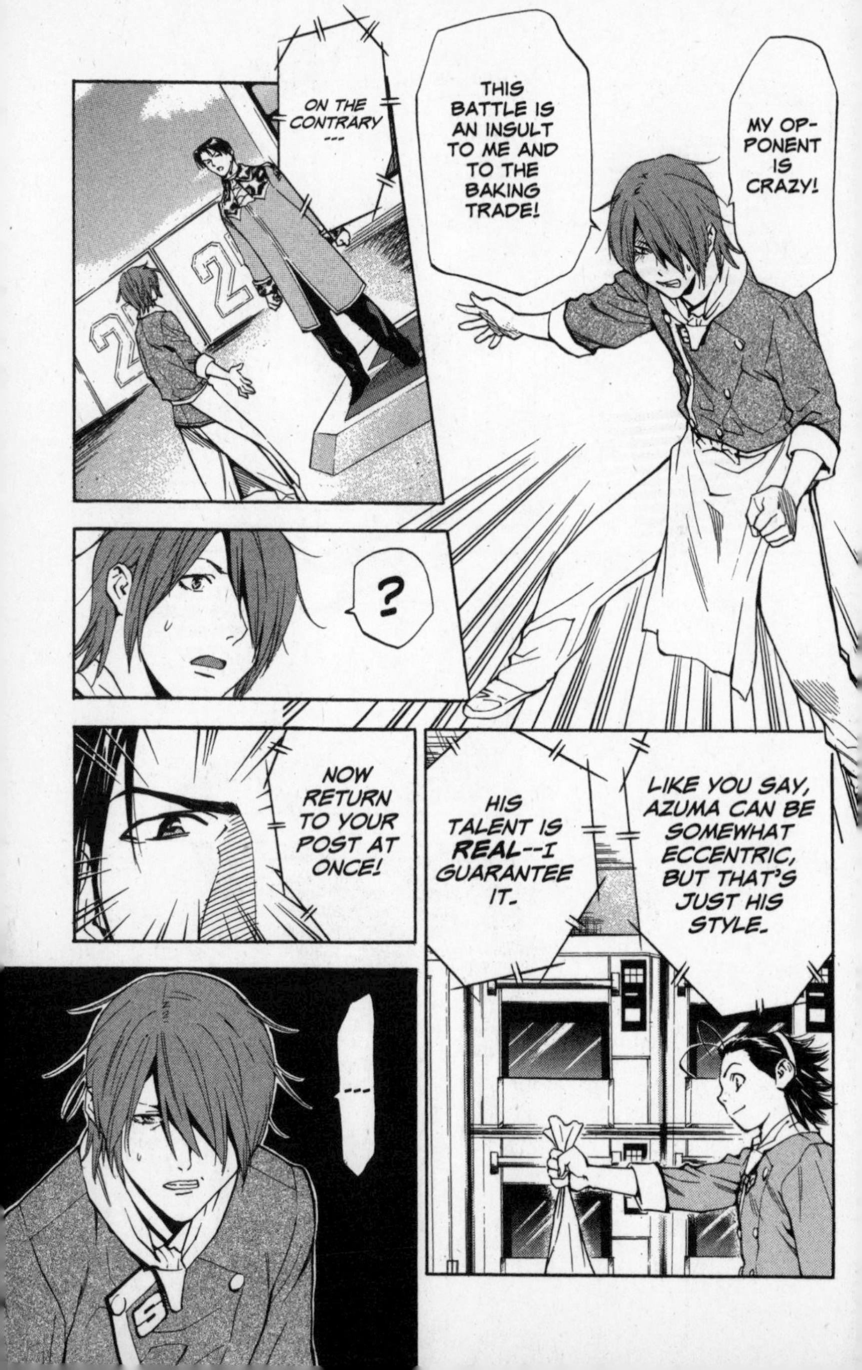
MY OP-PONENT IS CRAZY!
THIS BATTLE IS AN INSULT TO ME AND TO THE BAKING TRADE!
ON THE CONTRARY ---
?
LIKE YOU SAY, AZUMA CAN BE SOMEWHAT ECCENTRIC, BUT THAT'S JUST HIS STYLE.
HIS TALENT IS REAL--I GUARANTEE IT.
NOW RETURN TO YOUR POST AT ONCE!

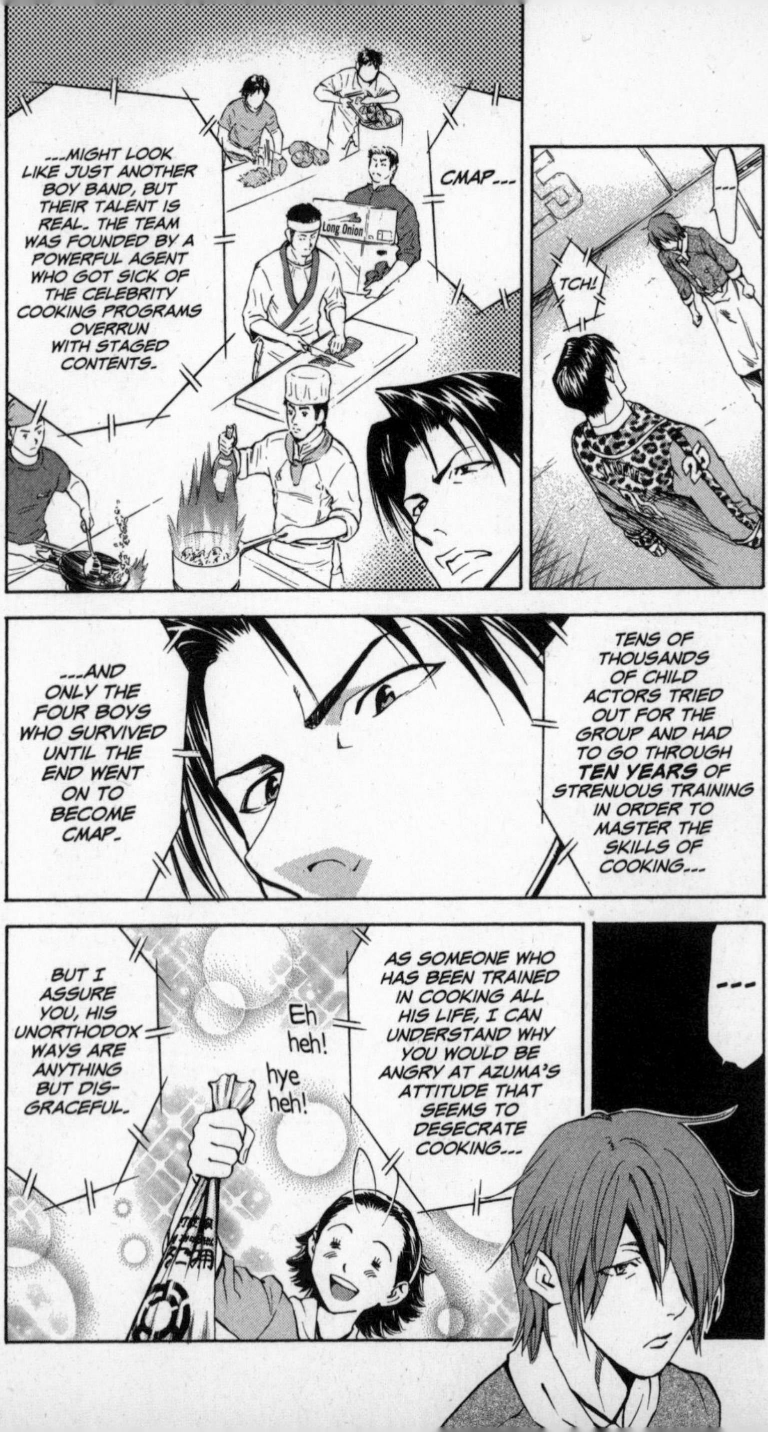
...
TCH!
CMAP...
...MIGHT LOOK LIKE JUST ANOTHER BOY BAND, BUT THEIR TALENT IS REAL. THE TEAM WAS FOUNDED BY A POWERFUL AGENT WHO GOT SICK OF THE CELEBRITY COOKING PROGRAMS OVERRUN WITH STAGED CONTENTS.
Long Onion
TENS OF THOUSANDS OF CHILD ACTORS TRIED OUT FOR THE GROUP AND HAD TO GO THROUGH **TEN YEARS** OF STRENUOUS TRAINING IN ORDER TO MASTER THE SKILLS OF COOKING...
...AND ONLY THE FOUR BOYS WHO SURVIVED UNTIL THE END WENT ON TO BECOME CMAP.
...
AS SOMEONE WHO HAS BEEN TRAINED IN COOKING ALL HIS LIFE, I CAN UNDERSTAND WHY YOU WOULD BE ANGRY AT AZUMA'S ATTITUDE THAT SEEMS TO DESECRATE COOKING...
Eh heh!
hye heh!
BUT I ASSURE YOU, HIS UNORTHODOX WAYS ARE ANYTHING BUT DIS-GRACEFUL.

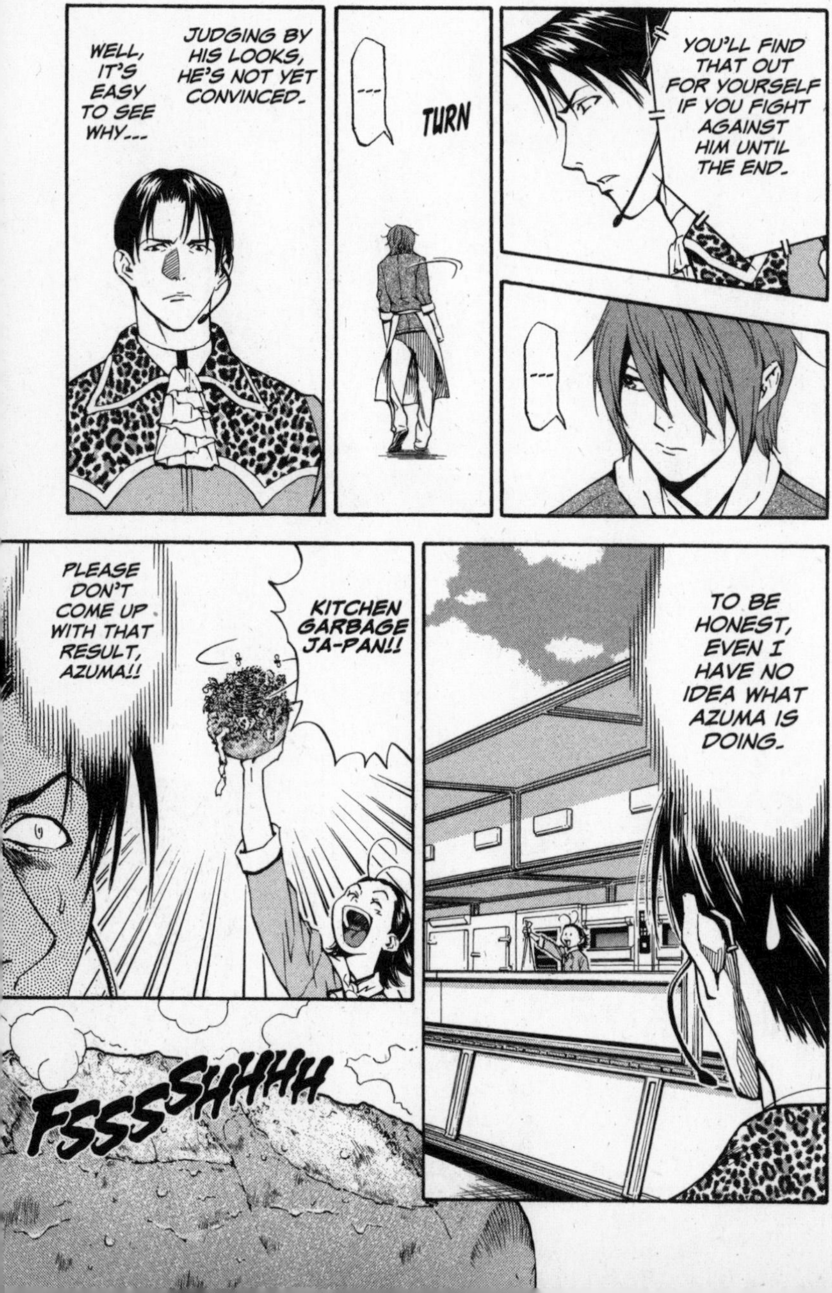
YOU'LL FIND THAT OUT FOR YOURSELF IF YOU FIGHT AGAINST HIM UNTIL THE END.
...
...
TURN
JUDGING BY HIS LOOKS, HE'S NOT YET CONVINCED.
WELL, IT'S EASY TO SEE WHY...
TO BE HONEST, EVEN I HAVE NO IDEA WHAT AZUMA IS DOING.
KITCHEN GARBAGE JA-PAN!!
PLEASE DON'T COME UP WITH THAT RESULT, AZUMA!!
FSSSSHHHH

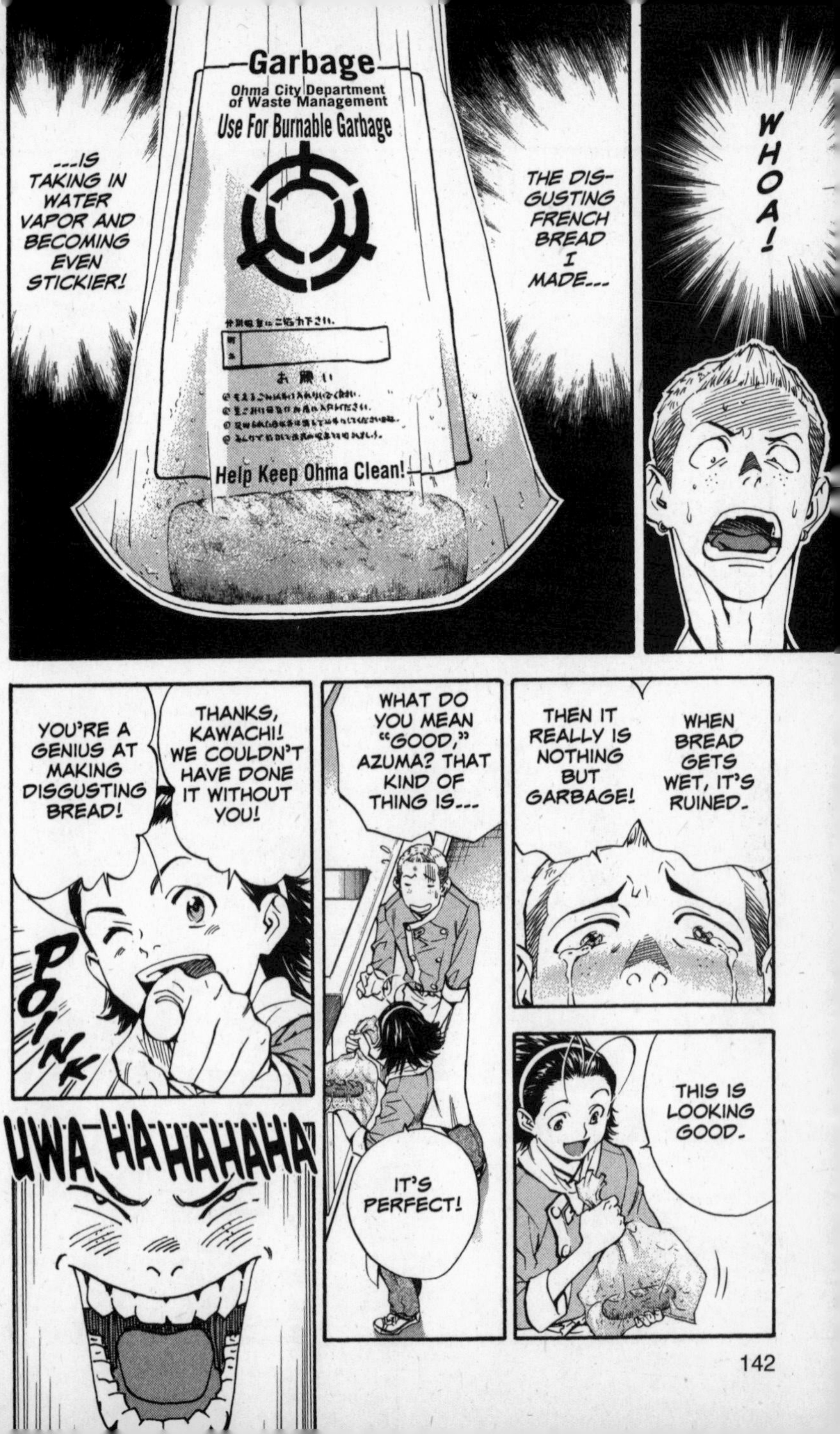
WHOA!
Garbage
Ohma City Department of Waste Management
Use For Burnable Garbage
Help Keep Ohma Clean!
THE DIS-GUSTING FRENCH BREAD I MADE...
...IS TAKING IN WATER VAPOR AND BECOMING EVEN STICKIER!
WHEN BREAD GETS WET, IT'S RUINED.
THEN IT REALLY IS NOTHING BUT GARBAGE!
THIS IS LOOKING GOOD.
WHAT DO YOU MEAN "GOOD," AZUMA? THAT KIND OF THING IS...
IT'S PERFECT!
THANKS, KAWACHI! WE COULDN'T HAVE DONE IT WITHOUT YOU!
YOU'RE A GENIUS AT MAKING DISGUSTING BREAD!
POINK
UWA HAHAHAHA

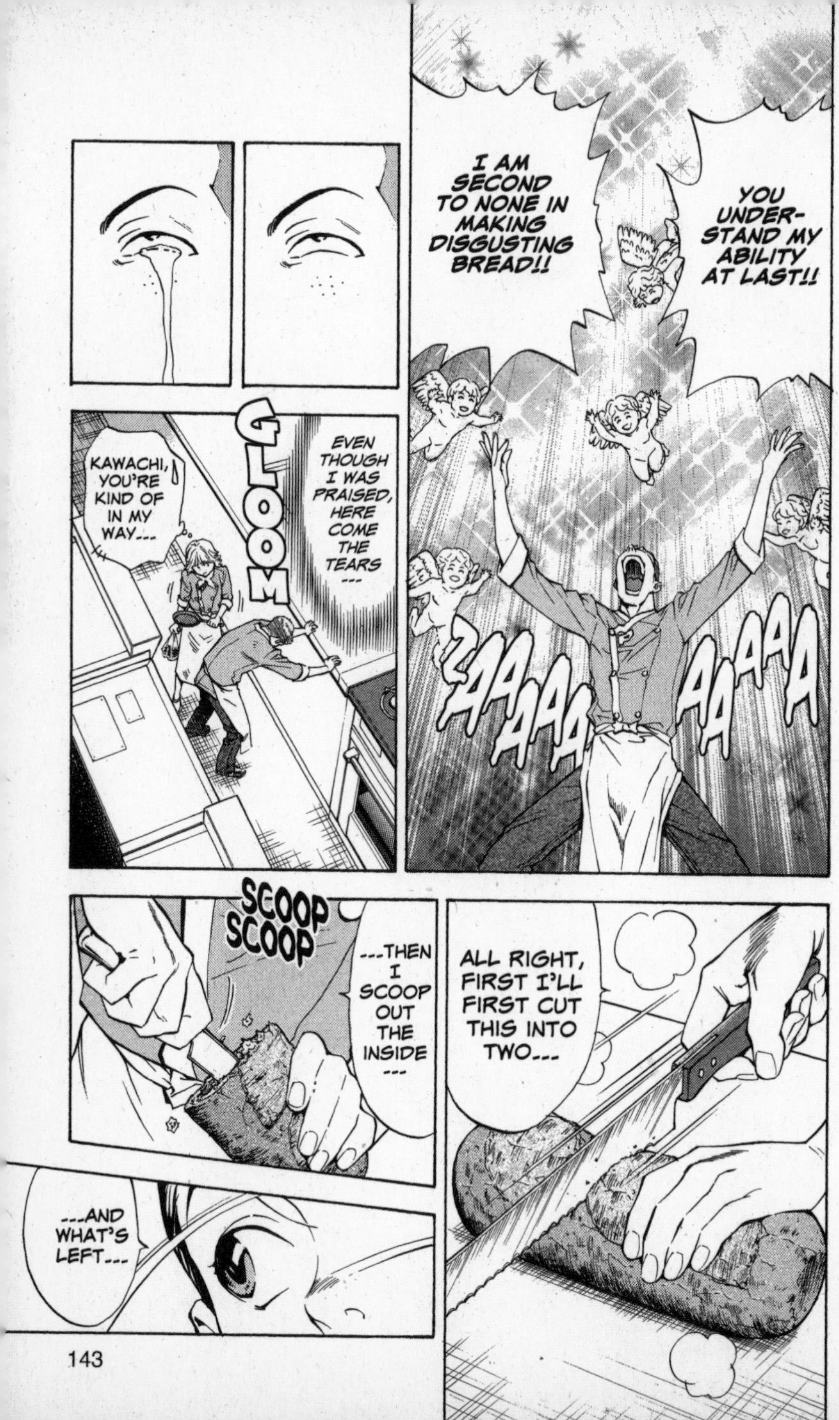
YOU UNDER-STAND MY ABILITY AT LAST!!
I AM SECOND TO NONE IN MAKING DISGUSTING BREAD!!
ZAAAAAAAAAAAAA
EVEN THOUGH I WAS PRAISED, HERE COME THE TEARS---
GLOOM
KAWACHI, YOU'RE KIND OF IN MY WAY---
ALL RIGHT, FIRST I'LL FIRST CUT THIS INTO TWO---
---THEN I SCOOP OUT THE INSIDE---
SCOOP SCOOP
---AND WHAT'S LEFT---

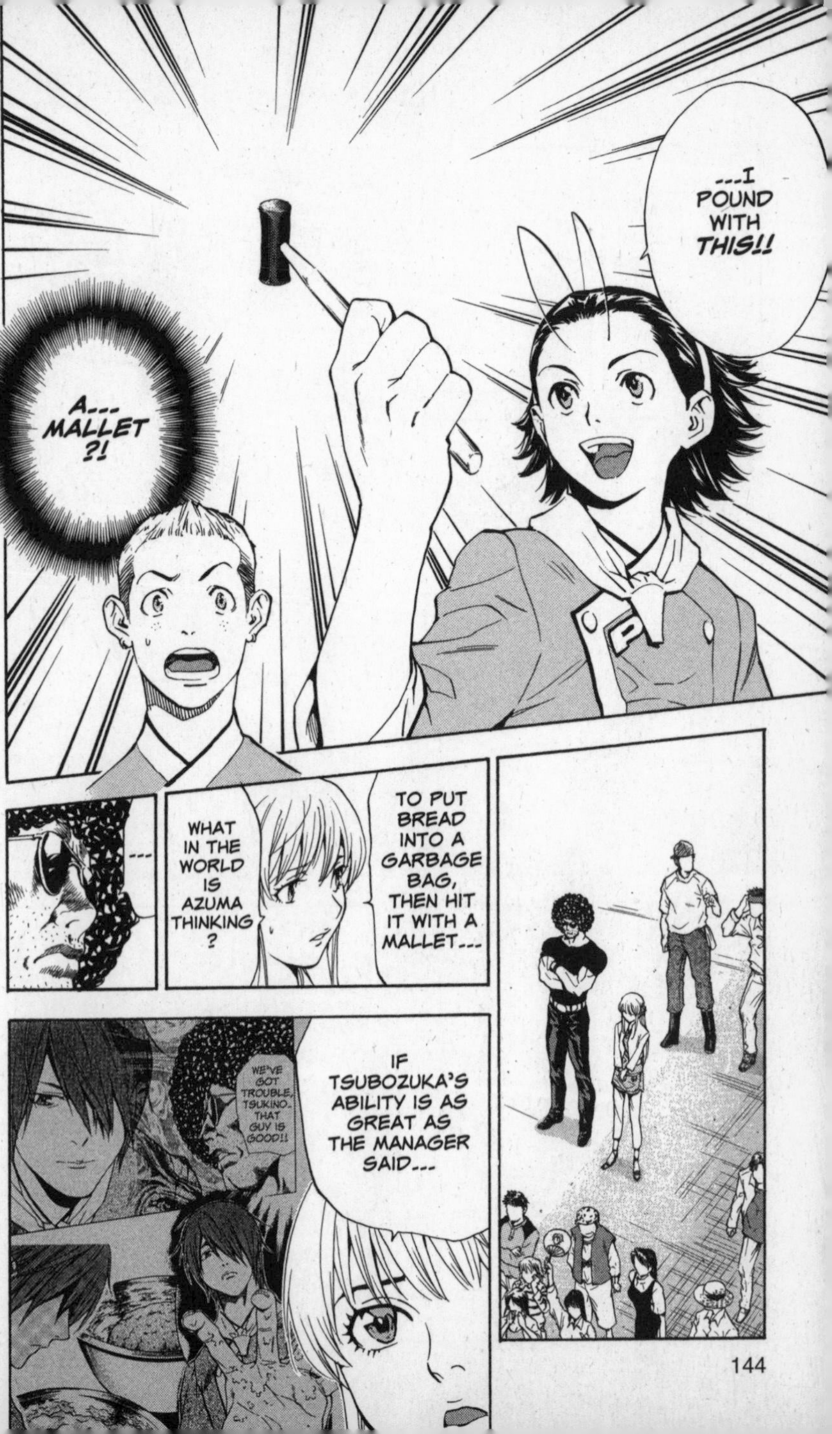
...I POUND WITH THIS!!
A... MALLET ?!
TO PUT BREAD INTO A GARBAGE BAG, THEN HIT IT WITH A MALLET...
WHAT IN THE WORLD IS AZUMA THINKING ?
...
IF TSUBOZUKA'S ABILITY IS AS GREAT AS THE MANAGER SAID...
WE'VE GOT TROUBLE, TSUKINO. THAT GUY IS GOOD!!

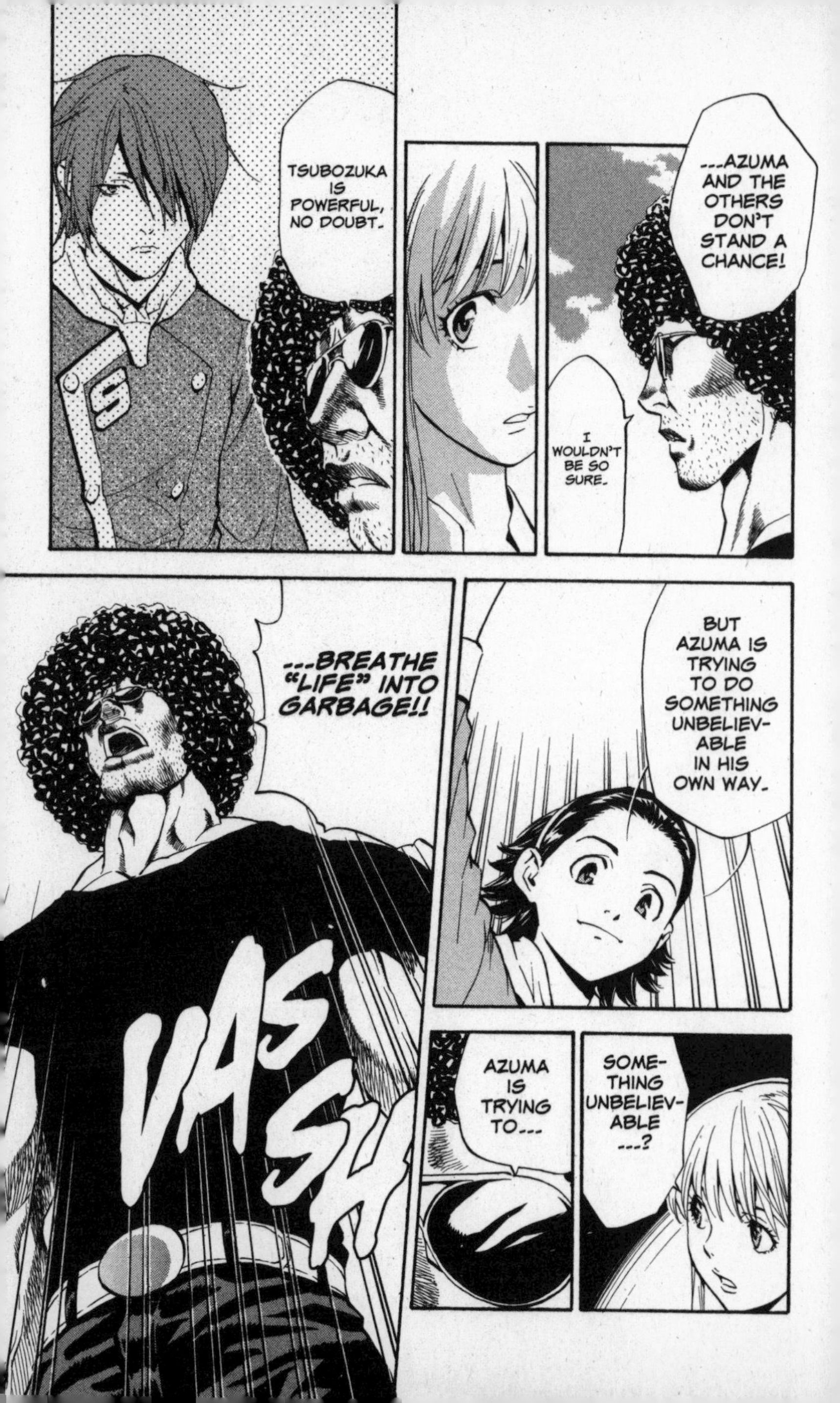
...AZUMA AND THE OTHERS DON'T STAND A CHANCE!
I WOULDN'T BE SO SURE.
TSUBOZUKA IS POWERFUL, NO DOUBT.
BUT AZUMA IS TRYING TO DO SOMETHING UNBELIEVABLE IN HIS OWN WAY.
SOMETHING UNBELIEVABLE...?
AZUMA IS TRYING TO...
...BREATHE "LIFE" INTO GARBAGE!!

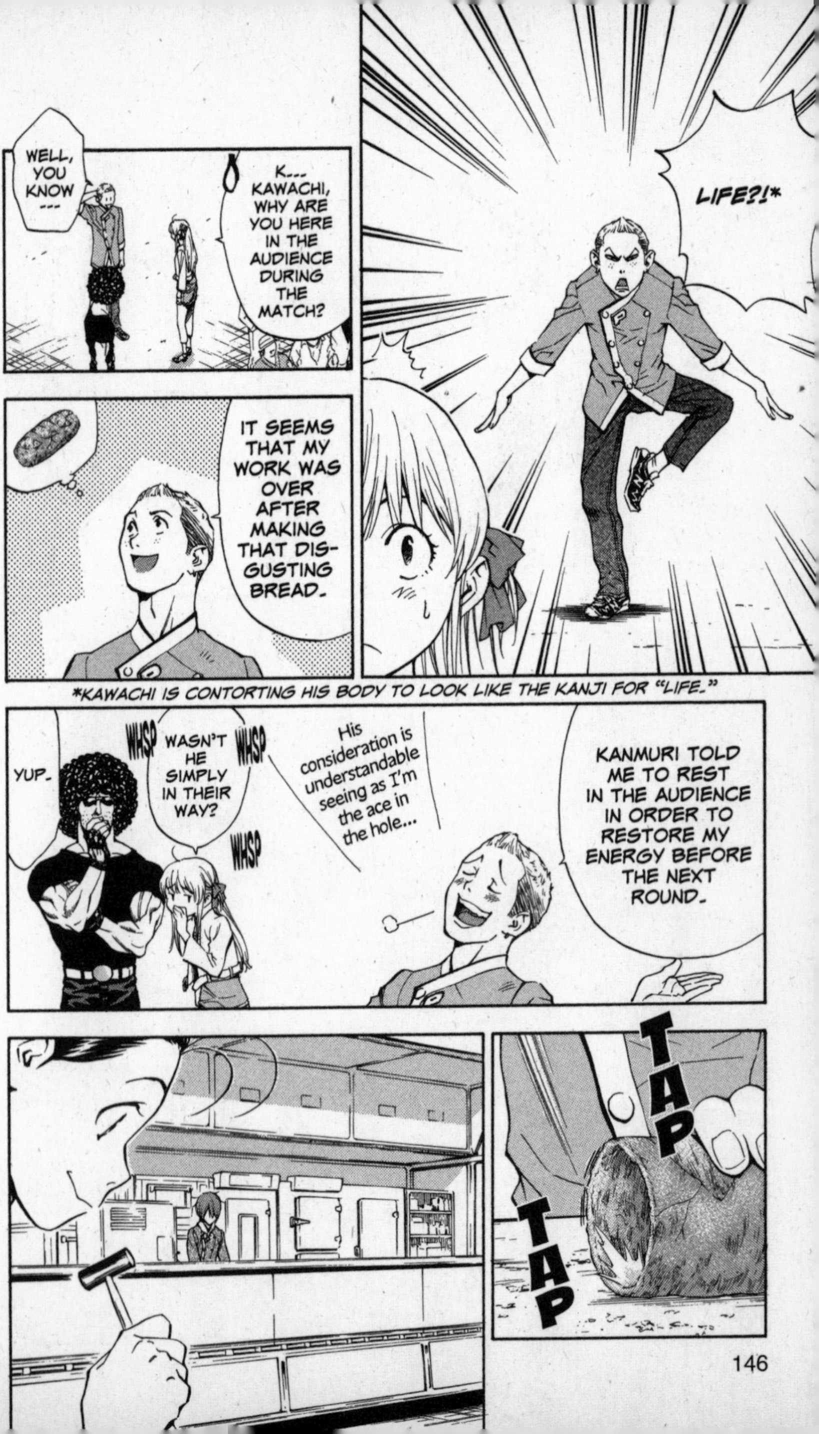
LIFE?!*
K... KAWACHI, WHY ARE YOU HERE IN THE AUDIENCE DURING THE MATCH?
WELL, YOU KNOW...
IT SEEMS THAT MY WORK WAS OVER AFTER MAKING THAT DIS-GUSTING BREAD.
KANMURI TOLD ME TO REST IN THE AUDIENCE IN ORDER TO RESTORE MY ENERGY BEFORE THE NEXT ROUND.
His consideration is understandable seeing as I'm the ace in the hole...
WHSP
WHSP
WASN'T HE SIMPLY IN THEIR WAY?
WHSP
YUP.
TAP
TAP

*KAWACHI IS CONTORTING HIS BODY TO LOOK LIKE THE KANJI FOR "LIFE."

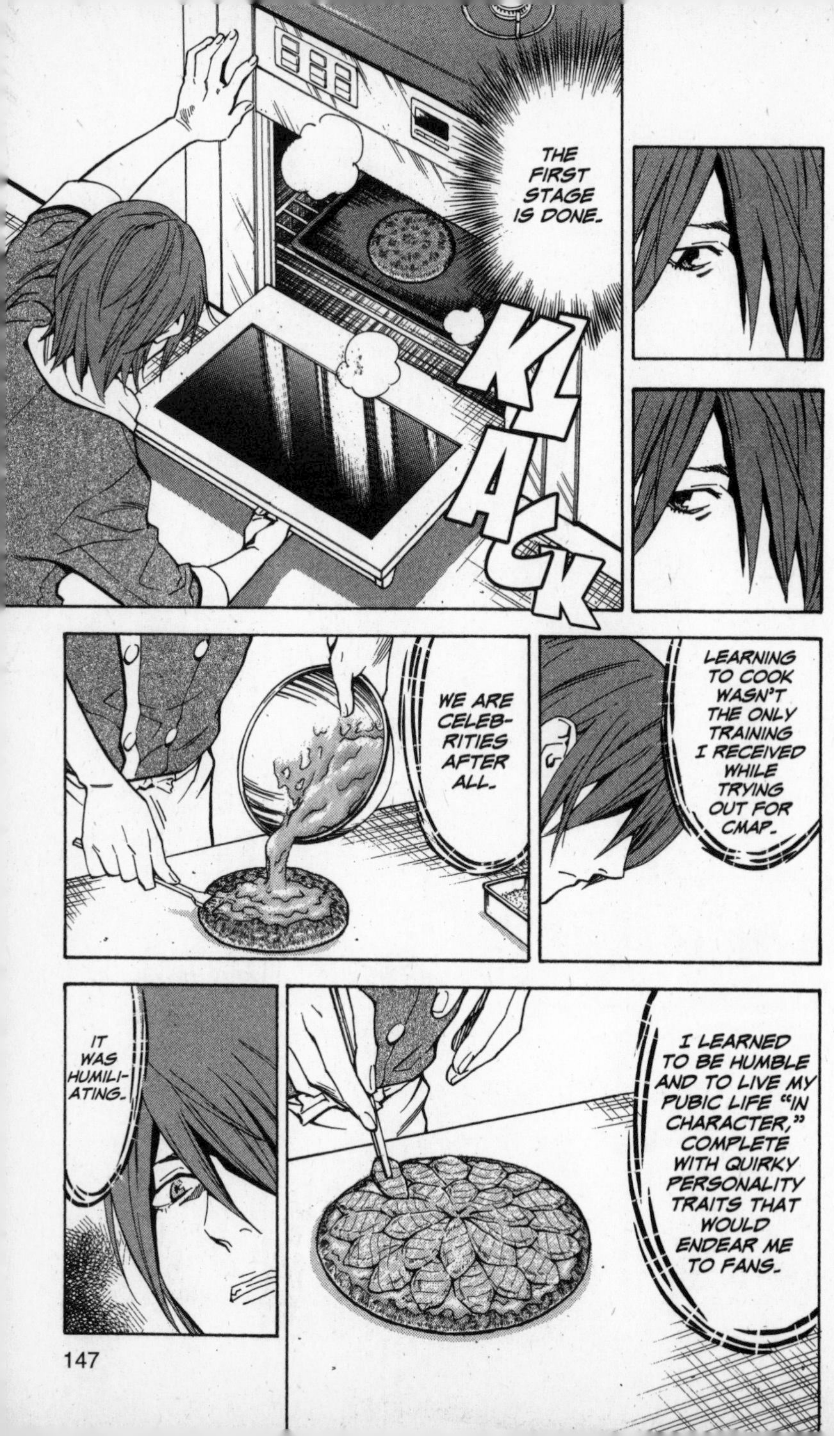
THE FIRST STAGE IS DONE.
KLACK
LEARNING TO COOK WASN'T THE ONLY TRAINING I RECEIVED WHILE TRYING OUT FOR CMAP.
WE ARE CELEB-RITIES AFTER ALL.
I LEARNED TO BE HUMBLE AND TO LIVE MY PUBIC LIFE "IN CHARACTER," COMPLETE WITH QUIRKY PERSONALITY TRAITS THAT WOULD ENDEAR ME TO FANS.
IT WAS HUMILI-ATING.

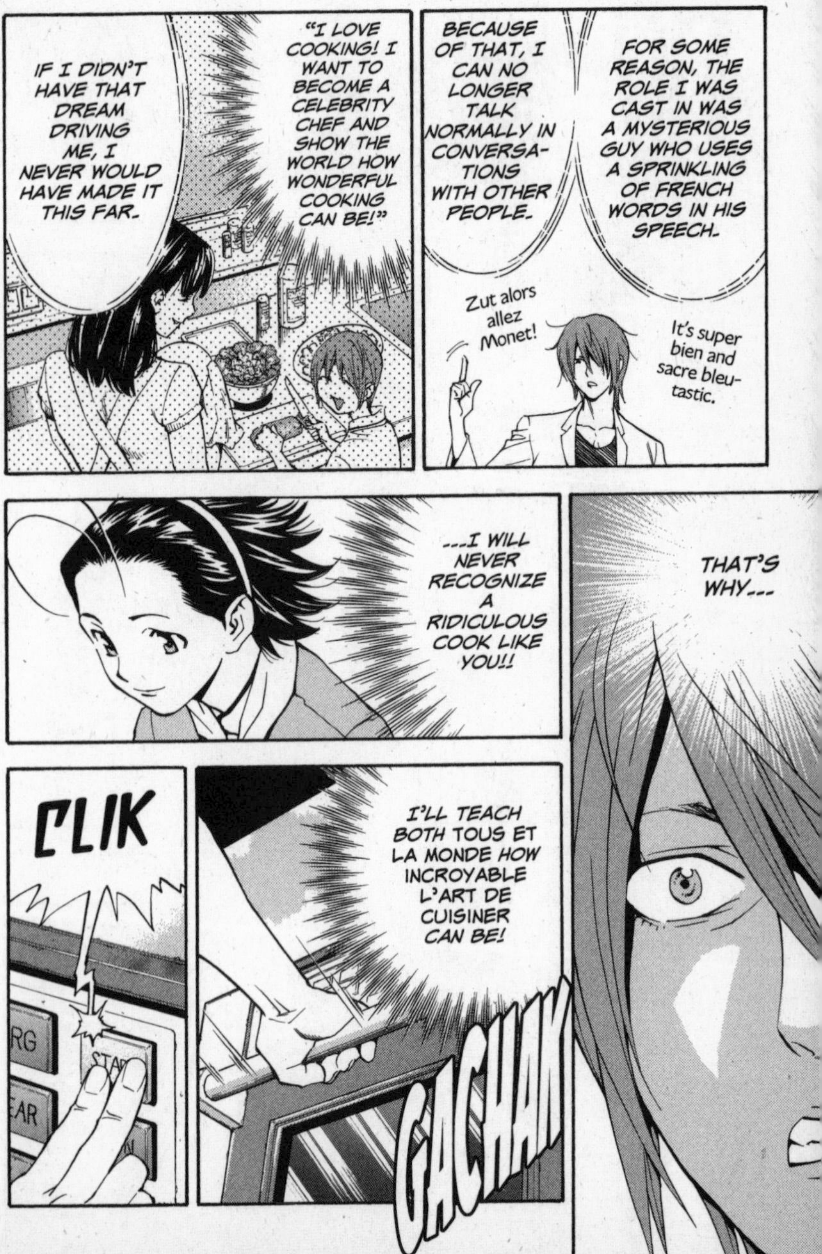
FOR SOME REASON, THE ROLE I WAS CAST IN WAS A MYSTERIOUS GUY WHO USES A SPRINKLING OF FRENCH WORDS IN HIS SPEECH.
BECAUSE OF THAT, I CAN NO LONGER TALK NORMALLY IN CONVERSATIONS WITH OTHER PEOPLE.
It's super bien and sacre bleu-tastic.
Zut alors allez Monet!
"I LOVE COOKING! I WANT TO BECOME A CELEBRITY CHEF AND SHOW THE WORLD HOW WONDERFUL COOKING CAN BE!"
IF I DIDN'T HAVE THAT DREAM DRIVING ME, I NEVER WOULD HAVE MADE IT THIS FAR.
THAT'S WHY...
GACHAN
...I WILL NEVER RECOGNIZE A RIDICULOUS COOK LIKE YOU!!
I'LL TEACH BOTH TOUS ET LA MONDE HOW INCROYABLE L'ART DE CUISINER CAN BE!
CLIK

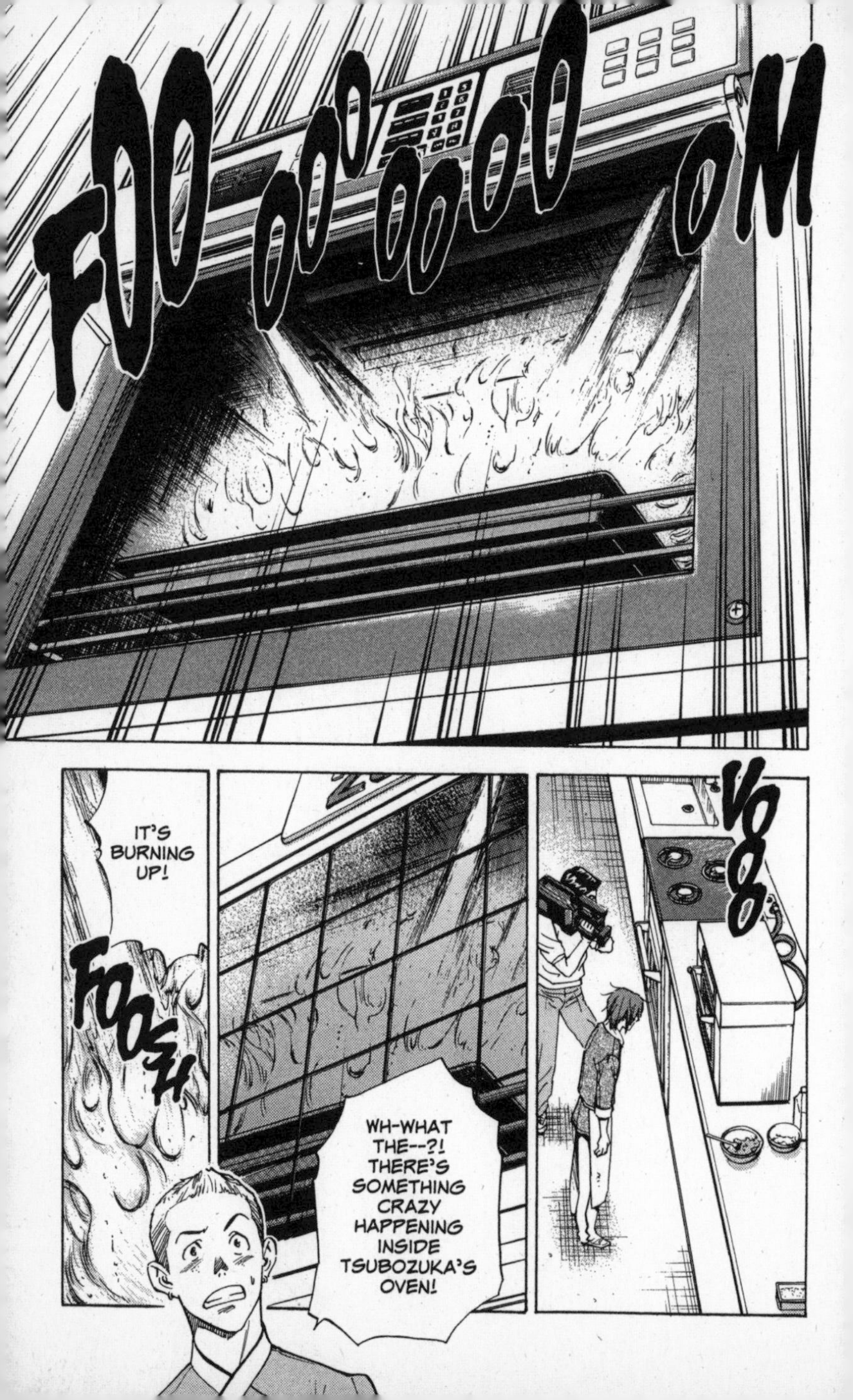
FOOOOOOOOOOOM
VOOO
WH-WHAT THE--?! THERE'S SOMETHING CRAZY HAPPENING INSIDE TSUBOZUKA'S OVEN!
IT'S BURNING UP!
FOOSH

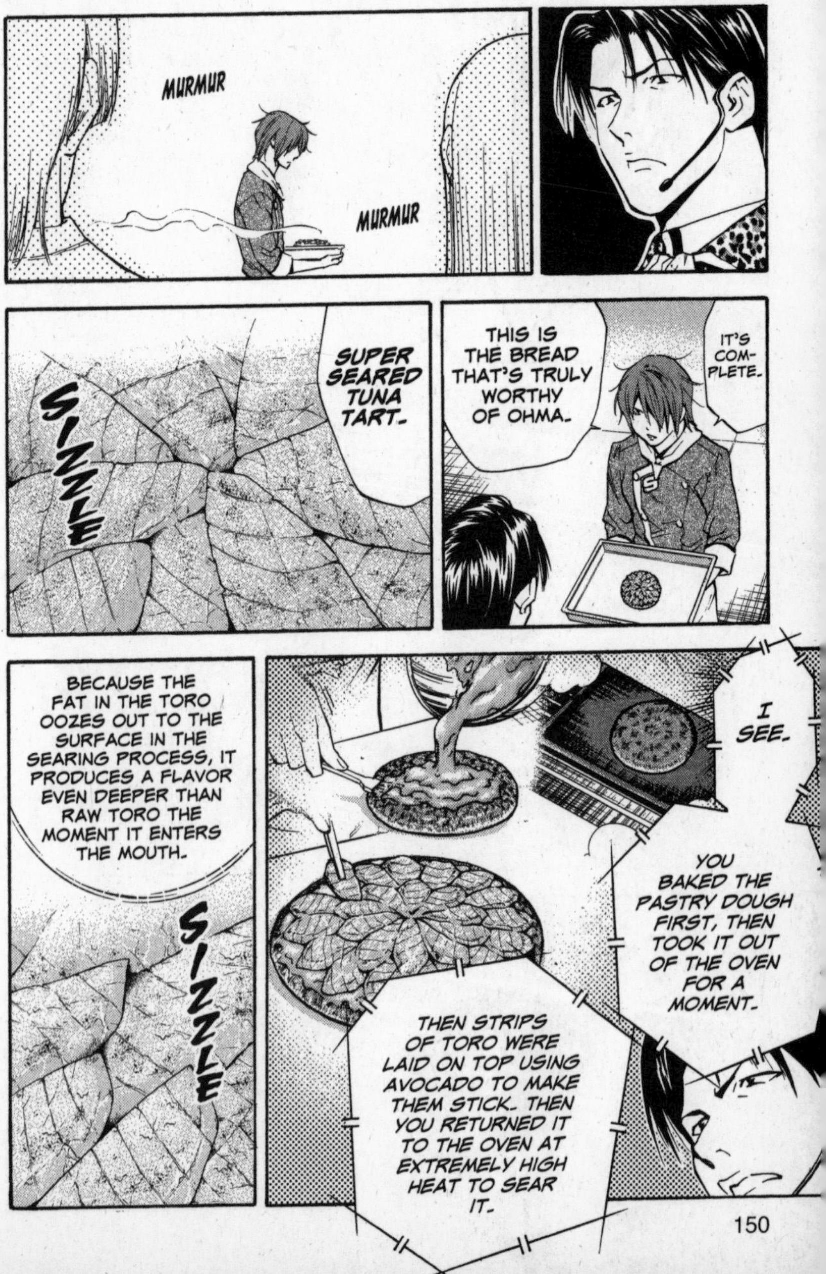
MURMUR
MURMUR
IT'S COMPLETE.
THIS IS THE BREAD THAT'S TRULY WORTHY OF OHMA.
SUPER SEARED TUNA TART.
SIZZLE
I SEE.
YOU BAKED THE PASTRY DOUGH FIRST, THEN TOOK IT OUT OF THE OVEN FOR A MOMENT.
THEN STRIPS OF TORO WERE LAID ON TOP USING AVOCADO TO MAKE THEM STICK. THEN YOU RETURNED IT TO THE OVEN AT EXTREMELY HIGH HEAT TO SEAR IT.
BECAUSE THE FAT IN THE TORO OOZES OUT TO THE SURFACE IN THE SEARING PROCESS, IT PRODUCES A FLAVOR EVEN DEEPER THAN RAW TORO THE MOMENT IT ENTERS THE MOUTH.
SIZZLE

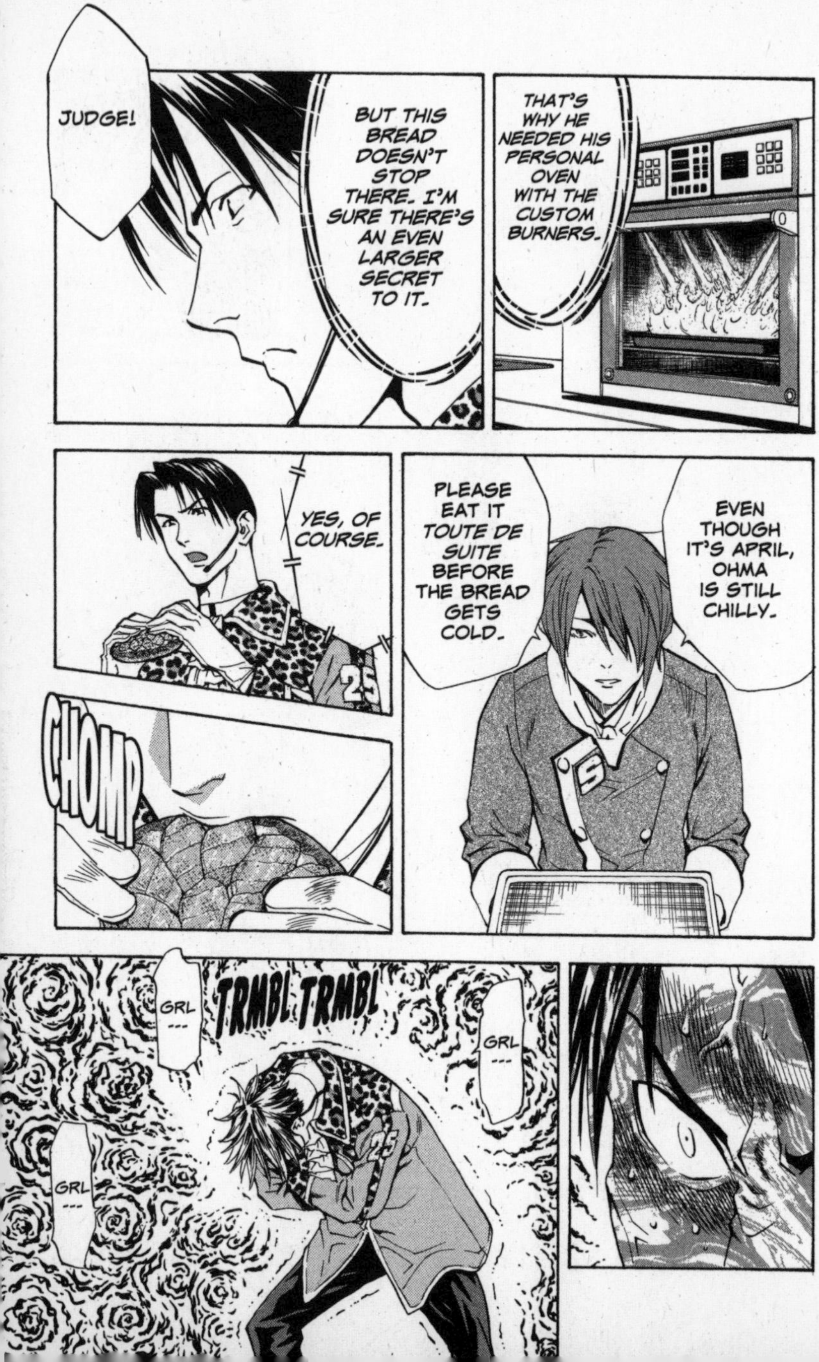
THAT'S WHY HE NEEDED HIS PERSONAL OVEN WITH THE CUSTOM BURNERS.
BUT THIS BREAD DOESN'T STOP THERE. I'M SURE THERE'S AN EVEN LARGER SECRET TO IT.
JUDGE!
EVEN THOUGH IT'S APRIL, OHMA IS STILL CHILLY.
PLEASE EAT IT TOUTE DE SUITE BEFORE THE BREAD GETS COLD.
YES, OF COURSE.
CHOMP
GRL ---
TRMBL TRMBL
GRL ---
GRL ---

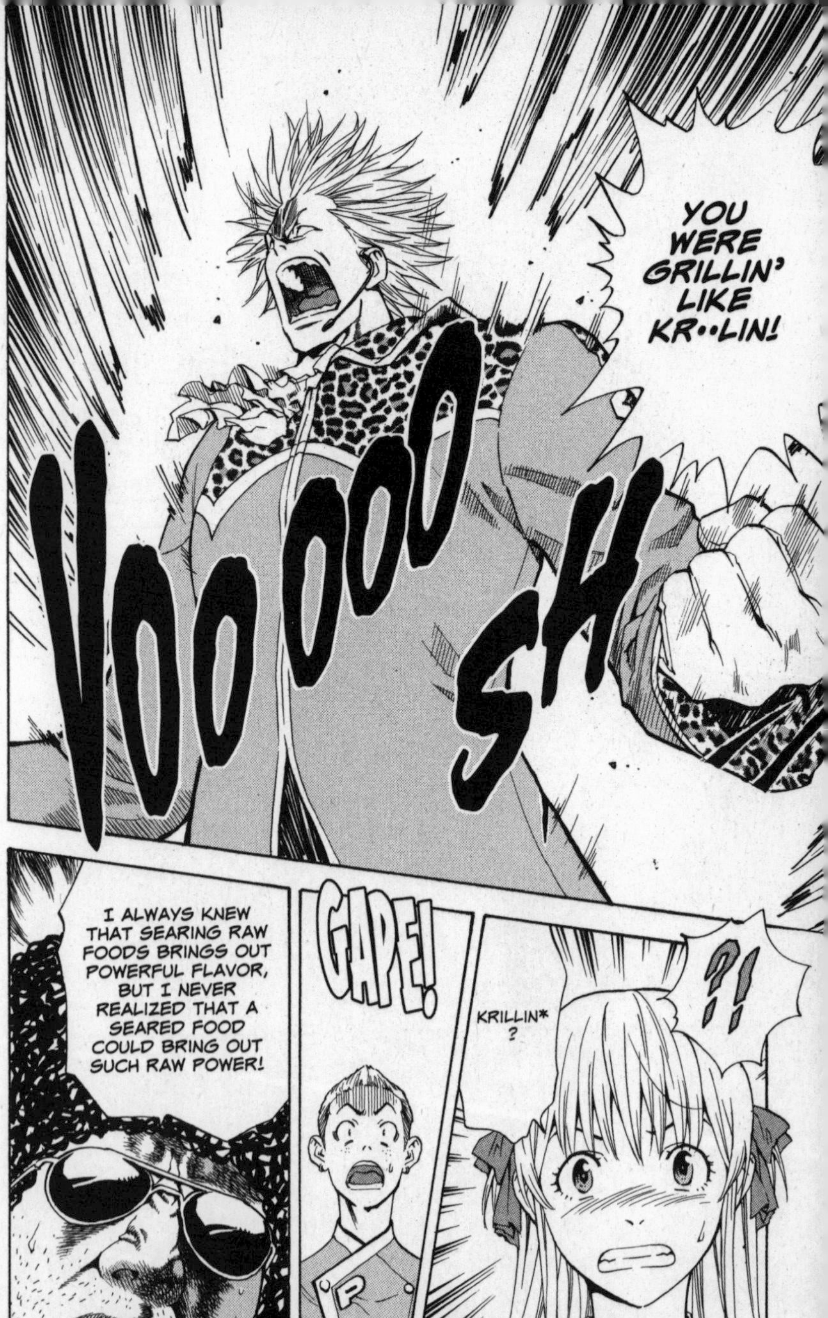
YOU WERE GRILLIN' LIKE KR••LIN!
VOOOOOOSH
?!
KRILLIN* ?
GAPE!
I ALWAYS KNEW THAT SEARING RAW FOODS BRINGS OUT POWERFUL FLAVOR, BUT I NEVER REALIZED THAT A SEARED FOOD COULD BRING OUT SUCH RAW POWER!

KR••LIN: AS IN THE BAD GUY FROM POPULAR MANGA AND ANIME SERIES D••GON B••L

Super Kure Yana Gari	←	Super Sured Tana Gart	←	Super Seared Tuna Tart

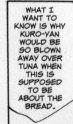

THEN... WHAT IS HE?!

?!

HE HAS **EVOLVED.** HE IS NO LONGER THE SAME KURO-YANAGI WE ONCE KNEW.

PANT PANT

I SHOULD HAVE EXPECTED NO LESS FROM A MEMBER OF CMAP. IT'S A WONDERFUL RESULT. ORA* -- NO, I-- WAS MOVED.

PANT PANT

PANT

WHAT DO YOU MEAN ?!

ZOOOSH

SUPER KURO-YANAGI !

WHAT I WANT TO KNOW IS WHY KURO-YAN WOULD BE SO BLOWN AWAY OVER TUNA WHEN THIS IS SUPPOSED TO BE ABOUT THE BREAD.

NEVER MIND ABOUT THAT.

WHAT ARE YOU TALKING ABOUT ?

"Ora" ...?

UH OH.... HE'S DRAWING ON PRETTY EXPLOSIVE MATERIAL FOR HIS REACTION.

153

*"ORA": A REFERENCE TO HOW G•KU IN D••GON B••L REFERS TO HIMSELF.

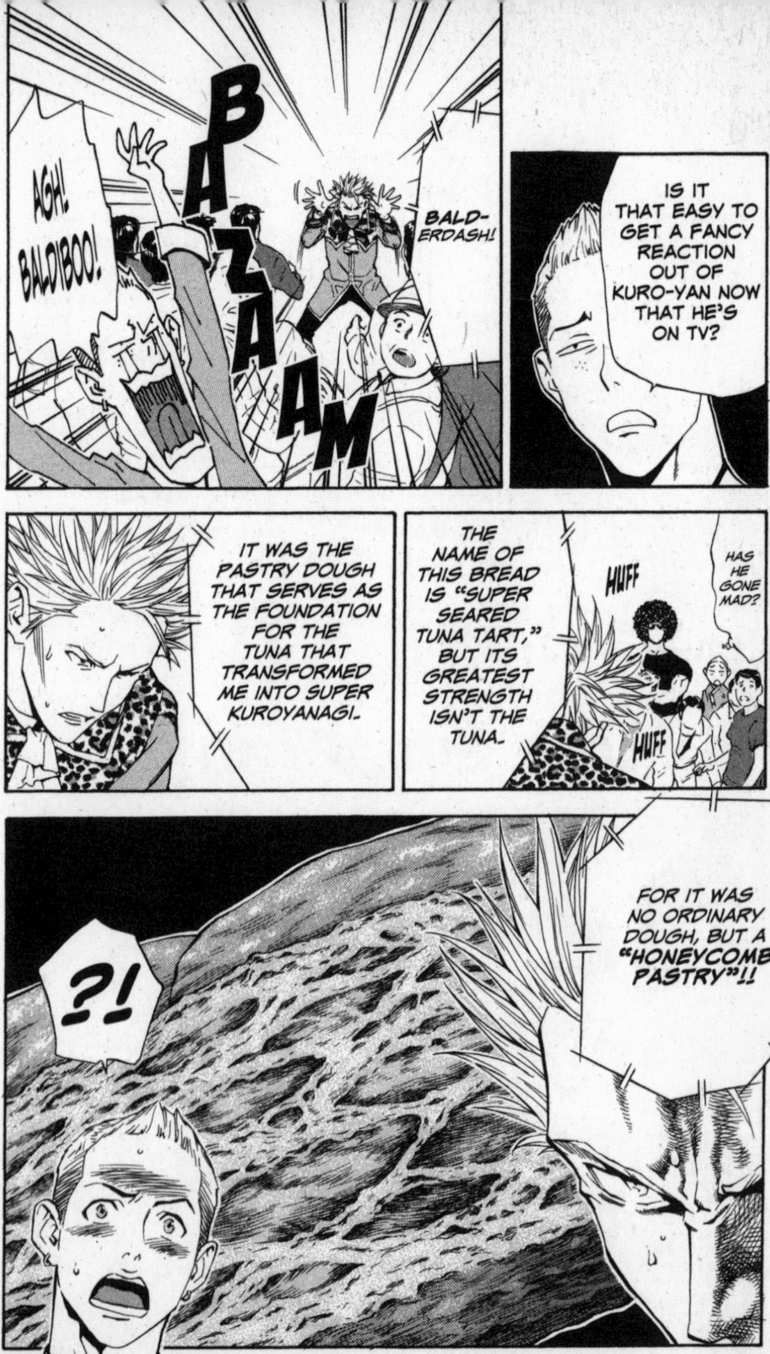
IS IT THAT EASY TO GET A FANCY REACTION OUT OF KURO-YAN NOW THAT HE'S ON TV?
BALD-ERDASH!
BAZAAM
AGH! BALDIBOO!
HAS HE GONE MAD?
THE NAME OF THIS BREAD IS "SUPER SEARED TUNA TART," BUT ITS GREATEST STRENGTH ISN'T THE TUNA.
HUFF
HUFF
IT WAS THE PASTRY DOUGH THAT SERVES AS THE FOUNDATION FOR THE TUNA THAT TRANSFORMED ME INTO SUPER KUROYANAGI.
FOR IT WAS NO ORDINARY DOUGH, BUT A "HONEYCOMB PASTRY"!!
?!

Story 132: Further Evolution

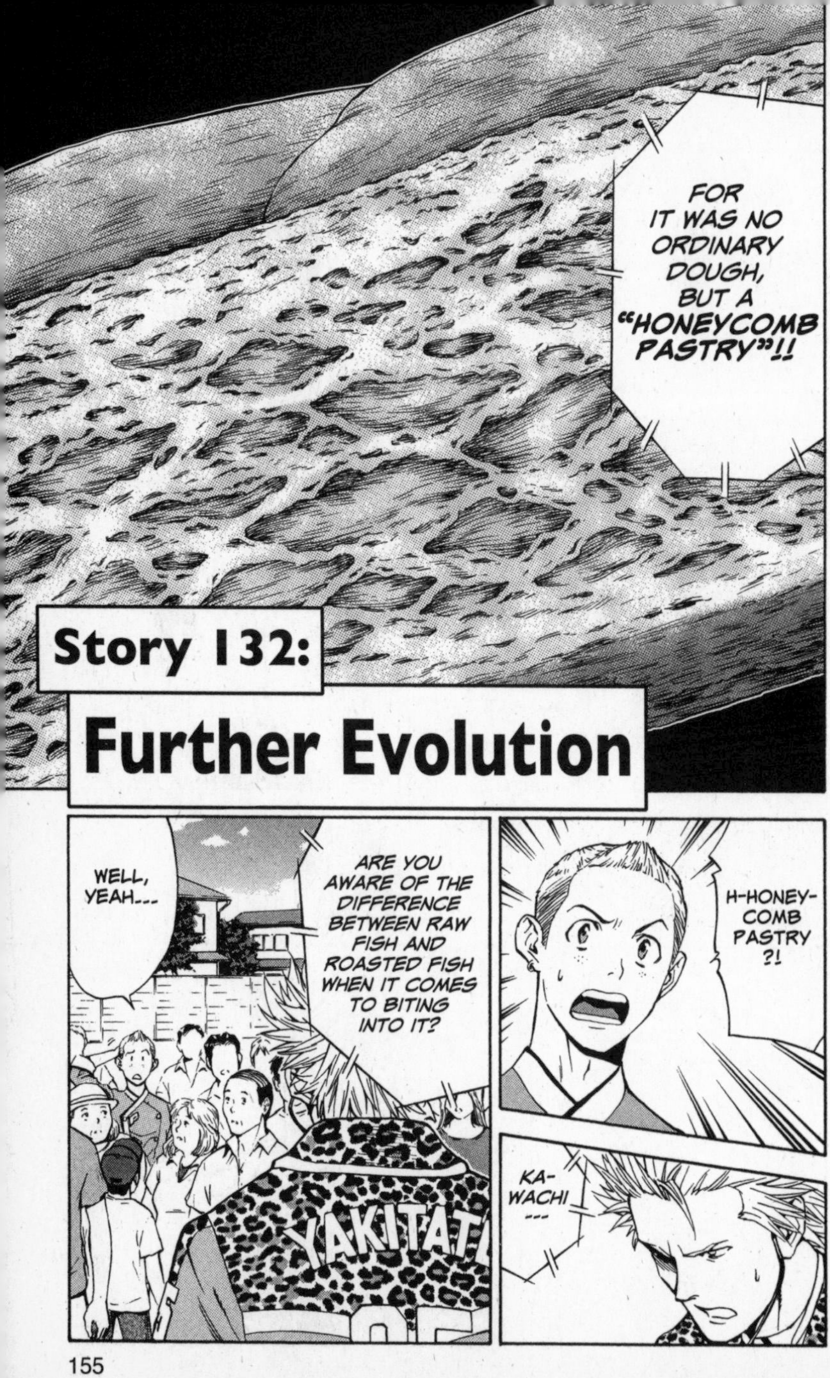
FOR IT WAS NO ORDINARY DOUGH, BUT A "HONEYCOMB PASTRY"!!
Story 132:
Further Evolution
H-HONEY-COMB PASTRY?!
KA-WACHI...
ARE YOU AWARE OF THE DIFFERENCE BETWEEN RAW FISH AND ROASTED FISH WHEN IT COMES TO BITING INTO IT?
WELL, YEAH...
YAKITATE

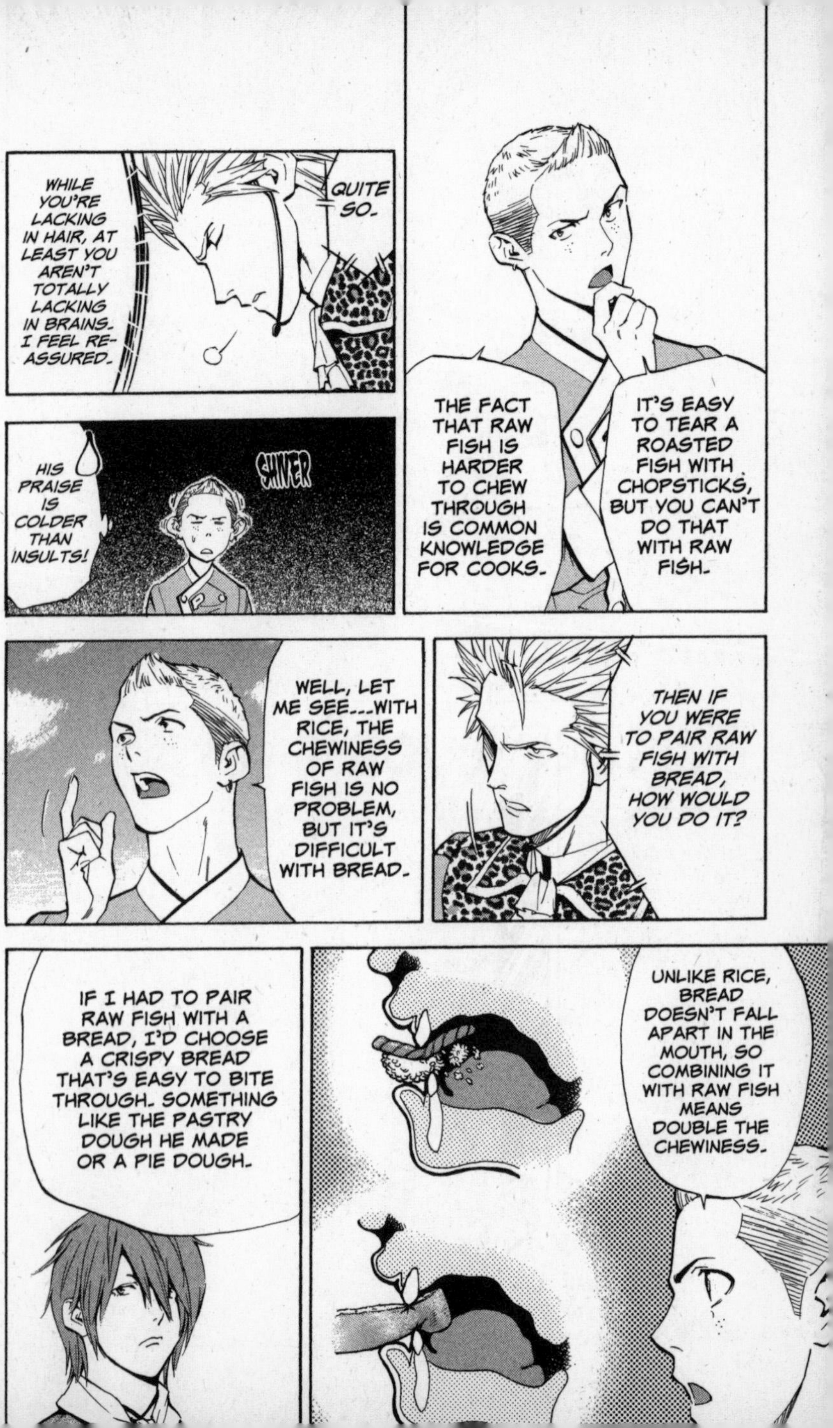
IT'S EASY TO TEAR A ROASTED FISH WITH CHOPSTICKS, BUT YOU CAN'T DO THAT WITH RAW FISH.
THE FACT THAT RAW FISH IS HARDER TO CHEW THROUGH IS COMMON KNOWLEDGE FOR COOKS.
QUITE SO.
WHILE YOU'RE LACKING IN HAIR, AT LEAST YOU AREN'T TOTALLY LACKING IN BRAINS. I FEEL RE-ASSURED.
SHIVER
HIS PRAISE IS COLDER THAN INSULTS!
THEN IF YOU WERE TO PAIR RAW FISH WITH BREAD, HOW WOULD YOU DO IT?
WELL, LET ME SEE...WITH RICE, THE CHEWINESS OF RAW FISH IS NO PROBLEM, BUT IT'S DIFFICULT WITH BREAD.
UNLIKE RICE, BREAD DOESN'T FALL APART IN THE MOUTH, SO COMBINING IT WITH RAW FISH MEANS DOUBLE THE CHEWINESS.
IF I HAD TO PAIR RAW FISH WITH A BREAD, I'D CHOOSE A CRISPY BREAD THAT'S EASY TO BITE THROUGH. SOMETHING LIKE THE PASTRY DOUGH HE MADE OR A PIE DOUGH.

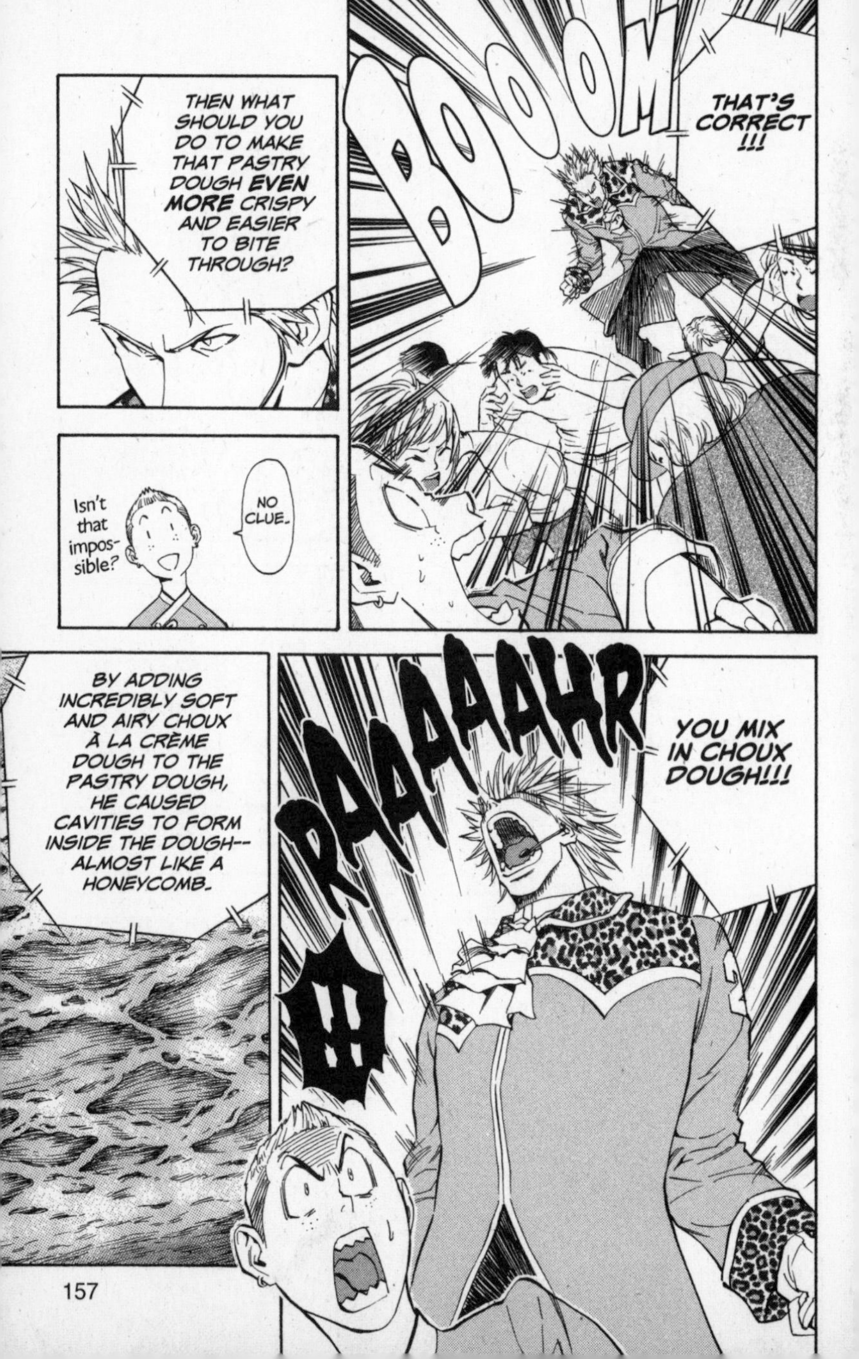
BOOOOM
THAT'S CORRECT!!!
THEN WHAT SHOULD YOU DO TO MAKE THAT PASTRY DOUGH **EVEN MORE** CRISPY AND EASIER TO BITE THROUGH?
NO CLUE.
Isn't that impossible?
RAAAAAHR
YOU MIX IN CHOUX DOUGH!!!
!!
BY ADDING INCREDIBLY SOFT AND AIRY CHOUX À LA CRÈME DOUGH TO THE PASTRY DOUGH, HE CAUSED CAVITIES TO FORM INSIDE THE DOUGH--ALMOST LIKE A HONEYCOMB.

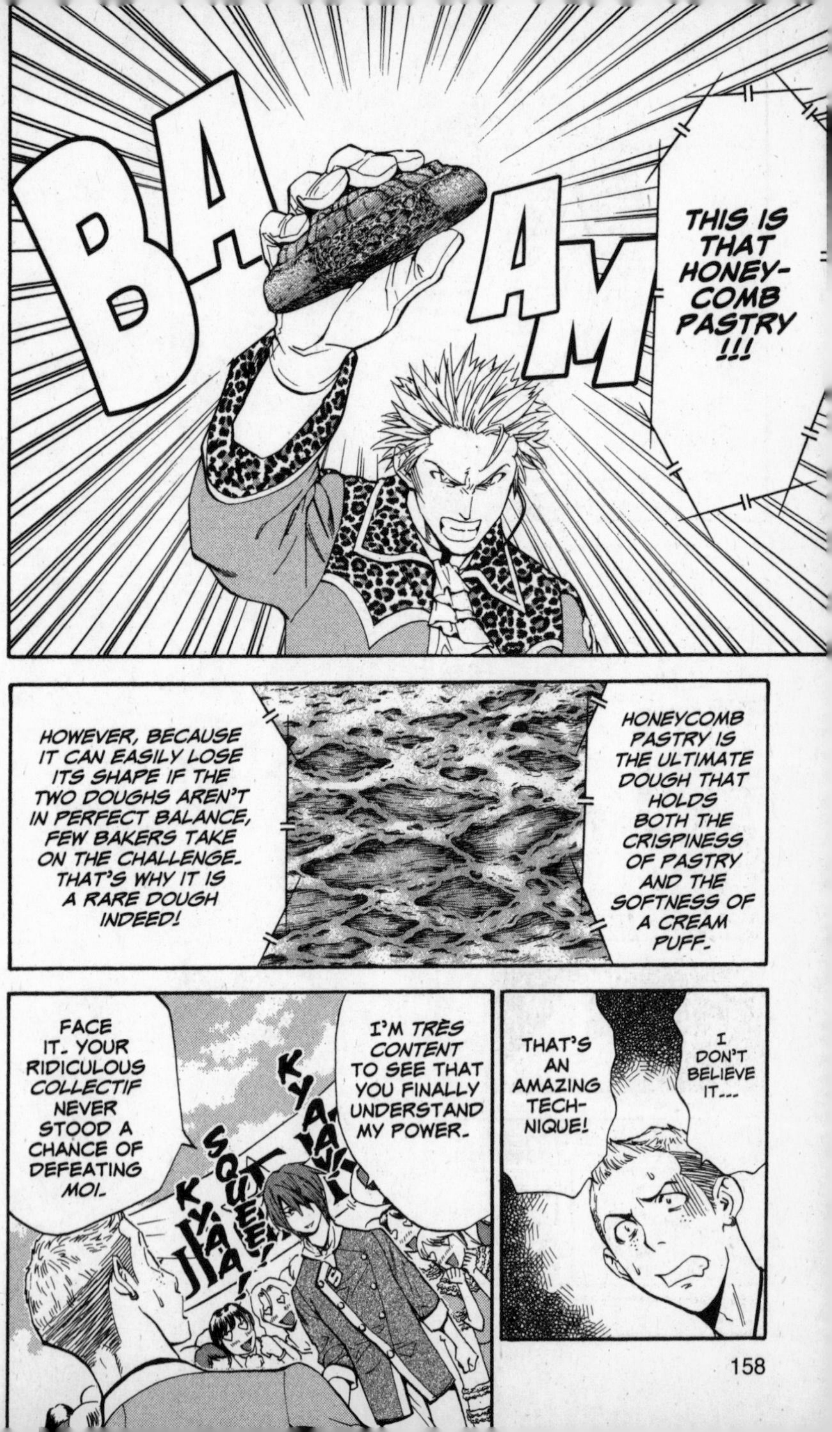
BAAM
THIS IS THAT HONEY-COMB PASTRY!!!
HONEYCOMB PASTRY IS THE ULTIMATE DOUGH THAT HOLDS BOTH THE CRISPINESS OF PASTRY AND THE SOFTNESS OF A CREAM PUFF.
HOWEVER, BECAUSE IT CAN EASILY LOSE ITS SHAPE IF THE TWO DOUGHS AREN'T IN PERFECT BALANCE, FEW BAKERS TAKE ON THE CHALLENGE. THAT'S WHY IT IS A RARE DOUGH INDEED!
I DON'T BELIEVE IT...
THAT'S AN AMAZING TECH-NIQUE!
I'M TRÈS CONTENT TO SEE THAT YOU FINALLY UNDERSTAND MY POWER.
KYAAA!
SQUEEE!
KYAAA!
FACE IT. YOUR RIDICULOUS COLLECTIF NEVER STOOD A CHANCE OF DEFEATING MOI.

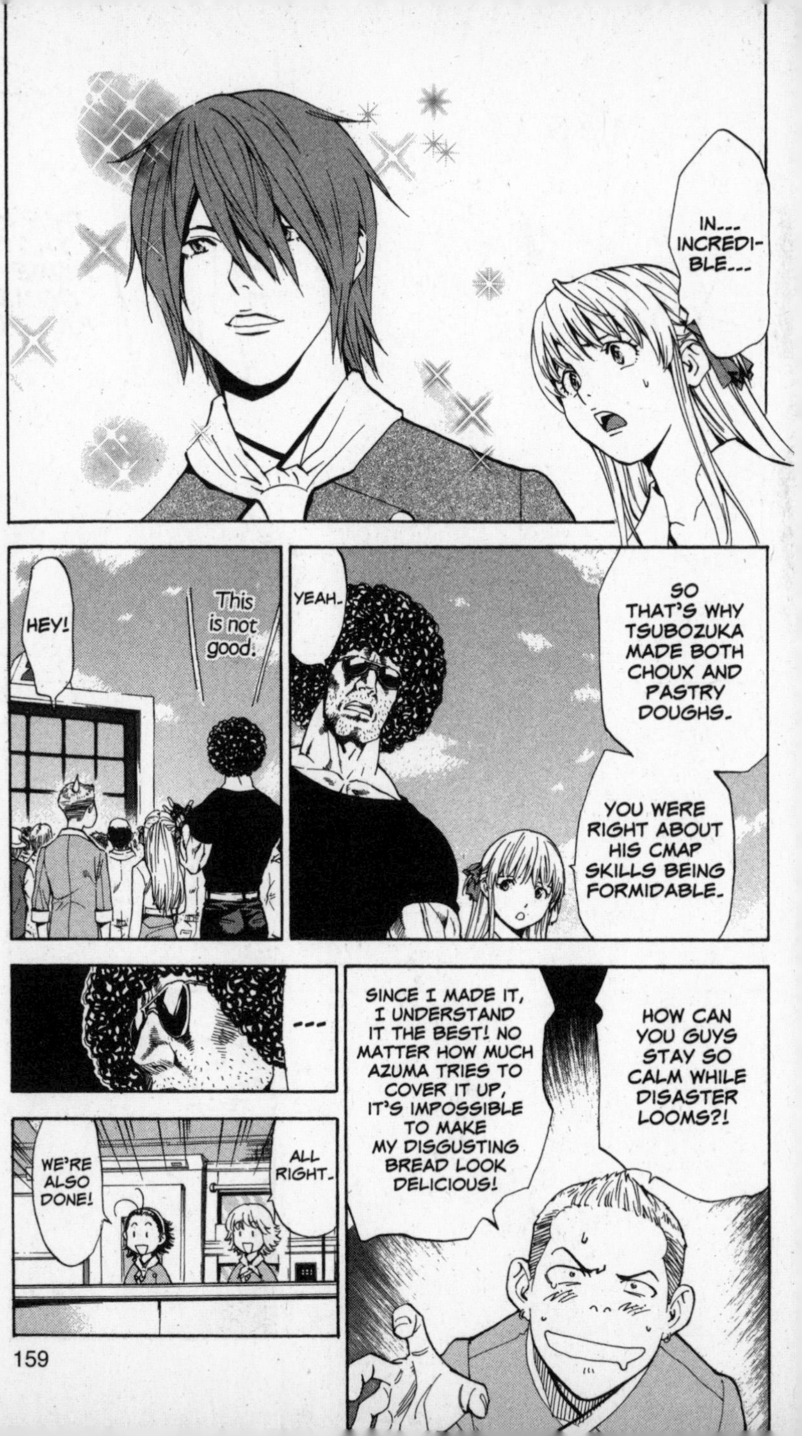

IN... INCREDIBLE...
SO THAT'S WHY TSUBOZUKA MADE BOTH CHOUX AND PASTRY DOUGHS.
YOU WERE RIGHT ABOUT HIS CMAP SKILLS BEING FORMIDABLE.
YEAH.
This is not good.
HEY!
HOW CAN YOU GUYS STAY SO CALM WHILE DISASTER LOOMS?!
SINCE I MADE IT, I UNDERSTAND IT THE BEST! NO MATTER HOW MUCH AZUMA TRIES TO COVER IT UP, IT'S IMPOSSIBLE TO MAKE MY DISGUSTING BREAD LOOK DELICIOUS!
...
ALL RIGHT.
WE'RE ALSO DONE!

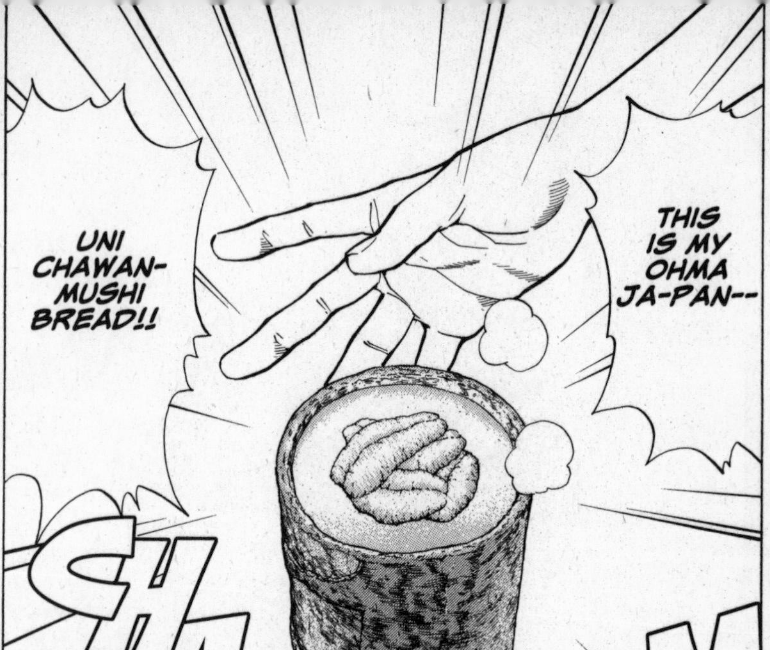
THIS IS MY OHMA JA-PAN--
UNI CHAWAN-MUSHI BREAD!!
CHA-WHAAAM

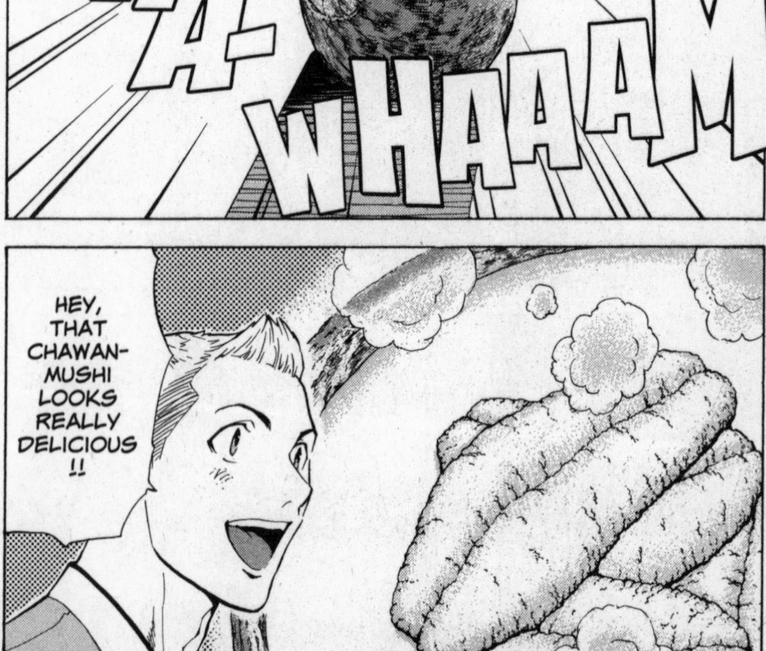
HEY, THAT CHAWAN-MUSHI LOOKS REALLY DELICIOUS!!

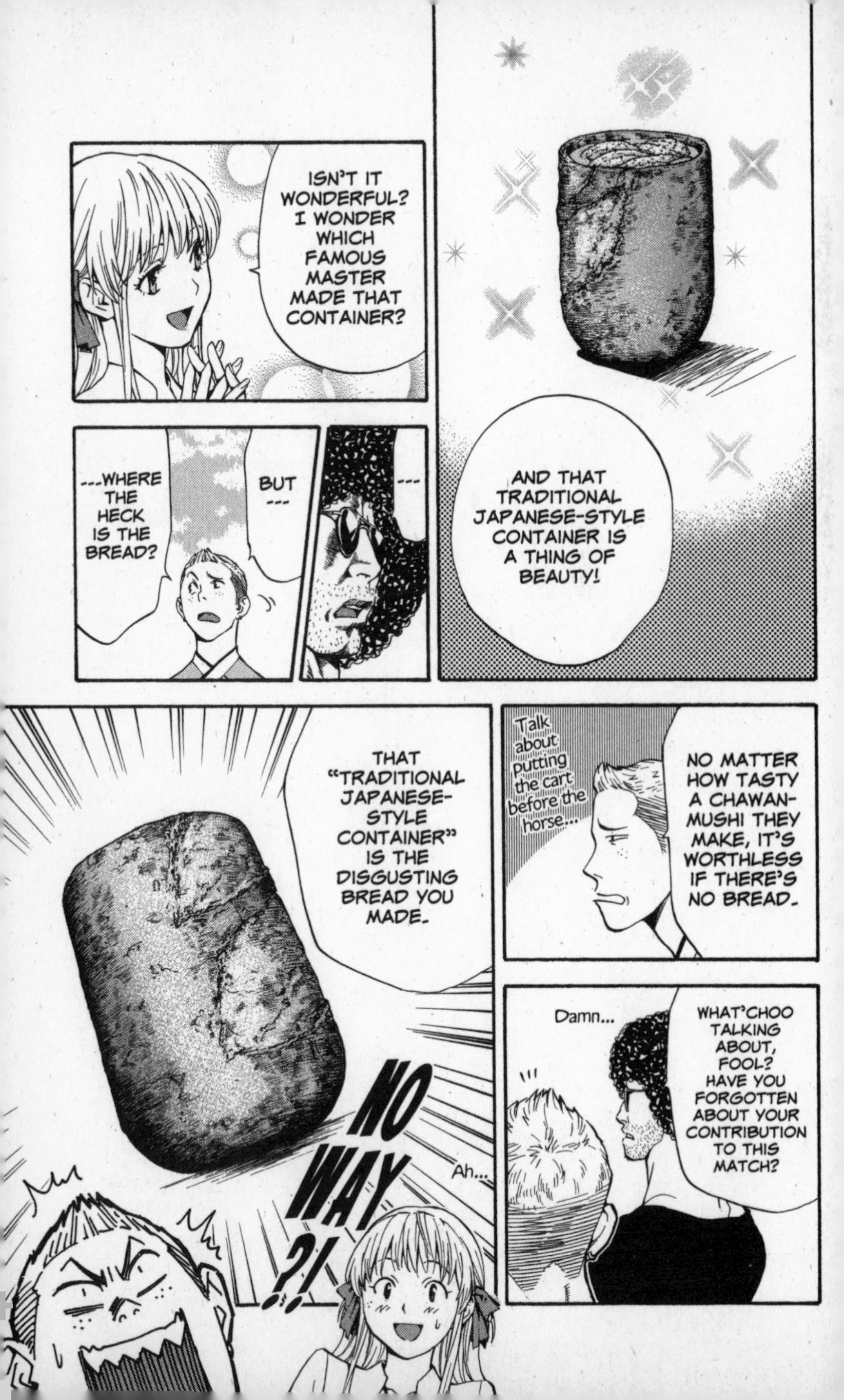
AND THAT TRADITIONAL JAPANESE-STYLE CONTAINER IS A THING OF BEAUTY!
ISN'T IT WONDERFUL? I WONDER WHICH FAMOUS MASTER MADE THAT CONTAINER?

BUT ---
---WHERE THE HECK IS THE BREAD?
NO MATTER HOW TASTY A CHAWAN-MUSHI THEY MAKE, IT'S WORTHLESS IF THERE'S NO BREAD.
Talk about putting the cart before the horse...
WHAT'CHOO TALKING ABOUT, FOOL? HAVE YOU FORGOTTEN ABOUT YOUR CONTRIBUTION TO THIS MATCH?
Damn...
THAT "TRADITIONAL JAPANESE-STYLE CONTAINER" IS THE DISGUSTING BREAD YOU MADE.
NO WAY?!
Ah...

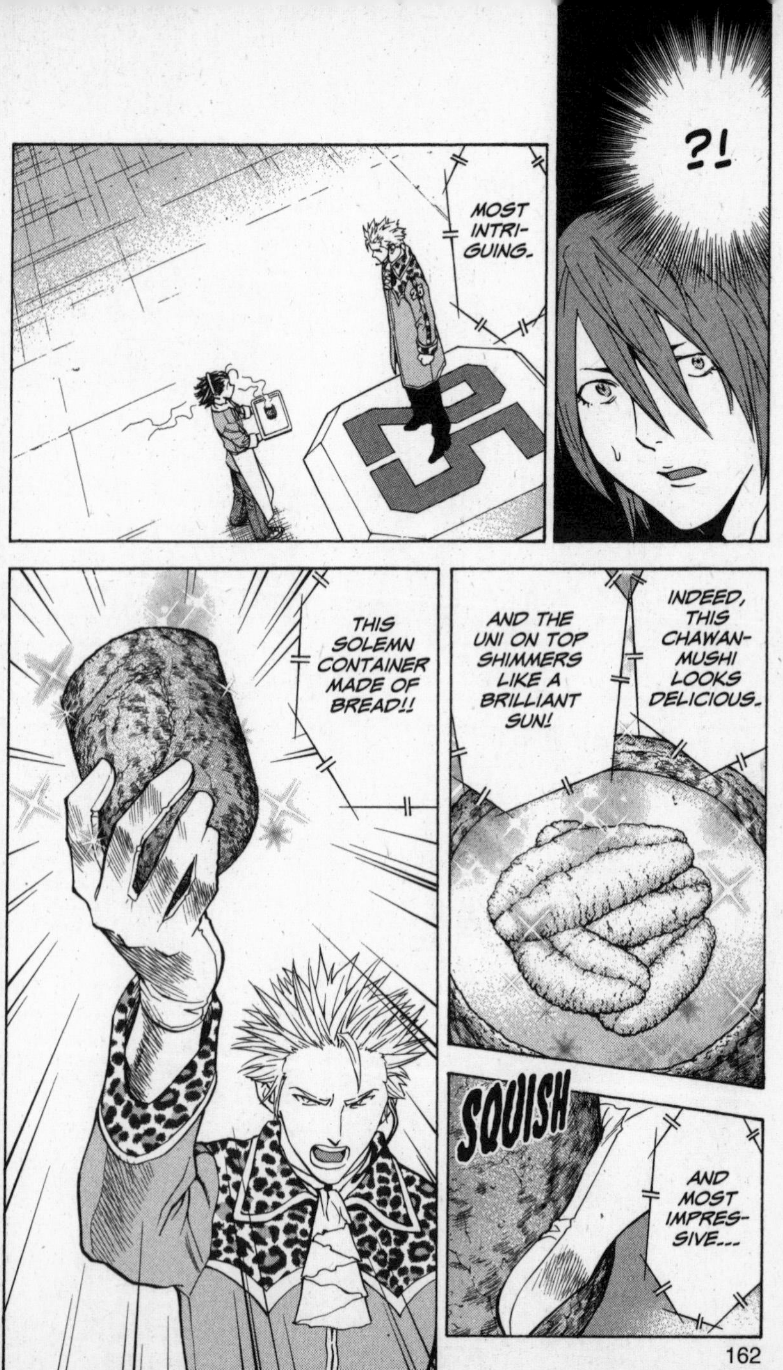
?!
MOST INTRI-GUING.
INDEED, THIS CHAWAN-MUSHI LOOKS DELICIOUS.
AND THE UNI ON TOP SHIMMERS LIKE A BRILLIANT SUN!
SQUISH
AND MOST IMPRES-SIVE...
THIS SOLEMN CONTAINER MADE OF BREAD!!

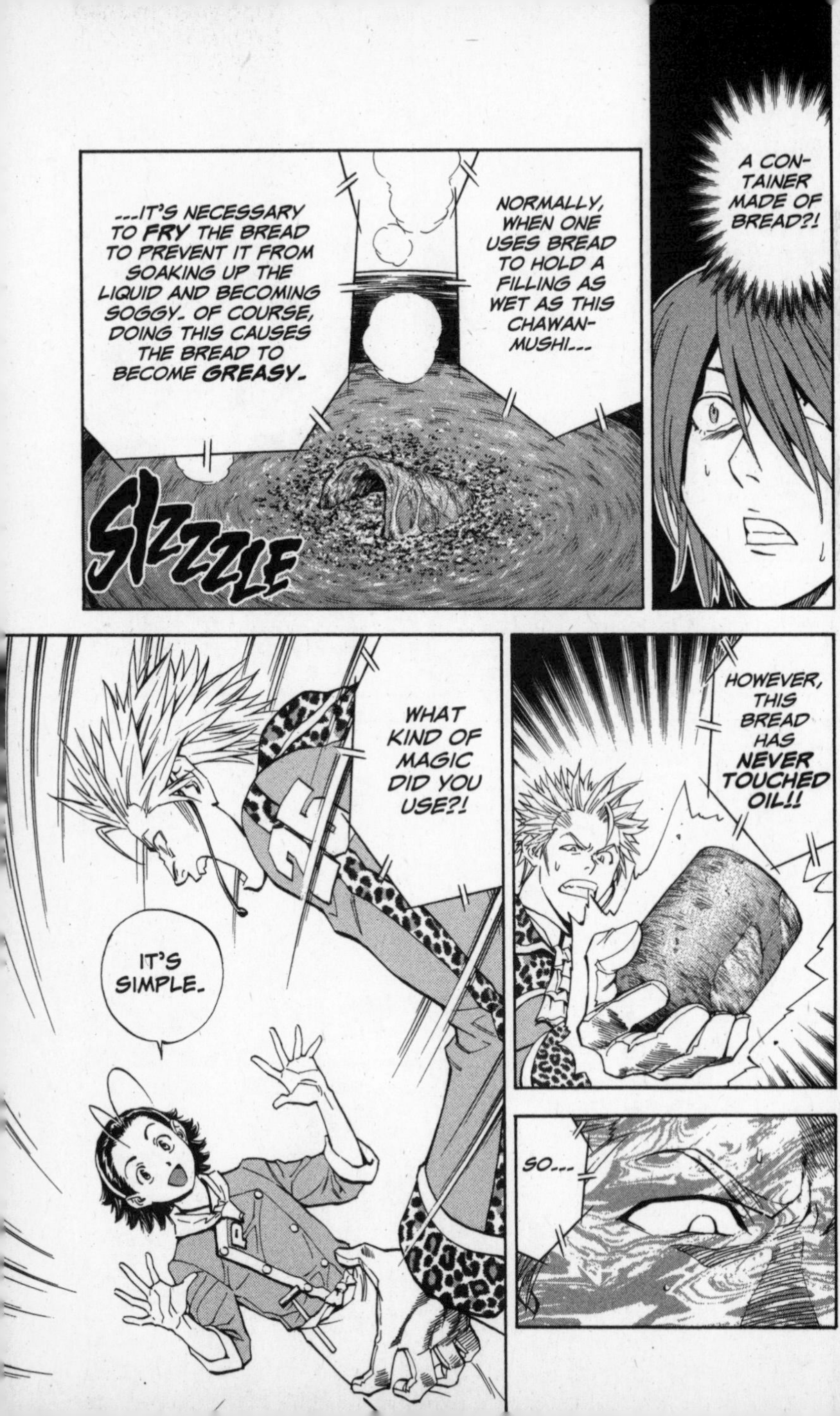
A CON-TAINER MADE OF BREAD?!
NORMALLY, WHEN ONE USES BREAD TO HOLD A FILLING AS WET AS THIS CHAWAN-MUSHI...
...IT'S NECESSARY TO **FRY** THE BREAD TO PREVENT IT FROM SOAKING UP THE LIQUID AND BECOMING SOGGY. OF COURSE, DOING THIS CAUSES THE BREAD TO BECOME **GREASY**.
SIZZZZLE
HOWEVER, THIS BREAD HAS **NEVER TOUCHED OIL!!**
SO...
WHAT KIND OF MAGIC DID YOU USE?!
IT'S SIMPLE.

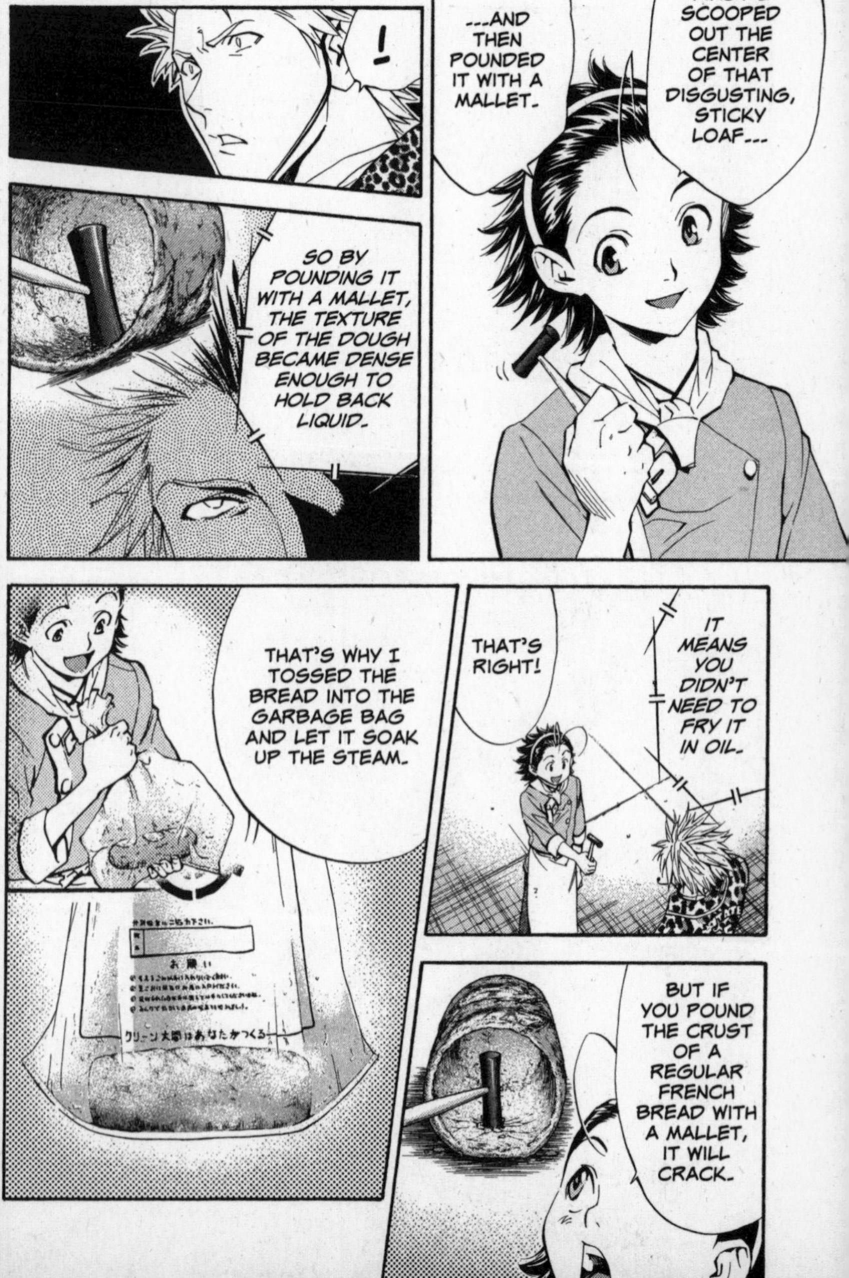
FIRST I SCOOPED OUT THE CENTER OF THAT DISGUSTING, STICKY LOAF...
...AND THEN POUNDED IT WITH A MALLET.
!
SO BY POUNDING IT WITH A MALLET, THE TEXTURE OF THE DOUGH BECAME DENSE ENOUGH TO HOLD BACK LIQUID.
IT MEANS YOU DIDN'T NEED TO FRY IT IN OIL.
THAT'S RIGHT!
BUT IF YOU POUND THE CRUST OF A REGULAR FRENCH BREAD WITH A MALLET, IT WILL CRACK.
THAT'S WHY I TOSSED THE BREAD INTO THE GARBAGE BAG AND LET IT SOAK UP THE STEAM.

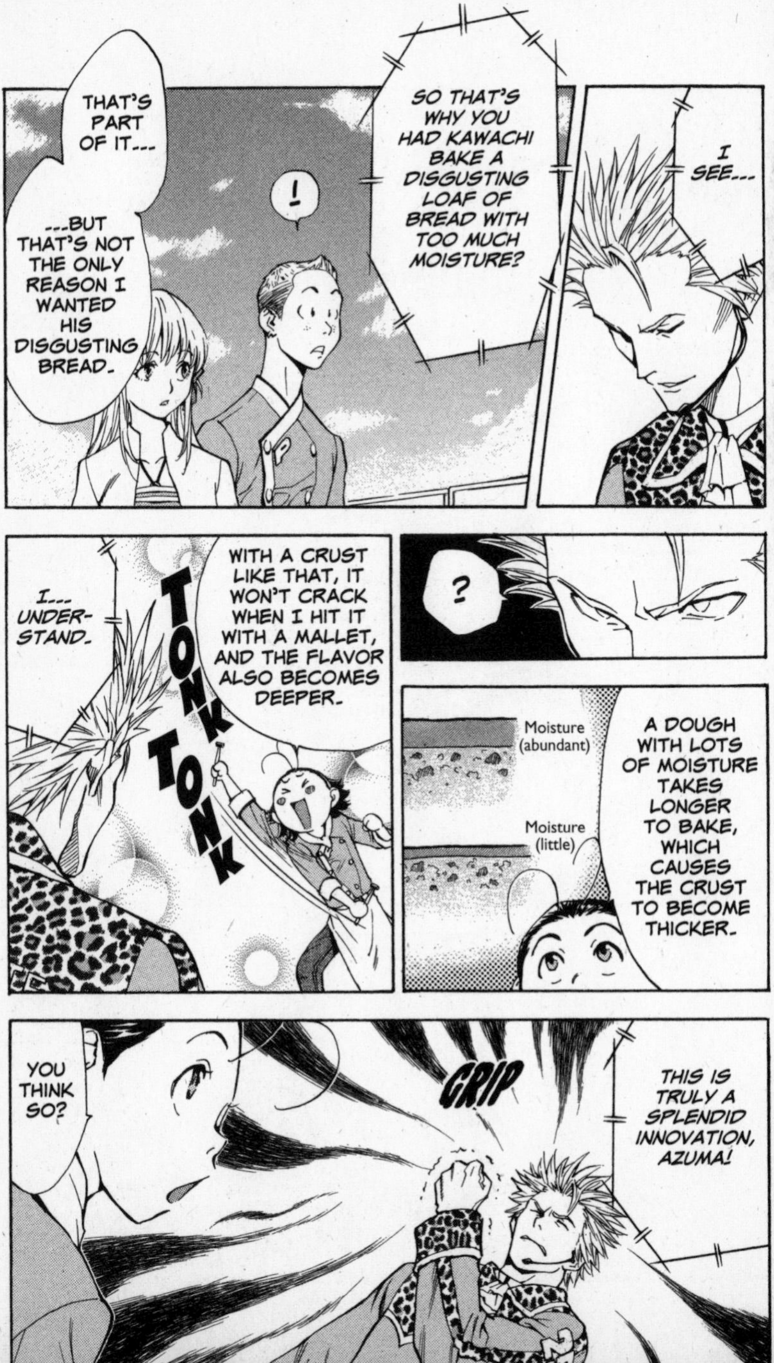
I SEE...
SO THAT'S WHY YOU HAD KAWACHI BAKE A DISGUSTING LOAF OF BREAD WITH TOO MUCH MOISTURE?
!
THAT'S PART OF IT...
...BUT THAT'S NOT THE ONLY REASON I WANTED HIS DISGUSTING BREAD.
?
A DOUGH WITH LOTS OF MOISTURE TAKES LONGER TO BAKE, WHICH CAUSES THE CRUST TO BECOME THICKER.
Moisture (abundant)
Moisture (little)
WITH A CRUST LIKE THAT, IT WON'T CRACK WHEN I HIT IT WITH A MALLET, AND THE FLAVOR ALSO BECOMES DEEPER.
TONK
TONK
I... UNDER-STAND.
THIS IS TRULY A SPLENDID INNOVATION, AZUMA!
GRIP
YOU THINK SO?

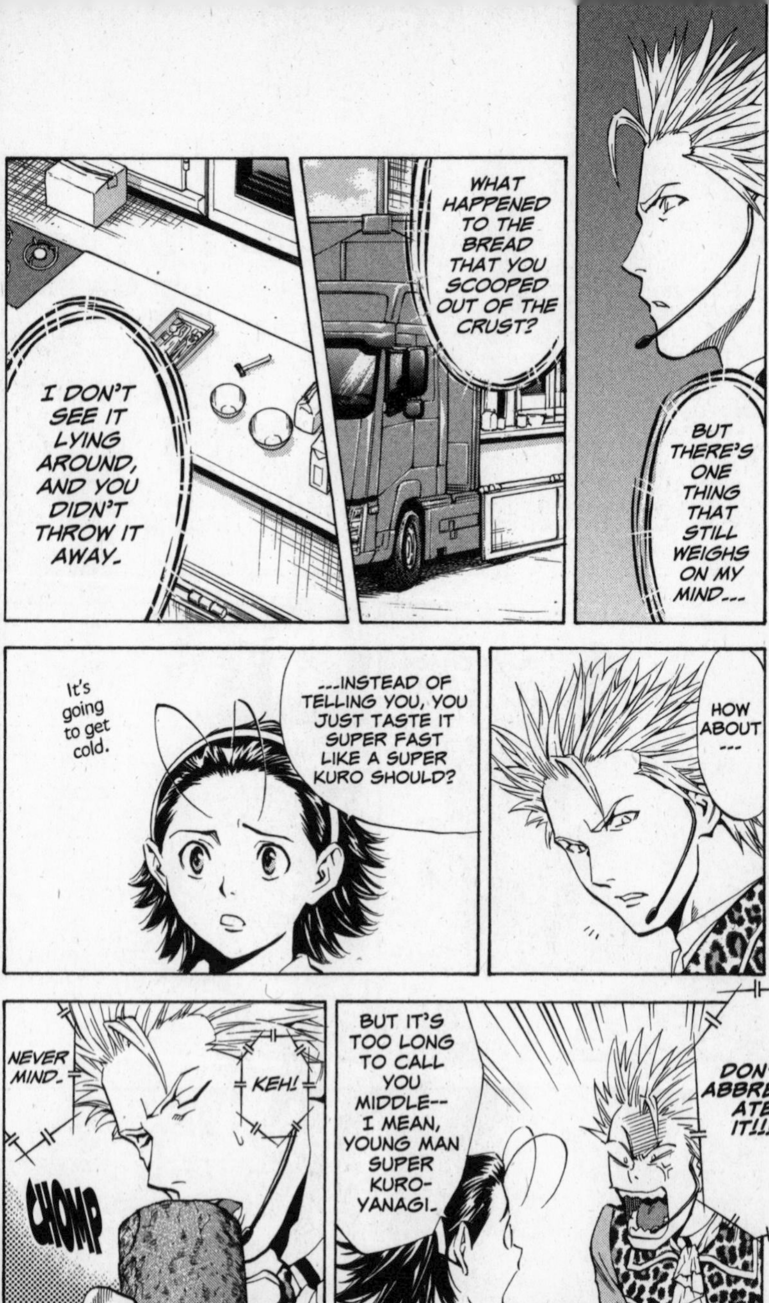
BUT THERE'S ONE THING THAT STILL WEIGHS ON MY MIND...
WHAT HAPPENED TO THE BREAD THAT YOU SCOOPED OUT OF THE CRUST?
I DON'T SEE IT LYING AROUND, AND YOU DIDN'T THROW IT AWAY.
HOW ABOUT...
...INSTEAD OF TELLING YOU, YOU JUST TASTE IT SUPER FAST LIKE A SUPER KURO SHOULD?
It's going to get cold.
DON'T ABBREVIATE IT!!!
BUT IT'S TOO LONG TO CALL YOU MIDDLE-- I MEAN, YOUNG MAN SUPER KURO-YANAGI.
KEH!
NEVER MIND.
CHOMP

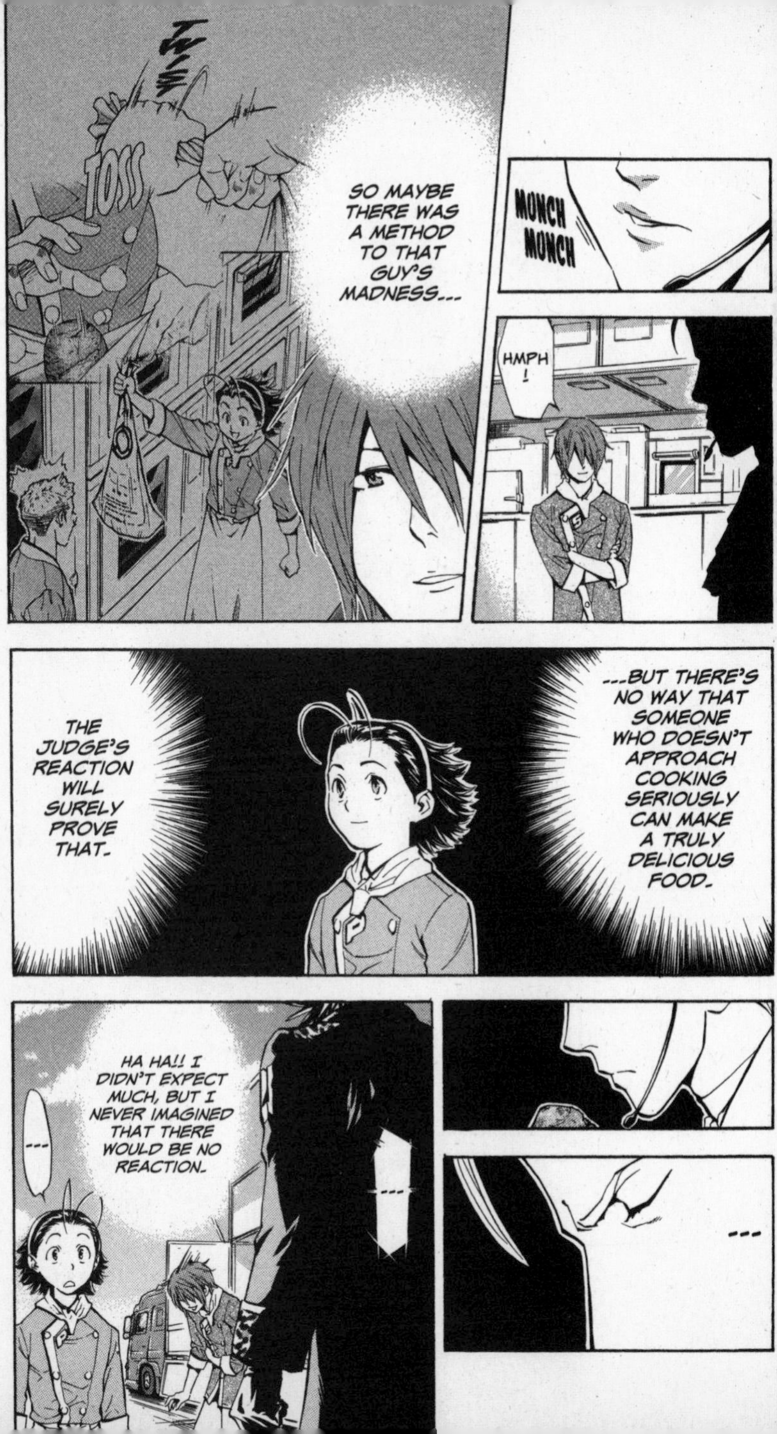
MUNCH MUNCH
HMPH!
TOSS
SO MAYBE THERE WAS A METHOD TO THAT GUY'S MADNESS...
...BUT THERE'S NO WAY THAT SOMEONE WHO DOESN'T APPROACH COOKING SERIOUSLY CAN MAKE A TRULY DELICIOUS FOOD.
THE JUDGE'S REACTION WILL SURELY PROVE THAT.
...
HA HA!! I DIDN'T EXPECT MUCH, BUT I NEVER IMAGINED THAT THERE WOULD BE NO REACTION.
...
...

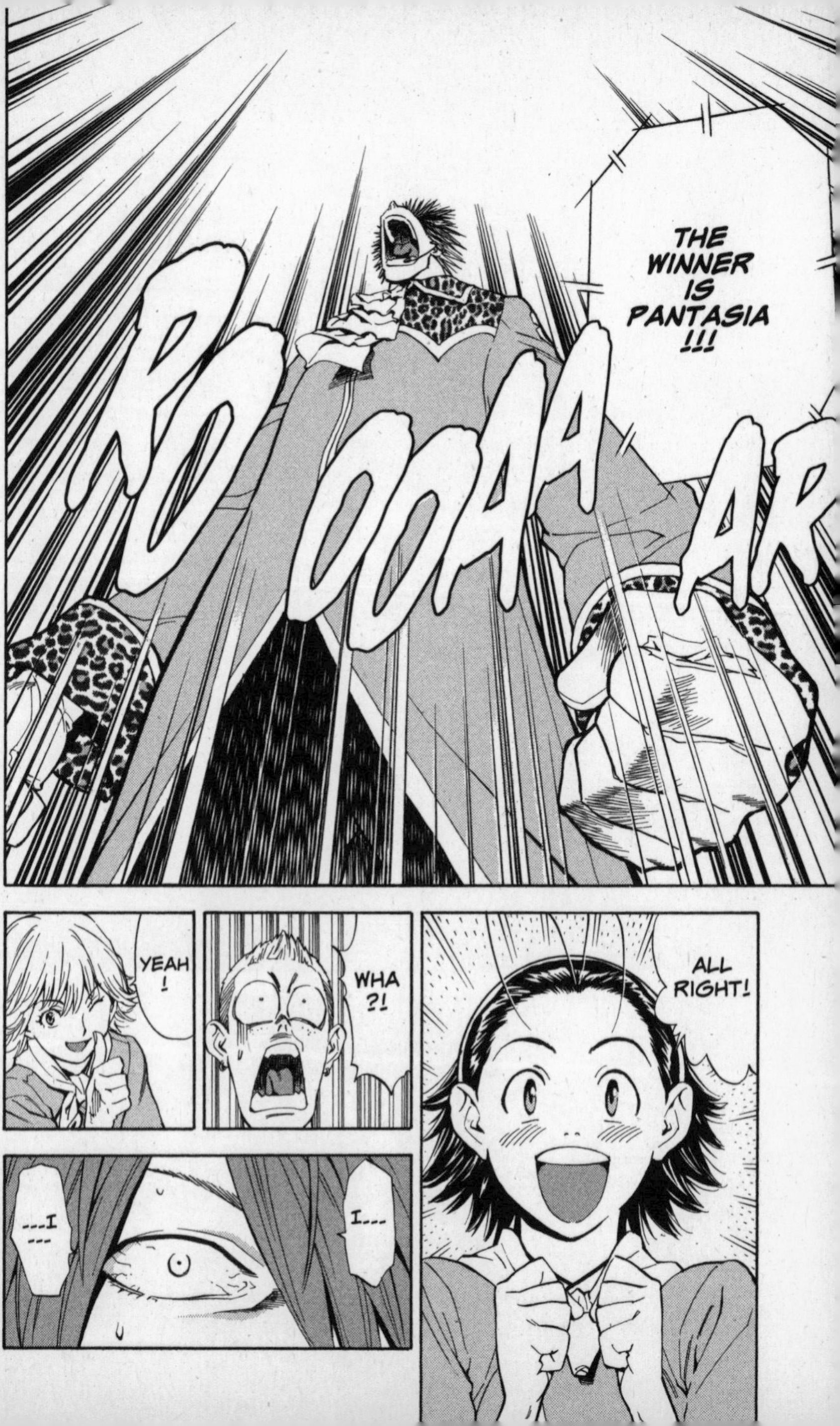
THE WINNER IS PANTASIA !!!
ALL RIGHT!
WHA ?!
YEAH !
I---
---I ---

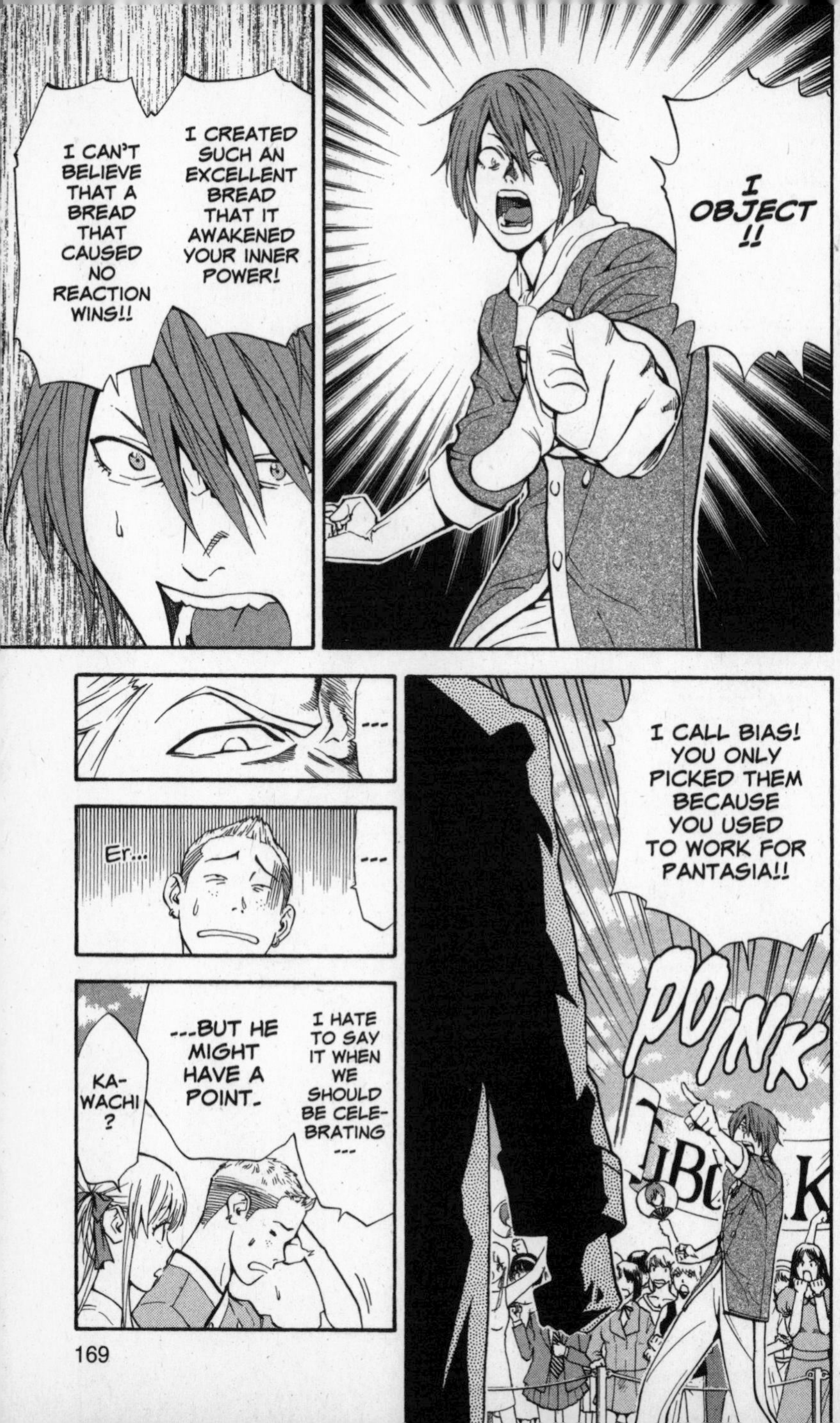
I OBJECT!!
I CREATED SUCH AN EXCELLENT BREAD THAT IT AWAKENED YOUR INNER POWER!
I CAN'T BELIEVE THAT A BREAD THAT CAUSED NO REACTION WINS!!
I CALL BIAS! YOU ONLY PICKED THEM BECAUSE YOU USED TO WORK FOR PANTASIA!!
POINK
...
...
Er...
I HATE TO SAY IT WHEN WE SHOULD BE CELEBRATING ...
...BUT HE MIGHT HAVE A POINT.
KA-WACHI?

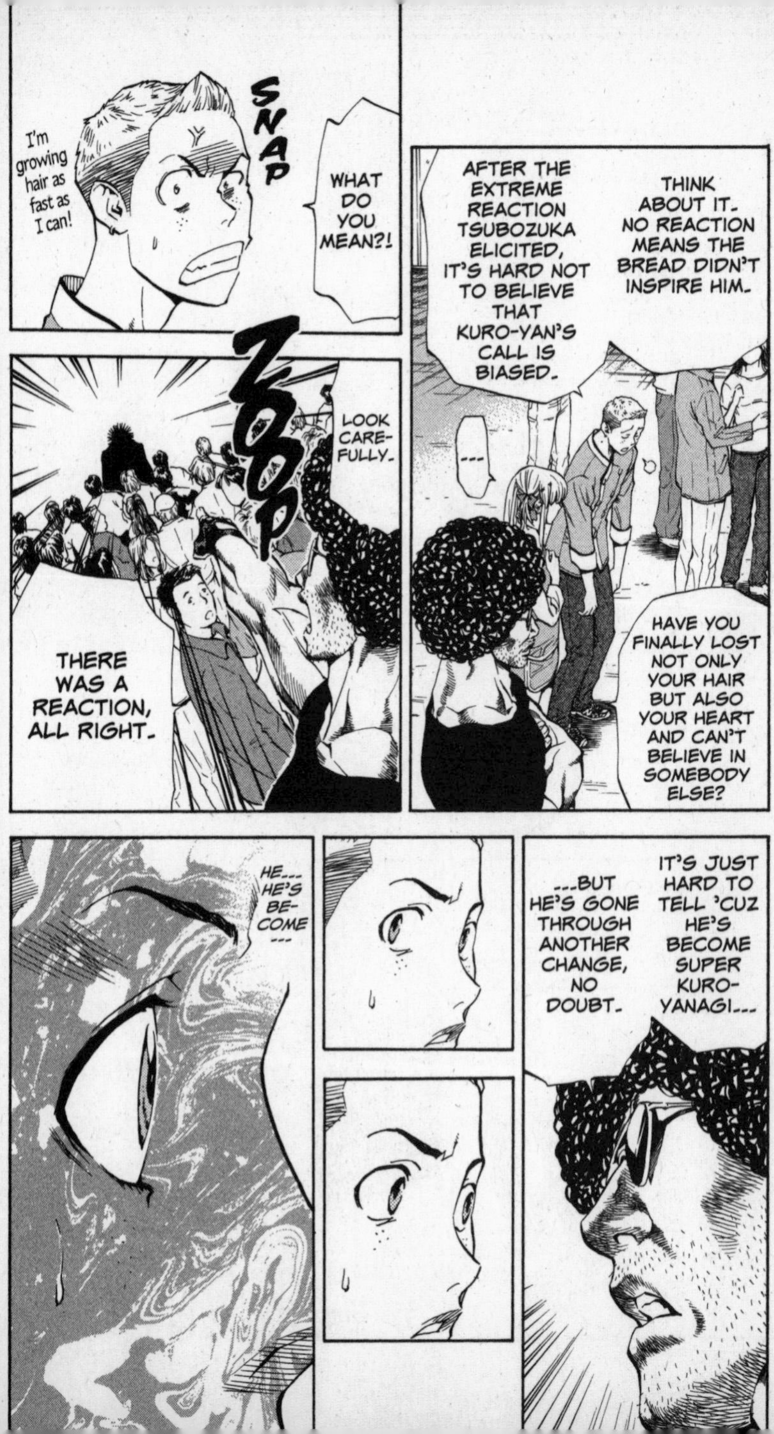
THINK ABOUT IT. NO REACTION MEANS THE BREAD DIDN'T INSPIRE HIM.
AFTER THE EXTREME REACTION TSUBOZUKA ELICITED, IT'S HARD NOT TO BELIEVE THAT KURO-YAN'S CALL IS BIASED.
...
HAVE YOU FINALLY LOST NOT ONLY YOUR HAIR BUT ALSO YOUR HEART AND CAN'T BELIEVE IN SOMEBODY ELSE?
WHAT DO YOU MEAN?!
SNAP
I'm growing hair as fast as I can!
LOOK CAREFULLY.
ZOOP
THERE WAS A REACTION, ALL RIGHT.
IT'S JUST HARD TO TELL 'CUZ HE'S BECOME SUPER KURO-YANAGI...
...BUT HE'S GONE THROUGH ANOTHER CHANGE, NO DOUBT.
HE... HE'S BE-COME...

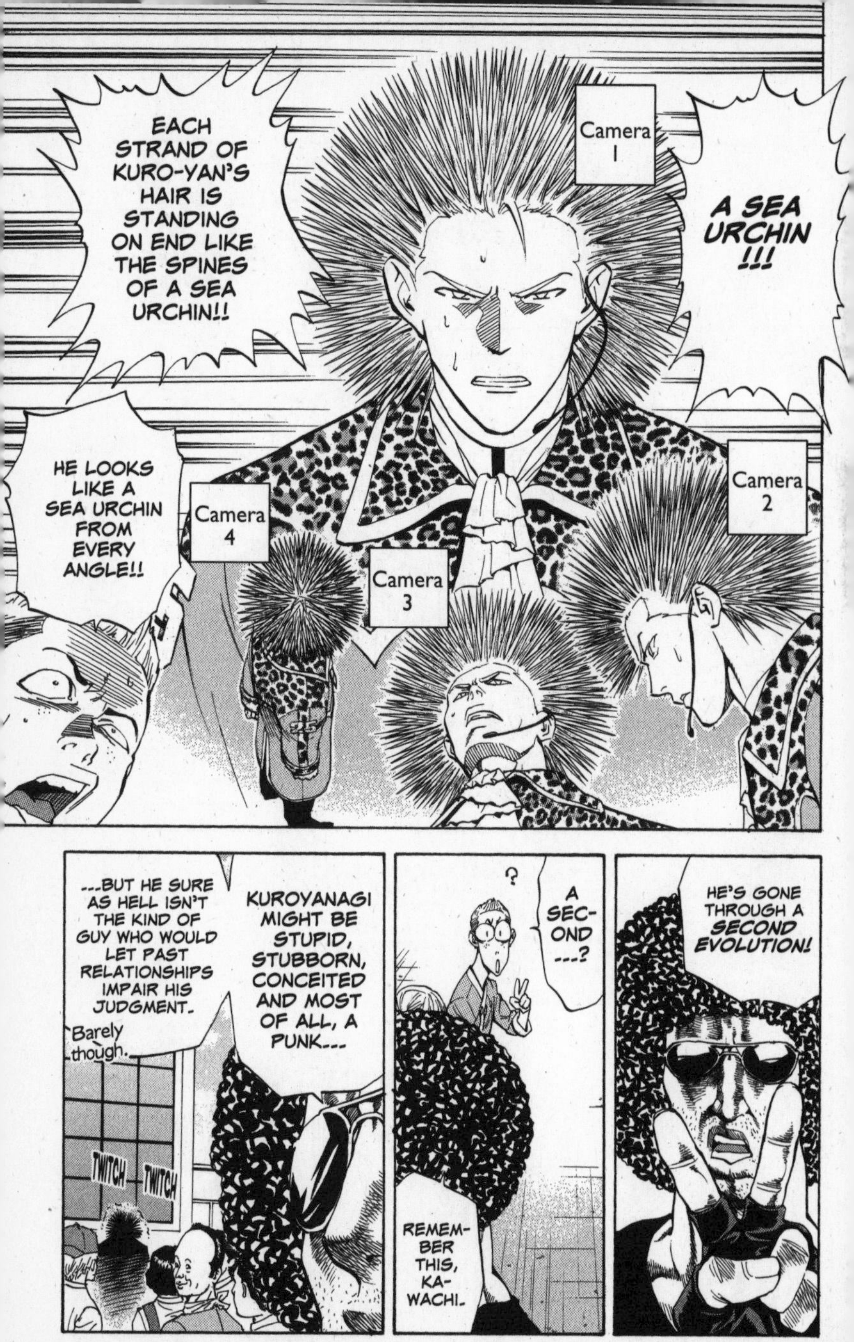

A SEA URCHIN !!!
Camera 1
EACH STRAND OF KURO-YAN'S HAIR IS STANDING ON END LIKE THE SPINES OF A SEA URCHIN!!
Camera 2
Camera 4
Camera 3
HE LOOKS LIKE A SEA URCHIN FROM EVERY ANGLE!!
HE'S GONE THROUGH A SECOND EVOLUTION!
A SEC-OND ---?
?
REMEM-BER THIS, KA-WACHI.
KUROYANAGI MIGHT BE STUPID, STUBBORN, CONCEITED AND MOST OF ALL, A PUNK---
---BUT HE SURE AS HELL ISN'T THE KIND OF GUY WHO WOULD LET PAST RELATIONSHIPS IMPAIR HIS JUDGMENT.
Barely though.
TWITCH TWITCH

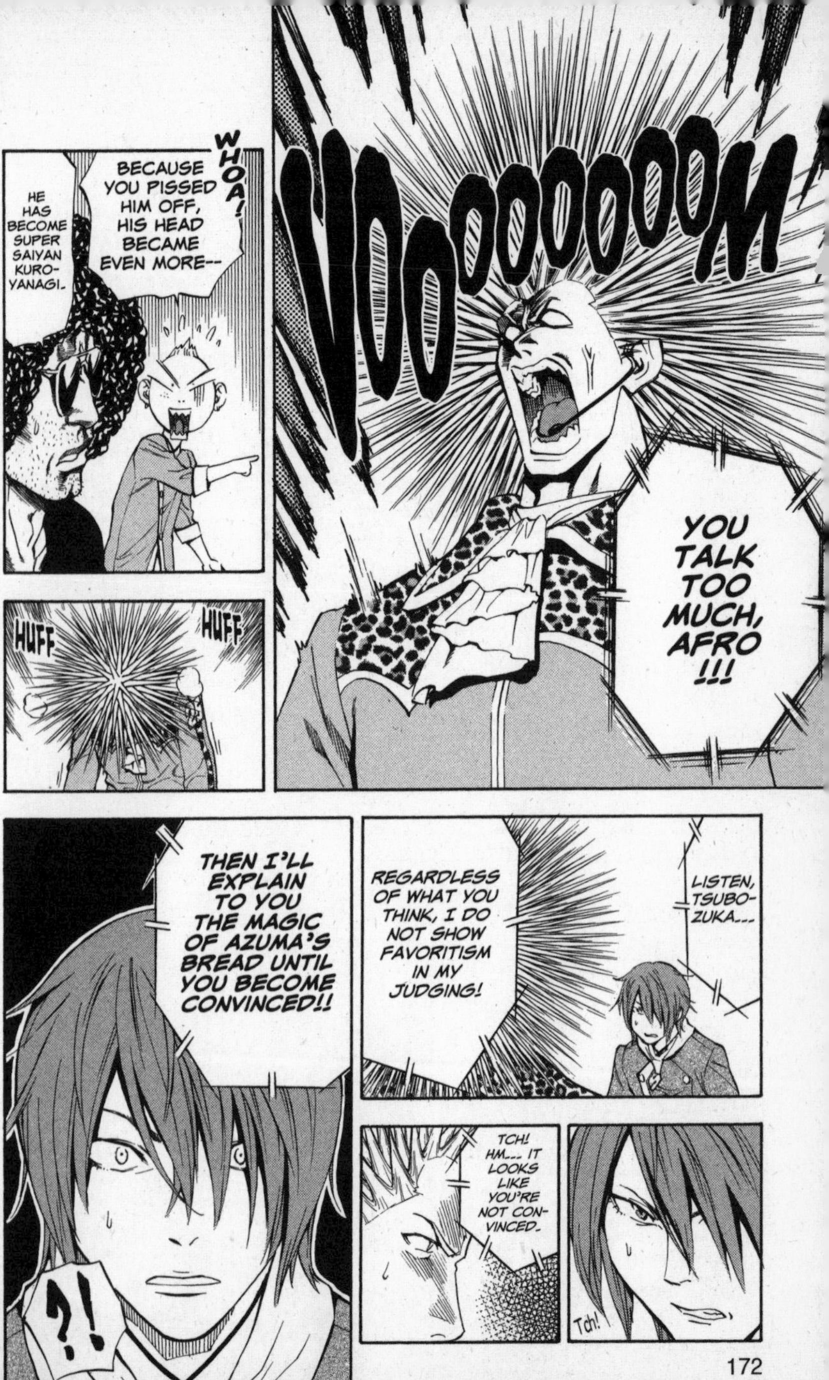
VOOOOOOOOM
YOU TALK TOO MUCH, AFRO!!!
WHOA!
BECAUSE YOU PISSED HIM OFF, HIS HEAD BECAME EVEN MORE--
HE HAS BECOME SUPER SAIYAN KURO-YANAGI.
HUFF
HUFF
LISTEN, TSUBO-ZUKA...
REGARDLESS OF WHAT YOU THINK, I DO NOT SHOW FAVORITISM IN MY JUDGING!
Tch!
TCH! HM... IT LOOKS LIKE YOU'RE NOT CON-VINCED.
THEN I'LL EXPLAIN TO YOU THE MAGIC OF AZUMA'S BREAD UNTIL YOU BECOME CONVINCED!!
?!

Story 133:

Bread Magic

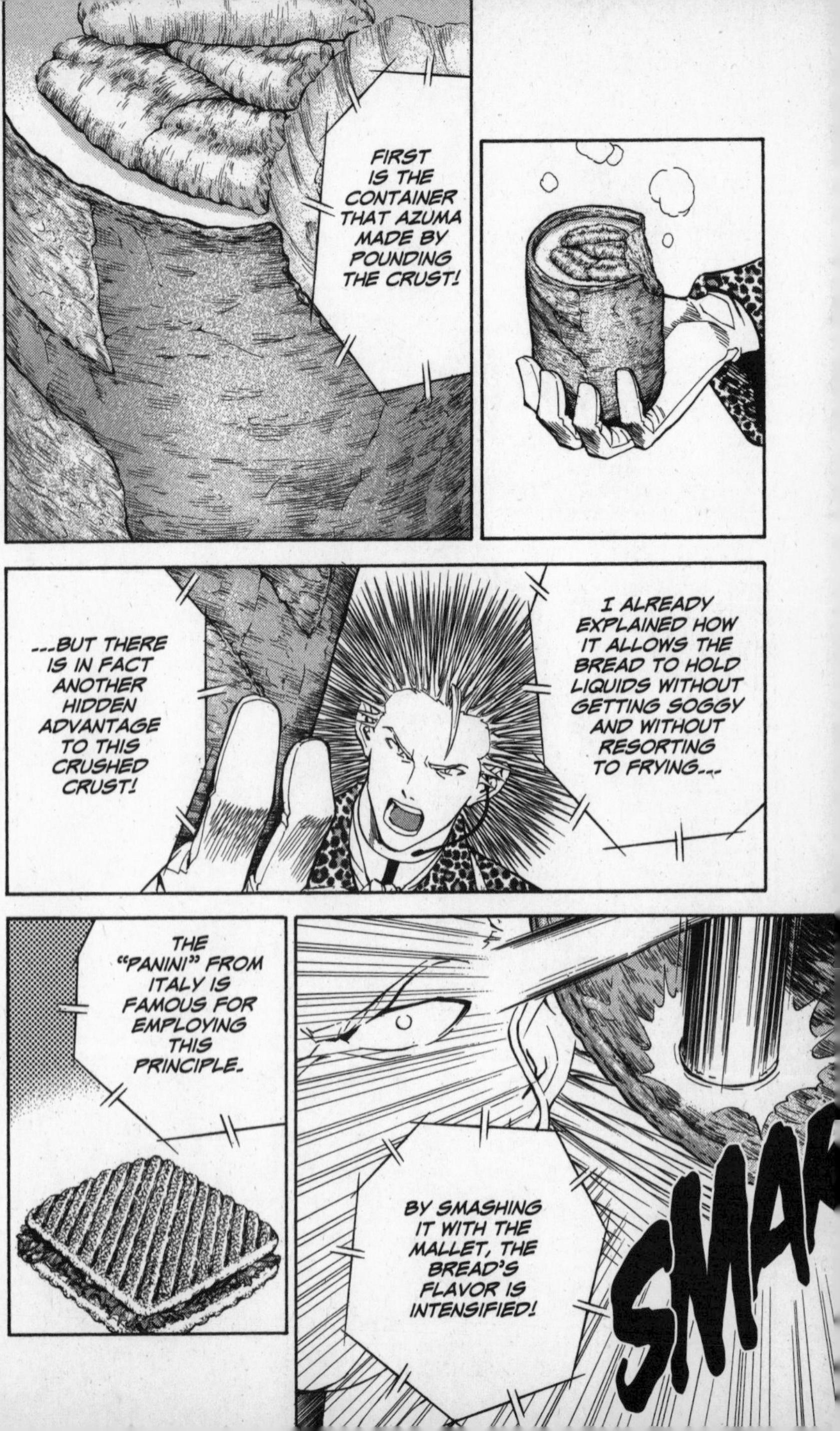
FIRST IS THE CONTAINER THAT AZUMA MADE BY POUNDING THE CRUST!
I ALREADY EXPLAINED HOW IT ALLOWS THE BREAD TO HOLD LIQUIDS WITHOUT GETTING SOGGY AND WITHOUT RESORTING TO FRYING...
...BUT THERE IS IN FACT ANOTHER HIDDEN ADVANTAGE TO THIS CRUSHED CRUST!
BY SMASHING IT WITH THE MALLET, THE BREAD'S FLAVOR IS INTENSIFIED!
SMA
THE "PANINI" FROM ITALY IS FAMOUS FOR EMPLOYING THIS PRINCIPLE.

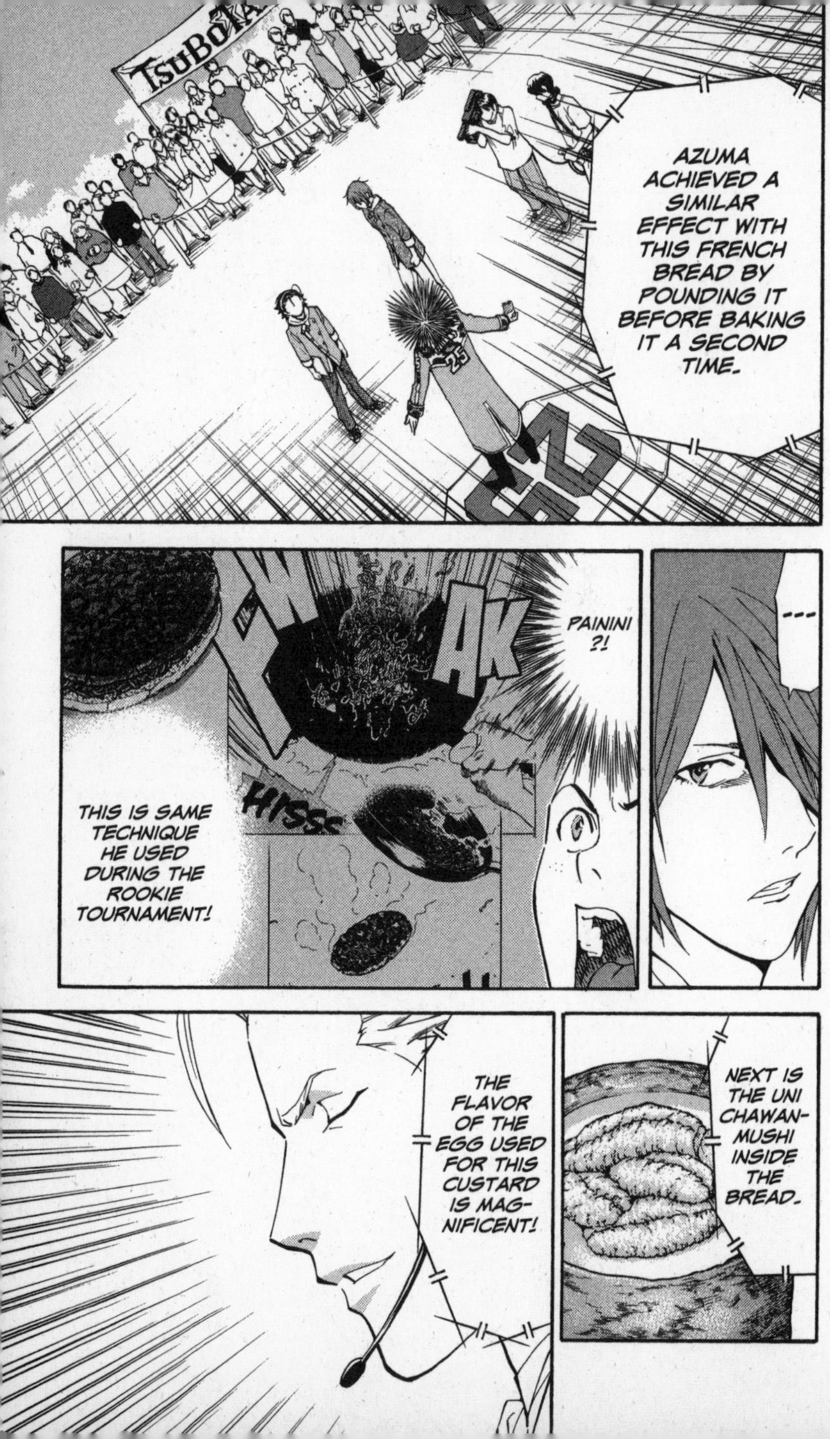
AZUMA ACHIEVED A SIMILAR EFFECT WITH THIS FRENCH BREAD BY POUNDING IT BEFORE BAKING IT A SECOND TIME.
...
PAININI ?!
HISSS
THIS IS SAME TECHNIQUE HE USED DURING THE ROOKIE TOURNAMENT!
NEXT IS THE UNI CHAWAN-MUSHI INSIDE THE BREAD.
THE FLAVOR OF THE EGG USED FOR THIS CUSTARD IS MAG-NIFICENT!

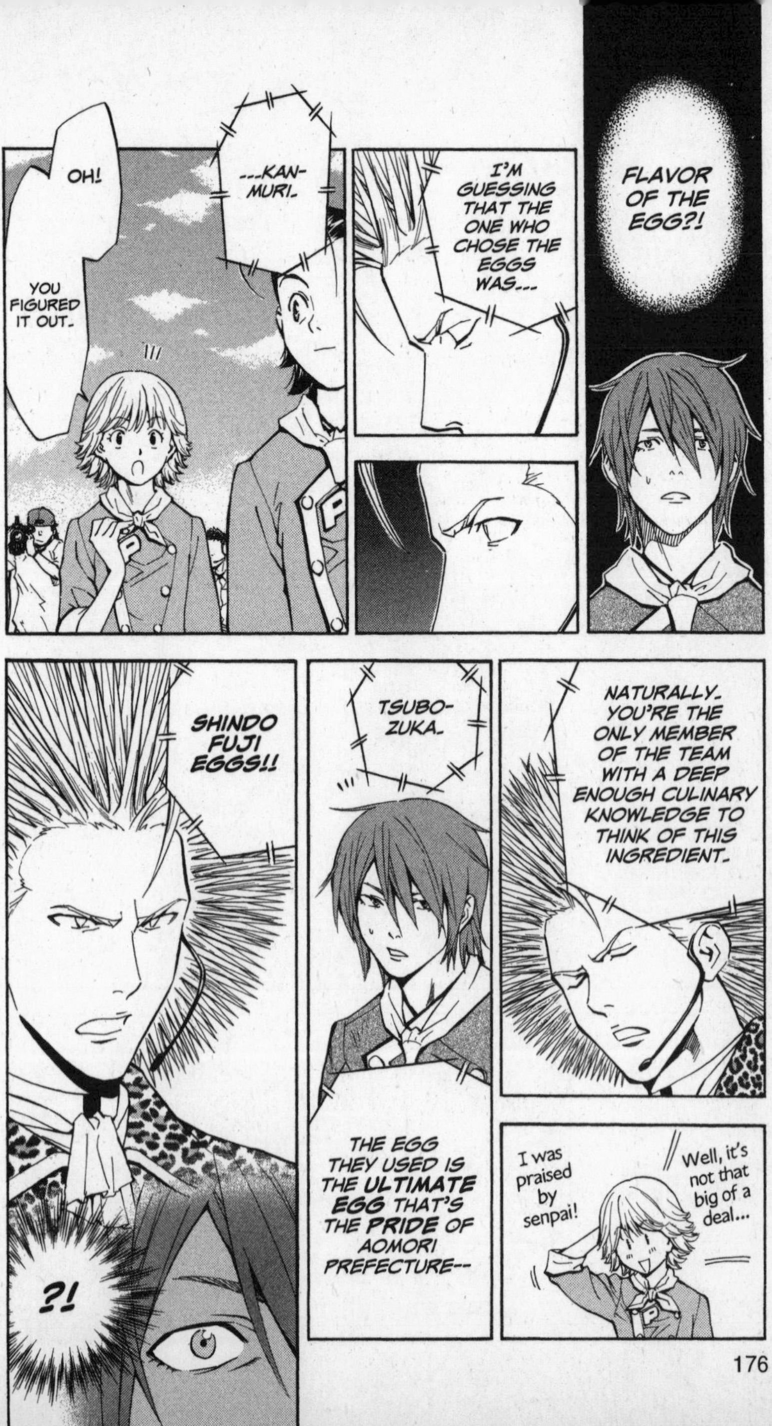
FLAVOR OF THE EGG?!
I'M GUESSING THAT THE ONE WHO CHOSE THE EGGS WAS...
...KAN-MURI.
OH!
YOU FIGURED IT OUT.
NATURALLY. YOU'RE THE ONLY MEMBER OF THE TEAM WITH A DEEP ENOUGH CULINARY KNOWLEDGE TO THINK OF THIS INGREDIENT.
Well, it's not that big of a deal...
I was praised by senpai!
TSUBO-ZUKA.
THE EGG THEY USED IS THE ULTIMATE EGG THAT'S THE PRIDE OF AOMORI PREFECTURE--
SHINDO FUJI EGGS!!
?!

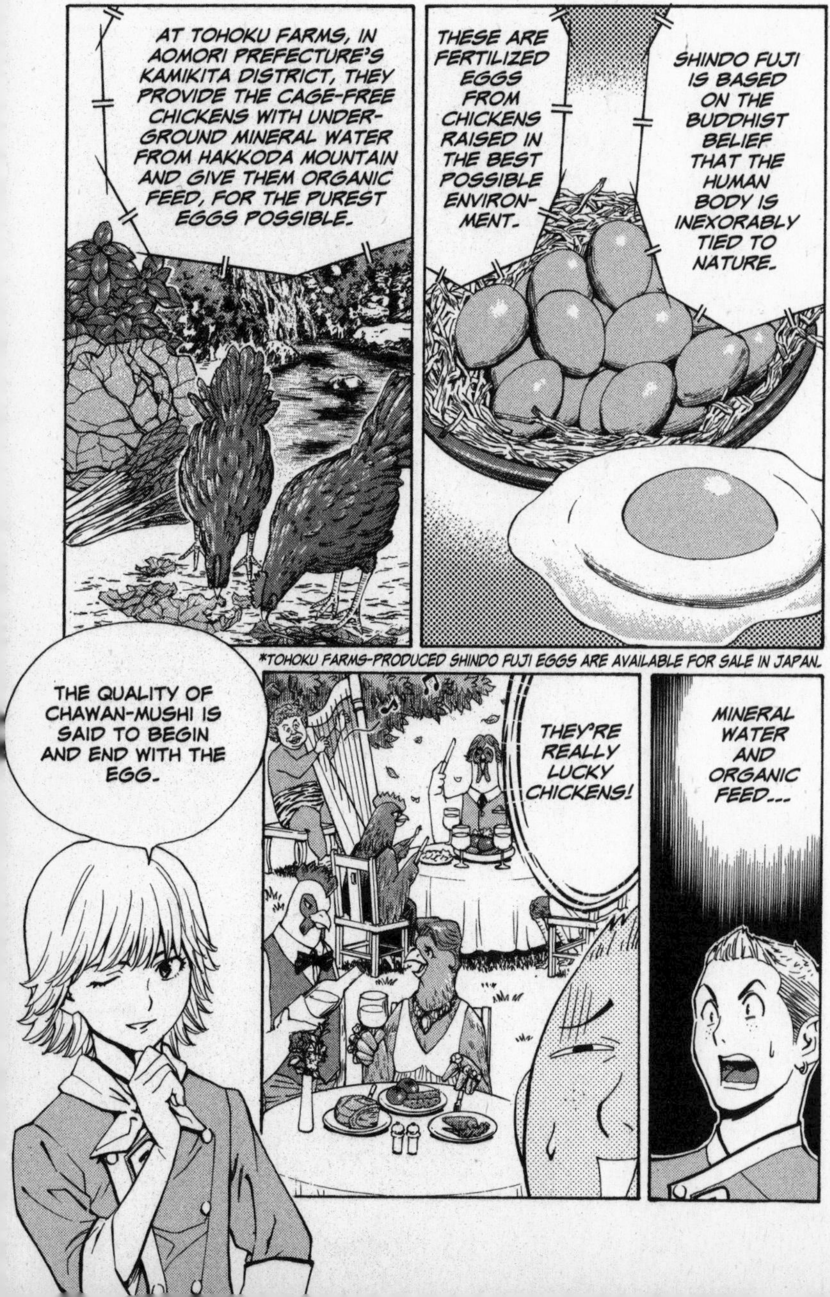
SHINDO FUJI IS BASED ON THE BUDDHIST BELIEF THAT THE HUMAN BODY IS INEXORABLY TIED TO NATURE.
THESE ARE FERTILIZED EGGS FROM CHICKENS RAISED IN THE BEST POSSIBLE ENVIRONMENT.
AT TOHOKU FARMS, IN AOMORI PREFECTURE'S KAMIKITA DISTRICT, THEY PROVIDE THE CAGE-FREE CHICKENS WITH UNDER-GROUND MINERAL WATER FROM HAKKODA MOUNTAIN AND GIVE THEM ORGANIC FEED, FOR THE PUREST EGGS POSSIBLE.
*TOHOKU FARMS-PRODUCED SHINDO FUJI EGGS ARE AVAILABLE FOR SALE IN JAPAN.
MINERAL WATER AND ORGANIC FEED...
THEY'RE REALLY LUCKY CHICKENS!
THE QUALITY OF CHAWAN-MUSHI IS SAID TO BEGIN AND END WITH THE EGG.

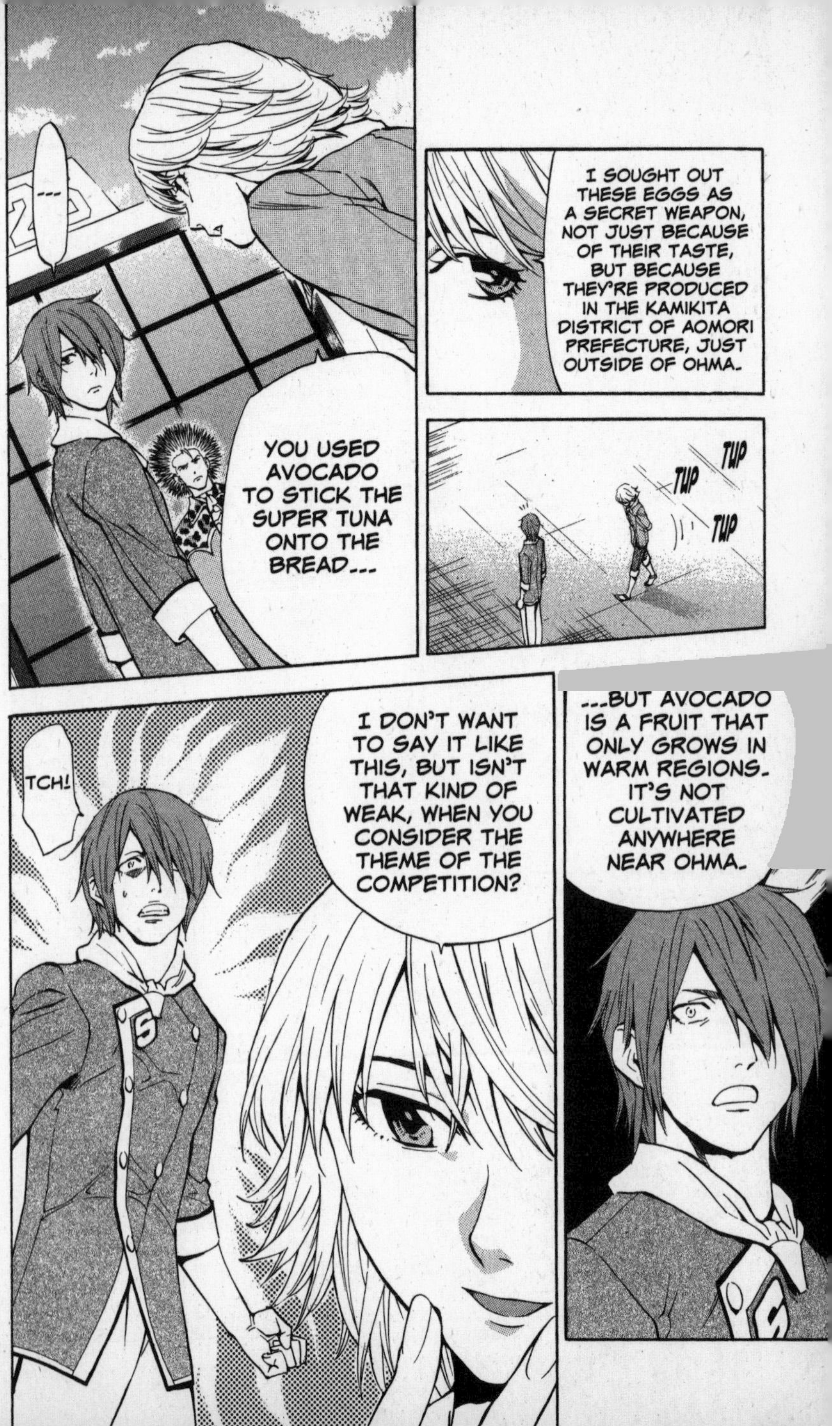
I SOUGHT OUT THESE EGGS AS A SECRET WEAPON, NOT JUST BECAUSE OF THEIR TASTE, BUT BECAUSE THEY'RE PRODUCED IN THE KAMIKITA DISTRICT OF AOMORI PREFECTURE, JUST OUTSIDE OF OHMA.
TUP
TUP
TUP
...
YOU USED AVOCADO TO STICK THE SUPER TUNA ONTO THE BREAD...
...BUT AVOCADO IS A FRUIT THAT ONLY GROWS IN WARM REGIONS. IT'S NOT CULTIVATED ANYWHERE NEAR OHMA.
I DON'T WANT TO SAY IT LIKE THIS, BUT ISN'T THAT KIND OF WEAK, WHEN YOU CONSIDER THE THEME OF THE COMPETITION?
TCH!

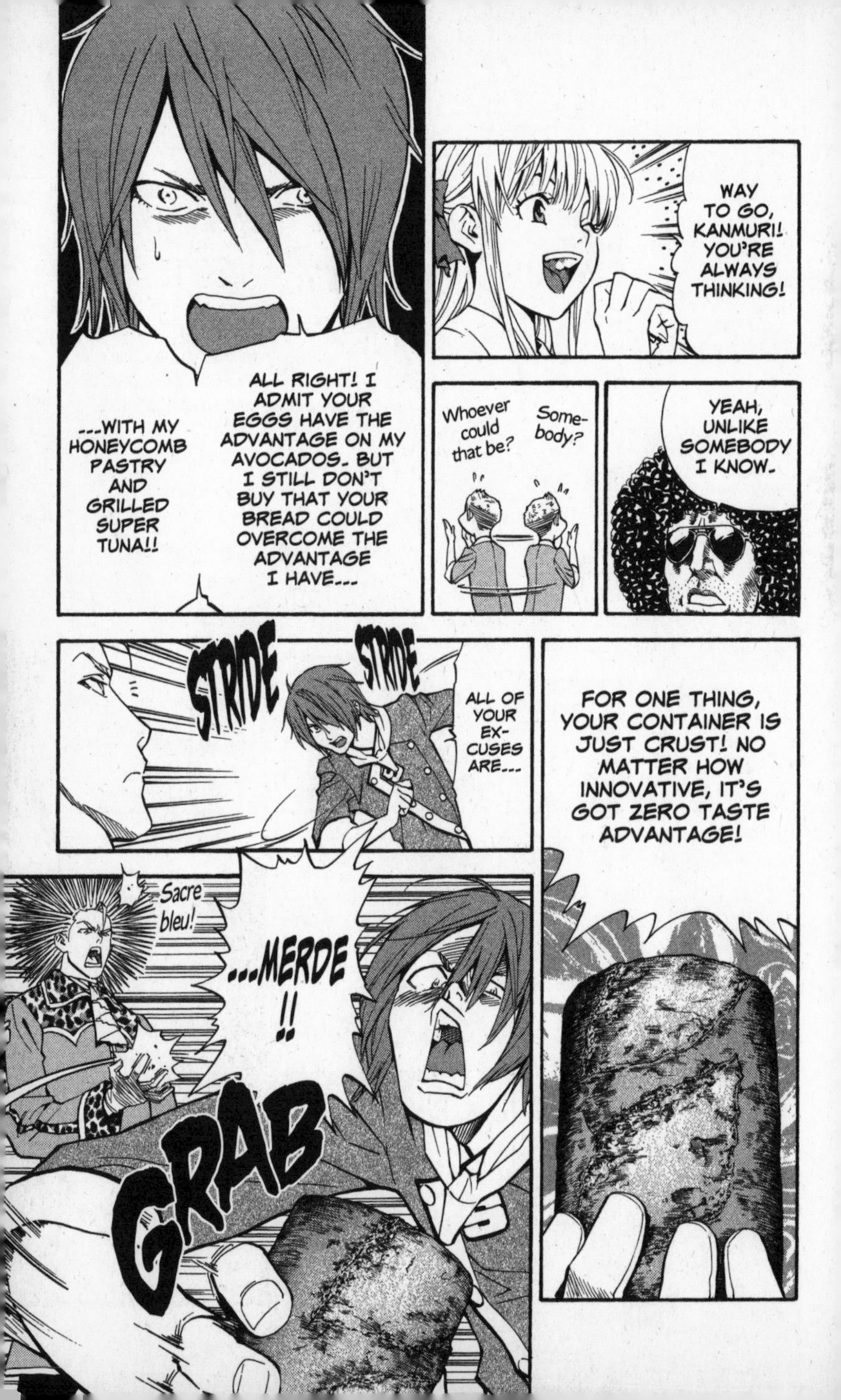
WAY TO GO, KANMURI! YOU'RE ALWAYS THINKING!
YEAH, UNLIKE SOMEBODY I KNOW.
Somebody?
Whoever could that be?
ALL RIGHT! I ADMIT YOUR EGGS HAVE THE ADVANTAGE ON MY AVOCADOS. BUT I STILL DON'T BUY THAT YOUR BREAD COULD OVERCOME THE ADVANTAGE I HAVE...
...WITH MY HONEYCOMB PASTRY AND GRILLED SUPER TUNA!!
FOR ONE THING, YOUR CONTAINER IS JUST CRUST! NO MATTER HOW INNOVATIVE, IT'S GOT ZERO TASTE ADVANTAGE!
STRIDE
STRIDE
ALL OF YOUR EXCUSES ARE...
...MERDE!!
Sacre bleu!
GRAB

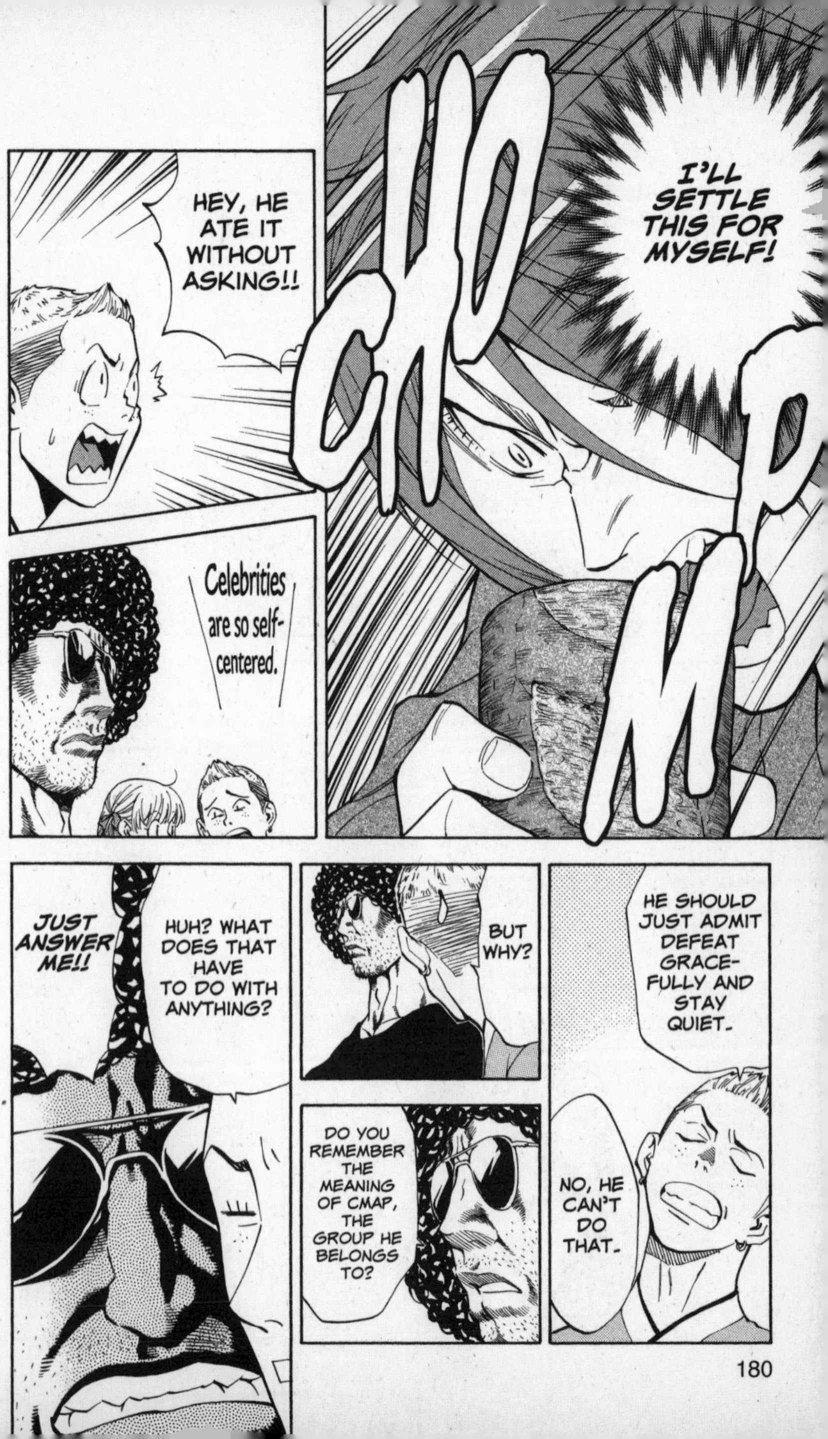
I'LL SETTLE THIS FOR MYSELF!
CHOMP
HEY, HE ATE IT WITHOUT ASKING!!
Celebrities are so self-centered.
HE SHOULD JUST ADMIT DEFEAT GRACEFULLY AND STAY QUIET.
NO, HE CAN'T DO THAT.
BUT WHY?
DO YOU REMEMBER THE MEANING OF CMAP, THE GROUP HE BELONGS TO?
HUH? WHAT DOES THAT HAVE TO DO WITH ANYTHING?
JUST ANSWER ME!!

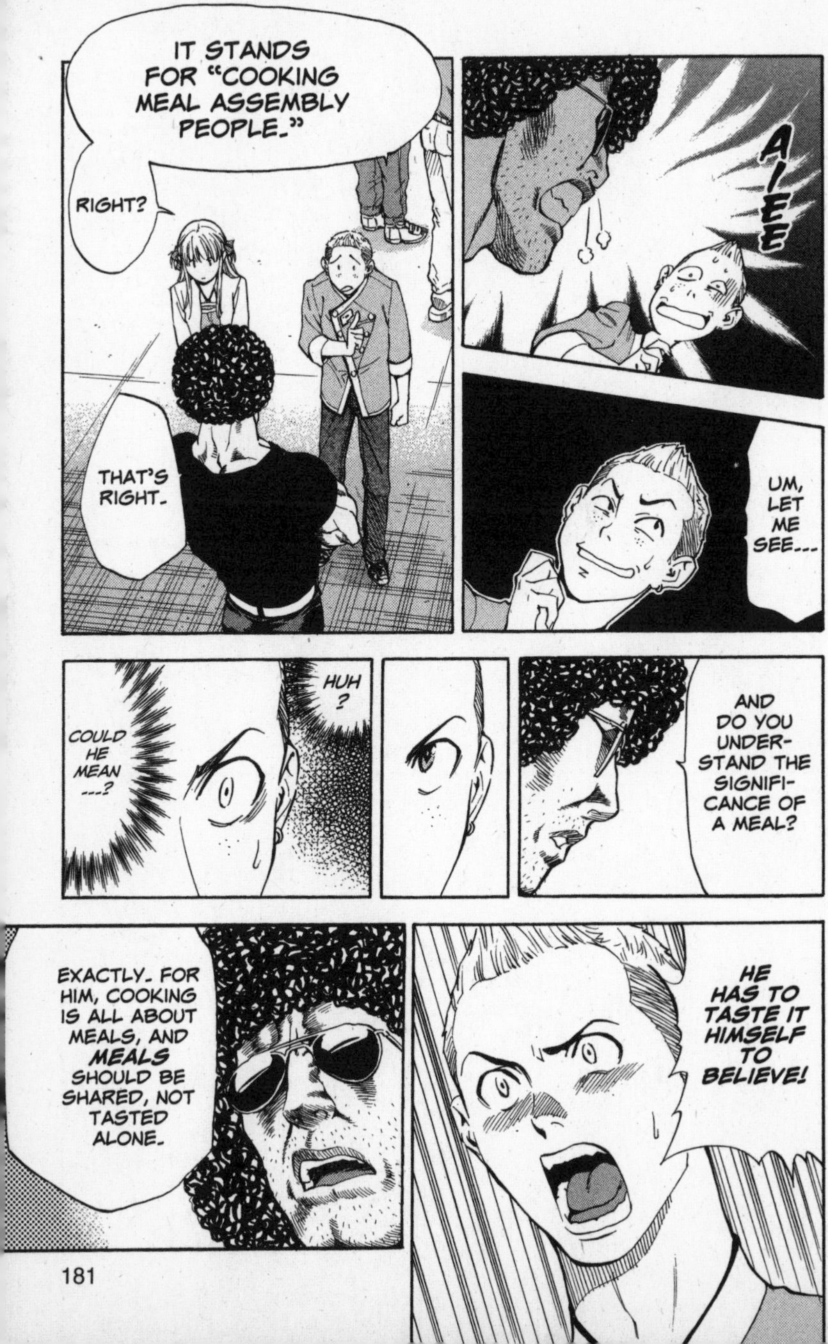
AIEEE
UM, LET ME SEE...
IT STANDS FOR "COOKING MEAL ASSEMBLY PEOPLE."
RIGHT?
THAT'S RIGHT.
AND DO YOU UNDERSTAND THE SIGNIFICANCE OF A MEAL?
HUH?
COULD HE MEAN...?
HE HAS TO TASTE IT HIMSELF TO BELIEVE!
EXACTLY. FOR HIM, COOKING IS ALL ABOUT MEALS, AND *MEALS* SHOULD BE SHARED, NOT TASTED ALONE.

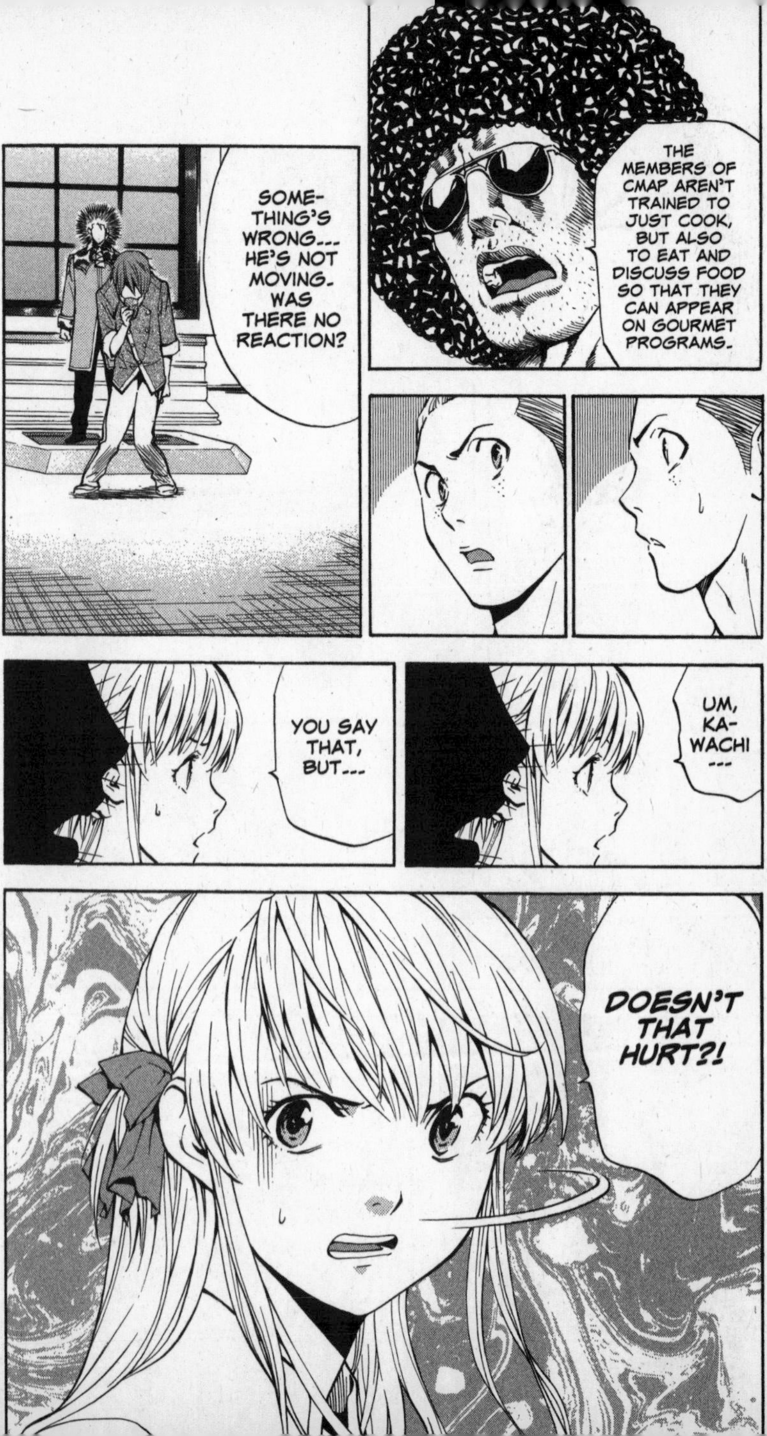
THE MEMBERS OF CMAP AREN'T TRAINED TO JUST COOK, BUT ALSO TO EAT AND DISCUSS FOOD SO THAT THEY CAN APPEAR ON GOURMET PROGRAMS.
SOME-THING'S WRONG... HE'S NOT MOVING. WAS THERE NO REACTION?
UM, KA-WACHI...
YOU SAY THAT, BUT...
DOESN'T THAT HURT?!

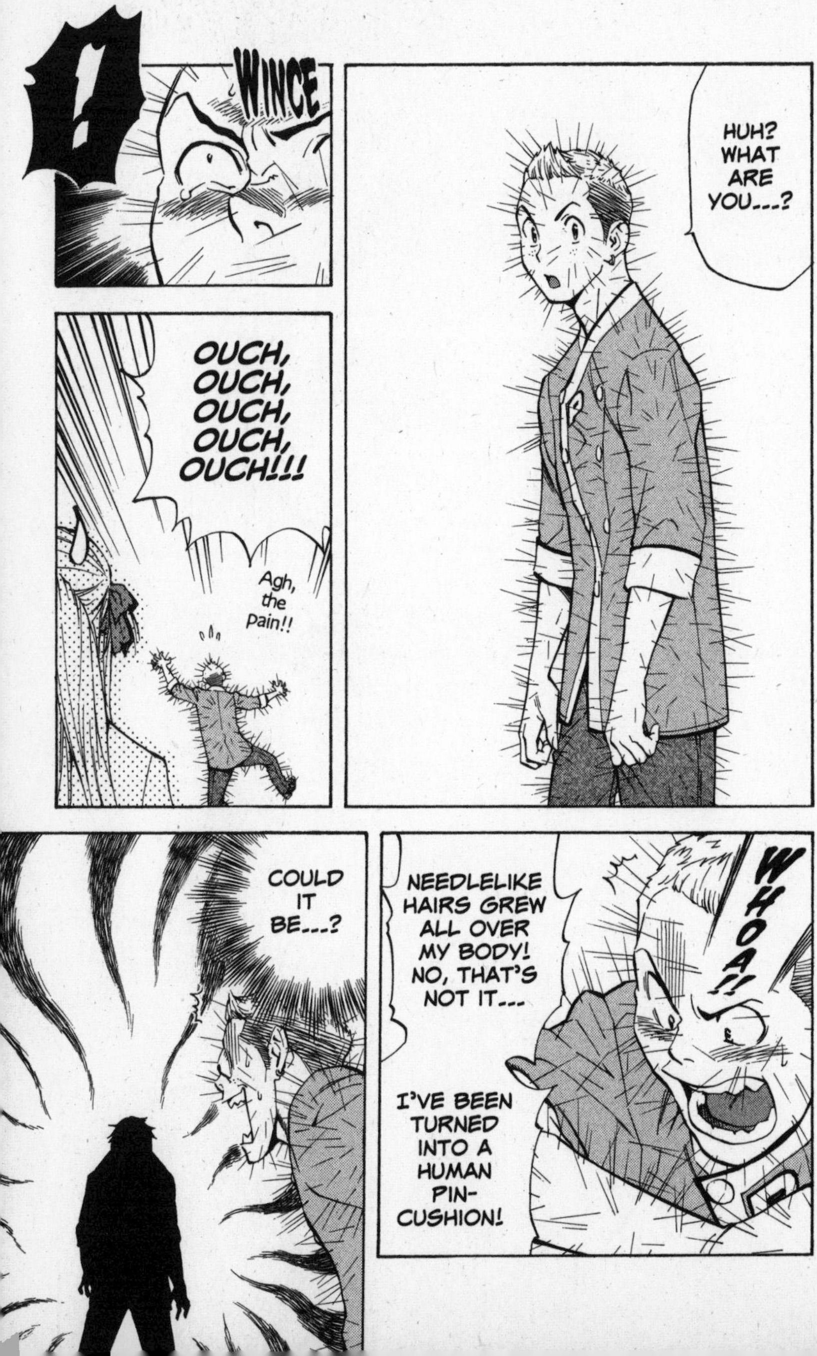
HUH? WHAT ARE YOU...?
WINCE
!
OUCH, OUCH, OUCH, OUCH, OUCH!!!
Agh, the pain!!
WHOA!!
NEEDLELIKE HAIRS GREW ALL OVER MY BODY! NO, THAT'S NOT IT...
I'VE BEEN TURNED INTO A HUMAN PIN-CUSHION!
COULD IT BE...?

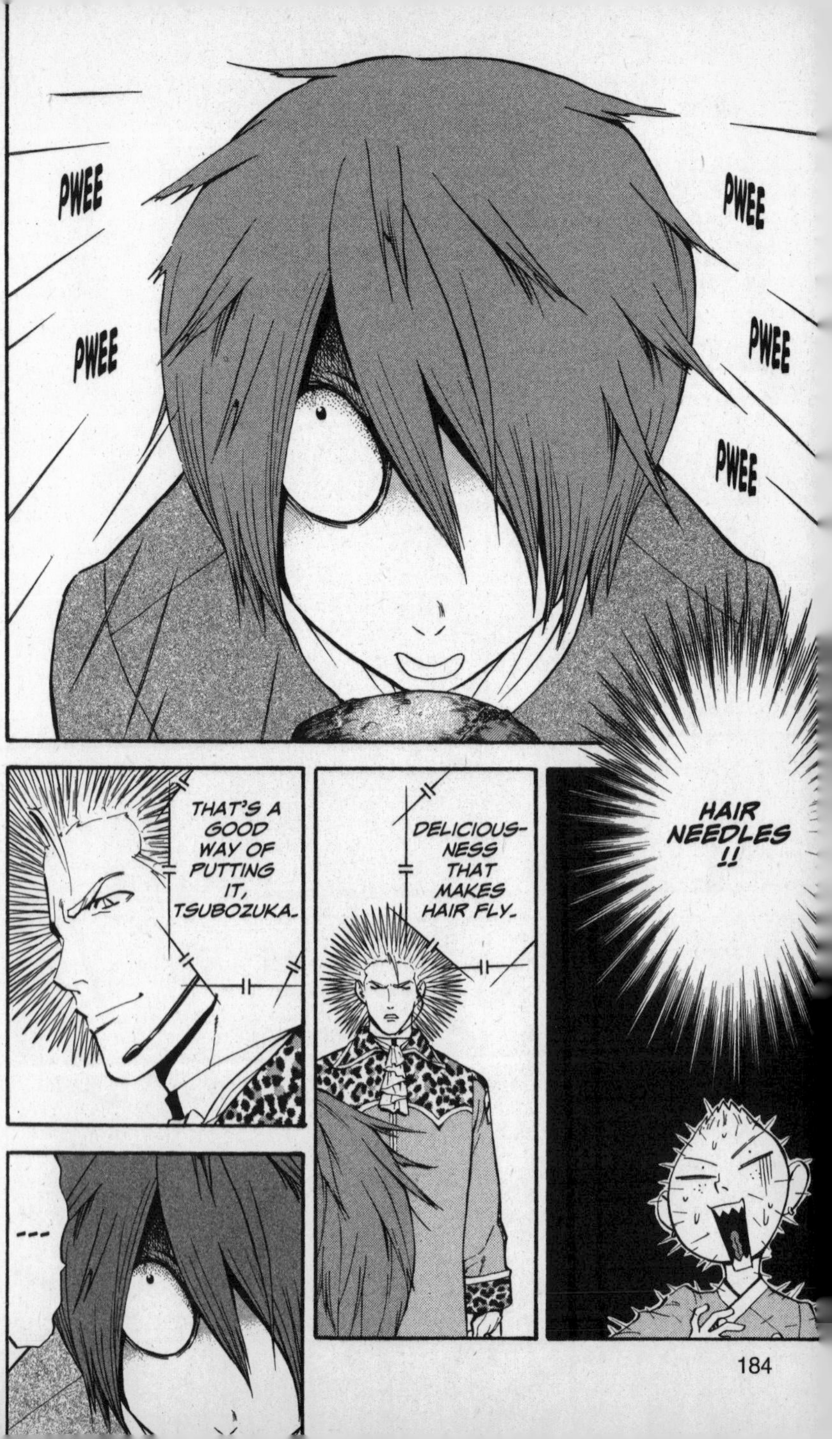
PWEE
PWEE
PWEE
PWEE
PWEE
HAIR NEEDLES!!
DELICIOUS-NESS THAT MAKES HAIR FLY..
THAT'S A GOOD WAY OF PUTTING IT, TSUBOZUKA..

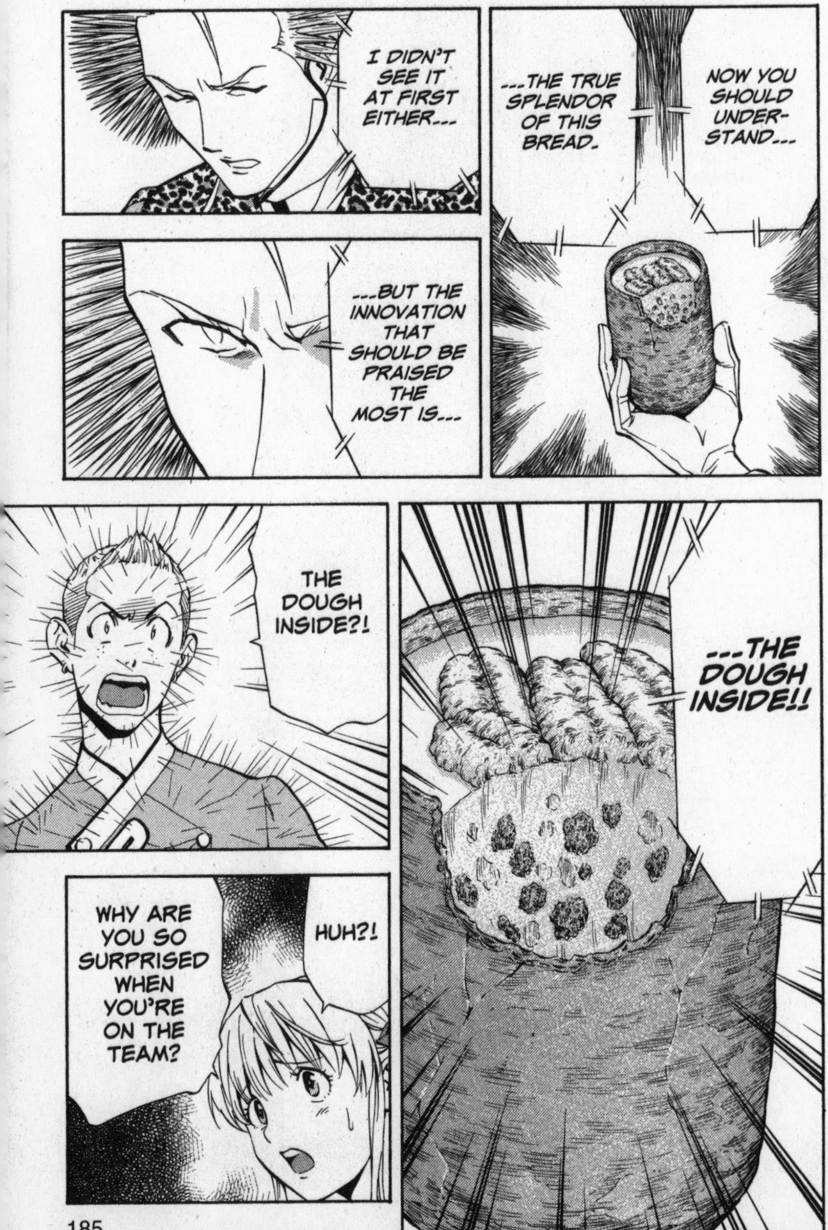
NOW YOU SHOULD UNDER-STAND...
...THE TRUE SPLENDOR OF THIS BREAD.
I DIDN'T SEE IT AT FIRST EITHER...
...BUT THE INNOVATION THAT SHOULD BE PRAISED THE MOST IS...
...THE DOUGH INSIDE!!
THE DOUGH INSIDE?!
HUH?!
WHY ARE YOU SO SURPRISED WHEN YOU'RE ON THE TEAM?

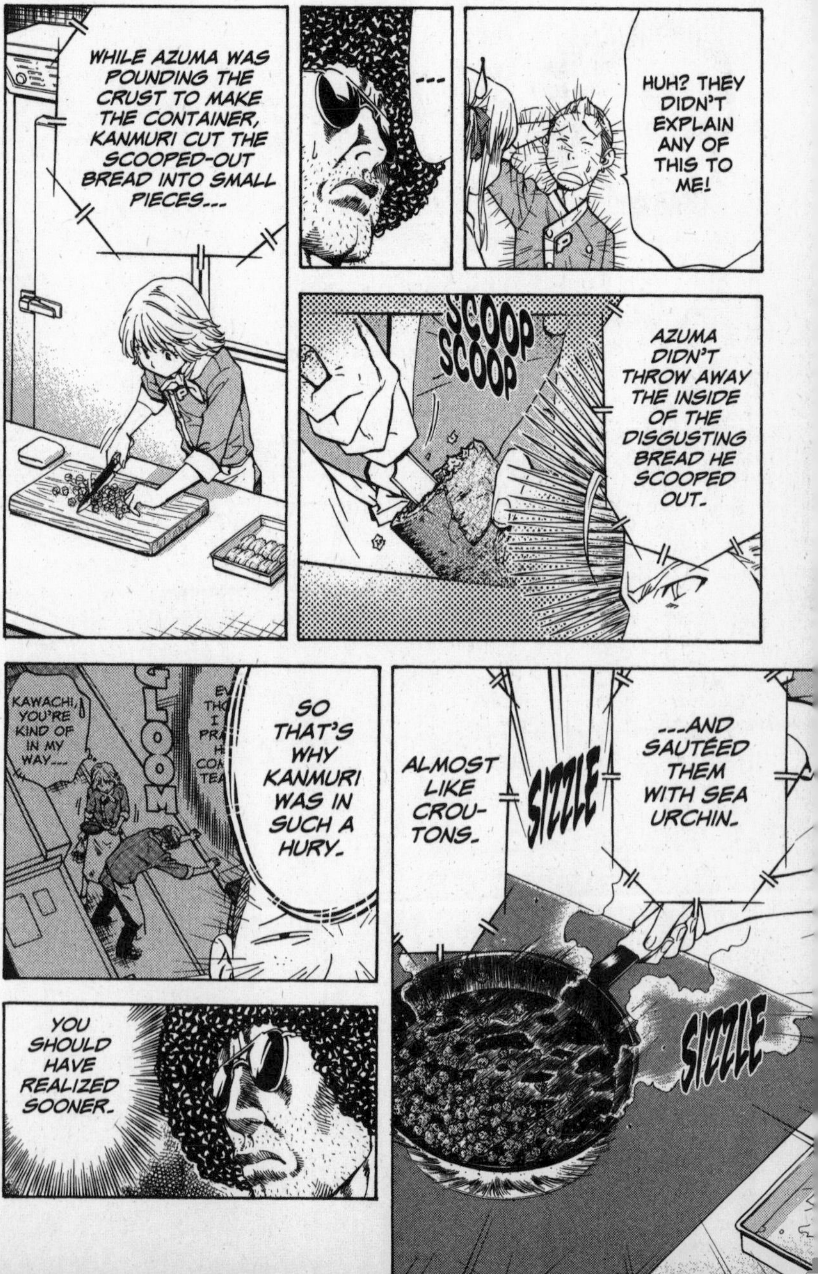
HUH? THEY DIDN'T EXPLAIN ANY OF THIS TO ME!
...
SCOOP SCOOP
AZUMA DIDN'T THROW AWAY THE INSIDE OF THE DISGUSTING BREAD HE SCOOPED OUT.
WHILE AZUMA WAS POUNDING THE CRUST TO MAKE THE CONTAINER, KANMURI CUT THE SCOOPED-OUT BREAD INTO SMALL PIECES...
...AND SAUTÉED THEM WITH SEA URCHIN.
SIZZLE
ALMOST LIKE CROUTONS.
SIZZLE
SO THAT'S WHY KANMURI WAS IN SUCH A HURY.
GLOOM
KAWACHI, YOU'RE KIND OF IN MY WAY...
YOU SHOULD HAVE REALIZED SOONER.

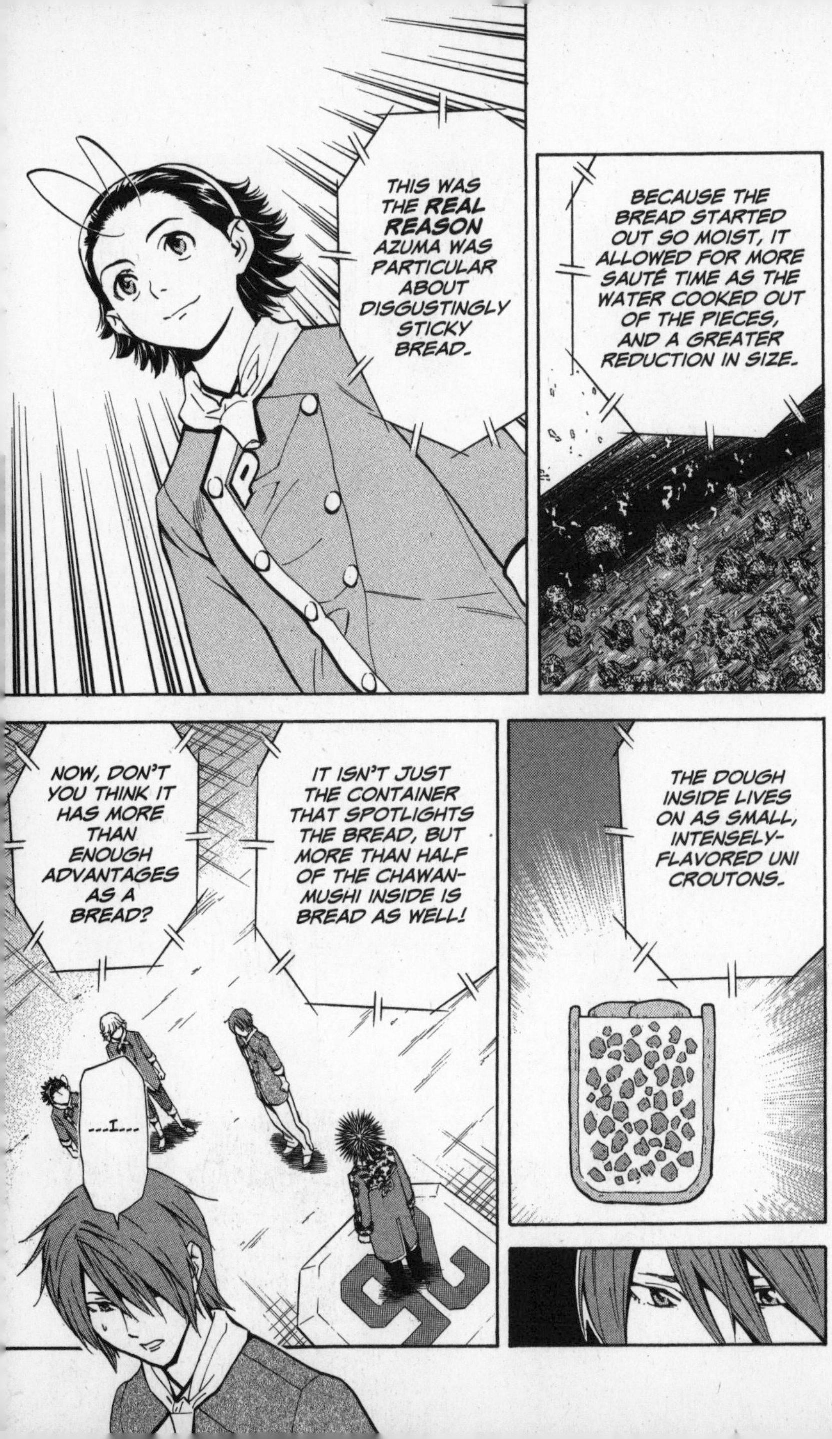
BECAUSE THE BREAD STARTED OUT SO MOIST, IT ALLOWED FOR MORE SAUTÉ TIME AS THE WATER COOKED OUT OF THE PIECES, AND A GREATER REDUCTION IN SIZE.
THIS WAS THE **REAL REASON** AZUMA WAS PARTICULAR ABOUT DISGUSTINGLY STICKY BREAD.
THE DOUGH INSIDE LIVES ON AS SMALL, INTENSELY-FLAVORED UNI CROUTONS.
IT ISN'T JUST THE CONTAINER THAT SPOTLIGHTS THE BREAD, BUT MORE THAN HALF OF THE CHAWAN-MUSHI INSIDE IS BREAD AS WELL!
NOW, DON'T YOU THINK IT HAS MORE THAN ENOUGH ADVANTAGES AS A BREAD?
...I...

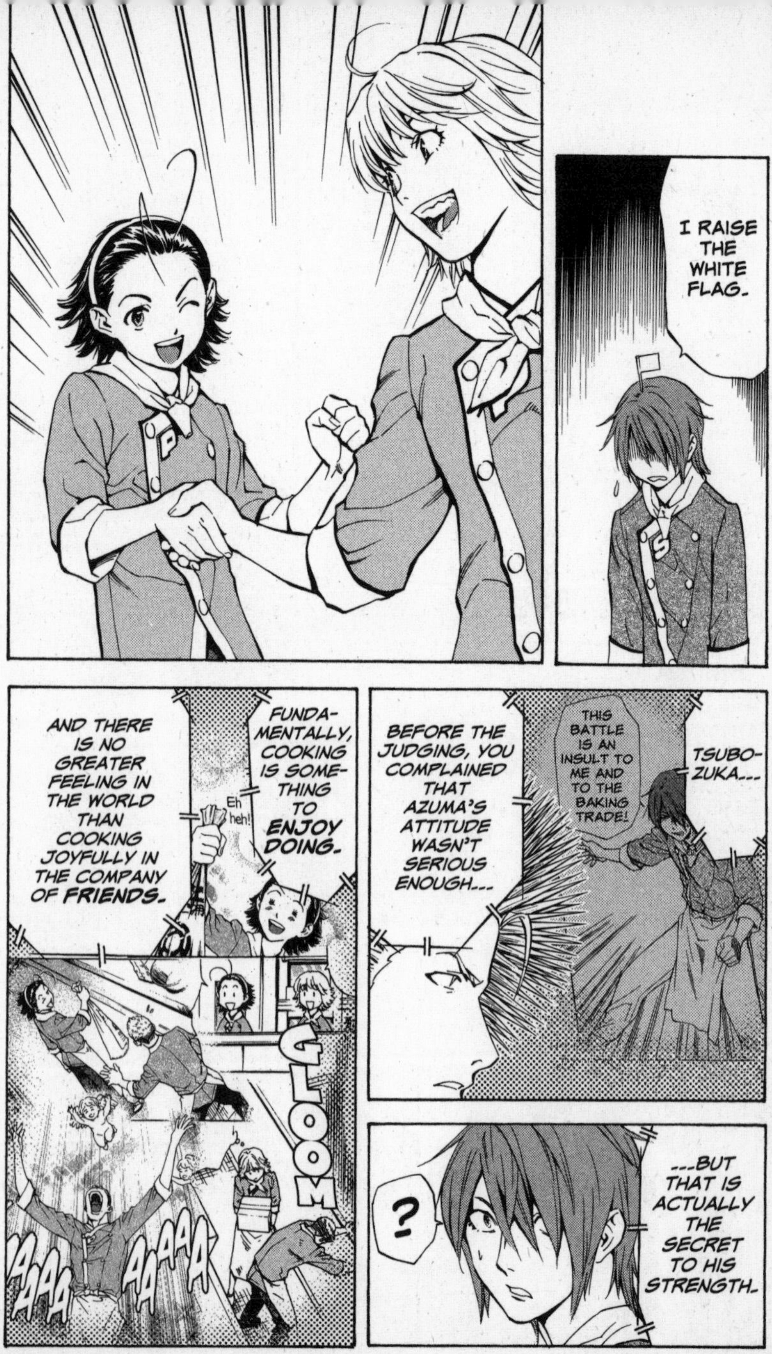
I RAISE THE WHITE FLAG.
TSUBOZUKA...
THIS BATTLE IS AN INSULT TO ME AND TO THE BAKING TRADE!
BEFORE THE JUDGING, YOU COMPLAINED THAT AZUMA'S ATTITUDE WASN'T SERIOUS ENOUGH...
FUNDAMENTALLY, COOKING IS SOMETHING TO ENJOY DOING.
Eh heh!
AND THERE IS NO GREATER FEELING IN THE WORLD THAN COOKING JOYFULLY IN THE COMPANY OF FRIENDS.
...BUT THAT IS ACTUALLY THE SECRET TO HIS STRENGTH.
?
GLOOM
AAAA
AAAA

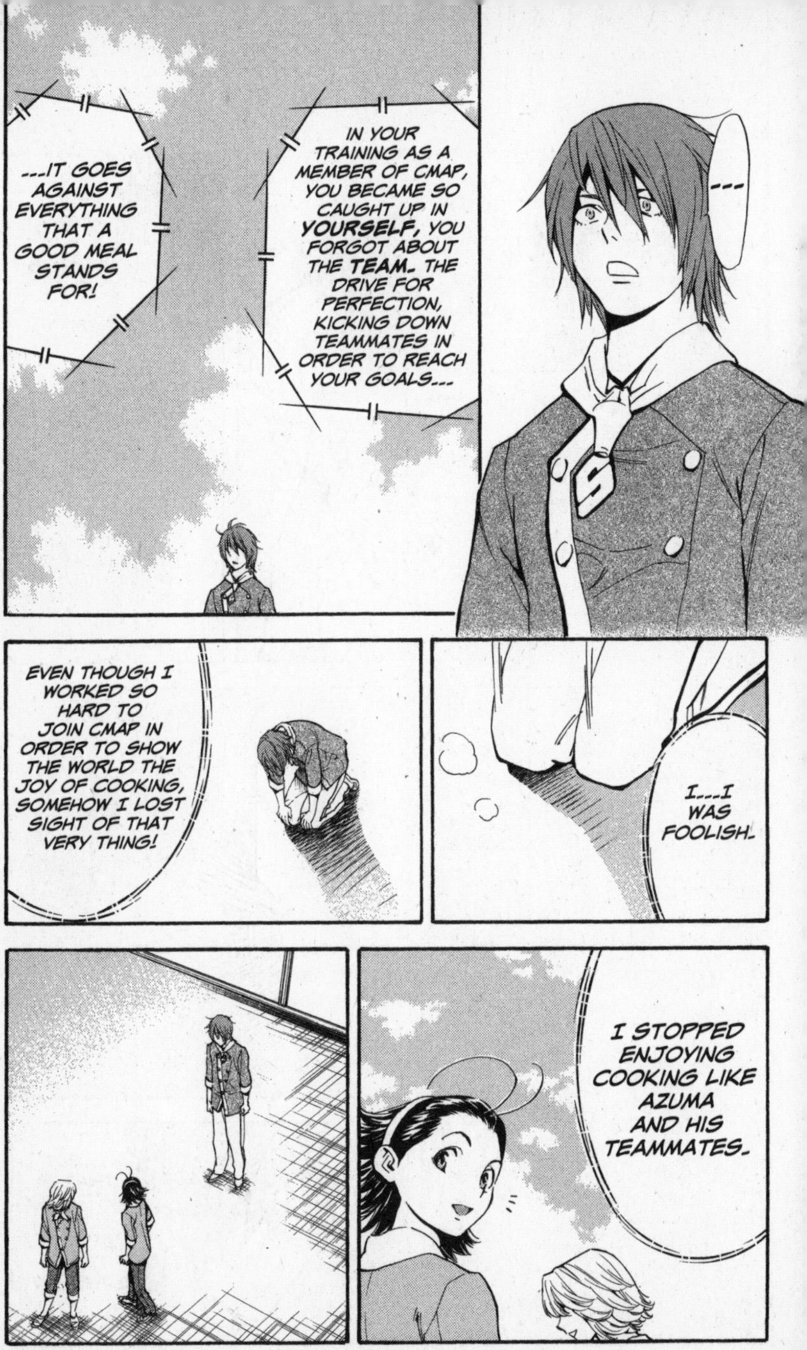
...
IN YOUR TRAINING AS A MEMBER OF CMAP, YOU BECAME SO CAUGHT UP IN **YOURSELF,** YOU FORGOT ABOUT THE **TEAM.** THE DRIVE FOR PERFECTION, KICKING DOWN TEAMMATES IN ORDER TO REACH YOUR GOALS...
...IT GOES AGAINST EVERYTHING THAT A GOOD MEAL STANDS FOR!
I...I WAS FOOLISH.
EVEN THOUGH I WORKED SO HARD TO JOIN CMAP IN ORDER TO SHOW THE WORLD THE JOY OF COOKING, SOMEHOW I LOST SIGHT OF THAT VERY THING!
I STOPPED ENJOYING COOKING LIKE AZUMA AND HIS TEAMMATES.

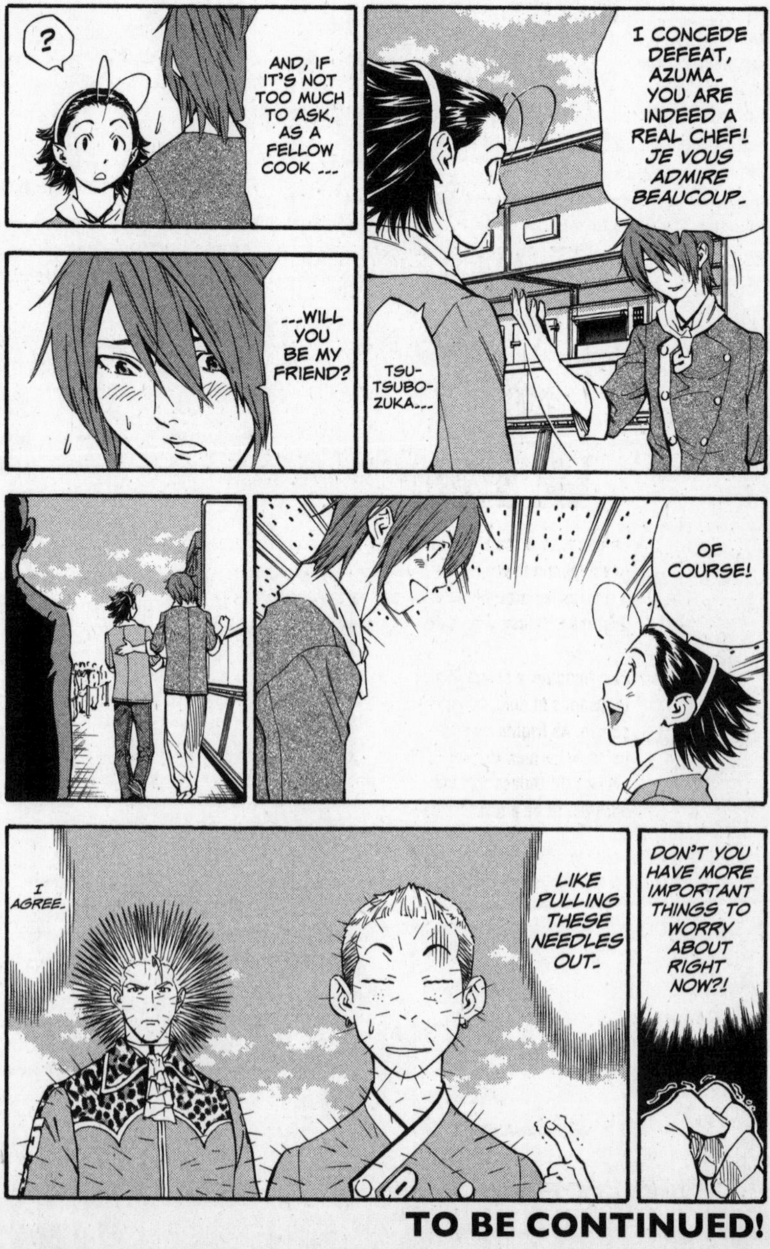
I CONCEDE DEFEAT, AZUMA. YOU ARE INDEED A REAL CHEF! JE VOUS ADMIRE BEAUCOUP.
TSU-TSUBO-ZUKA...
?
AND, IF IT'S NOT TOO MUCH TO ASK, AS A FELLOW COOK...
...WILL YOU BE MY FRIEND?
OF COURSE!
DON'T YOU HAVE MORE IMPORTANT THINGS TO WORRY ABOUT RIGHT NOW?!
LIKE PULLING THESE NEEDLES OUT.
I AGREE.

TO BE CONTINUED!

Freshly Baked!!
Mini Information

——— Tuna Fishing ———

Unless tuna is iced immediately after it's caught, *miyake* occurs (a phenomenon in which the protein of the fish starts to deteriorate if it thrashes around violently and its temperature rises above 40 degrees Celsius) and its sale price decreases drastically.

Just imagine, a single tuna can be sold for millions of yen (tens of thousands of dollars) and will suddenly become worthless if miyake sets in. As frightening as it is, miyake isn't all that rare, according to the fishermen I spoke to. There's so much money on the line with every fish! Unless you have a really strong heart, I don't think it's possible to be a tuna fisherman.

Photography/Alpina

YAKITATE!! JAPAN
VOL. 15

STORY AND ART BY
TAKASHI HASHIGUCHI

English Adaptation/Jake Forbes
Translation/Noritaka Minami
Touch-up Art & Lettering/Steve Dutro
Cover Design/Yukiko Whitley
Layout Design/Florian Fangohr
Editor/Megan Bates

Editor in Chief, Books/Alvin Lu
Editor in Chief, Magazines/Marc Weidenbaum
VP, Publishing Licensing/Rika Inouye
VP, Sales & Product Marketing/Gonzalo Ferreyra
VP, Creative/Linda Espinosa
Publisher/Hyoe Narita

YAKITATE!! 15 by Takashi HASHIGUCHI © 2005 Takashi HASHIGUCHI
All rights reserved.
Original Japanese edition published in 2005 by Shogakukan Inc., Tokyo.
The stories, characters and incidents mentioned in this publication are
entirely fictional.

Printed in the U.S.A.

Published by VIZ Media, LLC
P.O. Box 77010
San Francisco, CA 94107

10 9 8 7 6 5 4 3 2 1
First printing, January 2009

viz
media
www.viz.com   store.viz.com